Workbook for Introduction to Classical Nahuatl

Workbook for
Introduction to Classical Nahuatl
Revised Edition

J. RICHARD ANDREWS

UNIVERSITY OF OKLAHOMA PRESS : NORMAN

ALSO BY J. RICHARD ANDREWS

Juan del Encina: *Prometheus in Search of Prestige* (Berkeley, 1959)
(with Charles M. Vance) *Patterns for Reading Spanish* (New York, 1964)
Introduction to Classical Nahuatl, First Edition (Austin, 1975)
(trans. and ed. with Ross Hassig) *Treatise on the Heathen Superstitions and Customs That Today Live among the Indians Native to this New Spain, by Hernando Ruiz de Alarcón* (Norman, 1984)

Publication of this book is made possible through the generosity of Edith Kinney Gaylord.

ISBN 0-8061-3453-4

The paper in this book meets the guidelines for permanence and durability of the Committee on Production Guidelines for Book Longevity of the Council on Library Resources. ∞

Copyright © 2003 by the University of Oklahoma Press, Norman, Publishing Division of the University, Red River Books edition. All rights reserved. Manufactured in the U.S.A.

1 2 3 4 5 6 7 8 9 10

Contents

Preface	vii
Abbreviations and Symbols Used	ix

Exercises

1.	Linguistic Preliminaries	3
2.	Pronunciation. Orthography	4
3.	Particles	6
4.	Nuclear Clauses	7
5.	The Intransitive VNC Formula. Subject Pronouns. Tense Morphs	8
6.	The Transitive VNC Formula. Object Pronouns	9
7.	Verbstem Classes	10
8.	Further Remarks on VNCs. Basic Sentences	12
9.	The Optative Mood. Wish Sentences. Command/Exhortation Sentences	13
10.	The Admonitive Mood. Admonition Sentences	15
11.	Irregular VNCs	17
12.	The Absolutive-State NNC Formula. Subject Pronouns	19
13.	The Possessive-State NNC Formula. Subject and Possessor Pronouns	20
14.	Nounstem Classes	21
15.	Further Remarks on NNCs	23
16.	Pronominal NNCs	24
17.	Supplementation (Part One)	25
18.	Supplementation (Part Two)	27
19.	Supplementation (Part Three)	29
20.	The Nonactive Verbstem	31
21.	The Passive-Voice VNC	32
22.	Impersonal VNCs	34
23.	More on Verb Objects	36
24.	Causative Verbstems (First Type). Destockal Verbstems	37
25.	Causative Verbstems (Second Type)	38
26.	Applicative Verbstems	41
27.	Frequentative Verbstems	43
28.	Compound Verbstems: Verbal Embed	45
29.	Purposive VNCs	47
30.	Compound Verbstems: Nominal Embed	49
31.	Compound Nounstems	51

32. Affective NNCs	54
33. Honorific VNCs. Pejorative VNCs	55
34. Cardinal-Numeral NNCs	57
35. Nominalization of VNCs (Part One)	59
36. Nominalization of VNCs (Part Two)	61
37. Deverbal Nounstems (Part One)	64
38. Deverbal Nounstems (Part Two)	66
39. Deverbal Nounstems (Part Three)	68
40. Adjectival NNCs (Part One)	70
41. Adjectival NNCs (Part Two)	72
42. Adjectival Modification (Part One)	74
43. Adjectival Modification (Part Two)	76
44. Adverbial Nuclear Clauses	78
45. Relational NNCs (Part One)	80
46. Relational NNCs (Part Two)	81
47. Relational NNCs (Part Three)	84
48. Place-Name NNCs. Gentilic NNCs	86
49. Adverbial Modification (Part One)	88
50. Adverbial Modification (Part Two)	90
51. Complementation	92
52. Conjunction	94
53. The Notion of Similarity. Comparison	96
54. Denominal Verbstems (Part One)	98
55. Denominal Verbstems (Part Two)	99
56. Personal-Name NNCs	101
57. Miscellany (Part One)	103
58. Miscellany (Part Two)	105
Key to the Exercises	107
Introduction to the Vocabulary	203
Vocabulary	205

Preface

This support volume for the second edition of the *Introduction to Classical Nahuatl* consists of an exercise section, its key, and a vocabulary that lists entries taken only from the exercises.

The exercises follow the fifty-eight lessons of the *Introduction* and present to the student materials with which to become proficient in the grammatical principles and structures presented there. For the most part, this exercise material consists of unconnected sentences so that the patterns of the language can be brought into clear focus. This type of presentation, which is frowned on by many modern writers of foreign-language grammars, was chosen with the intention of getting the student to attend to the grammatical (morphological, morphosyntactical, or syntactical) point at issue without the distracting "help" of a context. It is precisely the reliance on suggestions thrown up by this kind of "help" and a concomitant lack of focus on grammatical rules and facts that have generated so much questionable translation of Nahuatl material. Translation must be made from grammatical strength, not from weakness that guesses its way along with the help of contextual high points. But gaining a competence in translating Nahuatl is not the real goal here. What is sought is an understanding of the language, a grasp of its particular communicational integrity.

That goal leads to another aspect of the workbook's presentation of exercise material that goes against the current of much modern foreign-language grammar-writing theory. The exercises are almost entirely of a "recognition" type. This strategy addresses the fact that Classical Nahuatl is no longer spoken, so the purpose of the lessons is to enable students to learn to read it rather than to speak or write it. The primary task of the student is to set oneself free of the temptation to impose one's own language upon a foreign communicational system, to get inside the language and become attuned to its own particular organizational principles. This means overcoming the barrier inherent in foreignness and refusing to be satisfied with mere equivalence (X = Y, without being concerned with the fact that the system supporting X is often vastly different from the system supporting Y, so that the meaning expressed by the two is really quite different). It is difficult to resist being satisfied to rest on the foreign language's outside surface. To accomplish a breakthrough, one must not simply repeat and repeat for a mindless acquisition but instead continually practice under the guidance of grammatical understanding. One must constantly train oneself to become familiar with the peculiarity present in the native speaker's way of processing the grammatical and semantic information expressed in morphs and their combinatorial patterns. It is to be hoped that this attention to the small-scale facts of the language will open the door into the foreign meaningfulness that has to be confronted when one later deals with the intriguing expressiveness of the language. The student's secondary task, that of learning to translate Nahuatl into English, is a subordinate concern.

Although Nahuatl-to-English exercises predominate, in the early lessons there are occasional English-to-Nahuatl ones. They aim at strengthening the learning of nuclear-clause structure, which is the essential difference between Nahuatl and English. Lessons 7–10, 14, and 15 each contain one exercise for translation from English to Nahuatl; also, Exercises 21D and 22C deal with problems of a transformational type. While separate-sentence exercises continue up to Lesson 56, exercises containing connected material begin in Lesson 47, and, in order to prepare the student to deal with texts, the reading selections are presented in traditional spelling in Lessons 57 and 58.

For the exercises to accomplish their purpose, they must be approached with the proper attitude. They should not be treated as one would treat a crossword puzzle. They are not to be "solved" and then set aside. As suggested above, internalizing a language depends on activating a knowledge of grammatical principles through the formation of habitual responses to forms and constructions structured by those principles. A one-time performance of an exercise item will obviously not accomplish this. Such hit-and-run tactics, in fact, accomplish very little, not even helping one to learn the vocabulary. One must drill oneself, do the same exercise over and over, practice with the persistence with which one practices a basketball shot or a musical composition—preferably with spaced training periods. The student should not, therefore, write English glosses over the Nahuatl items but should leave the item as something to challenge analytical and recognition abilities again and again, until one acquires ease and skill in performance.

Abbreviations and Symbols Used

abs-st = absolutive state
admon = admonitive
adv = adverb
advlzd = adverbalized
af = affinity
agen = agentive nounstem
anim = animate
applic = applicative
by extens = by extension
caus = causative
cl = clause
comp = compound stem
conn-*t* =connective-*t* compound stem
cuspres = customary present
defec = defective
derog = derogatory
dir = directional
emb = embed
freq = frequentative
fut agen s = future agentive stem
gen-use s = general-use stem
(H) = honorific
impers = impersonal
imprfv = imperfective
incorp = incorporated
instru = instrumentive
interrog = interrogative
intrans = intransitive
irreg = irregular
lit = literally
loc = locative

n = nounstem [*Not* "noun"; there are *No* nounwords in Nahuatl.]
neg = negative
NNC = nominal nuclear clause
nonac = nonactive
nonan = nonanimate
num s = numeral nounstem
obj = object
opt = optative
org-pos = organic possession
o.s. = oneself
(P) = pejorative
part = particle
pass = passive voice
pat = patientive nounstem
pers = person
pers name s = personal name stem
pl = plural
pos = possessive
pos pron = possessor pronoun
pos-st = possessor state
pref = prefix
pres = present
pret = preterit
pret agen = preterit-agentive nounstem
pret-as-pres = preterit-as-present
prfv = perfective
pron = pronoun
–QU- = *queh* (plural number dyad on certain VNCs)
(R) = reverential

redup = reduplicative stem/reduplication
reflex = reflexive
reflex-as-pass = reflexive as passive (i.e., an active-voice VNC with reflexive object pronoun used to express a passive-voice notion)
restr-use s = restricted-use stem
s = stem
sg = singular
s.o. = someone
sp = spelling
Span = Spanish
st = state
s.th. = something
subj = subject pronoun
-T- = -*tin* (plural-number dyad on certain NNCs)

T-O- ~ T-□- = any animate reciprocative object-pronoun
tradit sp = traditional spelling
trans = transitive
v = verbstem [*Not* "verb"; there are *No* verb-words in Nahuatl.]
var = variant
VNC = verbal nuclear clause
1st = first person
2nd = second person
3rd = third person
~ = or
/ = or
> = changes to; is transformed into
< = derives from

Ø = zero; morpheme or regular morph not phonologically represented; mute or silently present
□ = square zero; irregular morph not phonologically represented; mute or silently present
* = reconstructed, hypothetical, or unattested form
/. . ./ = phonemic representation of sounds
[. . .] = phonic or phonetic representation of sounds
(. . .) = fore and aft stem boundaries
#. . .# = fore and aft nuclear clause boundaries
= point of attachment of affix outside (either before or after) nuclear clause boundaries
+ = major boundary other than a stem boundary or nuclear clause boundary
- = minor boundary inside dyadic positions (or slots) as well as stem-internal boundary between components in a compound stem

Note: A hyphen is also used to indicate incomplete material. For example, in presenting a *stem* as a lexical item, -(. . .) indicates a transitive verbstem and (. . .)- indicates a nounstem, while (- . . .) indicates a stem occurring only as a matrix and (. . . -), one occurring only as an embed. The combination of a hyphen and a parenthesis is *never* used in analyzing nuclear clauses, since parentheses serve as replacements for hyphens as stem boundaries.

Workbook for Introduction to Classical Nahuatl

EXERCISE 1

Linguistic Preliminaries

1A. *Terms.* Define the following.

1. phoneme
2. phone
3. sigeme
4. morph
5. root
6. lexeme
7. morphology
8. instance level

1B. *Questions*

1. What is the difference between a syllable and a morpheme/morph?
2. What is the difference between derivation and inflection?
3. What is wrong with the widely-used expression "subject of the verb"?
4. What is the difference between a stem and a word in English or Spanish?

EXERCISE 2

Pronunciaton

2A. *The Correlation of Sound Symbols and Spelling Symbols.* Pronounce and spell the following vocables.

1. /we:i/
2. [ahko]
3. /ki:sa/
4. /kʷe:iλ/
5. [ahwi:k]
6. [¢ah¢i]
7. [kʷa:w̥temo:k¢in]
8. /te:ma:ki:štia:ni/
9. /a:ška:iλ/
10. [kʷeλa:čλi]
11. [nekʷλi]
12. /nosiwa:w/
13. [kikʷa:s]
14. [o:ničo:kak]
15. /kiyawiλ/
16. /mi:mikkeʔ/
17. [šikmo:λa]
18. [te:kʷ̥λi]
19. /ke:škič/
20. [nehwa:λ]
21. /to:kwaʔ/

2B. *The Importance of Vowel Length.* Pronounce. (Do not confuse *length* and *stress*.)

1. quipatla = he changes it
2. topan = it is above us
3. nocuauh = it is my tree
4. quitlatia = he burns it
5. chichi = it is a dog
6. quipiloa = he hangs it up
7. piltic = it is noble
8. teco = it is cut
9. notex = it is my flour
10. motema = he takes a steam bath
11. quipoloa = he loses it
12. quiyecoa = he tastes it

quipātla = he dissolves it
topān = it is our flag
nocuāuh = it is my eagle
quitlātia = he hides it
chīchi = it suckles
quipīloa = he makes it thinner
pīltic = it is thin
tēco = it is laid stretched out
notēx = he is my brother-in-law
motēma = it is put into a container
quipōloa = he kneads it (clay, etc.)
quiyēcoa = he finishes it

2C. *The Variant Sounds ([o] and [u]) Represented by the Letter o.* Pronounce.

1. ōmpa
2. nōchtli
3. tozcatl
4. ōquitzauc
5. tōtolin
6. conētl
7.
8.
9. xōpantli
10. cōztic
11. quitzopa
12. yōli
13. quitoca
14. tozan
15.
16.
17. āmoxtli
18. huīlōtl
19. cōtztli
20. mochi
21. tepoztli
22. tzopqui

Pronunciation 5

    7. quiyecoa   15. xocotl   23. coyōtl
    8. quihtzoma   16. tlaōcoya   24. ītepotzco

2D. What has happened when *tletla* became *tlatla* and *tepahzolli* became *tapahzolli*? What happens when *centli* becomes *cintli*?

2E. *Sound Changes Resulting from the Juxtaposition of Certain Consonants.* Join the indicated items, making any necessary changes in spelling. Pronounce the result.

Example: am- + ceyah = azceyah [asseyah]

1. am- + -cihuah
2. teuh- + -yoh
3. am- + -huih
4. tlāl- + -tli
5. ītech- + -tzinco
6. am- + -tzīnquīzah
7. mitz- + -chōctia
8. quim- + -xiccāhua
9. am- + -yezqueh
10. tēuc- + -yōtl
11. quim- + -zāzaca
12. oh- + -pitzactli
13. xāl- + -yoh
14. tepoz- + -chicōlli
15. nimitz- + -tzonhuilāna
16. tepoz- + -xomahtli
17. petlān- + -qui
18. am- + -tlaczah

EXERCISE 3

Particles

3A. Define "particle."

3B. *Particles*. Pronounce and translate.

1. anca
2. zan
3. quin
4. cuix?
5. nō
6. ye
7. ach
8. mā
9. ca
10. tēl

3C. *Particle Collocations*. Pronounce and translate.

1. aya
2. mā cazo
3. in tlā no zo
4. oc nō
5. ahzā zo
6. ayoc
7. mā zo tēl
8. ahca zo ah#
9. mā zā zo
10. ahzo

EXERCISE 4

Nuclear Clauses

4A. *Diagrammatic Formulas.* Rewrite from memory the linear format of VNC formula 1 and NNC formula 3 presented in § 4.5 in a diagrammatic format.

4B. *Features of Categories.* Name the features belonging to the following grammatical categories.

1. person
2. animacy
3. humanness
4. number
5. case

4C. *Terms.* Define the following terms.

1. deixis
2. anaphora
3. cataphora

EXERCISE 5

The Intransitive VNC Formula
Subject Pronouns
Tense Morphs

5A. *Diagrammatic Format of the Intransitive VNC Formula.* Write out from memory the diagrammatic format of the Intransitive VNC formula.

5B. *First-Person Subject Pronouns.* Write out from memory the various forms of the first-person singular (= "I") and first-person plural (= "we") of the Nahuatl subject personal pronouns occurring in VNCs.

5C. *Third-Person Subject Pronouns.* What change in the forms given in 5B would be required to change them to the third-person singular/common (= "he/she/it; it/they") and third-person plural (= "they")?

5D. *Tense-Morph Carriers.* Write down the Nahuatl indicative tense-morph carriers that convey the following pieces of information.

1. used to
2. at the present
3. long ago
4. in the future
5. at a time before now
6. was/were . . . ing
7. customarily nowadays
8. prior to some past time

EXERCISE 6

The Transitive VNC Formulas
Object Pronouns

6A. *Features of Categories.* Name the features belonging to the following grammatical categories.
   1. trajectory
   2. specificity
   3. prominence

6B. *Diagrammatic Formula for the Transitive VNC with Monadic Valence.* Write out from memory the diagrammatic format of the Transitive VNC formula with the monadic Valence position.

6C. *Monadic Valence Fillers.* Discuss the **tē** and **tla** fillers of the monadic Valence position.

6D. *Diagrammatic Formula for the Transitive VNC with Dyadic Valence.* Write out from memory the diagrammatic format of the Transitive VNC formula with the dyadic Valence position.

6E. *Objective-Case Projective Personal Pronouns.* Write out from memory the Nahuatl objective-case projective object personal pronouns for the following English verb-object pronouns.
   1. them
   2. me
   3. you (sg)
   4. us
   5. him/her/it (animate); it/them (nonanimate)
   6. you (pl)

6F. *Mainline Reflexive Object Personal Pronouns.* Write out from memory the Nahuatl mainline reflexive object personal pronouns for the following English reflexive pronouns.
   1. myself
   2. yourselves
   3. himself/herself/itself; itself/themselves (nonanimate)
   4. ourselves

EXERCISE 7

Verbstem Classes

7A. Analyze the following VNCs according to the diagrammatic format. Translate.
  1. tictēmoh
  2. tepēuhca
  3. ninīnāyaya
  4. tēpēuhca
  5. tēchihua
  6. ammotlāliānih
  7. tiquincuāzqueh
  8. tēchīhua

7B. Pronounce, identify the tense morph (all indicative), and translate the VNC.
  1. anquihtōzqueh
  2. miccah
  3. quitequi
  4. quihtlanini
  5. quīc
  6. nāhuix
  7. ticcuih
  8. titēchnōtzaya

7C. Pronounce, identify the verbstem class, and translate the VNC.
  1. ticchix, nimitzchiya, nēchchiyaz
  2. tiquihtoh, niquihtoa, quihtōz
  3. anquicacqueh, timitzcaquih, nēchcaquizqueh
  4. mozōmahqueh, titozōmah, ammozōmāzqueh
  5. nitlaczac, quicza, titlaczaz
  6. quintēmohqueh, tamēchtēmoah, antēchtēmōzqueh
  7. nihciuh, ihcihui, tihcihuiz
  8. tiquittaqueh, annēchittah, mitzittazqueh

7D. Using the following stems, translate the English clauses into Nahuatl.

Class A: tla-(mōtla) = to throw a rock at s.th.
Class B: tē-(nōtza) = to call/summon s.o.
Class C: tla-(tēm-o-ā) = to seek s.th.
Class C: m-o-(tlāl-i-ā) = to sit down; tla-(tlāl-i-ā) = to set s.th. down
Class D: tla-(māmā) = to carry s.th on one's back
  1. I threw a rock at it
  2. we sat down
  3. you (pl) customarily carry it on your backs
  4. they will summon me

5. you (sg) were seeking it/them
6. I shall set it down
7. they had carried things on their backs
8. I summoned you (pl)
9. we shall seek it/them
10. you (pl) throw rocks at things

EXERCISE 8

Further Remarks on VNCs
Basic Sentences

8A. Analyze and translate the following expanded VNCs.

1. huālquīzqueh
2. tontemoh
3. ōnichuālnōtzca
4. toconcaquizqueh
5. huāllamanaz
6. ōtiquimonnōtz
7. ōompēuh
8. ahōhuāllehcōc
9. tontāltīzqueh
10. ōnocottac
11. ōquihuālcuic
12. ōnocommēmeh

8B. Translate and insert first one and then the other directional prefix in the following VNCs. Translate the results.

1. panōqueh
2. ammīnāyah
3. tēihuāzqueh
4. ōtlachīuh
5. ticcuic
6. titotlālihqueh

8C. Pronounce and translate the following sentences.

1. Aya ōquichīuh.
2. Oc quimontēmoah.
3. Ye ōtocottaqueh.
4. Zan tlacua.
5. Cuix ōmic?
6. Ca ahniquihtoh.

8D. Translate the following English sentences into Nahuatl using the verbstems listed.

Class C: tla-(pol-o-ā) = to lose s.th., to waste s.th. (i.e., wealth)
Class A/B: tla-(pāca) = to wash s.th.
Class A: (tlehcō) = to ascend
Class A: (tzahtzi) = to shout
Class D: tē- ~ tla-(mā) = to capture s.o.; to hunt/catch s.th.

1. Indeed, he/she has already come up.
2. Didn't they shout hither?
3. He has already caught it.
4. Indeed, we will do the laundry
5. Perhaps you (sg) lost it.

EXERCISE 9

The Optative Mood. Wish Sentences Command/Exhortation Sentences

9A. *Past and Nonpast Optative VNCs.* Analyze and translate.

1. mā quipiyani, mā quipiya
2. mā nicpōhuani, mā nicpōhua
3. mā titotlāliānih, mā titotlālīcān
4. mā xicmāmānih, mā xicmāmācān

9B. *The Wish-Sentence Transformation (Affirmative and Negative).* (a) Analyze and translate the source assertion sentence. (b) Transform it into a wish sentence (analyzed version). (c) Write nonanalyzed version and translate.

Example 1: Titlapixqueh.

  a. #ti-Ø+tla(pix)Ø+qu-eh# = We guarded things.
  b. mā #ti-Ø+tla(piya)ni+Ø-h#
  c. Mā titlapiyanih. = If only we had guarded things. [The preterit optative is also possible: *Mā ōtitlapixqueh.*]

Example 2: Ahtiquihtlani.

  a. ah#ti-Ø+qu-Ø(ih-tlani)Ø+Ø-Ø# = You (sg) do not request it/them.
  b. mā ca#xi-Ø+qu-Ø(ih-tlani)Ø+□-Ø#
  c. Mā caxiquihtlani. = Would that you not request it. I hope you don't request it.

1. Titlanamacah.
2. Tictocac.
3. Quitlālīzqueh.
4. Ahōammotlalohcah.

9C. *Command/Exhortation–Sentence Transformation.* (a) Analyze and translate the source assertion sentence. (b) Transform it into the analyzed version of a direct-command sentence (if subject pronoun is 2nd person), an indirect-command sentence (if subject pronoun is 3rd person), or an exhortation sentence (if subject pronoun is 1st person). (c) Write the nonanalyzed version and translate the result.

Example 1: Anquipītzah.

  a. #an-Ø+qui-Ø(pītza)Ø+Ø-h# = You (pl) blow on it/them.
  b. mā #xi-Ø+c-Ø(pītza)Ø+c-ān#
  c. Mā xicpītzacān! = Blow (pl) on it/them!

Example 2: Ahtinēchīzahuia.
  a. ah#ti-∅+n-ēch(īz-a-hui-a)∅+∅-∅# = You don't surprise me. You don't shock me.
  b. mā ca#xi-∅+n-ēch(īz-a-hui)∅+☐-∅#
  c. Mā caxinēchīzahui! = Don't surprise me! Don't shock me!

1. Ahtitlapītzazqueh.
2. Quihtlani.
3. Ahanquiczah.
4. Tictlālia.

9D. *Wish Sentences and Command/Exhortation Sentences.* Pronounce and translate.

1. Mā tiquihtlanizqueh.
2. Mā caquihuāltepēhua.
3. Mā nicchīhuani.
4. Mā zan xiquitta!
5. Mā ōticpixqueh.
6. Tlā xiccaqui!
7. Mā catonquīzaz.
8. Mā tēl tiquihtōcān.
9. Mā quin ticpōhuaz.
10. Oc xicchiya.

9E. Using the verbstems listed, translate the English sentences into Nahuatl.

Class B: (pol-i-hui) = to become lost/destroyed, to perish/disappear
Class B: (miqui) = to die
Class A: tla-(namaca) = to sell s.th.
Class D: tla-(cuā) = to eat s.th.
Class C: tla-(zāl-o-ā) = to glue/solder s.th.

1. May I not perish! May I not die!
2. If only you (pl) had sold it.
3. Do (sg) not glue it.
4. Please eat (pl) it.
5. Let's not sell it.
6. If only they had not glued it!
7. Let them perish!

EXERCISE 10

The Admonitive Mood
Admonition Sentences

10A. *Admonitive VNCs.* Analyze and translate.

1. mā niccāuh, mā ticcāuhtin
2. mā timotēcah, mā ammotēcahtin
3. mā mozōmah, mā mozōmahtin
4. mā tlanelohtin, mā tlaneloh

10B. *Admonitive and Optative VNCs.* Identify the tense and mood of the VNC and translate.

Example: Mā ticchīuh. Mā ōticchīuh.

Mā ticchīuh. = *Admon.*: Beware (sg) of making/doing it.
Mā ōticchīuh. = *Pret. opt.*: If only you (sg) had made/done it.

1. Mā onquīz. Mā ōonquīz.
2. Mā caōninoquetz. Mā nēn ahninoquetz.
3. Mā titocāuhtin. Mā titocāhuacān.
4. Mā quixcah. Mā quixca.
5. Mā nēn anquiquetztin. Mā ōanquiquetzqueh.

10C. *The Admonition-Sentence Transformation.* (a) Analyze and translate the source assertion sentence. (b) Transform it into an (analyzed) admonition sentence. (c) Write out and translate the result.

Example 1: Anquichīhuah.

a. #an-∅+qui-∅(chīhua)∅+∅-h# = You (pl) are making it/them.
b. mā #an-∅+qui-∅(chīuh)∅+t-in#
c. Mā anquichīuhtin. = Beware (pl) of making it/them.

Example 2: Ahquicāhua.

a. ah#∅-∅+qui-∅(cāhua)∅+∅-∅# = He does not leave it/them.
b. mā nēn ah#∅-∅+qui-∅(cāuh)∅+□-∅#
c. Mā nēn ahquicāuh. = Let him beware of not leaving it/them. Let him be sure to leave it/them.

1. Ticquetza.
2. Ahantlaneloah.
3. Nipēhua.
4. Tlaxca.
5. Ahtitlamah.
6. Quiquēmih.

10D. *Admonition Sentences.* Pronounce and translate.
1. Mā annēchtzauctin.
2. Mā nēn quixcahtin.
3. Mā ticahhuahtin.
4. Mā nēn ahticpātzcah.

10E. *English-to-Nahuatl Translation.* Using the verbstems listed, translate the English sentences into Nahuatl.

Class B: tla-(tzacu-a) = to close s.th.
Class A: tē-(ahhua) = to scold/reprimand s.o.
Class C: tla-(tlā-ti-ā) = to hide s.th.; tē-(tlā-ti-ā) = to hide s.o.; *metaph.*, to kill s.o.
Class A: tla-(ī) = to drink s.th.
1. Let them be sure to close it.
2. Let's beware of killing them.
3. Beware of drinking it.
4. Beware (pl) of scolding him.
5. I must be sure to hide it.

10F. *Review.* Answer.
1. What information is conveyed by the Ø carrier in a subject pronoun's *pers*² subposition?
2. In the subject personal pronoun **ni-**Ø(... **+c-**Ø, what is the role of the **c** morphic carrier?
3. In an admonitive VNC's predicate, what information do the variant carriers **h** and Ø carry? What verbstem classes require which variant?

EXERCISE 11

Irregular VNCs

11A. *The Subject Pronoun's Number Position in Indicative VNCs formed from Irregular Verbs.* (1) Copy the following indicative VNCs. (2) Write out the morphic dyad filling the number position (if a morph is irregular rewrite the dyad in the regular shape). (3) Indicate the singular or plural value of the dyad. (4) Translate the VNC.

1. nicah
2. ticateh
3. ōtihuītzah
4. ōticmah
5. nonoc
6. tihuītzeh
7. nihuia
8. nicahcoc
9. tihcac

11B. *The Tense Morph in Indicative VNCs Formed from Irregular Verbs.* (1) Copy the following indicative VNCs. (2) Write out the tense morph (if it is irregular, rewrite it in the regular shape). (3) Name the tense (remember that the preterit-as-present and the distant-past-as-past are different tenses from the preterit and the distant past). (4) Translate the VNC.

1. ōcatca
2. anhuih
3. ōyahqueh
4. onoz
5. tihuālhuia
6. ayāc
7. cateh
8. huītzah
9. niyeni
10. tiyāyah
11. cahcocqueh

11C. *The Subject Pronoun's Number Position in Optative VNCs Formed from Irregular Verbs.* (1) Copy the following optative VNCs. (2) Write out the morphic dyad in the number position (if a morph is irregular, rewrite the dyad in the regular shape). (3) Indicate the singular or plural value of the dyad. (4) Translate the VNC.

1. mā capilcani
2. mā tiyecān
3. mā caxono
4. mā ōxihcanih
5. mā caxihuiān

11D. *Admonitive VNCs from Irregular Verbs.* Analyze and translate.

1. mā tiyahtin
2. mā nēn ahquimah
3. mā onohtin
4. mā nēn ahtiyah
5. mā cattin
6. mā nihcah

11E. *VNCs from Irregular Verbs Used in Sentences.* Pronounce and translate.
1. Cuix oc oncateh?
2. Ayoc ōhuītzah.
3. Cuix ye ōyah?
4. Quin ōnihuāllah.
5. Tlā xonyauh.
6. Cuix tiyāz?
7. Quin ōcommah.
8. Zan ōcahcoc.
9. Mā caye xihuiān.
10. At pilcaz.

11F. Explain why the VNCs *ōnitlamah*, *ōtitlamah*, and *ōtlamah* have the two different translation values (1) "I/you/he found s.th. out" and (2) "I/you/he hunted/captured s.th."

EXERCISE 12

The Absolutive-State NCC Formula
Subject Pronouns

12A. *The Absolutive-State NNC formula.* Write out from memory the diagrammatic format of the absolutive-state NNC formula.

12B. *Subject Personal Pronouns.* Write out from memory the morphic carriers of the various forms of the 1st person singular and 1st person plural of the Nahuatl subject personal pronouns occurring in absolutive-state NNCs.

12C. In what ways do Nahuatl NNCs differ from English nounwords with regard to the category of number?

EXERCISE 13

The Possessive-State NNC Formula
Subject and Possessor Pronouns

13A. *The Monadic State–Position.* Write out from memory the monadic state–position formula for a possessive-state NNC in the diagrammatic format.

13B. *The Dyadic State–Position.* Write out from memory the dyadic state–position formula for a possessive-state NNC in the diagrammatic format.

13C. *Subject Personal Pronouns.* Write out from memory the various forms of the 2nd person singular and 2nd person plural of the Nahuatl subject personal pronouns occurring in a possessive-state NNC.

13D. *The Possessor Pronouns.* Give from memory the Nahuatl possessor personal and indefinite pronouns for the following English possessive pronouns.

  1. our
  2. your (sg)
  3. his/her/its
  4. someone's
  5. my
  6. their
  7. something's
  8. your (pl)

13E. What information does the *st²* morph convey in: (1) n-o; (2) ī-∅ ?

13F. What information does the *st¹* morph convey in: (1) n-o; (2) ī-∅ ?

EXERCISE 14

Nounstem Classes

14A. *The Subject Pronoun in NNCs.* In order to fix in your mind the conviction that the number position in a Nahuatl NNC formula (as in the VNC formula) is a constituent of the subject personal pronoun and not a modifier of the nounstem, as is the fact in an English nounword, analyze the following NNCs according to the diagrammatic format. Translate the NNCs.

1. nicihuātl, īcihuāuh, ticihuah, amīncihuāhuān
2. noquichtli, noquichhui, amoquichtin, amoquichhuān
3. amocax, caxitl
4. tōcāitl, ītōcā
5. michin, nomich, mīmichtin, momichhuān

14B. *The Subject Pronoun Again.* Write out the morphic carriers of the subject personal pronoun in the following NNCs. Translate the subject pronoun. Translate the NNC.

1. cācālōtl, cācālōmeh, īncācālōuh, nocācālōhuān
2. māitl, nomā
3. nīcih, nicihtli, ticihtin, tocihhuān
4. moyac, yacatl
5. chichi, mochichi, chichimeh, amochichihuān
6. cītlalin, cīcītlaltin

14C. The State Position in the NNC Predicate. In order to fix in your mind the conviction that the State position in a Nahuatl NNC formula is a constituent of the predicate, analyze the following NNCs according to the diagrammatic format. In the absolutive-state NNCs, however (contrary to analyses elsewhere in these lessons), indicate the absolutive-state position by means of a plus mark followed by an empty underline (i.e., "+_"); for example, **camohtli**, "it is a sweet potato," is to be shown as having the absolutive-state predicate "+_(**camoh**)."

1. calli, nocal
2. īcac, cactli
3. cōlli, nocōl, cōltin, antocōlhuān
4. tēāhui, āhuitl, āhuimeh, timāhuihuān
5. amohhui, ohtli

14D. *The State Position Again.* Write out the morphic carriers of the predicate in the following NNCs using the same notation for an absolutive-state predicate as in Exercise 14C. Translate the predicate. Translate the NNC.

1. nīmal, titēmalhuān, nimalli, māmaltin
2. iyetl, miyeuh
3. metl, momeuh
4. etl, meuh
5. ticihuātl, tīcihuāuh, ancihuah, amocihuāhuān

14E. *The Affinity Stem and the Distributive/Varietal Stem.* Analyze and translate. Give the citation form of the stem.

1. tōōtztin
2. īncohconēhuān
3. tocahcax
4. antītīcih
5. īcuehcuē

14F. English-to-Nahuatl Translations. Using the nounstems listed, translate the following English clauses ("abs pl" = stem used to form absolutive-state NNCs with a plural subject pronoun).

(mōy-ō)-tl- > (mōy-ō)-uh-; *abs pl*, (mō-moy-o)-∅- = gnat, mosquito
(cac)-tli- > (cac)-∅- = sandal, shoe
(yaca)-tl- >(yac)-∅- = nose, point
(ītz)-tli- > (ītz)-hui- = obsidian, piece of obsidian
(iy-e)-tl- > (iy-e)-uh- = tobacco smoke, tobacco tube, tobacco, tobacco plant

1. it is your (pl) tobacco
2. they are mosquitoes
3. they are our (individually owned) shoes
4. they are your (sg) varied pieces of obsidian
5. they are varied kinds of tobacco
6. they are my mosquitoes
7. they are your sandals
8. it is her nose

EXERCISE 15

Further Remarks on NNCs

15A. *Peculiarities in the Predicates of Certain NNCs.* Write out the predicate of the following NNCs. If the predicate has a spelling irregularity, respell it in its regular shape. Translate the predicate. Translate the NNC.

1. tocuāuh
2. amonāhuān
3. notlācahuān
4. antocnīhuān
5. īpillo
6. tītēucyōhuān
7. tinonān
8. tocuāhuān
9. tinocnīuh
10. tlātlācohtin
11. nītēucyo
12. annopillōhuān

15B. *More Noteworthy Predicates in NNCs.* Analyze and translate the following NNCs.

1. tāxcā
2. amotētahhuān
3. mochān
4. ītēiccāhuān
5. totlamā
6. motlemāuh
7. tīiccāuh
8. motlātlahtōl
9. antotēāchcāhuān
10. ītlanacaz
11. tinoyāōuh
12. tīpohhuān

15C. *Sentences.* Pronounce and translate the following sentences.

1. Tlanacaztli.
2. Tonacaz.
3. Cuix ahtamonāhuān?
4. Ahīntiāchcāuh.
5. Ahzo īmāxcā.
6. Oc toyāōhuān.

15D. *English-to-Nahuatl Translations.* Using the nounstems given in Lesson 15, translate the following sentences.

1. Indeed, you are our lord.
2. Aren't we your lords (= liege lords; courtiers)?
3. He is only my slave.
4. They are no longer our friends.
5. I hope you are not his enemy.
6. You are not like me.

EXERCISE 16

Pronominal NNCs

16A. *Pronominal NNCs.* Pronounce, analyze, and translate the following NNCs.

1. tacah
2. antlehmeh
3. quēxquich
4. timiyequīntin
5. nitlah
6. izquīn
7. yehyehhuātl
8. achi
9. amehhuāntin
10. cātlein?
11. ixachīn
12. yehhuān
13. ammochīn
14. tiquēxquichtin
15. azcequīntin
16. titleh?

16B. *Pronominal NNCs in Sentences.* Pronounce and translate the following sentences.

1. Zan ye nō yehhuātl.
2. Oc nō ixquichtin.
3. Ahzo amacahmeh.
4. Cuix yehhuāntin?
5. Zan tiquēzquīntin.
6. Cuix ahtitleitin?
7. Ye amixquichtin.
8. Cuix amitlahmeh?
9. Zan oc achi.
10. Ca nehhuātl.

16C. *Review.* Add the directional/locative morph **on-** to the following "person-dyad plus object-dyad (~ object monad)" sequences. Translate the result morph by morph. [Indicate "nominative case" with "nom" and "objective case" with "obj."]

1. #ni-Ø+c-Ø(. . .
2. #ni-Ø+n-o(. . .
3. #an-Ø+qui-Ø+m-o(. . .
4. #an-Ø+tē(. . .
5. #ni-Ø+qu-in+n-o(. . .
6. #ni-Ø+tla(. . .

EXERCISE 17

Supplementation (Part One)

17A. *The Supplementary-Subject Function.* Analyze the constituent clauses of each sentence. Underline the head (the personal-pronoun subject in the principal clause) and its supplement (the adjunct clause). Translate the constituent clauses (again underlining the head and supplement). Translate the sentence.

Example 1: Ōnicoch nehhuātl. ō#ni-∅(coch)∅+☐-∅# #n-∅(eh-huā)tl-∅# = I-slept I-am-the-entity; i.e., I slept. [The underlined "I" in the translated sentence indicates English vocal stress (for emphasis). *Remember:* what English accomplishes with vocal stress, Nahuatl accomplishes with supplementation.]

Example 2: Ahtleh īmāxtli.

ah#∅-∅(tl-eh)∅-∅# #∅-∅+ī-∅(māx-tli)∅-∅# = It-is-nothing it-is-his-breechcloth; i.e., He has no breechcloth. He wears no breechcloth. He is not wearing a breechcloth.

1. Ōquichīuh nocōl.
2. Tzahtzih mochīntin.
3. Ahoncah cintli.
4. Ōtonocah timiyequīntin.
5. Tēihtlacoa peyōtl.
6. Ye huītzeh calpōltin.

17B. *The Supplementary-Object Function.* Analyze the constituent clauses of each sentence. Underline the head (the personal-pronoun object in the principal clause) and its supplement (the adjunct clause). Translate the constituent clauses (again underlining the head and its supplement). Translate the sentence.

Example: Ōquīc octli.

ō#∅-∅+qu-∅(ī)∅+c-∅# #∅-∅(oc)tli-∅# = He-drank-it it-is-pulque; i.e., He drank pulque.

1. Cuix ōtoconcuic nayoh?
2. Quimittac cīcītlaltin.
3. Quichīuhqueh īnhuīpil.
4. Ōquimpēuh oc cequīntin.
5. Nicnamaca cactli.
6. Cōyah cintli.

17C. *The Supplementary-Possessor Function.* Analyze the constituent clauses of each sentence. Underline the head (the personal-pronoun possessor in the principal clause) and its supplement (the adjunct clause). Translate the constituent clauses (again underlining the head and its supplement). Translate the sentence.

Example: Īncuen nopohhuān.

#Ø-Ø+ī-n(cuen)Ø-Ø# #Ø-Ø+n-o(poh)hu-ān# = It-is-<u>their</u>-tilled-land <u>they-are-my-equals</u>; i.e., It is the tilled land of my equals. They are the tilled lands of my equals.

1. Notōpīl nehhuātl.
2. Īteuh tōtōtl.
3. Īocuilhuān cuahuitl.
4. Īcōn nocih.
5. Māxcā titocnīuh.
6. Īmpilhuān mācēhualtin.

17D. *Multiple Supplements.* Identify the supplementary function of the adjunct clauses and translate the sentence. [SEN = sentence.]

Example: Ōquicuah niccāuh notlaxcal.

a. niccāuh = suppl subj.; *b.* notlaxcal = suppl obj; SEN = My younger brother ate my tortilla.

1. Ahōquīc ītah octli.
2. Quitēmoa nocuē nonān.
3. Ahtleh ītōcā īconēuh īcnīuh nocihuāuh.
4. Īnhuīpil īncihuāhuān tocnīhuān.
5. Ōtiquittaqueh īmohhui toyāōhuān.
6. Nicnechicoh īmahmā cuahuitl nehhuātl.

17E. *The Topicalization Transformation.* Identify the function of the supplement and translate the sentence.

Example: Tictōcah ayohtli. Ayohtli tictōcah.

a. ayohtli = suppl obj; SEN = We plant squash.
b. ayohtli = suppl obj as topic; SEN = As for the squash, we plant it.

1. Quīzah mochīntin. Mochīntin quīzah.
2. Cuix ōcān nochīmal? Nochīmal, cuix ōcān?
3. Mā moquetz yehhuātl. Yehhuātl mā moquetz.
4. Ca nīyāōuh mocnīuh. Mocnīuh ca nīyāōuh.
5. Mā xiccōhua cōmitl. Cōmitl mā xiccōhua.

17F. *Supplements in Information Questions.* Translate.

1. Quinequi ixquich. Quēxquich quinequi?
2. Ticcōhuaz cactli. Tleh ticcōhuaz?
3. Cānah mochi. Quēzqui cānah?
4. Quinechicōz ocotl. Tleh quinechicōz?
5. Yehhuātl īāxcā. Āc īāxcā?

17G. *Further Practice with Sentences.* Pronounce and translate.

1. Ca miyequīntin īpilhuān.
2. Tleh ōtiquihtoh?
3. Mā nēn tiquihtlacoh nocōzqui.
4. Īncal mā ticchīhuacān.
5. Cuix onhuetzqueh mochīntin?
6. Ahoc tleh quihtohqueh.
7. Cuix motah motah? Cuix monān monān?
8. Mā xichuālhuīca tletl.

EXERCISE 18

Supplementation (Part Two)

18A. *Marked Supplementation.* Write out the supplementary clause and identify its function. Translate the sentence.

   Example: Quināmicqueh in pīpiltin. [*In pīpiltin* = suppl subj.] = The nobles met him.

   1. Nictlālīz in notōcā.
   2. Quimāna in ocuiltin.
   3. Cuix ōtiquihneuc in xōchitl?
   4. Miquizqueh in ītlācahuān.
   5. Mā caxiccōhua in ōn.
   6. Ye quīzah in amoyāōhuān!
   7. Ca nāxcā in māxcā.
   8. Ca ōquimmictih in notōtolhuān in mochichi.
   9. Mā nēn tiquihtlacoh in īpetl in nonān.
   10. Xoconcui in īn.
   11. Mā cayāc tlaōcoya in īyōllo.
   12. Nēchcāhua in octli.

18B. *Marked Supplements in the Topicalized Transformation.* Write out the topic and identify its supplementary function. Translate the sentence.

   Example: In mochīntin ōmicqueh. [*In mochīntin* = suppl subj.] = All died.

   1. In nehhuātl nontlehcōz.
   2. In miztli quicua in nacatl.
   3. In tōtōtl ōniccac in īcuīc.
   4. In tōtōchtin ōmauhqueh.
   5. In yehhuāntin tocōlhuān.
   6. In īcal tlatlaya in īnteōuh.
   7. In zacatl quitquih.
   8. In nehhuātl nēchchiyah.

18C. *Ambiguity in Supplements.* Translate the following sentence showing each supplement in as many functions as possible.

Example: In Petoloh ōquicac in ītah. = Peter heard his father. His father heard Peter. Peter heard her father. Her father heard Peter. He/She heard Peter's father. Peter's father heard him/her. Peter's father heard it.

1. In ōcēlōtl quitta in mazātl.
2. In oquichtli in cihuātl ōquinōtz.
3. In nocnīuh quīmacaci in ītlah.
4. In īnyāōhuān ōquinxīcohcah.

18D. *Peculiarities in the Use of Supplements.* Identify the peculiarity of the supplementation and translate the sentence.

1. Tleh ōamāxqueh?
2. Cān īchān? [*Cān* = at what place? where? (see § 46.10).]
3. Tilmahtli contlāliāyah toquichtin.
4. Tichtec? Tiquichtec in cōzcatl?
5. Cuix ōantlatlātihqueh in pōchtēcatl?
6. Moch ōpanōqueh.

18E. *The Vocative Construction.* Pronounce and translate.

1. Tleh tāyi, in nocné?
2. Mā caxiquihto, nocnīhué.
3. Ca namēchitta, nopilhuāné.
4. Mā xiqui, noquich.
5. Mā nēn ticcuih, in niccāhué.
6. In tinotēlpōch, tlā xiccaqui in tlahtōlli.

EXERCISE 19

Supplementation (Part Three)

19A. *VNCs as Shared-Referent Supplements.* Write out the supplement and identify its function. Translate the sentence.

Example: Ontlatotōnih in tēcōānōtza. [*Tēcōānōtza* = suppl subj.] = The one who summons people as sharers warmed s.th., i.e., The host burned incense. [The verbstem *tē-(cōā-nōtza)* means "to summon s.o. as a sharer," i.e., "to invite s.o. to be a guest." The verbstem *tla-(to-tōn-i-ā)*, "to warm/heat s.th.," appears here with *tla*-fusion in the meaning "to burn/offer up incense."]

1. Ōniquimihuah in ōyahqueh.
2. Ahōniccac in ōtiquihtoh.
3. Huālmonechicohqueh in moyāhuacah.
4. Ye miquiz in ōteciya.
5. Ōniquittac ōticchīuh.
6. Oncateh in ōquināmoyāqueh.
7. In ōompanōqueh quimonahcizqueh.
8. Mā xicānacān in quitquih.
9. Ōquimpehpen in quipiyazqueh in teōtl.
10. Iz cah in tictēmoa. [*Iz* = here; see § 44.3.8.]
11. Nicchīhuaz tiquihtoa.
12. Ōmpa huih in huītecoh. [*Ōmpa* = to that place, there; see 46.10.]

19B. *Plural Constructions for īn, ōn, and āc.* Translate.

1. Mocuiltōnoah in ihqueh ōn.
2. In ihqueh īn, in īntēucyo ōquimīxcuep.
3. Āc mach ihqueh in quintzahtzilih? [*tē-(tzahtzi-liā)*, "to call to s.o."; for *mach*, see § 44.5.6.]
4. Ca popolocah in ihqueh ōn.
5. In ihqueh īn mozcaliah.
6. Āc ihqueh in ōquitlālihqueh?

19C. *Included-Referent Supplements.* Write out the supplement, identify its function, and indicate the personal-pronoun head for which it serves as referent. Translate the sentence.

Example: Cuix nelli ye ōhuāllahqueh? [Ye ōhuāllahqueh = suppl subj; referent for the personal-pronoun subject Ø-Ø(. . .)Ø-Ø of *nelli.*] = Is it true that they have already come?

1. Ahticmatih cuix quinamacaz.
2. Cuix nelli in ōquihcuiloh in āmoxtli.
3. Nēciya ye miquiz in ōteciya.
4. Cuix huelitiz in quimāmāzqueh in ixquich?
5. Ōquihtoh in ca ye huālahcizqueh.
6. Nēci octli qui.
7. Monequi in mā tiquīnāyacān.
8. Niquēlēhuia in mā monāmicti in nochpōch.
9. Niquihtlani in mā caxictlati.
10. Ca ahmō huel mochīhuaz in ōmpa tiyāzqueh. [*Ahmō* = not; see § 44.5.4. *Huel mochīhuaz* = *lit*, "it will be able to make itself."]
11. Nēci in titēlpōchtli.
12. Ahmō huelitiz in niccuāz.
13. Nicnequi in mā caniquitta.

19D. *Principal Clauses Involving the Notions of "knowing how to," "remembering to," etc.* Write out the supplement and identify the personal-pronoun head for which it indicates the referent.

1. Mā xiquilnāmiqui tichuīcaz in ēhuatl.
2. Cuix ticmati titlahtzomaz?
3. Ahquinequi māltīz.
4. Ōniquilcāuh niquīz in pahtli.
5. Ahnicmati in nicchīhuaz in ōn.
6. Cuix anquinequih ancontēmōzqueh?

19E. *Principal Clauses Involving the Notion of "saying."* Translate.

1. Quil mach mochi ōquitlatih.
2. Cuix ōtiquihtoh in onyāzqueh?
3. Oncān mihtoa in quēn in quixīnqueh īmācal. [*Quēn* = in what manner; see § 44.5.7.]
4. Quil quinnōtza in īnteōuh.
5. Quihtoh, "Mā nēn ahticchīuh."
6. Cuix oc tiquihtōz, "Mā xinēchonihua"?
7. Quil yeh in nāhualli.

19F. Explain the difference between shared-referent and included-referent supplementation.

EXERCISE 20

The Nonactive Verbstem

20A. *Derivation of the Nonactive Verbstem.* Give the meaning of the following active verbstems and then write out the imperfective nonactive stems that are derived from them.

1. tla-(icza)
2. (īlō-ti)
3. tla-(āyi)
4. tla-(cui)
5. tla-(mōtla)
6. (ē-hua)
7. (teci)
8. (yōli)
9. tla-(mati)
10. tla-(tequi)
11. tla-(ihnecui)
12. tla-(māmā)
13. (ca-h)
14. tla-(tlāza)
15. tla-(āna)
16. (huetzi)
17. (ahci)
18. tla-(tla-ti-ā)
19. (chōca)
20. (ciy-a-hui)
21. (huī-tz)

20B. *Following the Rules to form Nonactive Verbstems.* These active stems were not included in the examples given in § 20.2–§ 20.7. Follow the rules to form their nonactive counterparts.

1. (ihcuil-i-hui) = to become written/painted
2. tla-(cāhu-a) = to leave/abandon s.th.
3. tla-(quimil-o-ā) = to wrap s.th. up
4. tla-(tzacu-a) = to close/enclose s.th.
5. (tlal-i-hui) = to become hasty/speedy
6. tla-(pā) = to dye s.th.
7. (pol-i-hui) = to become lost/destroyed
8. (tlami) = to come to an end, to become finished

EXERCISE 21

The Passive-Voice VNC

21A. *The Difference between VNCs in the Active and Passive Voices.* Analyze and translate.

Example: quih, īhua

#∅-∅+qu-∅(i)∅+∅-h# = they drink it
#∅-∅(ī-hua)∅+∅-∅# = it is (undergoing the action of) being drunk

1. nicāna, āno, ānalo
2. amēchtocayah, antocōyah
3. niquimihcal, ihcalīlōqueh
4. mitzīmacaciz, tīmacaxōz
5. tāyiz, āyīhuaz
6. annēchnāmiquih, nināmico

21B. *The Relation of the Subject Pronoun in the Passive-Voice VNC to the Object Pronoun in the Active-Voice VNC.* Translate the passive-voice VNC. Identify the morphs of the subject pronoun and give the morphs of the object pronoun that serve as their source in an active-voice VNC.

Example: nitto = I am being seen; n-∅(. . . +∅-∅ = "I" < n-ēch = "me"

1. necōya
2. tānōc
3. huīcoh
4. nīmacaxōca
5. tipolōlōqueh
6. ancāhualōzqueh

21C. *The Relation of the Object Pronoun in the Active-Voice VNC and the Subject Pronoun in the Passive-Voice VNC.* Translate the active-voice VNC. Identify the morphs of the object pronoun and give the morphs of the subject pronoun that a passive-voice transform would use.

Example: tēchīmacaci = he fears and respects us; t-ēch = "us" > t-∅(...+∅-h = "we"

1. amēchhuīcaz
2. ōtiquīc
3. tiquimpolōzqueh
4. nēchānaz
5. mitztītlan
6. tēchmahca

21D. *The Passive Transformation.* (a) Translate the active-voice VNC. (b) Transform it into its passive-voice counterpart following the steps in the example. (c) Translate the resultant VNC.

The Passive-Voice VNC

Example: annēchīmacacih; (īmacax-ō)

a. annēchīmacacih = you (pl) fear and respect me
b. (1) #an-∅+n-ēch(īmacaci)∅+∅-h#   [Analyze active-voice VNC.]
   (2) ___+n-ēch(īmacaci)∅+___   [Delete subject pronoun.]
   (3) ... +n-ēch(īmacax-ō)∅+...   [Replace active stem with nonactive counterpart.]
   (4) #n-∅(īmacax-o)∅+∅-∅#   [Replace objective-case morphs of object pronoun with corresponding nominative-case morphs to create subject pronoun of passive-voice VNC.]
c. nīmacaxo = I am feared and respected

1. tēchhuīcah; (huīc-ō)
2. niquinnāmiqui; (nāmic-ō)
3. amēchihcalcah; (ihcalī-hua)
4. titozōzqueh; (zō-hua)
5. timitztlātihqueh; (tlā-ti-lō)

21E. *Sentences Manifesting Passive-Voice Focus.* Pronounce and translate. Give the active-voice stem.

1. Cuix ahōtiyōcolōc?
2. In īn, mā caquēmīhua.
3. Ahoc mamaliōhuaz in chālchihuitl.
4. At ōonānōc in tequitl.
5. Mochi ihcuanīhuaz.
6. Mā nēn timalohtin.
7. Ōcualōc in mētztli.
8. Mec ōtontītlanilōqueh.
9. Oc cequīntin ōittōqueh.
10. Cuix ōpolōlōc in īmāmox?
11. Quēzqui ōihcuilōlōz?
12. Ca ammalōzqueh amixquichtin.
13. Ca nihuālnōtzalo. Nēchhuālnōtza in Tōnatiuh.

21F. *The Reflexive to Express the Passive Notion.* Write out the VNC with the reflexive pronoun object and translate it literally. Translate the sentence.

Example: Oncān motēnēhua in quēn in ōahciqueh. [*Oncān* = there.]

[motēnēhua = it mentions itself.] = How they arrived is mentioned.

1. Ahmihtoa in cāmpa ōhuāllahqueh. [*Cāmpa* = from where?.]
2. Mocōhuaz in cōmitl.
3. Ahmomati in cuix ōpolōlōc.
4. Ca īmāxcā ōmocuic.
5. Quēxquich oc monequiz?
6. Oncān monamaca in cactli.
7. Ōmottaca in pāmitl.
8. Camohtli mopāhuaci.
9. Nō moxca.
10. Mohotqui in ācatl.
11. Mochīhuaya mītl. Ahtleh chicohuīyac. [(*chico-huī-ya-∅*)-*c*- = "a thing that is unequal in length."]

EXERCISE 22

Impersonal VNCs

22A. *The Difference between Inherently Impersonal VNCs and Nonanimate VNCs.* Analyze and translate. Indicate whether the personal-pronoun subject is normally supplementable or not.

1. cēhua
2. pixahuiya
3. tilāhua [as impers]
4. tilāhua [as nonan]
5. ōtēn
6. moyāhuac
7. yohuaya
8. chipīni
9. mani.
10. quiyahui
11. tlamiz
12. tecihuiya
13. tōnaya
14. mochīhuaz
15. ōchalān

22B. *The Difference between VNCs in the Active and Impersonal Voices.* Analyze and translate.

1. Tahcih. Ahxīhua.
2. Azciahuih. Ciaōhua.
3. Titeciz. Texohuaz.
4. Titozahuah. Nezahualo.
5. Ēhuaqueh. Ēōhuac.
6. Nitlacaqui. Tlacaco.
7. Antēchiyah. Tēchiyalo.
8. Pēhuaz. Pēōhuaz.

22C. The Impersonal Transformation. (a) Translate the active-voice VNC. (b) Transform it into its impersonal counterpart following the steps in the example. (c) Translate the resultant VNC.

Example: titēnōtzah; (nōtza-lō)

   a.: titēnōtzah = we are calling people
   b. (1) #ti-∅+tē(nōtza)∅+∅-h#   [Analyze active-voice VNC.]
     (2) __↓+tē(nōtza)∅+__↓   [Delete subject pronoun.]
     (3) . . . +tē(nōtza-lō)∅+ . . .   [Replace active stem with nonactive counterpart.]
     (4) #∅-∅+tē(nōtza-lo)∅+∅-∅#   [Import impersonal (nonspecific) subject pronoun from outside the source.]
   c. tēnōtzalo = s.o. is calling people; people are being called

1. antlatēmoah; (tēm-ō-lō)
2. ōticoch; (cochī-hua)
3. titīzahuiah; (īz-a-huī-lō)
4. tētocah; (toc-ō)
5. miquizqueh; (mic-o-hua)

Impersonal VNCs

22D. *The Difference between Passive-Voice and Impersonal-Voice VNCs.* Analyze and translate. [Remember: A passive-voice VNC has a specific subject pronoun (having any person and number) and an impersonal-voice VNC has a nonspecific one (3rd person singular only).]

1. cōhualo; tlacōhualo
2. tōcoh; tētōco
3. tlāxōc; tlatlāxōc
4. pītzalōc; tlapītzalōc
5. cuīhuaz; tlacuīhuaz
6. antzacualōzqueh; tētzacualōz

22E. *The Difference between an Active-Voice VNC and a VNC Built on a **tla**-Impersonal Stem.* Analyze and translate.

1. nēci; tlanēci
2. polihui; tlapolihui
3. yohua; tlayohua
4. onoc; tlaonoc
5. comōni; tlacomōni
6. niceceya; tlaceceya

22F. *Sentences Manifesting the Impersonal Focus.* Pronounce and translate.

1. Mā ye cuēl eh īlōcho.
2. Quin panōhuaz.
3. Cuix ōhuālhuechohuac?
4. Mā catlapolōlōz.
5. Aya ōtlathuica.
6. Cuix ye huālhuīlohuaz?
7. Ahzo ōpachiōhuaca.
8. Quin ōtōnac.
9. Mā nēn quīxohuah.
10. Cuix ahcēhuaz?

22G. *Sentences Contrasting Passive-Voice and Impersonal-Voice VNCs.* Pronounce and translate.

1. *a.* Cuix namacōz? *b.* Cuix tlanamacōz?
2. *a.* Mā catimalōcān. *b.* Mā catēmalo.
3. *a.* Quin ancāhualōqueh. *b.* Quin tlacāhualōc.
4. *a.* Ahzo tlapolōlōz. *b.* Ahzo nipolōlōz.
5. *a.* Mā nēn ahtēhuīcoh. *b.* Mā nēn ahhuīcoh.
6. *a.* Cuix ye cualōz? *b.* Cuix ye tlacualōz?

/ EXERCISE 23

More on Verb Objects

23A. *Kinds of Verbstems.* Name the three kinds of verbstems with transitive valence. Explain the difference between them (and the difference between the kinds of verb objects they require).
23B. *Verb Object Levels.* Explain the difference between mainline and shuntline objects.
23C. *Rules for Verb-Object Placement.* Write out from memory the four rules that govern the order of verb-object pronouns in a VNC.

EXERCISE 24

Causative Verbstems (First Type)
Destockal Verbstems

24A. *Transitivization of Intransitive Stems.* Analyze and translate the following pairs of VNCs. (Notice that some of the transitive stems are causative and some are applicative.)

1. nahci, nicahci
2. ac, caquih
3. mani, quimana
4. cuepi, mocuepa
5. tōca, quitōca
6. chihcha, quichihcha
7. tlan, quitlamih
8. ōnitēmic, ōnictēmic
9. cehuih, mocehuiah
10. ōnihuintic, ōtinēchihuintih

24B. *Intransitive and Causative VNCs Formed on Destockal Verbstems.* Analyze and translate.

1. chipīni, quichipīnia
2. ōchitōn, ōnicchitōnih
3. tomāhuah, quintomāhua
4. comōniya, mocomōniāyah
5. ōchalān, ōtitochalānihqueh
6. zālihui, niczāloa
7. ōmelāhuac, ōticmelāuhqueh
8. pixahui, anquipixoah

24C. *Sentences Containing VNCs Built on Intransitive and Transitivized Verbstems.* Pronounce and translate.

1. Ye ōihtlacauh in īnnemiliz. Ye ōquihtlacohqueh in īnnemiliz.
2. Mā nēn ahtiquimahcihtin. Mā nēn ahtahcihtin.
3. Cuix ye ōtiquixtlāuh? Cuix ye ōixtlāuh?
4. Mā xinēchcēhui. Tlā nicēhui.
5. Quin ōzāliōhuac. Quin ōzālōlōc.
6. Aya ōcotōn in mecatl. Aya ōquicotōnqueh in mecatl.
7. Cuix ōtecuīn in tletl?
8. Mā catitotecuīnīzqueh; mā catihuetzizqueh.
9. Ye ōpīnāuhqueh in noconēhuān.
10. Zan chipīniya. Ahzo quichipīniāyah yehhuāntin.
11. Cuix ye polihuiz? Cuix ye polōlōz?
12. Ahzo chipāhuaz in ātl. Ahzo ninochipāhuaz.
13. Ōhuītōliuh in tlacōtl. Ōnichuītōloh in tlacōtl.
14. Ye ōpachiuh in tenāmitl. In tōtōtl ōquipachoh in īteuh.
15. Tomi in nocac. Nictoma in nocac.

EXERCISE 25

Causative Verbstems (Second Type)

25A. *The Correspondence between Intransitive VNCs and Their Causative Derivatives.* Analyze and translate.

1. temo, nictemōhuia
2. tipano, mitzpanahuia
3. pēhua, nicpēhualtia
4. timahui, nimitzmauhtia
5. ninēci, ninonēxtia
6. nelti, nicneltilia
7. tiquīzah, tēchquīxtia
8. quīxōhua, nitlaquīxtia
9. nihuetzca, tinēchhuetzquītia
10. ehco, tiquehcahuiah

25B. *The Correspondence between Transitive VNCs and their Causative Derivatives.* Analyze and translate.

1. niquitta, tinēchittītia
2. ninopiya, nicnopiyaltia
3. quimatih, niquimmachīltia
4. nicnāmiqui, nicnonāmictia
5. nictepēhua, nēchtepēhualtiah
6. anquipoloah, namēchpolōltia

25C. *The Causative Transformation Carried Out on an Intransitive Source.* (1) Following the steps in the example, transform the source VNC into a causative VNC using the stem provided and the imported subject pronoun indicated. (2) Translate the result.

Example: ninemi; tē-(nemi-tiā); 3rd pl.

1.   a. #ni-Ø(nemi)Ø+Ø-Ø# = I am living   [Analyze and translate the source.]
    b. . . . +n-ēch . . . +tiā)   [Under the authority of the causative suffix, create a causative-object pronoun by replacing the nominative-case feature of the subject pronoun with an objective-case feature.]
    c. . . . +n-ēch(nemī-tia) . . .   [Create the causative core using the causative stem.]
    d. #Ø-Ø+n-ēch(nemī-tia)Ø+Ø-h#   [Import a new subject pronoun (here, 3rd pl).]

2. nēchnemītiah = they are causing me to live; i.e., they are sustaining me

Causative Verbstems (Second Type)

(1) pēhua; tla-(pēhua-l-tiā); 2nd sg
(2) tahci; tē-(ahxī-tiā); 1st pl
(3) temōhua; tla-(temō-huiā); 3rd sg
(4) ceceya; tla-(ce-ce-liā); 3rd pl
(5) tinēci; m-o-(nēx-tiā); 2nd sg

25D. *The Causative Transformation from a Transitive Source.* (1) Following the steps in the examples, transform the source VNC into a causative VNC, using the stem provided and the imported subject pronoun indicated. (2) Translate the result.

Example 1: nitlatta; tē+tla-(*itt-ī*-tiā); 2nd pl

1. *a.* #ni-∅+tla(tt-a)∅+∅-∅# =
I see s.th.   [Analyze and translate the source.]
b. ... +n-ēch ... +tiā ...   [Under the authority of the causative suffix, create a causative-object pronoun by replacing the nominative-case feature of the subject pronoun with an objective-case feature.]
c .... +n-ēch+tla(tt-ī-tiā) ...   [Create the causative core, using the causative stem and changing the mainline object of the source to a shuntline object (here the *tla* does not change shape).]
d. #an-∅+n-ēch+tla(tt-ī-tia)∅+∅-h#   [Import a new subject pronoun (here, 2nd pl).]

2. annēchtlattītiah = you (pl) are causing me to see s.th., you are showing me s.th.

Example 2: ticpoloah; tē+tla-(pol-ō-l-tiā); 2nd sg

1. *a.* #ti-∅+c-∅(pol-o-a)∅+∅-h# = we destroy it/them   [Analyze and translate the source VNC.]
b. ... +t-ēch+ ... -tiā ...   [Under the authority of the causative suffix, create a causative-object pronoun by replacing the nominative-case feature of the subject pronoun with an accusative-case feature.]
c. ... +t-ēch+☐-∅(pol-ō-l-tiā) ...   [Create the causative core, using the causative stem and changing the mainline object of the source to a shuntline object (here, c-∅ > ☐-∅).]

2. titēchpolōltia = you make us destroy it/them

(1) niquincaqui; tē+tē-(caquī-tiā); 2nd pl
(2) tlatepēhualo; tē+tla-(tep-ē-hua-l-tiā); 1st sg
(3) anquimāmah; m-o+tla-(māma-l-tiā); 2nd pl
(4) ticcua; tē+tla-(cua-l-tiā); 1st pl
(5) mozōma; tē+ne-(zōma-l-tiā); 3rd pl

25E. *Sentences Containing Causative VNCs.* Pronounce and translate.
1. Mā caxicmictiāni in tītlantli.
2. Ye ōchīhualtīlōc.
3. Ahnictemohuia in tlacualli.
4. Cuix ōmonemachtih?
5. Ayoc tēmachtīlo in cuīcatl.
6. Cuix ye ōquittītihqueh in chīmalli?
7. Ahno zo itlah quimonāmictīz.
8. Mā quintlapolōltīcān.
9. Mā nēn titēnezōmaltih.
10. Oc achi quicualtīz.
11. Cuix ōquītih in pahtli?
12. Ahquincua; zā quimmictia in tōtolmeh.
13. Quimauhtih in tētzāhuitl.
14. Cuix ye ōquitlācatilih?
15. Ōnittītīlōc in īcōzqui.
16. Mā motlacāhualtīcān...mā netlacāhualtīlo.
17. Īmācal mā tiquilactīcān.
18. Ticquīxtia in īxāyac.
19. Mec tētlehcahuīlo.
20. Mochi quiquīxtiah.
21. Tlachōctia; tlatlaōcoltia.

EXERCISE 26

Applicative Verbstems

26A. *The Difference between Nonapplicative and Applicative VNCs.* Analyze and translate.
1. conitta, quimonittilia
2. nināhuati, nimitznāhuatia
3. timihyāna, tinēchnehyānilia
4. nichōca, nicchōca
5. titlahtlani, tinēchtlahtlanilia
6. ēlcihcihui, quēlcihcihui
7. niccōhua, nicnocōhuia
8. titēmiquih, tictēmiquih

26B. *The Applicative Transformation.* (1) Following the steps in the example, transform the VNC into an applicative, using the stem provided and the imported applicative object indicated. (2) Translate the result.

Example: nicpōhua; tē+tla-(pōhui-liā); 2nd sg

1. *a.* #ni-∅+c-∅(pōhua)∅+∅-∅# = I am recounting it [Analyze and translate the source VNC.]
   b. ... +m-itz ... liā) ... [Import the applicative object pronoun sponsored by the applicative suffix.]
   c. ...+m-itz+□-∅(pōhui-lia)... [Create the applicative core, using the applicative stem and changing the main-line object of the source to a shuntline object (here, c-∅ > □-∅).]

2. nimitzpōhuilia = I recount it to you

(1) ticcōhua; tē+tla-(cōhui-liā); 1st sg
(2) niquihtoa; tē+tla-(iht-a-l-huiā); 3rd pl
(3) titotlātiah; tē+ne-(tlā-ti-liā); 2nd pl
(4) anquicaquih; tē+tla-(caqui-liā); nonspecif. human
(5) tēchnōtza; tē+tē-(nōchi-liā); 2nd sg

26C. *Recognizing the Source for Applicative VNCs.* Analyze and translate the VNC. Write out the source VNC and translate it.
1. mococoliah
2. quintlaquechilia
3. quitlāxilia
4. nictēquilia
5. nimitztlachīhuia
6. namēchchīhuilia
7. timotlahtlania

26D. *Sentences Containing Applicative VNCs*. Pronounce and translate.
1. Mā catecihuīlo in tomīl.
2. Ahzo quinānquilīzqueh.
3. Mā oc xicnemili.
4. Ca ahōnēchcaquilihqueh in toyāōhuān.
5. Cuix ahmococoliāyah?
6. Cuix ye ōtiquinchīhuilih?
7. Ahtleh nimitzcelilīz.
8. In nocōl ōconmottilih.
9. Mā nēn tiquintlapolhuih.
10. Quihuālmacayah in tlacualli.
11. Mā nēn ahtiquixtlāhuihtin.
12. Cuix tētzahtzilīlōc?
13. Tleh in tinēchmacaz?
14. Moch quincuīlihqueh.
15. Quinhuālcaquītih in ōquilhuih in teōtl.
16. Cuix ōtlapalēhuihqueh in tēlpōpōchtin?
17. Quinnezahuiliāyah in māmazah.

EXERCISE 27

Frequentative Verbstems

27A. *The Difference between Nonfrequentative and Frequentative VNCs.* Analyze and translate.

1. tzelihui, tzetzelihui
2. nitlacua, nitlacuacua
3. polōni, popoloca
4. tiquihxili, ticxihxili
5. chihcha, chihchihcha
6. ticteīnia, ticteteitza
7. nimitznōtza, nimitznohnōtza
8. mitznōchilia, mitznōnōchilia

27B. *Sentences Containing Frequentative VNCs.* Pronounce and translate.

1. Cuix ontlahtlamanalōc.
2. Huāllatōtocah in toquichtin.
3. Huāltotōcah in toquichtin.
4. Mā xihuālnehnemicān.
5. Quincuihcuīcatiah in īntēteōhuān.
6. Mā nēn contzahtzauctin.
7. Xichuihuixōcān in cuahuitl.
8. Mā quintzotzonilīcān in huēhuētl.
9. Cuix nelli in ōcontotōtz?
10. Quihtoh in ōquintēnahnāhuatilihqueh.
11. Nec tēxihxiliōhuac.
12. Oc popōcaya in tepētl.
13. In ichpōpōchtin quimomahmāmaltiāyah in cintli.
14. Quipohpolōltihqueh in ītlaōcol.
15. In mōmōyoh quiquinacayah.
16. Ca quitotōtzayah.
17. In tlācah tlahtlamāyah.
18. Totōcohuac.
19. Ye titocehcēhuihqueh.
20. Mec necehcēhuīlōc.
21. In tilmahtli quimmahmacac in tēuctli.
22. Nictohtomaz in īcac.
23. In acah ahquimotlahtlatilia in īāxcā.

24. Cuix chachapāni in quiyahuitl?—Ahmō, zan chichipīni. [*Ahmō* = "No."]
25. Mēxihcahé, mā huāllatotōca.
26. Quitlahtlattītiah in pōchtēcah.
27. Tiquintlahtlachiyaltiāyah in tēlpōpōchtin.

EXERCISE 28

Compound Verbstems: Verbal Embed

28A. *Compound Verbstems with an Intransitive Matrix.* Analyze and translate. Remember that the embed is always a preterit-tense predicate. Write out and translate the source VNCS.

Example: ninoquetztihcac

#ni-Ø+n-o(quetz-Ø-t-ihca)Ø+c-Ø# = I stand having got to my feet, I am standing in an upright position [*Ninoquetz*, "I got to my feet, I stood up"; *nihcac*, "I am standing."]

1. momimilohtiyah
2. quiyauhtimani
3. titopixtoqueh
4. quiquinacatiuh
5. ōquicuitihuetz
6. anquiquetztihuītzeh
7. ōtlanēztimanca
8. ihihcīcatihuītzah
9. momantiquīz
10. quimonitztoqueh
11. tocontēntihuih
12. ontlachixticatcah

28B. *Compound Verbstems with an Intransitivized-Reflexive Matrix.* Analyze and translate. Again, remember that the embed is always a preterit-tense predicate. Write out and translate the source VNCs.

Example: tōlohtimotlālīz

#Ø-Ø(tōl-o-h-Ø-ti-m-o-tlāl-ī)z+☐-Ø# = he will settle down to nodding, he will begin nodding [*Tōloh*, "he nodded"; *motlālīz*, "he will sit down/settle."]

1. ōnimictimotlālih
2. tlīliuhtimoquetzaz
3. xeliuhtimocāhua
4. ōihyāyatimotēcac
5. tlanēztimoquetz
6. ōtlamattimoman
7. tomāhuatimoquetza
8. tlayohuatimomana

28C. *Compound Verbstems of the Shared-Object Type.* Analyze and translate. Once more, remember that the embed is always a preterit-tense predicate. Write out and translate the source VNCs.

Example: nimitzēhuatitlālīz

#ni-Ø+m-itz(ē-hu-a-Ø-ti-tlāl-ī)z+☐-Ø# = I shall place you in a sitting position [*Nimitzēhuac* for *nimitzēuh*, I raised you up"; *nimitztlālīz*, "I shall place you."]

1. cololohtitlālihqueh
2. nictzaucticāuh
3. ōnēchhuilāntiquīxtih
4. quitēntimāyauhca
5. ninozauhtitēcaz
6. tictlapohticāhuazqueh

28D. *Compound Verbstems with a Future-Tense Embed.* Analyze and translate. Write out and translate the source VNCs. The embed is a future-tense predicate in an incorporated verb-object role.

Example: quihtōznequi

#∅-∅+qu-∅(iht-ō-z-nequi)∅+∅-∅# = it wants to say it; i.e., it means/signifies/denotes it

1. ticchīhuaznequih
2. nihuelitizquiya
3. mihtōtīzquiyah
4. quinecuilōznec
5. niquihnecuiznequi
6. ōhuetztoznecqueh
7. nicyōcoyazquiya
8. titotlalōznequiyah

28E. *Sentences Containing VNCs Built on Compound Verbstems.* Pronounce and translate.

1. Necoc micohuatiyah. [*Necoc* = on both sides; see § 44.6.]
2. Huālmocueptihuetzqueh in pīpiltin.
3. Cuix ahquilhuīznequi in ōāx?
4. In īntahhuān quintzahtzilihticateh.
5. Cuix ticnānquilīzquiya?
6. Tēchpalēhuīzquiyah in Mēxihcah.
7. Quimāntihuih mochīntin.
8. In īmicnīhuān quinhuālitztoqueh.
9. Ye tlathuiznequi.
10. Huāllamelāuhtihcac in ohtli.
11. Tlatzotzontihuītzeh in toyāōhuān.
12. In ohtli petzcauhtimoquetz. Zan nepehpetzcōlo.
13. Quimololhuihtihuih in māmaltin.
14. Toyāōhuān tēchyahualohtoqueh.
15. Īmīuh yeticah.
16. Quihuālpalēhuihtiyāzqueh oc cequīntin.
17. Cuecuepocatiuh tlexōchtli.
18. Monōnōtztocah in tītīcih.
19. Quicuitihuetz in tlahtōlli.
20. In tēteoh quiyahualohtimomanqueh in tlecuilli.
21. Chipāhuatimoquetz in ohtli.

EXERCISE 29

Purposive VNCs

29A. *Purposive VNCs in the Indicative Mood.* Analyze and translate. Write out and translate the future-tense VNC whose predicate fills the embed subposition.

1. quittītīto
2. quittato
3. quilhuīquīuh
4. ōcontzahtzacuacoh
5. huālmocuepatīhuih
6. tlacōhualōco
7. ōtitlehcōtoh
8. onahciquīhuih
9. niccaquītīco
10. tiquimpalēhuīcoh
11. tlahtlamātīuh
12. quīxohuato

29B. *Purposive VNCs in the Optative Mood.* Analyze and translate. Write out and translate the future-tense VNC whose predicate fills the embed subposition.

1. Mā quimontepēhuatīn.
2. Mā quināpalōqui.
3. Tlā xicnāmiquitīn.
4. Mā caticmahmacatīn.
5. Mā quinōnōtztihuetziquīn.
6. Mā xipahtiti.

29C. *Sentences with Purposive VNCs.* Pronounce and translate.

1. Concuitoh ohuatl.
2. Companahuīcoh in ātōyatl.
3. Quicāhuaquīuh tlacualli.
4. Tēchhuālmonāmictīcoh in toyāōhuān.
5. In tītlantin quittatoh ācalli.
6. Ītilmah ōtamēchmacaquīhuih.
7. Machiztico in ye huītzeh in pīpiltin.
8. Īmihīyo quicuitoh.
9. Totlatqui ōcānacoh.
10. Quittītītoh in tēuctli.
11. Conhuilānacoh in malli.
12. Nimitzilhuīco in ītlahtōl in totēucyo.
13. Mā xiquittati in motah.
14. Cuix ye cōyaquīhuih cintli?
15. Ca ahōnimitzihtlacōco.

16. Mā xinēchpalēhuīquih.
17. Cuix nelli in ahquintepēhuatoh in īnyāōhuān?
18. At mitzoncuīlītīuh in pahtli.
19. Ca ahmō huel mochīhuaz in ōmpa titlatlātlauhtītīhuih. Mā zan īc tiquincualānihtin. [*īc* = thereby, with that.]

EXERCISE 30

Compound Verbstems: Nominal Embed

30A. *The Incorporated-Object VNC*. Analyze and translate. Write out and translate the nounstem that serves as embed. Some of the compound stems in these VNCs require a novel way of thinking about the action signified.

Exa*mple:* nitlālcua = #ni-∅(tlāl-cua)∅+∅-∅# = I eat ground; i.e., I solemnly swear (by touching the earth and then bringing the fingers to the mouth) [< (tlāl)-li-, "land, earth, ground"]

1. quilhuiquīxtiliah
2. titlācamictihqueh
3. nitequicāhuaz
4. anquimohtlāxiliah
5. tlahuēlcui
6. niccuitlachīhuia
7. tēchohquechiliah
8. ticuauhaquiāya

30B. *The Incorporated-Adverb VNC with the Embed of the Compound Stem Coming from an Adverbial Source.* Analyze and translate. Write out and translate the nounstem that serves as embed.

Example: quitepachoah = #∅-∅+qui-∅(te-pach-o-a)∅+∅-h# = they are pressing down on him/her with rocks; i.e., they are stoning him/her [< *(te)-tl-*, "rock"]

1. quiteilpih
2. āpanoh
3. ticōlchipīnia
4. niquicxipolactia
5. ticmecapātzcah
6. timotequipachoa
7. niquinyacāna
8. ancalaquih

30C. *The Incorporated-Adverb VNC with the Embed of the Compound Stem Coming from a Nonadverbial Source.* Analyze and translate. Write out the possessive-state NNC that is the source for the embed.

Example: ōtzoniztaz = ō#∅-∅(tzon-izta-z)∅+☐-∅# = he/she became white at the hair; i.e., his/her hair became white [*Ītzon*, "it is his/her hair."]

1. ōiztehuehhuēiyac
2. ninometzpoztecca
3. ticcuātzayāna
4. quinmīlchīhua
5. monānmictih
6. quiquimilpatlac
7. timocxipāca
8. titocaccopīnah

30D. *The Incorporated-Complement VNC.* Analyze and translate. Write out the nounstem that serves as the embed and translate.

Example: nēchtlācamati = #Ø-Ø+n-ēch(tlāca-mati)Ø+Ø-Ø# = he knows me to be his master; i.e., he obeys me [< *(tlāca)-tl-*," person, master"]

1. ninotlācohcuepaz
2. quipilquīxtia
3. tiquinyāōchīhuah
4. timoxōlōpihcuepa
5. anquitētzāmmatih
6. mozōlnehnequi
7. namēchicnīuhtocaya
8. ticteōmatih

30E. *Sentences Containing VNCs with Nominal Embeds.* Pronounce and translate.

1. Zan ōēlcihciuhtinenca in malli.
2. Oc tēlpōchnēci.
3. Quitzīnquīxtihqueh in toquichtin.
4. Zan quitequicua in nacatl.
5. Zan huālmoyāōchihchīuhtiyah.
6. Mā camō amēchyōlihtlacōcān. [*Camō* = "not"; see § 44.5.4.]
7. Tiquimihcahuatztihuih in timācēhualtin.
8. Mā ximēllacuāhua, nocnīhué.
9. Quinyacatzacuilīzquiyah in īnyāōhuān.
10. Quīxnāmictimoquetzqueh in tlecuilli.
11. In tēuctli tēicnōitta.
12. Nicān tlālmahcēhualōco. [*Nicān* = here.]
13. Mā nēn tihuālnacaztlachix.
14. Ōquiztlacmīn in cōātl.
15. Cuix tehhuātl ōmitzcōānōtzqueh?
16. Ye ōnimazātlacualtih.
17. Ōnēchtōcātlālih notah.
18. Ihcoyocatiuh in ātl.
19. In Mēxihcah tlāltēmōtoh.
20. In cōātl ihzomocaya.
21. Zan ninotlāpachohtitēcaz.

EXERCISE 31

Compound Nounstems

31A. *The Embed-Before-Matrix Order in Compound Nounstems.* First, translate the components of the following compound stems literally (suggesting in the translation of the embed the nature of its modifying force on the matrix). Second, translate the compound stem freely. To foster an awareness of the difference between embed and matrix, the items are sequenced in chains.

Example: (cuā-te)-tl-

a. a rock in-the-form-of-a-head; *b.* hard-head [As in "You are a hard-head." Notice that this translation reverses the governed-before-governor order of the Nahuatl. Do not allow such translational reversals to confuse your grasp of the "embed precedes matrix" principle that controls all Nahuatl compound stems. Any reversal required by translation merely reveals a difference in the way the two languages envision the world.]

I. 1. (tzīn-tepoz)-tli-
    2. (tepoz-mī)-tl-
    3. (mī-cōmi)-tl-
    4. (cōn-tlīl)-li-
    5. (tlīl-ā)-tl-
    6. (ā-tōtol)-in-
    7. (tōtol-te)-tl-
    8. (te-cal)-li-
    9. (cal-oh)-tli-
    10. (oh-tēn)-tli-
    11. (tēn-tzon)-tli-
    12. (tzon-cal)-li-
    13. (cal-cuāi)-tl-
    14. (cuā-cuahui)-tl-
    15. (cuauh-māxa)-tl-
    16. (māx-tla)-tl-

II. 1. (tzīn-tlan)-tli-
    2. (tlan-cuāi)-tl-
    3. (cuā-naca)-tl-
    4. (naca-mōl)-li-
    5. (mōl-caxi)-tl-
    6. (cax-pech)-tli-

31B. *The Matrix in Compound Nounstems.* Translate the following nounstems in the same way as in Exercise 31A. Each group is formed on the same matrix.

I. Matrix stem: (cal)-li- = house, housing (enclosing framework), a structure
    1. (petla-cal)-li-
    2. (teoh-cal)-li-
    3. (ā-cal)-li-
    4. (xah-cal)-li-
    5. (cuauh-cal)-li-
    6. (tōtol-cal)-li-

II. Matrix stem: (te)-tl- = rock, egg
1. (xāl-te)-tl-
2. (teō-te)-tl-
3. (tzīn-te)-tl-
4. (tōtō-te)-tl-
5. (cōā-te)-tl-
6. (tēn-te)-tl-
7. (ā-te)-tl-
8. (īx-te)-tl-

31C. *The Embed in Compound Nounstems.* Translate the following nounstems in the same way as in Exercise 31A. Each group has the same stem as embed.

I. Embed stem: (tle)-tl- = fire
1. (tle-cal)-li-
2. (tle-cōmi)-tl-
3. (tle-caxi)-tl-
4. (tle-māi)-tl-
5. (tle-mōy-ō)-tl-
6. (tle-miy-ā-hua)-tl-
7. (tle-xō-ch)-tli-
8. (tle-cōā)-tl-
9. (tle-quiquiz)-tli-
10. (tle-cuahui)-tl-

II. Embed stem: (cal)-li- = house, housing (enclosing framework), a structure
1. (cal-īx)-tli-
2. (cal-lāl)-li-
3. (cal-mīl)-li-
4. (cal-nacaz)-tli-
5. (cal-coh-cōl)-li-
6. (cal-cuech)-tli-

31D. *Recursion in Compounding.* (a) Write out and translate the components of the compound stem; (b) state the formula used in the formation of the compound; i.e., a + (b + c) (i.e., with a compound matrix); (a + b) + c (i.e., with a compound embed); (a + b) + (c + d) (i.e., with both the matrix and the embed compound); etc.; (c) translate the compound.

Example: (ā-cal-chīmal)-li-

(a) (ā)-tl- = water; (cal)-li- = enclosing framework; (chīmal)-li- = shield: (b) formula: (a + b) + c: i.e., (ā-cal)-li- + (chīmal)-li-; (c) a shield in the form of a boat; i.e., a war dugout, a war canoe

1. (ā-cal-oh)-tli-
2. (te-mā-tla)-tl-
3. (xām-ā-cal)-li-
4. (xō-chi-chi-nān-cal)-li-
5. (ilhui-ca-ā-tēn)-tli-
6. (īx-tez-ca)-tl-
7. (ā-l-tepē-te-nāmi)-tl-
8. (mā-tle-quiquiz)-tli-

31E. *Sentences with Compound-Stemmed NNCs.* Pronounce and translate.
1. Cuix amoteōcuitl in īn?
2. Zan cequīntin companahuihqueh in ācalohtli.
3. Totōcah. Tequitlaneloah. Mācalhuītequih.
4. Īmmihmīcōn tehtēntiuh.
5. Quitlemīnah in teohcalli.
6. Toconācaltēnqueh in tlatquitl.
7. Niman quiquechcotōntihuetz in ītzontecon.
8. Ōquimacac in mōlcaxitl.
9. Quimahmamaltiuh ītlecuauh.
10. In ohtēntli quitocatiyahqueh.
11. Moquehquetza in tlenenepilli.

Compound Nounstems

12. In ātōtolin quinōtza in ehehcatl.
13. Moca cuahuiltetl ohōlīniz. [*Moca* = from/against/because of/by means of you.]
14. In tlequiquiztli quicāuhtiquīzqueh.

EXERCISE 32

Affective NNCs

32A. *NNCs Built on Affective Nounstems. Analyze and translate.*
1. āltepētl, āltepētōntli
2. nonān, nonāntzin
3. tochichiconēhuān, tochichiconēpipīlhuān
4. ācalli, ācalzolli
5. motah, motahtzin
6. cuācuahuitl, cuācuahuitōntli
7. īconēuh, īconētzin
8. tōtolin, tōtolpōl
9. cuitlapilli, cuitlapiltōntli
10. tēlpōchtli, tēlpōchtzintli [Also spelled *tēlpōttzintli*, as it is pronounced, as well as *tēlpōtzintli*.]
11. cōātl, cōātōntli
12. yōlcatl, yōlcatōntli

32B. *Sentences that Involve Affective NNCs.*
1. Zan mohuetztītihtoc in yōyōlitzin.
2. Tlālomitl ocuiltōn.
3. Quincua in zāyōltzitzin.
4. Tzapa quimehēllelquīxtiāya.
5. Cequi tepitōn.
6. In pīpiltotōntin quitquitinemih in temātlatl.
7. Mihtoa, "Cuix tOtompōl?"
8. Ahōquicac in ītlahtōl in nacaztzatza.
9. Quicencāhuiliah in īcuētōn in cihuātzintli
10. In pilpīl huehuetzca.
11. Conmaniliāyah tamaltepitōn.
12. Ohzolli in ahoc āc quitoca ohtli.
13. Chīmaltōntli quichīhuiliah in piltzintli.
14. Mā tlacāhua in amoyōllohtzin.

EXERCISE 33

Honorific VNCs
Pejorative VNCs

33A. *Honorific VNCs Built on Intransitive and Projective-Object Transitive VNCs.* Analyze and translate. Write out and translate the neutral VNC that serves as the source in each instance.

1. quimotlātilia
2. titēchmopiyalilia
3. ōquimocualtih
4. motlamauhtilia
5. mohuapāhuiltiah
6. nicnocelilia
7. ammahxiltihqueh
8. mā xinēchmopalēhuilīcān
9. anmocualāniltiah
10. motlamōchilīz
11. tiquimmihualtiāya
12. nēchmoxōxilih

33B. *Honorific VNCs Built on Reflexive-Object Transitive VNCs.* Analyze and translate. Write out and translate the neutral VNC that serves as the source in each instance.

1. molpihtzinoa
2. timopixtzinoāni
3. ammotolīnihtzinoah
4. mozōmahtzinoa
5. timozcalihtzinoa
6. ammotēcatzinōzqueh

33C. *Pejorative VNCs.* Analyze and translate. Write out and translate the neutral VNC that serves as the source in each instance.

1. nipolōnpōloa
2. nēchpolōnihpōloh
3. timitzmōtlapōlōzqueh
4. titlacuahpōloa
5. quimihxilpōloh
6. tictzomōnihpōloah

33D. *Sentences Containing Honorific, Reverential, and Pejorative VNCs.* Pronounce and translate.

1. Totēucyōé, notēlpōchtziné, mā xitēchmotlahtlātili!
2. Ca in ōmpa mitzonmotlapiyeliliah in mocōlhuān. [*Ōmpa* = there.]
3. Mā oc xicmocaquīti in notlahtōl, noxhuīuhtziné.
4. Mā oc tictotlahuehuetzquītilīcān in totēucyo.

5. At conmihcuanilīz in īpetlatzin.
6. Tleh ticmomachiltia?
7. Cuix ticmomaquilīz in mopiltzin in īntlatqui in tētēuctin?
8. Mā xicmocēhuilihtzino in monacayōtzin.
9. Ca motlahtlāhuāntihtinenca in pilli. Ca onmecānīlōc.
10. In notlahtōl xicmopiyaltīcān.
11. Nopiltzé, ca nicān mitzhuālmotlālilia in totēucyo. [*Nicān* = here.]
12. In īn, tlā xicmocuīli.
13. Mā xinēchmocnōittili. Mā xinēchmocnōmachīti in nimocnōtlācauh. Cuix ahtleh nimitznochīhuililia? Ca nitlachpāna. Ca nitlacuihcui. Nitletlālia in oncān nimitznotlahtōlchiyalia. [*Oncān* = there where.]
14. Mā camō ximomauhtīcān. Mā camō ximocuetlaxōcān. Ye neh nicmati anmochīntin antlamāzqueh. Zā zo quēxixquichtin tiquimmictīzqueh. [*Camō* = not.]
15. Xiyahpōlōcān! Xiquīzpōlōcān!
16. Cuix ōanquipolohpōlohqueh in nāmauh?

EXERCISE 34

Cardinal-Numeral NNCs

34A. *Numeral NNCs.* Analyze and translate.
1. caxtōltetl omōme
2. ōmpōhualli onchiucnāhui
3. mahtlācpāntli oncē
4. chiucnāuhōlōtl
5. yēpōhualtetl omēi
6. chicuacentlamantli
7. tlamic ommahtlāctli omōme
8. mahtlācpōhualli oncaxtōlli omēi
9. cempōhualli ommahtlāctli onnāhui
10. nāuhpōhualtetl ommācuīlli
11. caxtōlli-onnāuhpōhualli

34B. *Sentences Containing Cardinal-Numeral NNCs.* Pronounce and translate.
1. Zan mahtlāctli omōme nicnequi.
2. Cuix oc yēi?
3. Ye ōnicpoloh caxtōltetl.
4. Anquēxquichtin?—Tināhuintin.
5. Ahcaxtōltin omēi; zan caxtōltin.
6. Mā xinēchmaca chicuacentetl.
7. Cuix ētecpāntli ōpoliuh?
8. Zan nāuhmahpilli in conīz.
9. Nō nāhui in conmictih.
10. In xīhuitl huetz. Yēteyetiyah.
11. Mā oc ōme xinēchtēmoli.
12. Quēzqui īpatiuh in nāuhcuauhācalli?
13. Mā oc tiquinchiyecān in tēchpolōquīhuih. Ōntlamantin in ye huītzeh.
14. In centetl tecuāchtli īpatiuh catca mācuīlpōhualli in cacahuatl.
15. Ahzo nāuhtetl in cohololoah.
16. Mācuīlli mani.
17. Mozauhqueh ōmextin.

34C. Counting Exercise.
1. Count by fives from 15 to 35.
2. Count by tens from 10 to 60.

EXERCISE 35

Nominalization of VNCs (Part One)

35A. *Absolutive-State Preterit-Agentive NNCs.* Analyze and translate the preterit-agentive NNC. Write out and translate the preterit-tense VNC whose predicate serves as the nounstem of the NNC.

1. nicalpixqui
2. titemōc
3. titlanamacaqueh
4. tlamāmah
5. mīmicqueh
6. titlaneloh
7. tlapahqueh
8. antepāntlehcōqueh
9. titlahuēlīlōc
10. tlamīnqui
11. motolīnihqui
12. tētlacualtihqueh
13. nitlapixoh
14. titotlacuihqueh

35B. *Possessive-State Preterit-Agentive NNCs.* Analyze and translate. Write out the corresponding absolutive-state NNC.

1. tīcalpixcāhuān
2. nitiyahcāuh
3. tinotlahtohcāuh
4. nīnemachtihcāuh
5. antotlamāmahcāhuān
6. īneizcalihcāhuān
7. titotēyacāncāuh
8. nimotlamelāuhcāuh
9. ītōpīlehcāuh
10. amīnneihtōtihcāhuān

35C. *The Three Kinds of Preterit-Agentive NNCs of Ownerhood.* Analyze and translate. Write out the embed stem and translate it.

1. ezzoh
2. xocohuah
3. nochīllohcāuh
4. amīmīhuahcāhuān
5. titēnyoh
6. noyaquehcāuh
7. antequihuahqueh
8. temātleh
9. īmāyehcāuh
10. ticaquehqueh

35D. *Affective Forms of Preterit-Agentive NNCs.* Analyze and translate.

1. titlahuēlīlōcāpōl
2. miccātōntli
3. anteōpixcātzitzin
4. nimīlehcātōntli
5. īnemachtihcāpipīlhuān
6. netlacuihcāpōl

35E. *Compound-Stemmed Nuclear Clauses with Preterit-Agentive Nounstems as Embeds.* Analyze and translate.

1. nimauhcātlācatl
2. timotlamelāuhcāquetzaz
3. quimpāccātlahpalōtoh
4. nomīlehcāpoh
5. amēchmauhcāittah
6. tinēchtlahuēlīlōcāmati
7. ōanquinālquīzcācacqueh
8. īnnacayohcāpohtzin
9. ninococoxcānehnequi
10. nomiccātēx
11. chānehcāconētl
12. timomichhuahcāpohhuān

35F. *Sentences Containing Preterit-Agentive NNCs.* Pronounce and translate.

1. Tleh ītlahtohcātōcā?
2. In huēhuētqueh ahmō mihtōtiah. [*Ahmō* = not.]
3. Yahqueh in teōmāmahqueh.
4. In ācalchīmalehqueh totōcah.
5. In tilmahtli cōāxāyacayoh.
6. Tōtolnamacac tōtoleh.
7. Quinhuīcac in calpixqueh.
8. Quil ahtlācacemēleh.
9. In īntēnteuh in tlahtohqueh teōcuitlatēntetl.
10. In ītilmah tēntlapalloh.
11. In ihqueh īn, mīlehqueh.
12. In ichtilmahtli xohxōchitēnyoh.
13. In piltōntli nāneh.
14. In acah conmottilia tlācahuah yez.
15. Cuauhtenāmehtoc. Cuauhtenānyohtoc. [Explain why the embeds are not preterit-agentive NNCs.]

EXERCISE 36

Nominalization of VNCs (Part Two)

36A. *Customary-Present Agentive NNCs.* Analyze and translate the following pairs of VNCs and NNCs.

Example: nipanōni, nipanōni

   a. #ni-∅(panō)ni+∅-∅# = I customarily cross rivers
   b. #ni-∅(panō-ni)∅-∅# = I am one who customarily crosses rivers; i.e., I am a boat passenger

1. nitlahtoāni, nitlahtoāni
2. itzcuincuāni, itzcuincuāni
3. antlamatinih, antlamatinih
4. tēcuānih, tēcuānimeh
5. titozcaliānih, titozcaliānih
6. mānehneminih, mānehneminih
7. titlamatini, titlamatinitōn
8. tlāhuānani, tlāhuānanipōl
9. titēcuāni, tītēcuāniuh

36B. *Absolutive-State Instrumentive NNCs.* Analyze and translate the following pairs of VNCs and NNCs.

Example: panōhuani, panōhuani

   a. #∅-∅(panō-hua)ni+∅-∅# = all customarily cross a river
   b. #∅-∅(panō-hua-ni)∅-∅# = it is the means by which people cross a river, i.e., it is a passage on a boat, it is a bridge

1. tlālpōhualōni, tlālpōhualōni
2. texōni, texōni
3. tlacōhualōni, tlacōhualōni
4. nemachtīlōni, nemachtīlōni
5. nelpīlōni, nelpīlōni
6. tlatlapōlōni, tlatlapōlōnitōn
7. netlālīlōni, netlālīlōni
8. tlapātzcōni, tlapātzcōni

9. tlapātzcalōni, tlapātzcalōni
10. tlatlāxōni, tlatlāxōni

36C. *Possessive-State Instrumentive NNCs.* Analyze and translate the following pairs of VNCs and NNCs.

Example: tētlahpaloāya, ītētlahpaloāya

a. #∅-∅+tē(tlahpal-o-ā)ya+∅-∅# = he used to urge people to be healthy; i.e., he used to greet people
b. #∅-∅+ī-∅(tē-tlahpal-o-ā-ya)∅-∅# = it is his means of greeting people, i.e., it is his salutation, they are his words of greeting, it is his greeting gift, they are his greeting gifts

1. nitlanequiya, notlanequiya
2. titlacuāya, motlacuāya
3. ceyaya, īceyaya
4. titlamātocayah, totlamātocaya
5. tēmīnaya, ītēmīnaya
6. ammomānahuiāyah, amonemānahuiāya
7. tlahnecuiyah, īntlahnecuiya
8. niyōliya, noyōliya

36D. *Passive-Action NNCs (the Possessive State is Obligatory).* Analyze and translate the following pairs of VNCs and NNCs.

Example: ōnecōca, īnecōca

a. ō#∅-∅(nec-ō)ca+∅-∅# = it/they had been needed
b. #∅-∅+ī-∅(nec-ō-ca)∅-∅# = it is its/their being needed; i.e., it is its/their usefulness; it is useful, they are useful; there is a need for it/them

1. ōpalēhuīlōca, īpalēhuīlōca
2. ōnitlapōlōca, notlapōlōca
3. ōtīximachōcah, tīximachōca
4. ōmictīlōca, īmictīlōca
5. ōnemictīlōcah, īnnemictīlōca

36E. *The First Type of Active-Action NNCs (the Possessive State is Obligatory).* Analyze and translate the following pairs of VNCs and NNCs.

Example: ōlīnca, īōlīnca

a. #∅-∅(ōl-ī-n)ca+∅-∅# = it/they had moved/budged
b. #∅-∅+ī-∅(ōl-ī-n-ca)∅-∅# = it is its/their action of moving/budging

1. ōihtlacauhcah, īmihtlacauhca
2. ōmocuepca, īnecuepca
3. ōniyōlca, noyōlca
4. ōtinēzcah, tonēzca
5. ōtihuelnēzca, mohuelnēzca

Nominalization of VNCs (Part Two)

36F. *Sentences Containing Customary-Agentive, Instrumentive, Passive-Action, and First-Type Active-Action NNCs.* Pronounce and translate.

1. Ca nō miyec in īnnēzca.
2. In cihuātl ōquicelih in nepahtīlōni.
3. Ahommocāhua in tepoztlatecōni.
4. Cuix amītēyāōchīhuanih anyeznequih in tlahtoāni?
5. Ahtleh īnecōca.
6. In tlohtli tlahtlamāni.
7. Iz catqui in īmihtlacauhca in Otomih. [*Iz* = here.]
8. In cuauhtechalōtl quicua in cuahuitl īyacacelica.
9. Yāōtēcani in teōtl.
10. In ozomahtli moquichtlāliāni.
11. Īcualōca in tōnatiuh ōquīmmauhtih.
12. Cuix oncah ātlīhualōni?

EXERCISE 37

Deverbal Nounstems (Part One)

37A. *The Second Type of Active-Action NNCs.* Analyze and translate the VNCs and their active-action NNCs.

1. tzahtzi, ītzahtziliz, tzahtziliztli
2. titētlahpaloa, motētlahpalōliz, tētlahpalōliztli
3. titonēxtiah, tonenēxtīliz, nenēxtīliztli
4. antēxōxah, amotēxōxaliz, tēxōxaliztli
5. mocuepa, īnecuepaliz, necuepaliztli
6. quēlēhuia, ēlēhuīztli
7. chichiya, īchichiliz, chichiliztli
8. ninocāuhtiquīza, nonecāuhtiquīzaliz, necāuhtiquīzaliztli
9. quinequi, nequiztli

37B. *Passive-Patientive NNCs.* Analyze and translate the active-voice VNCs, their passive-voice counterparts, and the deverbal NNCs formed from stems derived from the latter.

1. annēchtītlanih, nitītlano, nitītlantli
2. quipiyah, piyalo, piyalli
3. ticnāhuatiah, nāhuatīlo, tonāhuatīl
4. quitzacua, tzacualo, tzacualli
5. quimahcēhua, mahcēhualo, mahcēhualli
6. ticpozōnah, pozōnalo, pozōnalli
7. nicpa, palo, palli
8. nictēmaca, tēmaco, notēmac

37C. *Sentences Containing Passive-Patientive and Second-Type Active-Action NNCs.* Pronounce and translate.

1. Cuauhtenāmehtoc in ithualli.
2. Quichīuhqueh in īn tītlantin.
3. Quimihua in nānāhualtin.
4. Malmiquih in pōchtēcah. Malmicohua.
5. Quimotequitiah in tēihpītzaliztli.

Deverbal Nounstems (Part One)

6. Quihtlanilīz in ītēicnēlīliz.
7. Ahzo cocolizcuizqueh.
8. Ye nāhualquīzah in amoyāōhuān!
9. Nō quimāhuiltiah in tēxōxaliztli.
10. Cuix ahtitēnāmichuān?
11. "Ca nimitztlahtlātīz."—"Ca ye cualli. Tlā xihuāllauh."
12. Cequīntin tzacualli quitlehcahuihqueh.

EXERCISE 38

Deverbal Nounstems (Part Two)

38A. *Impersonal-Patientive NNCs.* Analyze and translate the impersonal-voice VNC and the patientive NNC. Give the active-voice verbstem.

1. chihchalo, chihchalli
2. tlatataco, tlatatactli
3. tlalpīlo, tlalpīlli
4. tlaxcalo, tlaxcalli
5. necuiltōnōlo, necuiltōnōlli

38B. *Compound NNCs Built on Passive- or Impersonal-Patientive VNCs.* Analyze and translate. Give the active-voice verbstem.

1. cuauhhuātzalo, cuauhhuātzalli
2. neīxcāhuīlo, neīxcāhuīlli
3. nāhuatīlo, teōtl īnāhuatīl, teōnāhuatīlli
4. cuahchico, cuahchictli
5. tlaquetzalo, tlaquetzalli tetl, tetlaquetzalli

38C. *Sentences Containing Impersonal-Patientive NNCs and Compound NNCs Built on Passive- or Impersonal-Patientive VNCs.* Pronounce and translate.

1. Cuix ye neteōithualtēmalōc?
2. Māpozōnalnehnequi in īn.
3. Āc in tlaxcalixcac?
4. Cuix titlaxcalchīhuaznequi?
5. Tlaāltīlmicohuaya. Tēātiāyah in pōchtēcah.
6. Quihua tlahtōlitquic.
7. Quihuālcaquītiāyah in ītlahtōl.
8. Huālquīzah in cuācuahchictin.
9. Quimmacah izquitlamantli.
10. Zan in tlahtoāni īneīxcāhuīl.
11. In ihqueh īn, īntlacual in etl.
12. Zan quimātlatēmah in tlaōlli.
13. In cuauhhuātzalli huetztoc.

14. In chapolin chihchaleh.
15. Ye ontēcuāncualōzqueh; tēcuāncualtin; tēcuānimeh īntlacualhuān.
16. Quitzacualtihqueh in tōnatiuh.
17. In īn tōnalli mihtoāya ahmō cualli; tēcuāntōnalli. [*Ahmō* = not.]
18. In mochīntin tēteoh quiyahualohtimomanqueh in tlecuilli.

EXERCISE 39

Deverbal Nounstems (Part Three)

39A. *Perfective-Patientive NNCs.* Analyze and translate the following VNCs and their derived NNCs.

1. ōtlaquēn, tlaquēntli
2. ōtlequiquiz, tlequiquiztli
3. ōtēnōtz, tlanōtztli
4. ōtlaquetz, tlaquetztli
5. ōnitlachīuh, notlachīuh
6. ōyōl, yōlli
7. *ōyōlloh, yōllohtli
8. *ōtlazoh, tlazohtli
9. ōnen, īnen
10. ōnitlalcāuh, tlalcāuhtli

39B. *Contrast between Preterit-Agentive NNCs and Perfective-Patientive NNCs.* Analyze and translate.

1. titonōtzqueh, nenōtztli
2. tlamelāuhqui, tlamelāuhtli
3. tlachīuhqui, tlachīuhtli
4. poztecqui, poztectli
5. tlahtlalpītzqui, tlahtlalpītztli
6. tlanamacac, tlanamactli
7. tēihxilqui, tlahxilli
8. tlacāuhqui, tlacāuhtli

39C. *Imperfective-Patientive NNCs.* Analyze and translate the following VNCs and their derived NNCs.

1. nitlatqui, notlatqui
2. tlazo, tlazōtl
3. quiyahui, quiyahuitl
4. tlazaca, zacatl
5. tlatechaloa, techalōtl
6. nitlacuihcui, tlacuihcuitl
7. tlaquēmi, tlaquēmitl
8. cepayahui, cepayahuitl

39D. *Imperfective-Patientive NNCs Whose Nounstems have (-yō)-tl- as a Matrix.* Analyze and translate.

1. tlahtōlli, tlahtōllōtl
2. ahtlācatl, ahtlācayōtl
3. oquichtli, oquichyōtl
4. nāntli, nānyōtl
5. mahuiztli, mahuizzōtl
6. tēntli, tēnyōtl
7. tlahtohqui, tlahtohcāyōtl
8. ichcatl, ichcayōtl

39E. *The Difference between Adventitious and Organic Possession.* Analyze and translate.

1. īchiquiuh, īchiquiuhyo
2. noxināch, noxināchyo
3. motohmiuh, ītohmiyo
4. monac, monacayo
5. īxōchihcual, īxōchihcuallo
6. īnex, īnexxo

39F. *NNCs Built on Root- and Stock-based Patientive Nounstems.* Analyze and translate the following VNCs and their derived NNCs.

1. xoxōhui, xoxoctli
2. cualāni, cualactli
3. catzāhua, catzactli
4. tlapechoa, tlapechtli
5. tzapīni, tzaptli
6. tlacomōloa, tlacomōlli
7. malacachihui, malacachtli
8. tlahpalihui, tlahpalli
9. ilacachihui, ilacachtli
10. petzihui, petztli

39G. *Sentences Containing Perfective-Patientive NNCs, Imperfective-Patientive NNCs, and Root- or Stock-based NNCs.* Pronounce and translate.

1. Cocoya in īnacayo.
2. Ōmotlahtōlhuelittac in teōpixqui.
3. Ye ōquipoloh in ītlatqui.
4. Quīximatih xihuitl in iihīyo.
5. Quimatiyah in īmihīyo cīcītlaltin.
6. Conquēntia in quetzalquēmitl.
7. In tēlpōpōchtin īntequiuh catca in cōātequitl.
8. Tepoztli in īntlahuītōl.
9. In īmezzo in miquiyah huel ōmpa huālahciya. [*Huel ōmpa* = all the way to there.]
10. Ōquitēcaqueh tlapechtli.
11. Monequi amotlahpal.
12. In ahyōllohtlahpalihui zan motlaloa.
13. Xicchīuhtihuetzi in tleh in tichīhuallano.
14. Oncān ihīyōcuiqueh. In īmihīyo quicuiqueh. [*Oncān* = in that place, there.]
15. Quihuīcatiyahqueh cuauhtlapechtli.
16. In ītecollo in ocotl ōcontōcaqueh.
17. Zā cē īntlahuītōl yetinenca. In īmmīcōn quimāmahtinencah. [Here *(nemi)* has a distant-past-as-past tense formation; see § 11.4.9.]
18. Ca ītequimācēhuallo māyītia. [Said of a lord guilty of alcohol abuse. Remember that when the personal-pronoun object of *tla-(āyi)* is specific, it is only silently present.]
19. Mā xoconmotlaōcolnōnōchilīcān in totēucyo.
20. Itlah quimomachitoca.
21. Teh xiccuitihuetzi in tleh in ticuitlano.
22. In Mēxihcah quimilhuih, "Nopilhuāné, mā titlachcuitequicān. Mā achihtzin tictlālīcān tlachcuitectzintli."

EXERCISE 40

Adjectival NNCs (Part One)

40A. *Patientive NNCs as Adjectival NNCs.* Analyze the following NNCs. Translate them, first with a noun in the English predicate and then with an adjective. Write out the source verbstem and translate it.

Example: tlīlli

#Ø-Ø(tlīl)li-Ø# = (a) it is ink; (b) it is black [< (tlīl-i-hui), "to become inky"]

1. cōztli
2. tlapahtīlli
3. tzōlli
4. yēctli
5. catzactli
6. tlatlactli
7. tlacohcopīntli
8. melactli
9. tlaāntli
10. neīxcāhuīlli

40B. *Preterit-Agentive NNCs Translated as Adjectives.* Analyze the following preterit-agentive NNCs. Translate them, first with a noun in the English predicate and then with an adjective. Write out the source verbstem and translate it.

Example: huācqui

#Ø-Ø(huā-c-Ø)qui-Ø# = (a) it is a dry thing; (b) it is dry [< (huā-qui), "to become dry."]

1. tlīliuhqui
2. catzāhuac
3. ichtic
4. yacahuitztic
5. tlanqui
6. tlatlactic
7. teuhyoh
8. tilāhuac
9. tlapānqui
10. huēiyac

40C. *Nominalized Obsolete Preterit-Agentive NNCs Translated as Adjectives.* Analyze the following obsolete preterit-agentive NNCs. Translate them, first with a noun in the English predicate and then with an adjective. Write out the source verbstem and translate it.

Example: iztāc

#Ø-Ø(iztā-Ø)c-Ø# = (a) it is a white thing; (b) it is white [< (izta-ya), "to become like salt," i.e., "to become white"]

Adjectival NNCs (Part One)

1. ihyāc
2. ātic
3. chichic
4. yancuic
5. ītztic
6. xococ
7. cōztic
8. cecec

40D. *The Nominalized Customary-Present Passive VNC Translated as an Adjective.* Analyze and translate the following NNCs as adjectives. Write out and translate the active-voice source verbstem.

1. chiyalōni
2. pōhualōni
3. necōni
4. chōquilīlōni
5. namacōni
6. ichtecōni
7. cualōni
8. chīhualōni

40E. *Sentences with Adjectival NNCs.* Pronounce and translate.

1. Tenāmeh in āltepētl.
2. Miyec in tlamantli.
3. Zan tiyohqueh in tihuēhuētqueh.
4. In īmitzcuinhuān huehhuēintin.
5. Yehhuāntin ahīmel. Tlatziuhqueh.
6. In tlaquetzqui tlahtōlhuēlic.
7. In tlālchīuhqui chicāhuac.
8. In īpōcyo ihyāc.
9. Cequīntin tlīltic in īntzon.
10. Ahhuēiyac in īncuē.
11. Ēintin motolīnihqueh.
12. In oquichtin tlazohtli in īncac.
13. Nehhuātl ezzoh in noxāyac.
14. Nepāpan in cōlōtl. [*Cōlōtl* is being used generically.]
15. In ītēntzon huīyac.
16. In īn ahīhuani.
17. Mizquitl in ītlaaquīllo exōtic.
18. Īmacaxōni in yāōquīzcāyacānqui. [Here *(yāō)-tl-* stands for *(yāō-yō)-tl-*.]
19. Īahtlapal pōccōztic.
20. Mahuiztic in tlahmachtilmahtli.

EXERCISE 41

Adjectival NNCs (Part Two)

41A. *Intensified Stems in Adjectival NNCs.* Analyze and translate the following pairs of adjectival NNCs.

1. chamactli, chamaccaltic
2. huitztli, huitztōntli
3. cōztli, cōzpōl
4. huapactli, huapacpahtic
5. huehhuēintin, huehhuēipopōl
6. ītztic, ītzticāpahtic
7. tapayoltic, tapayolticātōntli
8. tlahpaltic, tlahpalticāpōl

41B. *Adjectival NNCs Involving Various Kinds of Compound-Stem Formations.* Analyze and translate the following pairs.

1. niztāc, nicuāiztāc
2. tlahuēlīlōc, tēntlahuēlīlōc
3. huitztic, tzīnhuitztic
4. tichicāhuac, tiyōllohchicāhuac
5. titlahuēlīlōqueh, tiyāōtlahuēlīlōqueh
6. niztalli, nicuāiztalli
7. huāctli, tlālhuāctli
8. huācqui, cuauhhuācqui
9. huīyac, tlācahuīyac
10. ihyāc, xoquihyāc
11. tilāhuac, ihhuitilāhuac
12. tilāhuac, ihhuiyōtilāhuac
13. ololtic, cuitlaololtic
14. ancatzactin, anteōcatzactin
15. tecontic, cuātecontic
16. pitzactotōntin, māpitzactotōntin

41C. *Adjectival Embeds in Compound-Stemmed NNCs.* Analyze and translate the following pairs.

1. tlazohtli, tlazohcuēitl
2. tepoztli, īntepoztōpīl
3. tlahuēlīlōc, tlahuēlīlōcātlahtōlli
4. ichtli, īmichtilmah
5. cocoxqui, mococoxcānān
6. mauhqui, mauhcāmicqui

41D. *Sentences Involving NNCs Formed with Adjectival Components.* Pronounce and translate.

1. Ahyōllohchicāhuac in īcnīuh.
2. Īmichcamāxtli yetinemi.
3. Tlazohtlanqui in ti!mahtli.
4. In īmitzcuinhuān huehhuēipopōl.
5. Huālquīza in īhuēitlatqui. [Here *(huē-i)-∅-* has the meaning "important."]

6. Ēllahuēlīlōc in tēlpōchtli.
7. Quimmacayah in tlazohtilmahtli.
8. Ōtlālhuāccāquīzacoh.
9. Ye nicuāiztaleh.
10. In tlanōtztli tlahtōlhuēlic.

EXERCISE 42

Adjectival Modification (Part One)

42A. *The Adjectival-Modification Transformation.* In each of the following pairs of sentences, the first serves as the source for the second. Translate the first as a structure of supplementation and the second as a structure of adjectival modification.

Example: Huēi in calli. Calli huēi.
   a. The house is big. [The adjectival NNC is the principal.]
   b. It is a house that is big. It is a big house. [The adjectival NNC is the adjunct.]

1. Huēiyac in īncuē. Īncuē huēiyac.
2. Neucyoh in tlaxcalli. Tlaxcalli in neucyoh.
3. Ihyāc in pōctli. Pōctli ihyāc.
4. Ītztic in ehcatl. Ehcatl in ītztic.
5. Cualli in petlatl. Petlatl cualli.
6. Yēctli in ātl. Ātl yēctli.
7. Tichicāhuac in titlālchīuhqui. Titlālchīuhqui tichicāhuac.
8. Tlatziuhqueh in notlācahuān. Notlācahuān in tlatziuhqueh.

42B. *The Problem of Ambiguity in Structures of Supplementation and Structures of Adjectival Modification.* In the following sentences, translate the adjunct clause first as a supplement and second as an adjectival modifier.

Example: Tohmitl in huēiyac.
   a. That which is long is fur.
   b. It is fur that is long. It is long fur.

1. Titlācatl in timozcalih.
2. Tletl in tictlālihqueh.
3. Nimoxhuīuh in nicualli.
4. Calli in quichīuhqueh.
5. Tlālli in huācqui.
6. Tlātlācohtin cihuah.

42C. *The Preposing Transformation.* Translate the source and the transform. (Remember: Translation violates the source sentence, so English is free to translate both constructions the same way.)

Example: Quih in octli in cualli. Quih in cualli octli.
   a. They drink pulque that is good. They drink good pulque.
   b. They drink good pulque.

Adjectival Modification (Part One) 75

    1. Yah in calpixqui in huēi. Yah in huēi calpixqui.
    2. Monequi in tlaxcalli iztāc. Monequi in iztāc tlaxcalli.
    3. Cocoliztli in huēi mochīuh. Huēi cocoliztli mochīuh.
    4. Quitataca in teōcuitlatl in cōztic. Quitataca in cōztic teōcuitlatl.
    5. Quinamaca in tilmahtli in tlazohtli. Quinamaca in tlazohtli tilmahtli.

42D. *Further Sentences Involving Adjectival Modification.* Pronounce and translate.
    1. Zan mocenchīhuaya in tlacualli in quicuāyah.
    2. Quinamaca in nepāpan ihhuitl.
    3. In cōātl quimitta in onoqueh mācēhualtin.
    4. In īauh ītztic ātl.
    5. Quimīximatiyah in ōmpa onoqueh cīcītlaltin. [*Ōmpa* = in that place, there.]
    6. Ca nō miyec in īnnēzca in quichīuhqueh.
    7. Quinhuīcac oc cequīntin calpixqueh.
    8. Quicaquih in tlahtōlli in quihtohtihuih in huēhuētqueh.
    9. Yehhuāntin īntlaīximach in ōmpa mochīhua peyōtl.
    10. Tomāhuac in cuahuitl ihcaca.
    11. Quimittītihqueh in quihuālcuiqueh cōzcatl.
    12. Ōntetl in ācalli in concalaquihqueh.
    13. Ixquich tlācatl quicac.
    14. Quimmacah in izquitlamantli quitquiqueh.

42E. What does the compound-stemmed NNC *xāyacatlachihchīhualli*, "it is a mask," tell one about the syntax of the concatenate construction *tlachihchīhualli xāyacatl*, "it is a mask"? Translate the two expressions literally.

EXERCISE 43

Adjectival Modification (Part Two)

43A. *The Nonpreposed Adjectival Modifier.* First translate every component in each sentence literally and then give a free translation of the sentence.

Example: Ca nehhuātl in niquimahman.

   a. Indeed I-am-the-one adjr I-upset-them.
   b. I am indeed the one who disturbed them.

1. In cihuah, ca tlazohtli in huīpilli in quichīuhqueh.
2. Ca yehhuātl in quitlālih in zāzanīlli.
3. Momauhtihqueh in nānāhualtin in quimictihqueh in pōchtēcatl.
4. Tlatziuhqueh in mācēhualtin in ōmpa cah īmmīl. [*Ōmpa* = it-is-at-that-place, i.e., there.]
5. In tamalli quinamaca, yehhuātl in tōtoltetamalli.
6. Quicuiqueh in ixquich in quittaqueh.

43B. *Both Preposed and Nonpreposed Adjectival Modifiers in the Same Sentence.* First translate every component in each sentence literally and then give a free translation of the sentence.

1. Cē ātlacuic cihuātl in quimittac.
2. In īn tlatquitl in monec quipiyayah in pīpiltin.
3. Quinamaca in nepāpan ihhuitl in tlazohtli.
4. Conānqueh cē huēi tiyahcāuh in chicāhuac.
5. Quipiya cē tezcatl in malacachtic.

43C. *The Topicalization of the Head of a Structure of Modification.* For both the source sentence and its transform, first translate every component literally and then translate the sentence freely.

1. Nimitzmaca mochi in necuiltōnōlli. Mochi nimitzmaca in necuiltōnōlli.
2. Ihīyoh in octli in quīyah. In octli ihīyoh in quīyah.
3. Quinhuālhuīcac miyequīntin Españoles. Miyequīntin quinhuālhuīcac Españoles. [The Spanish word *Españoles* must be given a Nahuatl NNC structure to work in the sentences, namely: #∅-∅(Españoles)□-□#, "they are Spaniards." The Nahuatlization could have been more complete with *Españolesmeh*, i.e., with a sounded plural-number dyad: #∅-∅(Españoles)m-eh#.]

Adjectival Modification (Part Two)

4. Oncah ixquich in tōnacāyōtl. Ixquich oncah in tōnacāyōtl.
5. Micqueh miyequīntin in tiyahcāhuān. Miyequīntin micqueh in tiyahcāhuān.
6. Momauhtihqueh mochīntin in toyāōhuān. Mochīntin momauhtihqueh in toyāōhuān.
7. Yehhuāntin īntlaīximach mochi in āxcān nemi. Mochi yehhuāntin īntlaīximach in āxcān nemi. [*Āxcān* = it-is-at-the-present; i.e., at the present.]
8. Quincuīlihqueh moch in īnyāōtlatqui. Moch quincuīlihqueh in īnyāōtlatqui.
9. Quitlatia in āmatl tlaōlchipīnīlli. In āmatl quitlatia tlaōlchipīnīlli.
10. Ca pitzāhuac in tlacōtl in ticpiya. In tlacōtl ca pitzāhuac in ticpiya.

43D. *Āc* **and** *Tleh* **as Heads in Structures of Modification.** First translate each component in the sentence literally and then translate the sentence freely.

1. Nicmacac in tleh in quinec.
2. In āc in quīzaznequi ōmpa quihuālxihxilih. [*Ōmpa* = it-is-at-that-place, i.e., at that place, there.]
3. Ōniquittac in āc in ōquichtec.
4. In tleh in ōtiquihtoh, ca nelli.
5. Ōquittac in tleh in ticchīhuazqueh. [Translate the future tense as a future-in-the-past.]
6. Cuix quimati in tleh in quimomachtia?

43E. *Further Sentences Involving Adjectival Modification.* Pronounce and translate.

1. Cemeh tehhuāntin tiquimmacatihuih in tlatquitl.
2. Ixquich oncah in xōchihcualli.
3. In īn mochi nanacatl ahxoxōuhcācualōni.
4. In āc in miyec quicua, miyec tlamantli quitta tēmahmauhtih.
5. Mochi oncah in nepāpan ichcatl.
6. Ahoc āc tlācatl ōquīz in mācēhualli.
7. Mochi quīximati in nepāpan tlazohtetl.
8. Ixquich ōlīn in huēhuēntzin.
9. In chīlli quinamaca in cualli.
10. In pahtli quīximati in micohuani.
11. Miyec in quitquiqueh in teōcuitlatl.
12. In quitquiqueh in tētlahpalōliztli, cuix miyec?
13. Ahzo acah ye huītz cemeh in tocnīhuān.
14. Cē notiāchcāuh ōtitomictihqueh.
15. Ca ahmō cē namēchhuelitta. Ca ahmō azcemeh annēchyōlpachihuiltiah.

EXERCISE 44

Adverbial Nuclear Clauses

44A. *Adverbial Expressions.* Analyze and translate the following adverbial expressions. Identify each as a particle, an adverbialized VNC, or an adverbialized NNC. If it is an NNC, state whether it is a first- or second-degree adverb.

1. cencah
2. ahmō
3. necoc
4. ye
5. ahhuel
6. mōztla
7. tlaōcoxcā
8. tlacuāuh
9. yēhua
10. iz
11. oc nohmah
12. tlahcah
13. nēn
14. nel
15. cemilhuitl
16. īchān
17. cuēl
18. cemihcac
19. cenyohual
20. chico
21. tlācaēhuatl
22. tlamelāuhcā
23. iuh
24. tēlpōchcalli

44B. *Sentences Containing Adverbialized Nuclear Clauses.* Pronounce and translate. (The sentences given here anticipate the description of adverbial modification in Lesson 49.)

1. Ahhuel nicmāma.
2. Necoc huālhuetzih.
3. Iuh cah noyeliz.
4. Tlahcah nēcini.
5. Nel monequi.
6. Īnchan yauh in īn ohtli.
7. Cuix cemihcac ninemiz?
8. Ommaquiāyah tlācaēhuatl.
9. Mā huāllauh ihciuhcā.
10. Nōncuah momanah in tēlpōpōchtin.
11. Īxtlapal onoc.
12. Tēlpōchcalli caquihqueh.

Adverbial Expressions 79

13. Niman quihtoh in Quetzalcōātl, "Tleh in īn? Ca cencah cualli. In cocoliztli, ca ōcompoloh. Cāmpa ōyah cocolli? Ca ahoc mō ninococoa." [*Cāmpa* = to where?]
14. Mā cuēl eh niccēhuihto in nonacayo! [The VNC is an optative form of a connective-**t** compound verbstem.]
15. In ōachto ommicqueh māmaltin.
16. Cenyohual itztoc.

EXERCISE 45

Relational NNCs (Part One)

45A. *Relational Nounstems That Permit Only Option One.* Analyze the following NNCs and translate, first literally and then freely.

Example: amohuān

#Ø-Ø+am-o(huān)Ø-Ø# = it is your (pl) company; in your (pl) company, with you (pl)

1. ītloc
2. īmpal
3. mohuān
4. notloc
5. topal
6. īnhuān

45B. *Sentences Involving Relational Nounstems That Permit Only Option One.* Pronounce and translate.

1. Ahmō īhuān tlatlah in tlahtoāni.
2. Yehhuāntin zan quēmman totloc cateh.
3. Tleh in ticchīhuazqueh in īc huel tiquīzazqueh?
4. Mā cualli īc ninemini!
5. Zan īpaltzinco titīximaticoh in totēucyo.
6. Ca oc cē. Xoconi. Ca cualli in pahtli; īc chicāhuaz in monacayo.
7. Īc cen yauh in ilaquīlo.
8. Achi huel cemmātl in īc huīyac.
9. Cualli īc xinemi in īc cualli īc timiquiz.
10. Yeh in īc huēi!
11. In īc mihtoah "miccāzāyōlin": quil īntōnal in tomiccāhuān.
12. Īnhuān nitlacuāz.
13. Quimacatīuh in īhuān yōlqui; īc quinēxtia in netlazohtlaliztli.
14. Ahmō īnhuān yōlqueh in quimānayah.
15. In īc tetecuica motleuh!
16. In monān, īhuān in mohuēltīuh, ōmitzmocencāhuililih.

EXERCISE 46

Relational NNCs (Part Two)

46A. *The Preterit-Agentive Nounstem as Embed to the Matrix Nounstem (-n)-tli.* Analyze and translate the following NNCs. Write out both the restricted-use and general-use preterit-agentive stems (the latter serves as the embed for the compound-stemmed locative nounstem).

Example: āhuahcān

#∅-∅(ā-huah-∅-cā-n)☐-∅# = it is a place of water owners [< (ā-huah-∅)-☐- > (ā-huah-∅-cā)-tl-, "a water owner"]

1. tēpahpāquiltihcān
2. tōllohcān
3. cacnamacacān
4. tēchōctihcān
5. tlaxcalchīuhcān
6. tēcuiltōnohcān

46B. What is the difference in formation between the locative NNCs in Exercise 46A and a possessive-state locative NNC such as *īonocān*?

46C. *Locative (or Temporal) Nounstems Formed on the Matrix Nounstem (-n)-tli- with the Imperfect-Tense Core of Active and Impersonal VNCs Filling the Embed Subposition.* Analyze and translate the following NNCs.

1. īneāltiāyān
2. calacōhuayān
3. īquīzayān
4. tlayohuayān
5. panōhuayān
6. tlaxcalnamacōyān
7. tlapiyalōyān
8. moyeyān

46D. *Locative Nounstems Formed on the Matrix Nounstem (-tlah)-tli-.* Analyze and translate the following NNCs.

1. nohpallah
2. ohōztōtlah
3. cuauhyohuacātlah
4. cahcallah
5. netlah
6. zoquitlah

46E. *Locative Nounstems Formed on the Matrix Nounstem (-co)-☐- or (-c)-tli.* Analyze and translate the following NNCs.

1. ātlacomōlco
2. quimilco
3. īquiyāhuatēnyōc
4. tiānquizco
5. īxiquipilco
6. nohuamīlco
7. īmīxco
8. tlachco
9. amomāc
10. ahpilōlco

46F. *Nounstems Formed on the Matrix Nounstems (-pa)-☐- (Direction), (-pa)-☐- (Frequency), and (-teuh)-☐-.* Analyze and translate the following NNCs.

1. tlacōchcalcopa
2. mācuīlpa
3. zacateuh
4. noceyalizcopa
5. quiyāhuacpa
6. tlaxcalteuh
7. nāuhpa (also: nāppa)
8. mātlateuh
9. mahtlācpa omōme
10. īmāōpōchcopa
11. ihhuiteuh
12. caxtōlpa

46G. *Sentences Formed with Relational Nounstems That Permit Only Option Two.* Pronounce and translate.

1. Mā caōppa xinōtzalo.
2. Cuauhyohuacātlah ōquīzqueh.
3. Nāuhcān xeliuhticah.
4. Cuauhtlah īmochīhuayān.
5. Huālmotzonicquetz in yōlcatzintli.
6. Texcalco in īchān.
7. Conmana tleco in oncān ithualco.
8. Teohtlālli iihtic ōmic.
9. Ayāc tleh contēnquīxtīz. Zan amihtic.
10. Mā tlapiyelo in nōhuiyān ātēnco.
11. Ōmpa huālpēuh in tōnatiuh īcalaquiyāmpa.
12. Ca ye ixquich cāhuitl in cencah īīxco titlachiyaznequih.
13. Ye īmonequiyān in nitlacuāz.
14. Achi cōntōnco contēca in ātl.
15. Calihticpa ōnontlachix.
16. Cuix ōticteteuhilpih?
17. Ahcohuetzi in īnyōllo.
18. Cuix totlocpa ēhuazqueh?
19. Ceccān ixtlāhuacān motēcatoh.
20. Yehhuān īmīxcohyān īncatiyān, ca īncalpōllōc.
21. Ōnahcico in nahciyān.
22. Īnnetōcayān catca tlahtohqueh.
23. In īnteōuh quimilhuih, "Oc nachca in tihuih." Niman yahtiyahqueh in tōnatiuh īcalaquiyāmpa.
24. Ahoc mō huel molnāmiqui in quēxquich oncān onocah.
25. Quēxquich cāhuitl in ixtlāhuacān nenqueh ahoc mō āc quimati.

Relational NNCs (Part Two)

26. Monechicoah in īcalnāhuac tlācah.
27. Oncān yōli in tlacuechāhuayān. [The *tla-* is an impersonalizing *tla-*. The intransitive verbstem *(cuech-ā-hua)* is translated as "to become damp/moist."]
28. Cuauhtlah tlatzmolīniyān. [The intransitive verbstem *(itz-mol-ī-ni)* is translated "(for trees, etc.) to sprout."]
29. Cāmpa cah nomahcuex?—Cuix nīxnāhuac?
30. Mā oc xonpilhuahcāteuhtlamattocān.

46H. *The Deer*

In mazātl cuācuahueh, ca oquichtli. Cuācuauhtihtīcectic, cuācuammātzōltic. In ōtlatziuh īcuācuauh, mocuācuauhtlāza. Cuammāxac caquia in īcuācuauh; niman tzīntlacza; oncān quicuappoztequi in īcuācuauh. Īc quipilquīxtihtiuh.

In mazātl in ahmō cuācuahueh, ca cihuātl.

EXERCISE 47

Relational NNCs (Part Three)

47A. *Relational Nounstems That Permit Options One and Two.* Analyze and translate the following NNCs.

1. tōltzālan
2. mohuīctzinco
3. amotzālan
4. xōchitzālan
5. ātōyahuīc
6. tomahpiltzālan

47B. *Relational Nounstems That Permit Options One and Three.* Analyze and translate the following NNCs.

1. caxtica
2. mocpac
3. teōyōtica
4. cuauhtica
5. ōztōticpac
6. noca

47C. *Relational Nounstems That Permit Options One, Two, and Three.* Analyze and translate the following NNCs.

1. notechpa
2. motlan
3. īcaltechyo
4. topan
5. mīxtlan
6. nocxititlan
7. tēnepantlah
8. tepāntitech
9. tletitlan
10. tocamapan

47D. *Associated-Entity NNCs.* Analyze and translate.

1. tepēpancatl
2. callahcatl
3. ātezcatēncatl
4. zoquitlahcatl
5. tlālcāhualpancatl
6. tōnalcatl

47E. *NNCs of Pertinency.* Analyze and translate.

1. tepēpancayōtl
2. tiānquizcayōtl
3. tōnalcayōtl
4. tepētlahcayōtl
5. ōztōcayōtl
6. tlālli-īyōllohcayōtl

47F. *Sentences Involving Relational NNCs That Permit the Options of This Lesson, as well as Sentences Containing Associated-Entity NNCs and NNCs of Pertinency.* Pronounce and translate.
1. Huel huehcapan cateh in cīcītlaltin.
2. Achtopa quipēhualtia in tzahtzi; niman quinānquiliah in nepāpan tōtōmeh ātlan nemih.
3. Nōhuiyān mochīhua tepēpan.
4. Īnca ommomōtlayah in īnyāōhuān.
5. Oncān tēīxpan quitlāz in īmāxtli.
6. In cān in īmpan yohuatiuh, oncān quitēmoah in ōztōtl.
7. Tlapanco huālhuetziz.
8. Mochīntin īmpan cepayauh.
9. Ahtlatica tlamīnah.
10. Tetica ōnicmōtlac. Īca tetl ōnicmōtlac.
11. In tiyahcāhuān mopachoah tenāntitlan.
12. Ītech onahcitoh in īmācal.
13. Ōppa ontlachix in īcpac tōtōtl.
14. Mā tlāltitech mahxītīcān in totēucyōhuān.
15. Huēi-ātēnco xāltitlan in tlapāni.
16. Cuauhtica ōquihuītec.
17. Ōquihuīcaqueh īīxpan in tlahtoāni.
18. Tocalpōlpan pōhui.
19. Onahci ōmpōhualxihuitl īpan mahtlācxihuitl omōme.
20. Huel ilhuicayōllohtitech ahcitihcac.
21. Izquīntin īn in īmīxpan miquiyah in Huitztzilōpōchtli.
22. In tōtolin īahāztitlan quimaquia in īpilhuān.
23. . . . in iuh niman ye onnēciz tlani tlaīxpan.
24. In māmaltin in motlepantlāzazqueh nō mihtōtihtihuih.
25. Quēn nel? Ca ahoc tleh īpahtica.
26. Tlāllan tlacoyocco in mopilhuahtia.
27. Cacatl in ītōcā ītlahtōl ītech tlaāntli. Ahtlamini in ītlahtōl; "cacaca" quihtoa.
28. Tōctitlan calactihuetz.
29. Totech ōquicāuhqueh in īncocoliz.
30. Ye neh nicmati in tleh in mopan nicchīhuaz.

47G. *The Tree Squirrel*

Cuauhtechalōtl, yehhuātl in cuauhtlah nemi techalōtl. Cuauhticpac in tlacua. Zan mochipa cuauhtitech in nemi, auh in īc motōcāyōtia "cuauhtechalōtl." Mochi quicua in ococintli. Quicua in cuahuitl īyacacelica. Nō quincua in cuauhocuiltin. Quixihxīpēuhtinemi in cuahuitl; oncān quimāna in cuauhocuiltin. Māpipitzoa. [*Auh* = "and"; see § 52.3.]

EXERCISE 48

Place-Name NNCs

48A. *Place-Name NNCs.* Analyze and translate.

1. Ācatzintitlan
2. Āmalīnalpan
3. Necoquīxehcān
4. Yohuallān
5. Tetamazolco
6. Ātl-Ícholoāyān
7. Tlaōllāntōnco
8. Tecpayohcān
9. Ehcatepēc
10. Pāntitlan
11. Ācōlnāhuac
12. Chīmalhuahcān

48B. *Gentilic NNCs.* Analyze and translate. Write out the stem of the place-name source and translate.

Example: Tetlanmēcatl

#Ø-Ø(Te-tlan-mē-☐-ca)tl-Ø# = he/she is a dweller in Tetlanman [< (Te-tlan-mā-n)-☐-, "In the Area of the Stone Teeth"]

1. Āyacac calqueh
2. Itzcuincuitlapilcatl
3. nĀcalhuah
4. tiTōchpanēcah
5. Āmāxtēcatl
6. Nōchtlān tlācah
7. Tlatilōlcatl
8. tiTlapaltēcatl
9. Tōnatiuh-Ílxco tlācatl
10. anCholōltēcah

48C. *Gentilic-Collectivity NNCs.* Analyze and translate. Write out the stem of the place-name source and translate.

1. Xīlōtepēcayōtl
2. Huāuhpanēcayōtl
3. Tziuhcōācayōtl
4. Cuetlaxtēcayōtl
5. Āztacalcayōtl
6. Ocuiltēcayōtl

48D. Sentences Involving Place-Name NNCs. Pronounce and translate.

1. Ahcico cecni Cuauhtitlan.
2. Ōmpa nemi Teōtl-Ílxco īhuīcpa in ātēnco.
3. Niman ye īc tlehcoh in īcpac Cōātepētl. [Not a place-name; a terrain-feature name.]
4. Quimonhuīcaqueh in Tōlpetlac.

Place-Name NNCs

5. Yehhuātl in huēi ātl totlan mani nicān Mēxihco.
6. Quittītītoh in tlahtoāni Tlīllān calmecac.
7. In Teohcalhuīyacān oncalacqueh.
8. Chicuēi Calli xihuitl īc onmihcuanihqueh in Nexticpac in Mēxihcah.
9. Nicān oc ceppa tetatacōtoh in Malīnalco.
10. Onahciqueh cecni ītōcāyōcān Calacohuayān.
11. In oquichtin quintihtītlani zan nō iuh quimocuitlahuīzqueh in Mictlān.
12. Iz catqui īc tonquīzaz in Ītzehehcayān.

48E. *Sentences Involving Gentilic NNCs.* Pronounce and translate.

1. In Tlīliuhqui-Tepēcah oncān quimonnelōcoh in Teohcalhuīyaqueh.
2. In Tōltēcah nō mihtoah Chīchīmēcah.
3. In ihqueh īn, achi mocuextēcanequih.
4. Quil in Tōltēcah ahcān in huehca quimatiyah.
5. In Mātlatzincah ītech momatiyah in temātlatl.
6. Ca toyāōuh in Tepanēcatl.
7. In Tlaxcaltēcah yēppa mochalānihticatcah in Cholōltēcah.
8. Mochīntin micqueh in Tlaxcaltēcah īmOtonhuān.
9. In ixquichtin in Tenōchcah cencah momauhtihqueh.
10. Nicān poliuhqueh in Xōchitlān tlācah.
11. Īc quimatih in ātlahcah, ca cencah quiyahuiz in huāllathuiz
12. Īpan mochīuh in īc pēhualōc Āzcapōtzalcatl.

48F. *A Blood-Offering Ceremony*

In ōīpan ommihzōc [in āmatl], niman ye īc huālquīza in ithualnepantlah. Achtopa ontlatlāza. In ilhuicac contlāza in īezzo. Niman ye ōmpa in tōnatiuh īquīzayān, mihtoāya "Tlapcopa," nāppa in contlāza īezzo. Niman ye ōmpa in tōnatiuh īcalaquiyān, mihtoāya "Cihuātlāmpa," nō nāppa in contlāza īezzo. Niman ye ōmpa in īmāōpōchcopa tlālli, mihtoāya "Huitznāhuacatlālpan," nō nāppa in contlāza īezzo. Niman ye ōmpa in īmāyauhcāmpa tlālli, mihtoāya "Mīmixcōah īntlālpan," nō nāppa in contlāza in īezzo. Zan ōmpa ommocāhuaya, in īc nāuhcāmpa ommihzo.

EXERCISE 49

Adverbial Modification (Part One)

49A. *Sentences Using NNCs with First-Degree Adverbialization.* Pronounce and translate.
1. In nochān ōhuālmohuīcac in teōpixqui.
2. Onactihcaca in īnāhual.
3. Nepanōtl mohottah.
4. Huālmauhcāquīzqueh in īmāltepēuh.
5. Zan tequitl ōnātlīc.
6. In tlequiquiztli huetzi in īnnāhuatīl.
7. Zan nāppōhualilhuitl tlahtohcāt.
8. Cuīcatl tiyōlqueh.
9. Ōcalac in tēlpōchcalli.
10. Ninozohzōhua quechōlli.
11. In īnchān cencah cēhua. [Translate *(chān)-tli-* as "homeland."]
12. Acah īchān ōcalacqueh.
13. Tlahtohcāt nāuhxihuitl.
14. Īntlāhuiz quimonaquiāyah.
15. Cemilhuitl ōtinehnenqueh.

49B. *Sentences Using NNCs with Second-Degree Adverbialization.* Pronounce and translate.
1. Ca nel ōconittac.
2. Mā zan cuēl tontlaēlēhuih in tlālticpac.
3. Huīptla cēhuaz.
4. In oc cectlapal ahtleh huāllah in ācalli.
5. In teōtlāc ōtlālōlīn.
6. Cencah ye huehcāuh mococoa.
7. In ye huehcāuh yehhuātl in īnteōuh catca.
8. Tlacuāuh tlahtohqueh.
9. In ētlamanixtin huel mīz. [*Ētlamanixtin* shows first-degree adverbialization.]
10. Ca nel no zo topilneccāyo tēchmāyītilia in Totēucyo.
11. Cuix mōztla tonīlōtiz?
12. Zan cuēl ōmic.

Adverbial Modification (Part One) 89

    13. Ichtacā nēchilhuīco.
    14. Chico xiquihcuani in ōn tetl.

49C. *Multiple-Nucleus Structures in the Adverbial Function.* Pronounce and translate.
1. Mochīntin huih in tōnatiuh īchān.
2. Ixquich cāhuitl mocuāilpihtinemih.
3. Ōcalac in huēi tēlpōchcalli.
4. Zan ōme ilhuitl ōmpa mocēhuihqueh.
5. In ixquich in mētztli monequi.

49D. *The Adverbial Clause Functioning as Principal Clause.* Pronounce and translate.
1. Cēcemilhuitl in huālnehnenqueh.
2. Cēceyohual in quitzaucqueh.
3. Īc in tzonquīzaz in īnnezahualiz?
4. Ca xāltitlan in īchān.
5. Cān in mochīhua in īn xihuitl?
6. Chīllohcān in huāllauh.
7. Quēn in quihuālmonequiltīz in Totēucyo?
8. Ca nicān in mihtōtīzqueh.
9. Ayāxcān in mocāuh.

49E. *Sentences Involving Complex Structures of Adverbial Modification.* Pronounce and translate.
1. Huel cē xihuitl in huālmoquetzaya.
2. Huel ōmpa mochīhua in īnchān in mohmōchitl.
3. Oc huehca yohuan in quīza.
4. In peyōtl zan iyoh ōmpa in mochīhua in teohtlālpan.
5. Huel iuh cemilhuitl in calacohua.
6. Tēcuitlaxcolyēctih, oc cencah ihcuāc in aya tleh mocua.
7. Zan tlamachtzin in ōquīzqueh. [Also spelled *tlamatzin*.]
8. Cencah īhuiyān in yahtihuītzeh.
9. In āc in quicuāz ahoc mō quēlēhuīz in tlacualli ixquichca in miquiz.
10. Huel nōhuiyān in canah motlālīz in topanēhuayo īpan, niman palāni.
11. Ahmō īnnemachpan in mictīlōqueh.
12. Īquēzquilhuiyōc ye nō ceppa tēchcentlahtalhuih.

49F. *An Aztec Warrior*

Ōtzahtzīhuac. "Mēxihcahé, mā ye cuēl yehhuātl!" Niman īc quihuālīxtih in Tlapanēcatl Ehcatzin, Otomitl. Īnca ommomōtlac. Quihtoh, "Tiyahcāhuāné, Tlatilōlcahé, mā ye cuēl! Āc ihqueh in tenimeh? Xihuālnehnemicān!" Niman īc, īca cē māyahuito in Español. Tlālli īc quihuītec. Yehhuātl in huālyacattihuia in quimāyahuito, in quihuālyacatihtihuia. Auh in ōquimāyahuito, nec conhuilānato in Español. [*Auh* = "and." The final *a* on *huālyacattihuia* is the reduced form of the distant-past-as-past tense morph *ca*; see § 11.5.2.*a.iii*. Also notice the formally unjustified applicative *tē-(māy-a-hui)*, "to give a push/shove against s.o.," i.e., "to knock s.o. down," along with its source intransitive *(māy-a-hui)*, "to give a shove," which is accompanied by the adverbial NNC *īca*, "against him," formed on the relational nounstem *(ca)-◻-*.]

EXERCISE 50

Adverbial Modification (Part Two)

50A. *Adverbial Modification: Time and Place.* Pronounce and translate.
1. In ōhuālihzac, niman ye chōca.
2. In onahcico in oncān ōquitlatēnēhuilih, niman ōquittac in tepetlatl. [For *oncān* here, see § 46.3.2.*b*.]
3. In īc in mozōmaz, quihuālpachōz in ilhuicatl.
4. Ahtleh ohhuih in quichīhuayah.
5. In ōonyah, niman ye īc quitēilhuia, "Nicnottilīznequi in tlācatl Quetzalcōātl."
6. In ihcuāc cuīcatlāzaya, zan niman quinānquiliāyah.
7. Ēxcān in huih in ihcuāc miquih.
8. Ontlayohuaticah in oncān ontlacāuhtēhuac.
9. In oncān in quil cencah netolīnīlo.
10. In oncān Chiucnāuhmictlān, oncān ōn cempohpoliōhua.
11. In ihcuāc quizōhua īcuitlapil, ihcuāc in huālnēci cōztic.
12. In ihcuāc miquiyah tlahtohqueh, ōmpa quimontōcayah; niman īmpan quintlāliliāyah centetl tzacualli.
13. Oncān achihtōncā onhuehcāhuaqueh in oc īc conchihchīuhqueh tlequiquiztli.

50B. *Adverbial Modification: Consideration and Purpose.* Pronounce and translate.
1. Momati ahzo piltzintli in chōca.
2. Huel ximotlachiyelti in cātlehhuātl achtopa mocui.
3. Huih tēnāmiquizqueh.
4. Momatqueh ca oncān quimictīzqueh.
5. Huih in quiquetzazqueh in īcal in īnteōuh.
6. Oc cequīntin huāllahqueh in quimpalēhuīzquīyah.
7. Ye yauh quimmomacaz in tēteoh.
8. In ixquich mācēhualli cenhuetzi in motamalhuia.
9. Huel ixquich tlācatl ōyah in tēnāmiquito.
10. Momatiya ca ōmpa in yāōmiquizqueh.
11. Yauh in māltīz.
12. Ōtlamatqueh, āc yeh in mahuizcuic.
13. Mā tihuiān tātatacazqueh, in oncān tātlīzqueh.

Adverbial Modification (Part Two)

14. Huītz tēnāhualittaz.
15. Mā catichtequicān in mā titepachōlohtin.
16. Mā caxitētlanxīma in mā titetzotzonaloh.

50C. *Adverbial Modification: Condition and Concession.* Pronounce and translate.

1. In tlā oc piltōntli, oc quihuīcah in pilhuahqueh.
2. In tlā zā nēn quēmman nēciya ahzo octli qui, niman quitzauctihuiah. [The *a* in *–huiah* is a variant of the distant-past-as-past tense morph [ca].]
3. In mā nel huehca nemiyah, ihciuhcā onahcitihuetziyah.
4. In āxcān mā zo ihui in ahoc mō cencah monequi tlāhuiztli, ca zan motocatiuh in tlachīhualli.
5. In tlā canah itlah mochīhuaz, huel oc yohuan in huīlohua.
6. In tlā canel mō tichicāhuac, huel ticmāmāz.
7. Ahīmel, mā zo ihui in ichtiqueh.
8. In tlā caoc tleh quitta quitlāhuāntīz, quinamaca in ītilmah.
9. In tlā catleh mohuen, ahhuel ticalaquiz.
10. In mā nel ōtlālmic, ca oquichtli.
11. In mā nel yehhuāntin in tēcōāchīhuah, mihtōtiah.
12. In tlā ye cahmana in quitlathuitia, quilhuia, "Xinēchcāhua."

50D. *Assuring the Growth of a Tooth*

In ihcuāc huetzi īntlan pīpiltotōntin, in tēnānhuān ītlacoyocco contlāzah in quimichin. Ahno zo eh īmpilhuān quimilhuiah, "Ītlacoyocco xictlāli in quimichin." Yeh īca quil in tlā camō iuh quichīhuazqueh, ahmō huel ixhuaz in ītlan piltzintli. Zan tlancotoctic yez.

50E. *The Tree That Broke*

In ōahcicoh in cuahuitl ītzīntlan, niman ye īc ītzīntlan oncān onmotlālihqueh. In oncān ihcac cencah tomāhuac in cuahuitl in āhuēhuētl. Niman oncān contlālihqueh in tlālmomoztli. Īpan quitlālihqueh in tētzāhuitl Huitztzilōpōchtli, in ōcontlālihqueh. Auh in ye īquēzquilhuiyōc, niman conmanilihqueh in īmihtac. Niman ye tlacuāzquiyah, niman ye quicaquih āc in quinnōtza. In īcpac huāllahtoa āhuēhuētl. Quimilhuia, "In oncān ancateh ōn, ximihcuanīcān, ahmō amopan huetziz. Ca mōztla huetziz in āhuēhuētl." Niman īc quicāuhqueh in quicuāyah. Cencah huehcāuh in tohtōlohticatcah.[1] Niman īc ōmihcuanihqueh; ōquitlālcāhuihqueh in āhuēhuētl. Ōneltic, in ōtlathuic, ōmotzīnēuh in īmpan poztec in cuahuitl in āhuēhuētl.

Oncān oc nāuhxiuhtihqueh in catcah Āztēcah Mexihtin in īc oncān motlālīcoh ītzīntlan mocēhuiāyah in āhuēhuētl.

---

1. There is an intransitive verbstem *(tōl-o-ā)*, "to bow the head/nod," and a transitive verbstem *tla-(tol-o-ā)*, "to swallow s.th." The intransitive stem has a long vowel in its root, the transitive one a short vowel. It is extremely rare for a transitive verbstem to appear in a VNC without an object pronoun; nevertheless, since the preceding sentence mentions eating, translations have assumed that swallowing is the intended meaning. In this meaning, if properly written, the VNC would be *tlatohtolohticatcah*, "they were each swallowing (something)." The intransitive VNC *tohtōlohticatcah*, which is the form chosen here, is rendered "they were each bowing their heads."

EXERCISE 51

Complementation

51A. *The Object-Complement Construction.* Pronounce and translate.
1. Ītlahtohcāhuān mochīhuah in tōnatiuh.
2. Mochīntin tlamacazqueh mochīhuah.
3. Āc timomati?
4. Xoxōuhqui niccua.
5. Tētepoztin mochīuhtihuītzeh.
6. Pāpalōmeh mocuepah.
7. Huel melāhuac quimocaquītīz.
8. Tixōlōpihtin titocuepah.
9. Yehhuātl īīxxīptla mochīuh.
10. Yehhuātl pehpenalo in teōpixqui mochīhua.

51B. *The Subject-Complement Construction.* Pronounce and translate.
1. Īcel ihcatihuītz.
2. Cihuātl ōtlācat in īconētōn.
3. In tlecuilli nexxoh catca.
4. At īntlacōch catca.
5. Tomāhuac ihcac in cuahuitl.
6. Cuix oc ichpōchtli nēci?
7. In īntlaquēn catca ichtli.
8. In ācalchīmalli cuahuitl ahnēci.
9. Ye nihuēhueh ninēci.
10. In īntlaquēn catca in tēcuānēhuatl.
11. Xomahtli cuahuitl cah.
12. In īnteōuh catca ītōcā Iyocippa.

51C. *The Adverbial-Complement Construction.* Pronounce and translate.
1. Moca xālli. Xālloh.
2. Niman pēhua in tlamīnqui quimīna.
3. Ompēhua motlaloa.
4. Moca zacatl. Zacayoh.

Complementation

    5. Pēhua tepēhui.
    6. Titocāhuazqueh ticuīcah.
    7. Timoca tlālli. Titlālloh.
    8. In ye huāllāznequi quiyahuitl, ihcuāc pēhua in tlahtoa in īn tōtōtl.
    9. Ahmō huehcāhuazqueh yāōquīzatīhuih.
  10. Pēhua ahhuachquiyahui.
  11. Ōmach mocah tlāllōhuaqueh.
  12. Zā mocah tlāltin.
  13. In īxāyac moca eztli.
  14. Cencah ōlloh. Moca ōlli.

51D. *Advantage from Adversity*

    Auh niman ōquinnāhuatih in ītlahtohcāhuān in Coxcoxtli in Cōlhuahqueh. Quimilhuia, "Cāmpa in yezqueh?" Ōquilhuihqueh in ītlahtohcāhuān, "Tlācatlé, Tlahtoānié, mā ōmpa huiān, mā ye ōmpa yetīnl in tepētitlan in nicān Tīzaāpan." Niman ōmpa quincāhuatoh; ōquintlālītoh in ōmpa Tīzaāpan. Auh niman ōquinōnōtzqueh in tlahtoāni in Coxcoxtli. Quilhuiah, "Tlācatlé, Tlahtoānié, ca ōtiquincāhuatoh in Tīzaāpan in Mēxihcah." Niman ōquihtoh in Coxcoxtli, "Ca ye cualli. Ca ahmō tlācah. Ca cencah tlahuēlīlōqueh. Ahzo ōmpa tlamizqueh, cōācualōzqueh. Ca cencah īnchan in cōcōah."

    Auh in yehhuāntin in Mēxihcah cencah ōpahpācqueh in ōquimittaqueh in cōcōah. Zan moch yehhuāntin in quinmopāhuaxiliah, in quinmotlehuāchiliah, in quincuah yehhuāntin Mēxihcah.

    Auh niman ye quihtoa in Coxcoxtli ōquilnāmic. Ye quimilhuia, "Cōlhuahquehé, in anquincāhuatoh, tlā xiquimittatīn cuix ōmicqueh." Niman ōquilhuihqueh, "Ca ye cualli, Tlācatlé, Tlahtoānié. Mā tiquimittatīn." Auh in ōquimonittaqueh tlapopōtztoqueh; pōctli mani; tlatlatiah in īmpan onahciqueh. Niman quimilhuihqueh, "Ōanquihīyōhuihqueh, Mēxihcayé. Zan tamēchittacoh. Tamēchtlahpalōcoh. Quēn ancateh?" Niman ōquinhuālnānquilihqueh, ōquimilhuihqueh, "Ōantēchmocnēlilihqueh. Ca tipācticateh." Quimilhuihqueh, "Ca ye cualli. Ye tihuih." Huāllahqueh in tēcpan. Niman ye quinōnōtzah in Coxcoxtli. Ye quilhuiah, "Tlācatlé, Tlahtoānié, ca ōtiquimonittatoh. Ca ōquintlahtlamihqueh in cōcōah in ōquincuahqueh. Ca ayoc āqueh in cōcōah. Ca ōtlanqueh." Niman ōquihtoh in Coxcoxtli, "O! Tlā xiquimittacān. Ca tlahuēlīlōqueh. Mā quichīuhtiyecān. Mā caxiquinnōtzacān."

    1. *Yetīn* is an optative outbound purposive VNC with a 3rd-pers plural subject pronoun: *mā #∅-∅(ye-☐-t-ī)∅+∅-n#*, "let them go in order to be" (see § 29.3.3).

EXERCISE 52

Conjunction

52A. *Marked and Unmarked Conjunction.* Pronounce and translate.
1. Mahmāeh, ihicxeh.
2. Motema ēxpa, nāppa.
3. Auh niman quinnōtz in tlahciuhqueh.
4. Ahmō quīz in *vinoh* in octli.
5. Auh in tlahtoāni quimilhuih, "Ximocēhuīcān."
6. Tzahtzitiquīzah, ihcahuacah, motēnhuītequih.
7. Ca nicān amīxtzinco amocpactzinco ōnō ceppa nitlachix. [*Amīxtzinco* is traditionally spelled *amitzinco*.]
8. In ōpahtic, niman īc calaqui in temāzcalco, auh ōmpa coni in iztāc pahtli.
9. Cencah moyōlic in xinehnemi, auh cencah moyōlic in xiyauh, in xohtlatoca.

52B. *Adverbial Particles and NNCs That Can Appear in Structures of Unmarked or Marked Conjunction.* Pronounce and translate. Remember: *īhuān* is NOT a conjunctor; it does NOT mean "and"! It is an adverbialized NNC that is translated "in its company," and more freely, "in addition (to it)," "along with (it)," "moreover," "furthermore," etc. (see § 52.4.1.*a*).
1. Cecni in oquichtli, īhuān oc cecni in cihuātl.
2. Cemilhuitl īhuān cenyohual zan connequiya in cāmpa yeh ohtli quitocaz.
3. Ahtleh in ītlatqui, ahtleh iāxcā, tēl cualli tlācatl.
4. Nāuhtetl ahno zo mācuīltetl in īteuh.
5. Zan nō cococātlālpan in onoqueh, auh yēceh nō chālchiuhīximatinih.
6. Cuix ōticcōuh, cuix no zo ōticchīuh?
7. Ayāc quimati in ahzo huel neltiz in ahca no zo mō.
8. Auh in īc tiyāz, in īc tohtlatocaz, in īc ohtli ticnāmiquiz, ahmō titōlōz, ahmō nō tahquetzaz. Ca ahnezcalihcāyōtl. Zan huel titlamelāuhcāihcatiyāz.

52C. *Sentences with Lexical Items Created by Conjunction (i.e., Biclausalisms).* Pronounce and translate.
1. Nicān ticah in ticuāuhtli in tōcēlōtl.
2. Auh iz ye tonoc tehhuātl in ticuēitl in tihuīpilli.

Conjunction

    3. Cōzcatl quetzalli īpan nimitzmati.
    4. Cōzcateuh quetzalteuh īpan nimitzmati.
    5. Mohuīctzinco quitquitihuītz, quihtohtihuītz, quihuenchīuhtihuītz in nāntli in tahtli.
    6. In tēcocoliāni ātl tlacualli īpan quitētolōltia in īc tēyōllohtlahuēlīlōcātilia.
    7. Yehhuātl tōnatiuh īnān ītah mochīhua.
    8. Quinemactia in petlatl, in icpalli, in tlatcōni in tlamāmalōni.

52D. *The Turkey Vulture*

Tzopilōtl tlīltic, catzāhuac, cuāchīchīltic, xotihtīcectic. Moch ītlacual in tleh in micqui, in ihyāc, īhuān in tlahyelli.

52E. *First Paragraph to the Introduction to the* <u>Mexican Chronicle</u>

Nicān mihtoa motēnēhua in quēn in ōahcicoh ōcalaquicoh in huēhuētqueh in mihtoah motēnēhuah Teōchīchīmēcah, Āztlān tlācah, Mexihtin, Chicōmōztōcah, in tlāltēmōcoh in tlālmahcēhuacoh in nicān īpan huēi āltepētl, *ciudad*, Mēxihco Tenōchtitlan, in ītenyōcān īmachiyōcān, in tenōchtli īmancān in ātlihtic, in cuāuhtli īnequetzayān, in cuāuhtli īpipitzcayān, in cuāuhtli īnetomayān, cuāuhtli ītlacuāyān, in cōātl ihzomocayān [the possessor pronoun *ī-Ø* has lost its length because of the following glottal stop], in michin īpatlāniyān, in mātlālātl in tozpalātl in īnepaniuhyān, in ātlatlayān, in oncān in ihīyōtl machōco in tōltzālan in ācatzālan, in īnnāmicōyān in īnchiyelōyān nāuhcāmpa in nepāpan tlācah, in oncān ahcicoh motlālīcoh in mahtlāctlomēintin Teōchīchīmēcah in cococāyōtica motlālīcoh in īc ōahcicoh.

52F. *Protection from Hail*

In ihcuāc quiyahui, in cencah tecihui, in āc in oncān īmīl, ahno zo īchīlcuen, ahno zo īecuen, īchiyan, tleco nextli quiyāhuac quihuāltepēhua īithualco. Quil mach īc ahmō tecihuīlōz in īmīl; quil īc polihui in tecihuitl.

52G. *The Broken Grinding Stone*

In yehhuātl metlatl quimotētzāhuiāyah in nicān tlācah. In ihcuāc acah oncān teztoc, in[1] huālpoztequi, īc nēciya, quil mach, ye miquiz in ōteciya, ahno zo eh[2] yehhuātl in chāneh, ahno zo īmpilhuān, ahno zo eh cemeh miquizqueh in īchān tlācah.

    1. *in* = "if."
    2. Traditionally written *anoce*.

EXERCISE 53

The Notion of Similarity Comparison

53A. *The Expression of Comparison.* Pronounce and translate.

1. In ītzontecon huēi, ixquich in nicān tohuehxōlōuh.
2. In pōchtēcah in ōztōmēcah zan centetl catca in īmmahuizzo.
3. Ahmō cualli ōn, yeh cualli īn.
4. Oc tāchcāuh in īc titlāhuānqui, in ahmō in motah.
5. Oc achi nichicāhuac, in ahmō mach iuhqui tehhuātl.
6. Oc huālcah tāxcāhuah, titlatquihuah, in ahmō nehhuātl.
7. Oc cencah miyec in māxcā in motlatqui in ahmō nehhuātl.
8. Oc yeh huehhuēi in amotlahtlacōl in antlahtohqueh, in ahmō yeh īntlahtlacōl in amotlapachōlhuān.
9. Cencah huehhuēi in īmācal in quin ōhuāllahqueh, in ahmō mach iuhqui catca in īmācal in achto ōhuāllahqueh.
10. In cepayahuitl tlacempanahuia in īc iztāc; ahoc tleh iuhqui in īc iztāc.
11. In tlā āxcān xōpantlah ticecmiqui, quēn zan yeh ticecmiquiz in cehuetzilizpan?
12. Zan ye nō yeh in īnāhual īnecuepaliz in tlācatecolōtl Tezcatl-Ihpōca.
13. Oc huālcah in īc cuauhtic in ahmō nehhuātl.

53B. *The Cuitlamiztli*

Cuitlamiztli cuauhtlah nemi. Ca zan ye nō yeh in miztli. In īc motōcāyōtia "cuitlamiztli": in ōcahcic centetl mazātl, quipēhualtia in quicua; quitequicua; quicuahtoc; huel quitlamia. Ōmilhuitl, ēilhuitl in īc ahmō tlacua; zan quicencua; zan huetztoc; tlatemōhuihtoc. Īc mihtoa "cuitlamiztli": īpampa xihxicuin īhuān īpampa in ahmō motlātia. In yohualtica quinhuālcua in tōtolmeh; quintlamia, in tlā nel centecpāntli. In ōixhuic, zā quinmictia īhuān in ichcameh.

53C. *The Ringtail*

Itzcuincuāni, ca zan ye nō yeh in cuitlamiztli. In īc motōcāyōtia "itzcuincuāni": in yohualtica huāllauh in cahcallah. Chōca. Auh in ōchōcac, niman mochīntin quinānquiliah in chichimeh. Mochīntin tzahtzih. In ixquichtin quicaquiliah[1] ītzahtziliz; niman īhuīcpa huih. Auh in ōītlan mocentlālihqueh, in ōcololhuihqueh, oncān cāna in quēzquitetl huelitiz. Quincua. Cencah huel ītlacualhuān in chichimeh.

---

1. Notice the applicative: "they hear it [i.e., its cry] from it [i.e., the ringtail]."

53D. *Peyote*

In īn peyōtl iztāc. Auh zan iyoh ōmpa in mochīhua in tlacōchcalcopa in teohtlālpan in mihtoa Mictlāmpa. In āc in quicua īn, in ahno zo qui, ītech quīza iuhqui in nanacatl. Nō miyec tlamantli quitta in tēmahmauhtih, ahno zo tēhuetzquītih. Ahzo cemilhuitl, ahno zo ōmilhuitl in ītech quīza, tēl zan nō concāhua. Yēceh, ca quihtlacoa in īyōllo. Tētlapolōltia; tēihuintia; tētech quīza.

EXERCISE 54

Denominal Verbstems (Part One)

54A. *Derivation of Denominal Verbstems.* Analyze the following VNCs. Write out the source nounstem and explain the derivation. Translate the VNC.

Example: nitlāltiz = #ni-∅(tlāl-ti)z+☐-∅# = I shall become earth.
  Source: the nounstem *(tlāl)-li-*, "earth, land, dirt." *Derivation:* by means of the inceptive/stative verbstem-forming suffix *ti* (see §54.2.1).

1. centeti
2. nicnemactia
3. cehui
4. tizoquiyōhua
5. quitōcāyōtia
6. tēlpōchyahcāti
7. cōztiya
8. tequihuahcāti
9. xīlōti
10. mizhuayōtia
11. nicnotechtia
12. nimitznocihuāpohtia

54B. *Sentences with VNCs Formed on Denominal Verbstems.* Pronounce and translate.

1. Huexōcanauhtli xohuehhuēiyaquiya.
2. Āzōlin tēnhuīyac, xohuihhuīyac.
3. In ihcuāc ōmocencāuh xīcohcuitlatl, zā tēpan itztapaltepan mocanāhua, momimiloa īca cuauhmāitl mimiltic.
4. In ye imman, in ōtlaimmantic in īc tēmictīzqueh in Españoles, niman ye īc huālquīzah.
5. Ahzo itlah tolhuiltiz, tomahcēhualtiz.
6. Cuix momatiyāntic in ōn tēmictīliztli?
7. Conmotlatquitih in quetzalpatzactli.
8. Quihtoāyah, "Quiteuhyōtīz, quitlahzollōtīz."

54C. *A Rabbit in the House*

Nō īhuān, netētzāhuilōya in tōchin in ihcuāc acah īchān calaquiya. Quihtoah in mīllahcah, in mīlpan tlācah, "Ye tlālpolihuiz in īchān. Ahno zo ye acah cholōz. Ye contocaz in tōchtli, in mazātl īohhui; ye tōchtiz, ye mazātiz; ye motōchtilīz, ye momazātilīz."

EXERCISE 55

Denominal Verbstems (Part Two)

55A. *Derivation of Denominal Verbstems.* Analyze the following VNCs. Write out the source nounstem and explain the derivation.

Example: nātōyapanoa = #n-∅(ā-tōy-a-pan-o-a)∅+∅-∅# = I ford a river. *Source:* the locative nounstem *(ā-tōy-a-pan)-▢-*, "over a river," formed from *(ā-tōy-a)-tl-*, "river," and the relational nounstem *(pan)-▢-*, "upper surface/superior location." *Derivation:* intransitive verbstem-forming suffixal cluster *o-ā* (see § 54.9).

1. tlanahui
2. quitīzahuia
3. timācuīlmētztihqueh
4. nitlaizhuahuia
5. motlehuia
6. ōmpōhualxiuhtia omōme
7. quineuchuiah
8. ticxōchihuia

55B. *Sentences with VNCs Formed on Denominal Verbstems.* Pronounce and translate.

1. Nāuhxiuhtihqueh in Pāntitlan in Mēxihcah.
2. Ōnonehuiyānhuih nixōlōpihtli.
3. In teponāzcuīcanimeh quintlatzotzoniliah, quinteponācilhuiah, quincuīcatlāxiliah in tlātlācohtin.
4. Ōhuel quicnōpilhuih in tlālticpacayōtl.
5. Ahtictlazohtla in mēlchiquiuh in motzontecon in īc ticmōtla in texcalli in ātlauhtli, in tepētl, in ixtlāhuatl.
6. Tlahcahuatztihuih, motēmpahpahuihtihuih, oyouhtihuih. Mihtoa coyohuihtihuih, yāōhuih.
7. Notlahtzitzinhuāné, ōanquihīyōhuihqueh; ōanquiciyauhqueh.
8. In īc yēcahui, achto molpia in colohtli; zā tēpan mīxcuāchhuia īc chicāhua.

55C. *Panning for Gold*

In cān in ātōyapan ōmpa huetzticah īohhui teōcuitlatl, in ātōyatl quitqui, cātoctia teōcuitlatl. Īc, īpampa, in aya mō huālhuih Españoles, in Mēxihcah, in Ānāhuacah, in tlaīximatinih, ahmō quitatacayah in cōztic in iztāc teōcuitlatl; zan ātōyaxālli quicuiyah, quicuauhxīcalhuiah. Oncān quittayah in cōztic teōcuitlatl, in canah huetztihuītz in iuhqui, ixquich in tlaōlli. Niman ye oncān quicuiyah in iuhqui xālli. Zā tēpan cātiliāyah; quipītzayah, quihmatiyah, quitlāliāyah in cōzcatl, in mahcuextli, in nacochtli, in tēntetl.

55D. *Stepping over a Child*

In ihcuāc tlā acah melāhuatoc piltōntli, necuiliuhtoc, in tlā acah ōconcuencholhuih, niman cahhuah in āc in ōtēcuencholhuih. Quilhuiah, "Tleh īpampa in ticcuencholhuia?"

Quil mach īc ayoc mō mānaz in piltōntli. Zā ixquichtōn yez. Auh in īc compahtiāya, in īc ahmō īpan mochīhuaz piltōntli, oc ceppa quihuālpancholhuia. Īc ompahtiya.

EXERCISE 56

Personal-Name NNCs

56A. *Personal-Name NNCs.* Analyze and translate.

1. Mahmahuini
2. niHuēi-Īmīuh
3. Iztāc-Tōtōtl
4. tiNecoc-Yāōtzin
5. Xōchitōnal
6. tAyāc-Tlācatl
7. Nezahualcoyōtl
8. niTotlehuīcōl
9. Itzcuincua
10. tiToyāōtzin
11. Ācatōnaleh
12. niZacatitech-Cochi
13. Tlacōxīnqui
14. niXiuhtlahtoh
15. Tōchāmi
16. tiTlāltēcatzin
17. Ilancuēitl
18. niChālchiuhcua

56B. Spanish-language and English-language writers dealing with Aztec topics give the nonhonorific form of the name of the tenth ruler/king of Mexihco Tenochtitlan as "Cuitlahuac" (e.g., in the Nahuatl text of the *Florentine Codex* we find "Cuitlahua," but in their English translation Anderson and Dibble write "Cuitlahuac"). On the other hand, the honorific form is always written "Cuitlahuatzin." Analyze and translate both "Cuitlahuac" and "Cuitlahuatzin." [This is the traditional spelling of "Cuitlahuatzin." Remember that a glottal stop is almost never written in traditional spelling.] Explain the mistake the English and Spanish writers make. Since the honorific form is written correctly, what should the nonhonorific form be? If "Cuitlahuac" were the correct form, what would the honorific form be?

The mistaken writers may have been confusing the king's personal name with the place name traditionally written "Cuitlahuac." Here the final –*c* is the relational noun-stem *(-c)-tli-*.

56C. *Sentences Involving Personal-Name NNCs.* Pronounce and translate. [The double-nucleus name (see § 55.4) in the first five sentences has been traditionally treated as if two gods are being mentioned. Notice, however, how clearly the Nahuatl indicates that there is only one; i.e., the name is formed as a biclausalism, a conjoined NNC lexical item (for the conjoined NNC lexical item *nonān notah*, see § 52.6).]

1. Mā xichuālmochihchīhui, mā xichuālmihpīchili in titlācatl, in tŌmetēuctli in tŌmecihuātl.
2. Ōmitzihmah, ōmitzyōcox in monān in motah, in Ōmetēuctli in Ōmecihuātl, in ilhuicacihuātl.
3. Quēn ōmitztlamahmacac in monān in motah, in Ōmetēuctli in Ōmecihuātl.
4. Cuāuhtli ōcēlōtl, tiyahcāuh, tēlpōchtli, noxocoyōuh, ōtimahxītīco in tlālticpac; ōmitzhuālmihualih in monān in motah, in Ōmetēuctli in Ōmecihuātl.
5. Ca ōehcoc in mahcēhualli. Ah! Ca ōquihuālmihualih in tonān in totah, in Ōmetēuctli in Ōmecihuātl, in Chiucnāuhnepaniuhcān, in Ōmeyōcān.
6. Xicmati, xiccaqui. Ahmō nicān mochān. Ca ticuāuhtli, ca tōcēlōtl. Ca tīquechōl, ca tīzacuān in Tloqueh Nāhuaqueh.
7. Mā ītech ximahxīti in monāntzin in Chālchihuitl-Īcuē, in Chālchiuhtlatōnac. Mā mitzmānili. Mā mitzmopahpāquili; mā mitzmahāltili. Mā chico tlanāhuac quihuīca, quitēca in catzāhuacāyōtl in ītechpa tichuālcuic in monān, in motah.
8. Nimitznōtza, nimitztzahtzilia in tēteoh tīnnan, in tiCītlallatōnac, in tiCītlalli-Īcuē.
9. Ca ye quicēhuihtoqueh in ītloc in ināhuac in tonān in totah, in Mictlān-Tēuctli.
10. Zā tēpan, in ōhuālpēuhqueh, in ohtlica īmpan ōahcicoh in tlātlācatecoloh; huēi cōmitl ītlan huehhuetztoqueh. . . . Yehhuāntin, in quintōcāyōtiah "Mīmixcōah," chicōmentin. Īn cē tlācatl ītōcā Xiuhneltzin; in īc ōme ītōcā Mīmichtzin; in īc ēi, in cihuātl, īnhueltīuh, ītōcā Teōxāhual. Auh in oc nāhuintin ahmō huel momati in īntōcā.

56D. *A Fateful Name*

Auh in ihcuāc, īpan mochīuh Motēuczōma, toxiuh molpilih, cencah nōhuīyān īc tlanāhuatih in īc tēmōlōz malli in ītōcā "Xihuitl." In zā zo cāmpa yeh ānōz. Auh cē ahxīhuac. Huexōtzincatl, tlazohpilli. Ītōcā "Xiuhtlamīn." Tlatilōlco malli mochīuh. In tlamāni ītōcā "Itzcuin," auh īc tōcāyōtīlōc, īc nōtzalōc "Xiuhtlamīnmāni."

Ca yehhuātl īēlpan huetz in tlecuahuitl īmal. Mochi tleco tlan in īnacayo. Auh zā tzohualli in īc quīxxīptlayōtih in īpan quipōuh. Tlaōlpāhuaxtli īpan quitlahtlālih in īc quitēcualtih.

56E. *After Kingship Ended in Tlatilolco*

In ihcuāc ōmomiquilih Moquihuixtzin, ahoc āc tlahtoāni motlālih in Tlatilōlco. Oncān ōtzīntic in zā cuāuhtlahtōlo. Auh nicān ompēhua in zā cuāuhtlahtōlo in Tlatilōlco. Nicān cateh in cuāuhtlahtohqueh in īpan onmotlālihqueh en īpetl in īcpal in concāuhtiyah tlahtoāni Moquihuixtzin; in contlapiyelihqueh, yehhuāntin īn: tlācatēccatzintli Tzihuacpopōcatzin, tlacōchcalcatzintli Ītzcuāuhtzin. Ōmextin tlazohpīpiltin. Auh niman ye tlacōchcalcatzintli Tezcatzin, tlācatēccatzintli Tōtōzacatzin. Ōmextin cuāuhpīpiltin, Mēxihcah pīpiltin.

EXERCISE 57

Miscellany (Part One)

In the sections of this exercise and the next, attention is turned toward the problem of reading texts in traditional spelling. Study Appendix F and § 57.8. Rewrite the following in the standardized spelling presented in Lesson 2 and used throughout the Lessons. Translate the result.

57A. *Selected items.* Since these items are not constrained by a context, some may permit more than one spelling.

1. teuhyoa
2. nouia
3. teuiutica
4. imaquicac
5. ca
6. yua
7. tullin
8. ece
9. teoaiulque
10. yoliliço
11. moiaoa
12. qvicoloua
13. ihyotl
14. matlalqueie
15. i Necatitlan
16. yvjoc
17. tlanellitoani
18. ye
19. aieciotl
20. tlayuani

57B. *The Owl (Florentine Codex,* Facsimile Ed., Bk. 3, fol. 46v)

Tecolotl: ololtic, tapaioltic cujtla ololtic, ixtemamalacachtic, ixpechtic, quaquave hi vitica: quateololtic, quatecontic, hi vitilaoac, hiviotilaoac, ixmjmjqujnj intlaca. texcalco; quavitl itic intlacati iooaltica, in tlaquaqua: ipampa occenca vella chia in iooan. tlatvmaoa injc tlatva; qujtva, tecolo, tecolo, o.o.

57C. *A Skirmish (Florentine Codex,* Facsimile Ed., Bk. 3, fol. 64)

Mexicae maie cuel: njman ieic tlacaoaca, yoan tlapitzalo yoan chimallaça in iau tlachixquj: njman ieic qujntoca in Españoles, qujmaiauhtivi yoa qujmantivi, caxtoltin inanoque in Españoles: njmã ic qujnoalhujcaque: auh injmacal nimã ic qujtzin qujxtique. a nepantla contecatv. Auh ino quimaxitico caxtvltin omei in vncan mjqujzque itoca: tlacuchcalco: njmã ieic qujn pepetlaoa, much qujn cujlique in in iao tlatquj, yoã ini michcavipil, yoan injxqujch in in tech catca, moch qujntepeoaltique: njman ieic tlacoti quin mictia: auh inj mic njoan qujn valitztvque anepantla.

57D. *A Messenger from the Hereafter* (*Florentine Codex*, Facsimile Ed., Bk. 2, fol. 2v–3r)

Ce tlacatl çihoatl ichan tenochtitlan mjc ica cocoliztli, njman motocac yitoalco ipan qujtemanque, ieiuh nauilhuitl motocac in cihoatl micquj mozcali ioaltica, cenca tlamauhti in vncan motocaca tlatatacco motlapo, auh intetl icmotemanca ve'ca veuetzito: auh iniehoatl cihoatl in o iuh mozcali, njman qujnonotzato, qujlhujto in motecuçuma intlein qujttac qujpouili, qujlhuj. Cainic onjnozcali njmjtzilhujco. Caieixqujch catehoatl mocatzonqujça intlatocaiotl in mexico catehoatl mopan mantiaz in altepetl mexico. Aqujque inieuitze caieho antin tlalmaceoaqujuj, iehoantin onozque in mexico: auh in iehoatl mjcca çihoatl ienocempoalxiujtl oçe inen ioan occe qujchiuh iconeuh oquichtli.

EXERCISE 58

Miscellany (Part Two)

58A. *A Few Errors in Siméon's Diccionario de la lengua nahuatl o mexicana.* In addition to writing the Nahuatl in the standardized spelling, explain why the "root" that Siméon gives is incorrect.

1. inoquimonequian, *adv.*, "while the moment is propitious, favorable." *Root:* inoquic monequian.
2. icnelilmachitia: nite *or* ninote, "to thank someone for a favor he/she has done you...." *Root:* icnelilia, machitia.
3. yacauictic, *adj.*, "one who has a large, long nose." *Root:* yacauitzoa.
4. Uetzcatocatzin, *s.*, "One of the chiefs of the merchants of Tlatelolco." *Root:* uetzcayotl, tocaitl.
5. yamaztia: ni, "to become soft, to be moved to pity." *Root:* yamania.
6. cococ, *adj.*, "hot, something that burns the mouth, ..." *Root:* cocoa.
7. çoquittiuitz, *intrans. verb*, "for there to be a storm, a great tempest." *Roots:* çoquitia, uitz.
8. elleltia: nin (*for* nino), "to repent, ..." *Root:* elleloa.
9. yecaui, *intrans. verb*, "to end, finish...." *Roots:* ye, caua (?).
10. icica: n (*for* ni), "to pant; to be out of breath, winded." *Root:* iciui.
11. cacayachilia: nitetla, "to destroy/take to pieces or make scraps/crumbs of something for someone." *Root:* cacayaca.
12. cecepatic, *adj.*, "very cold, frozen...." *Root:* cepayaui.
13. copactli, *substantive*, "palate, upper part of the mouth...." *Roots:* comitl, paqui.
14. cuecuetzoca, *frequentative of* cuechoa: ni, "to have an itch, to be agitated." [Siméon claims that *cuechoa* is the root.]
15. çolotza: nitla, "to suck something up, to gulp something down." [The problem is in the entry itself (incidentally, Siméon took the entry from Molina). What is the "root" (better, the "source stem")? Hint: A better translation of the verbstem is "to slurp s.th."]

58B. *Huitzilopochtli (Florentine Codex*, Facsim. Ed., Bk.1, fol. 1r)

Vitzilubuchtli: çan ma ceoalli, çan tlacatl catca: naoalli, tetzaujtl, atla ca cemelle, teixcuepanj: qujiocoianj in iaoiutl, iaotecanj, iao tlatoanj: caitechpa mjtoaia. tepan qujtlaça yn xiuhcoatl, in ma malhoaztli.q.n. iaoiutl, teuatl, tlachinolli. Auh ynjquac, ilhuj qujxtiloia, malmjcoaia, tlaaltilmjcoaia: tealtiaia, yn pochteca. Auh ynjc muchichioa ia; xiuhtotonacoche catca, xiuhcoa naoale, xiuhtlalpile, matacaxe, tzitzile, oiuoalle.

58C.   *The Eagle Falcon* (*Florentine Codex*, Facsim. Ed., Bk. 11, fol. 47r)

Quauhtlotli: yoan tloquauhtli, achivei in cioatl: auh ino quichtli çan achi tepitvn. In cioatl cencaie tlamani: itvca, Alcon: tecoztic, inj hivio mu chi tlilnextic; injcujtlapil, ma tlactli o mume: icxi coztic. In ic tlama: çan ica injzti. Inj quac impã mocacanauhtiuh tvtvme macivi in impan mocacanaoa amo ic qujnvitequj inj ama tla pal: çan iztitica qujn motzo loznequj. Auh in iehoantin tvtvme: aocmo vel patlanj, inpatlaniznequj: aocmo vel vi, ça cha chapanti vetzi. Auh in tla centetl vel caci: çan njman ielpã, qujmotzoltzitzquja; njmã quj quechcoionja, catli injezço, vel qujtlamja; amotle cana i tla qujchipinja, in eztli. Auh inj quac vel tlaqua; achtvpa quj vivitla, inhivio tvtvtl; in cemjl hujtl expan tlaqua. Injcceppa iquac in aiamo valqujça, tvna tiuh. Injc vppa: nepantla tvnatiuh. Injc expa: iquac in onca lac tonatiuh, mopilhuatia; vel ovican, texcalcamac in mochã tia: çan vnteme injpilhoan Yoan iniehoatl tlootli: quj iollotiaia in vitzilobuchtli. Ipã pa caqujtvaia: in iehoantin tlotlhotin, injc espa tlaqua incemilhujtl: iuhqujn ma catlitia in tvnatiuh, yoan ipã pa: iniquac catli eztli, mochquj tlamja: amo qualonj inj naca io. Auh injc maci tlhotlotin: ix pan qujtlalilia canauhtli, yoã ielpan, ielchiqujpan qujtlali lia tzoaztli: auh in cequjntin, çan quj iaoalochtia intzõ oaztli.

58D.   *Distracted Messengers* (*Florentine Codex*, Facsim. Ed., Bk. 6, fol. 183v)

. . . qujl mach quetzalcoatl, tullan tlatoanj catca: qujl vmentin cioa mahaltiaia injn nealtiaian: inoquin oalittac: ic njman qujn oalioa cequjntin qujmittazque, inaqujque maaltia: auh in ie hoantin titlanti: çaie qujmjitzti cate, in maaltia cioa: amoma qujnonotzato. Inquetzalcoatl: occeppa çatepan conjoa injxolouh, quitoznequj, ititlan: inquimittaz aqujque in maaltia: çan no iuhqujchiuh, aiocmo qujcue pato injnetitlaniz: ic vncan tzin tic, neloaiooac; inmjtoa: moxoxolotitlanj.

Key to the Exercises

Note: This key is selective. It does not always illustrate all aspects of the task set up for a given exercise, nor does it always present the steps underlying the solution for a given task. As Nahuatl sentences are prone to ambiguity, it is unfeasible for a key of this nature to give all the translational possibilities of an item. The translations given here were chosen in order to exploit the purpose of the exercise. For this reason, the student is advised to be alert to other possible translations.

EXERCISE 1

1A. 1. Phoneme = a type-level meaning-carrying sound that achieves its identity by standing in contrast with other such elements in a language's phonological system.
2. Phone = a token-level representation of a phoneme.
3. Sigeme = a type-level meaning-carrying silence whose existence is hypothesized because a phoneme (or phoneme sequence) occurs at the same place in a contrasting form; e.g., a sigeme is hypothesized to exist at the end of /kid-Ø/ because of the presence of the phoneme /s/ at the end of /kid-s/, since the /Ø/ and the /s/ contrast as carriers of number (singular and plural respectively).
4. Morph = a token-level element that is an amalgam of token-level carrier elements and a token-level meaning element.
5. Root = a major morpheme/morph of which a stem is made; e.g., in "fool-" the root and the stem coincide; in "fool-ish" the root "fool-" is the base for the formation of the stem; in "fool-ish-ness-" the root "fool-" is the ultimate base for the formation of the base from which the stem is formed.
6. Lexeme = the type-level meaning component of a stem.
7. Morphology = the study of the formation of stems or words (in English) or of stems (in Nahuatl). In Nahuatl the existence of nuclear clauses requires morphosyntax (instead of mere morphology) to study their formation.
8. Instance level = the level of utterance, of actual occurrence of language use (either spoken or written). It is the only phenomenally real level of language. The other two levels are abstractions, hypothetical constructs derived from depurations of the extremely rich facts of the instance level so that these can be analyzed and described more easily.

1B. 1. A syllable is a *meaningless* structure unit formed with elements of only the phonological or graphological systems (i.e., only with phonemes/phones or graphemes/graphs). The center of a Nahuatl syllable must be a vowel. On the other hand, a morpheme/morph is a *meaningful* structural element that is a composite of elements of the carrier system and the meaning system. Since the carrier system is involved (and not just the phonological/graphological system, as in the case of a syllable), the meaning resident in a morpheme/morph can be carried not only by a phoneme/phone but also by a sigeme/sig. Furthermore, a morpheme/morph whose carrier is phonological can consist of a single vowel, a single consonant, two vowels, two consonants, or any combination of vowels and consonants. While it is possible for a morpheme/morph to coincide with a syllable, it is more common for a morpheme/morph to disregard syllabic structure.

2. Derivation adds affixes INSIDE the boundaries of a stem to create a new *stem*. Inflection adds prefixes *and/or* suffixes OUTSIDE stem boundaries to create *words* (in English or Spanish) or *nuclear clauses* (in Nahuatl).

3. The term "subject" names a grammatical *function unit*, but "verb" names a grammatical *category*. While grammarians of English can ignore the lack of logic involved in coupling two incompatible terms because the constituent (pronoun, noun, phrase, clause) functioning as a subject in English always stands separate from the verbword, in speaking of other kinds of languages (Greek, Latin, Spanish, Nahuatl, Arabic, etc. it is nonsensical to use the expression because the subject is always included INSIDE the finite verbword (in the form of personal-pronominal suffixes, prefixes, or circumfixes). Consider Spanish: for example, corren (i.e., corre+∅-n, "run+3rd-pl"), "they run." If the affixal subject ∅-n, "they," needs to be emphasized or more exactly identified or clarified, a supplementary subject must be added: e.g., ellas corren ~ corren ellas, "they (feminine) run" (the fact that the basic subject is feminine is made clear by the addition of the supplementary subject); las muchachas corren ~ corren las muchachas, "the girls run"; Juana y María corren ~ corren Juana y María, "Jane and Mary run"; etc. The false belief generated by the expression "subject of the verb" blocks any understanding of what is going on in languages that are not of the English type.

4. A stem is a hypothetical construct from which a word (in English) or a nuclear clause (in Nahuatl) is formed. Nonparadigmatic words always have the same morphemic/morphic makeup as their stems (e.g., the stem "(frank-ly)" and the word "frankly"). Paradigmatic words always differ from their stems in morphemic/morphic makeup (even if this is not apparent on the instance level (e.g., the singular form "sheep" and the plural form "sheep," while having the same sound, are actually quite different, a fact that becomes clear on the morphic level: the *stem* "(sheep)-" forms the contrasting *words* "(sheep)∅" and "(sheep)□"; in the former the singular morph has as its carrier the regular sig "-∅", and in the latter the plural morph has as its carrier the irregular sig "-□", which is here occurring as a replacement for the regular plural morphic carrier "-s").

EXERCISE 2

2A.
1. huēi
2. ahco
3. quīza
4. cuēitl
5. ahhuīc
6. tzahtzi
7. Cuāuhtemōctzin
8. tēmāquīxtiāni
9. āxcāitl
10. cuetlāchtli
11. neuctli
12. nocihuāuh
13. quicuāz
14. ōnichōcac
15. quiahuitl/quiyahuitl
16. mīmicqueh
17. xicmōtla
18. tēuctli
19. quēxquich
20. nehhuātl
21. tōchuah

2C.
1. [u:mpa]
2. [nu:čλi]
3. [tuskaλ]
4. [o:ki¢ak^{w}]
5. [to:tulin]
6. [kune:λ]
7. [kiyekoa]
8. [kih¢uma]
9. [šu:panλi]
10. [ku:stik]
11. [ki¢upa]
12. [yu:li]
13. [kitoka]
14. [tusan]
15. [šokuλ]
16. [λao:kuya]
17. [a:muxλi]
18. [wi:lu:λ]
19. [ku:¢λi]
20. [muči]
21. [tepusλi]
22. [¢upki]
23. [kuyu:λ]
24. [i: tepu¢ko]

2D. In the first two, /e/ has been lowered to [a]. In the third, /e/ becomes raised to [i].

2E.
1. azcihuah
2. teuhyoh
3. anhuih/ahuih
4. tlālli
5. ītetztzinco/ītettzinco/ītetzinco [Also spelled *ītechtzinco.*]
6. antzīnquīzah
7. michchōctia/michōctia [Also spelled *mitzchōctia.*]
8. quixxiccāhua [Also spelled *quinxiccāhua.*]
9. anyezqueh/ayezqueh
10. tēucyōtl
11. quizzāzaca [Also spelled *quinzāzaca.*]
12. ohpitzactli
13. xālloh
14. tepochchicōlli/tepochicōlli
15. nimitztzonhuilāna, nimitzonhuilāna
16. tepoxxomahtli [Also spelled *tepozxomahtli.*]
17. petlānqui [peλa:ŋki]
18. antlaczah

EXERCISE 3

3A. Particle = a minor lexical item that has no morphological structure and is invariant. It is the only kind of Nahuatl word (sentence fragment), since all other items in the language are nuclear clauses (i.e., units that can serve as full sentences).

3B.
1. therefore; if that is the case, then . . .
2. only (unqualified by prior situation); just; nothing else but
3. just now (i.e., in the recent past); presently (i.e., in the near future)
4. perhaps? perchance?
5. also
6. already
7. possibly; I don't know . . .

8. if only, would that
9. indeed
10. nevertheless; despite that

3C. 1. not yet
2. if only perhaps; since in as much as . . .
3. and if perhaps, if by chance, if maybe; but if
4. and moreover, and also [Literally, "still also."]
5. perhaps, maybe
6. no longer
7. supposing that . . . ; even if . . .
8. perhaps . . . not; perhaps not . . .
9. be that as it may, regardless
10. perhaps

EXERCISE 4

4A. 1. VNC formula 1:

#pers^1-pers^2+ . . . +num^1-num^2#	Subject	
+va^1-va^2(STEM)	core	Predicate
)tns	tense	

2. NNC formula 3:

#pers^1-pers^2(. . .)num^1-num^2#	Subject
(STEM)	Predicate

4B. 1. person = first; second; third (i.e., speaker; addressee; the other)
2. animacy = animate; nonanimate
3. humanness = human; nonhuman
4. number = singular; plural; common
5. case = nominative; objective; possessive

4C. 1. Deixis = an identification of a mention INSIDE language by pointing to or otherwise indicating a person, thing, time, place, etc., OUTSIDE in nonlinguistic reality (e.g., "I" points to the speaker or writer).
2. Anaphora = the reference back to an antecedent identification in a text (spoken or written) in order to clarify or explain a subsequent unidentified mention (e.g., "I told Mary that she should do it.").
3. Cataphora = the reference forward to a subsequent identification in a text in order to clarify or explain a prior unidentified mention (e.g., "I've told him a hundred times, but, as you know, Bill never listens.")

EXERCISE 5

5A.

#pers^1-pers^2(. . . +num^1-num^2#	Subject	
(STEM)	core	Predicate
)tns	tense	

Key to the Exercises

5B. 1. For present, customary present, imperfect, or distant-past indicative:
   1st-sg: #n-∅(. . . +∅-∅#
   1st-pl: #t-∅(. . . +∅-h#
2. For future or preterit indicative:
   1st-sg: #n-∅(. . . +c-∅# (pret. only) ~ #n-∅(. . . +qui-∅# ~ #n-∅(. . . +□-∅#
   1st-pl: #t-∅(. . . +qu-eh#
3. For nonpast optative:
   1st-sg: #n-∅(. . . +□-∅#
   1st-pl: #t-∅(. . . +c-ān#
4. For past optative:
   1st-sg: #n-∅(. . . +∅-∅#
   1st-pl: #t-∅(. . . +∅-h#
5. For nonpast admonitive:
   1st-sg: #n-∅(. . . +□-∅#
   1st-pl: #t-∅(. . . +t-in# ~ #t-∅(. . . +t-ih#

5C. Change the person dyads from "n-∅" and "t-∅" to "∅-∅."

5D. 1. yā ~ ya   5. ∅
     2. ∅   6. yā ~ ya
     3. cā ~ ca   7. ni
     4. z   8. cā ~ ca

EXERCISE 6

6A. 1. trajectory = projective; reflexive; reciprocative
    2. specificity = specific; nonspecific
    3. prominence = mainline; shuntline

6B.

#pers¹-pers²+ . . . +num¹-num²#	Subject
va(STEM)	core
)tns	tense

{ Predicate

6C. The morphs *tē* and *tla* are indefinite pronouns; they are nonspecific thir-person projective object morphs having the meanings "someone/anyone/people (in general)/everyone" and "something/anything/things (in general)/everything" respectively. *Tē* refers to human beings only; *tla* refers to animate nonhuman beings or to nonanimate things.

6D.

#pers¹-pers²+ . . . +num¹-num²#	Subject
va¹-va²(STEM)	core
)tns	tense

{ Predicate

6E. 1. qu-im ~ qu-in   4. t-ēch
    2. n-ēch   5. c-∅/qu-∅ ~ qui-∅
    3. m-itz   6. am-ēch

6F. 1. n-o ~ n-□   3. m-o ~ m-□
    2. m-o ~ m-□   4. t-o ~ t-□

EXERCISE 7

7A.

1.

#ti-Ø+ ... +□-Ø#	Subject	
+c-Ø(tēm-o-h)	core	} Predicate
)Ø+	tense	

"you (sg) sought it/them"

2.

#Ø-Ø(... +Ø-Ø#	Subject	
(tep-ē-uh)	core	} Predicate
)ca+	tense	

"it/they had spilled (onto the ground)"

3.

#ni-Ø+ ... +Ø-Ø#	Subject	
+n-□(īnāya)	core	} Predicate
)ya+	tense	

"I used to hide (myself)." ~ "I was hiding."

4.

#Ø-Ø+ ... +Ø-Ø#	Subject	
+tē(pēuh)	core	} Predicate
)ca+	tense	

"he had conquered people"

5.

#Ø-Ø+ ... +Ø-Ø#	Subject	
+t-ēch(ihua)	core	} Predicate
)Ø+	tense	

"he sends us (as messengers)"

6.

#am-Ø+ ... +Ø-h#	Subject	
+m-o(tlāl-i-ā)	core	} Predicate
)ni+	tense	

"you (pl) customarily sit down"

7.

#ti-Ø+ ... +qu-eh#	Subject	
+qu-in(cuā)	core	} Predicate
)z+	tense	

"we shall eat them"

8.

#Ø-Ø+ ... +Ø-Ø#	Subject	
+tē(chīhua)	core	} Predicate
)Ø+	tense	

"he engenders people"

Key to the Exercises

7B. 1. z = future; "you (pl) will say it"
2. ca = distant past; "they had died"
3. Ø = present; "he cuts it/them"
4. ni = customary present; "he usually asks for it"
5. Ø = preterit; "he drank it"
6. Ø = preterit; "I became content"
7. Ø = present; "we take it/them"
8. ya = imperfect; "you (sg) used to call us"

7C. 1. Class B; "you (sg) waited for him/her," "I am waiting for you (sg), "he will wait for me"
2. Class C; "you (sg) said it," "I am saying it," "he/she will say it"
3. Class B; "you (pl) heard it," "we hear you (sg)," "they will hear me"
4. Class D; "they frowned in anger," "we are frowning in anger," "you (pl) will frown in anger"
5. Class A; "I stepped on s.th.," "he steps on it/them," "you (sg) will step on s.th."
6. Class C; "they sought them," "we are seeking you (pl)," "you (pl) will seek us"
7. Class B; "I hurried," "he is hurrying," "you (sg) will hurry"
8. Class A; "we saw him/her/it," "you (pl) see me," "they will see you (sg)"

7D. 1. nicmōtlac
2. titotlālihqueh
3. anquimāmānih
4. nēchnōtzazqueh
5. tictēmoāya
6. nictlālīz
7. tlamāmahcah
8. namēchnōtz
9. tictēmōzqueh
10. antlamōtlah

EXERCISE 8

8A. 1. #Ø-Ø+huāl(quīz)Ø+qu-eh# = they came out
2. #t-Ø+on(temo)Ø+Ø-h# = we descend thither, we go down
3. ō#ni-Ø+c-Ø+huāl(nōtz)ca+Ø-Ø# = I had come to summon him/her
4. #to-Ø+c-Ø+on(caqui)z+qu-eh# = we went to hear him/her/it
5. #Ø-Ø+huāl+la(man-a)z+☐-Ø# [Or with *tla*-fusion: #Ø-Ø+huāl(la-man-a)z+☐-Ø#, "he/she will come to make an oblation."]
6. ō#ti-Ø+qu-im+on(nōtz)Ø+☐-Ø# = you summoned them thither
7. ō#Ø-Ø+om(pēuh)Ø+☐-Ø# = he/she/it has started off
8. ah#ō#Ø-Ø+huāl(lehcō)Ø+c-Ø# = he/she has not climbed up hither
9. #t-Ø+on+t-☐(ā-l-tī)z+qu-eh# = we shall go to bathe (ourselves), we shall bathe there
10. ō#no-Ø+c-Ø+o(tt-a)Ø+c-Ø# = I went to see him/her/it
11. ō#Ø-Ø+qui-Ø+huāl(cui)Ø+c-Ø# = he/she has brought it/them; he/she has come to get it/them
12. ō#no-Ø+c-Ø+om(mēmeh)Ø+☐-Ø# = I carried/have carried it/them thither on my back

8B. 1. they crossed over
huālpanōqueh = they came across
ompanōqueh = they went across
2. you (pl) hide
anhuālmīnāyah = you (pl) come to hide
amommīnāyah = you (pl) go to hide
3. they will send s.o.

huāltēihuāzqueh = they will send s.o. hither
ontēihuāzqueh = they will send s.o. thither
4. he has made s.th.
ōhuāllachīuh = he has come to make s.th.
ōontlachīuh = he has gone to make s.th.
5. you took it/them
tichuālcuic = you came to take it/them
toconcuic = you went to take it/them
6. we sat down/settled
tihuāltotlālihqueh = we came and sat down/settled
tontotlālihqueh = we went and sat down/settled

8C. 1. He has not yet made it.
2. They are still seeking them thither.
3. We have already gone to see him.
4. He/She/It just eats. He/She/It doesn't do anything but eat.
5. Has he/she/it died?
6. Indeed, I did not say it.

8D. 1. Ca ye huāllehcōc.
2. Cuix ahhuāltzahtziqueh?
3. Ye ōquimah.
4. Ca titlapācazqueh.
5. Ahzo ticpoloh.

EXERCISE 9

9A. 1. mā #∅-∅+qui-∅(piya)ni+∅-∅# = if only he had guarded it/them
mā #∅-∅+qui-∅(piya)∅+☐-∅# = if only he may guard it/them
2. mā #ni-∅+c-∅(pōhua)ni+∅-∅# = if only I had counted them
mā #ni-∅+c-∅(pōhua)∅+☐-∅# = if only I may count them
3. mā #ti-∅+t-o(tlāl-i-ā)ni+∅-h# = if only we had sat down
mā #ti-∅+t-o(tlāl-ī)∅+c-ān# = if only we may sit down
4. mā #xi-∅+c-∅(māmā)ni+∅-h# = if only you (pl) had carried it on your backs
mā #xi-∅+c-∅(māmā)∅+c-ān# = if only you (pl) may/would carry it on your backs

9B. 1. *a.* #ti-∅+tla(namaca)∅+∅-h# = We sell things.
b. mā #ti-∅+tla(namaca)∅+c-ān#
c. Mā titlanamacacān. = If only we may sell things.
2. *a.* #ti-∅+c-∅(toca)∅+c-∅# = You followed/pursued him.
b. ma #xi-∅+c-∅(toca)ni+∅-∅#
c. Mā xictocani. = If only you had followed/pursued him. [The preterit optative is also possible: *mā ō#ti-∅+c-∅(toca)∅+c-∅#, Mā ōtictocac*, "If only you had followed/pursued him."]
3. *a.* #∅-∅+qui-∅(tlāl-ī)z+qu-eh# = They will set it down.
b. mā #∅-∅+qui-∅(tlāl-ī)∅+c-ān#
c. Mā quitlālīcān. = If only they may set it down. [The future optative is also possible: *mā #∅-∅+qui-∅(tlāl-ī)z+qu-eh#, Mā quitlālīzqueh*, "If only they set it down (at a later time)."]

Key to the Exercises

    4. *a.* ah#ō#am-∅+m-o(tlal-o-h)ca+∅-h# = You (pl) had not run.
       b. mā ca#ō#xi-∅+m-o(tlal-o-ā)ni+∅-h#
       c. Mā caōximotlaloānih. = If only you (pl) had not run.

9C. 1. *a.* ah#ti-∅+tla(pītza)z+qu-eh# = We shall not blow on things.
       b. mā ca#ti-∅+tla(pītza)∅+c-ān#
       c. Mā catitlapītzacān. = Let's not blow on things. [The future optative is also possible: *mā ca#ti-∅+tla(pītza)z+qu-eh#*, *Mā catitlapītzazqueh*, "Let's not blow on things (in the future)."]
   2. *a.* #∅-∅+qu-∅(ih-tlani)∅+∅-∅# = He asks for/requests it/them.
       b. mā #∅-∅+qu-∅(ih-tlani)∅+☐-∅#
       c. Mā quihtlani. = Let him ask for/request it/them. [Or: "Have him. . . ."]
   3. *a.* ah#an-∅+qu-∅(icza)∅+∅-h# = You (pl) don't tread on it/them.
       b. mā ca#xi-∅+qu-∅(icza)∅+c-ān#
       c. Mā caxiquiczacān. = Don't (pl) tread on it/them.
   4. *a.* #ti-∅+c-∅(tlāl-i-a)∅+∅-∅# = You (sg) set it down.
       b. mā#xi-∅+c-∅(tlāl-i)∅+☐-∅#
       c. Mā xictlāli. = Set (sg) it down.

9D. 1. Let's ask for/request it/them (later).
   2. Let him not scatter it/them in this direction.
   3. I wish I were making it. I wish I had made it.
   4. Just look at it.
   5. If only we had guarded it/them.
   6. Please listen (to him/her/it). ~ Please hear him/her/it.
   7. Don't go out (at a later time).
   8. Let's just go on and say it.
   9. Count it/them later.
  10. Wait a while. [Lit., "Wait for it still/yet."]

9E. 1. Mā canipolihui. Mā canimiqui.
   2. Mā ōxicnamacanih.
   3. Mā caxiczālo.
   4. Tlā xiccuācān.
   5. Mā caticnamacacān.
   6. Mā caōquizāloānih.
   7. Mā polihuicān.

EXERCISE 10

10A. 1. mā #ni-∅+c-∅(cāuh)∅+☐-∅# = let me beware of leaving it/them
      mā #ti-∅+c-∅(cāuh)∅+t-in# = let's beware of leaving it/them
   2. mā #ti-∅+m-o(tēca)h+☐-∅# = beware of stretching out
      mā #an-∅+m-o(tēca)h+t-in# = beware (pl) of stretching out
   3. mā #∅-∅+m-o(zōmah)∅+☐-∅# = let him/her beware of frowning in anger
      mā #∅-∅+m-o(zōmah)∅+t-in# = let them beware of frowning in anger
   4. mā #∅-∅+tla(nel-o-h)∅+t-in# = let them beware of stirring things
      mā #∅-∅+tla(nel-o-h)∅+☐-∅# = let him/her beware of stirring things

10B. 1. Mā onquīz. = *Admon.*: Let him beware of going out.
Mā ōonquīz. = *Pret. opt*: If only he had gone out.
2. Mā caōninoquetz. = *Pret. opt*: If only I had not stood up.
Mā nēn ahninoquetz. = *Admon.*: Let me beware of not standing up. Let me be sure to stand up.
3. Mā titocāuhtin. = *Admon.*: Let's beware of hushing up/ceasing/stopping over (somewhere).
Mā titocāhuacān. = *Nonpast opt*: Let's hush up/cease/stop over.
4. Mā quixcah. = *Admon.*: Let her beware of baking it/them.
Mā quixca. = *Nonpast opt.*: Let her bake it/them.
5. Mā nēn anquiquetztin. = *Admon.*: Beware (pl) of erecting it/them.
Mā ōanquiquetzqueh. = *Pret. opt.*: If only you (pl) had erected it/them.

10C. 1. *a.* #ti-∅+c-∅(quetza)∅+∅-∅# = You (sg) are erecting it/them.
b. mā #ti-∅+c-∅(quetz)∅+☐-∅#
c. Mā ticquetz. = Beware of erecting it/them.
2. *a.* ah#an-∅+tla(nel-o-a)∅+∅-h# = You (pl) don't stir things.
b. mā nēn ah#an-∅+tla(nel-o-h)∅+t-in#
c. Mā nēn ahantlanelohtin. = Beware (pl) of not stirring things. Be sure to stir things.
3. *a.* #ni-∅(pēhua)∅+∅-∅# = I am beginning.
b. mā #ni-∅(pēuh)∅+☐-∅#
c. Mā nipēuh. = Let me beware of beginning.
4. *a.* #∅-∅+tla(xca)∅+∅-∅# = She is baking things.
b. mā #∅-∅+tla(xca)h+☐-∅#
c. Mā tlaxcah. = Let her beware of baking things.
5. *a.* ah#ti-∅+tla(ma)∅+∅-h# = We are not hunting anything.
b. mā nēn ah#ti-∅+tla(mah)∅+t-in#
c. Mā nēn ahtitlamahtin. = Let's beware of not hunting something. Let's be sure to hunt something.
6. *a.* #∅-∅+qui-∅(quēmi)∅+∅-h# = They are putting them on. They are wearing them.
b. mā #∅-∅+qui-∅(quēn)∅+t-in#
c. Mā quiquēntin. = Let them beware of putting them on. Let them beware of wearing them.

10D. 1. Beware (pl) of locking me up.
2. Let them beware of baking it/them.
3. Let's beware of scolding him/her.
4. Beware of not squeezing liquid from it. Be sure to squeeze liquid from it.

10E. 1. Mā nēn ahquitzauctin.
2. Mā tiquintlātihtin.
3. Mā nēn tiquih.
4. Mā ancahhuahtin.
5. Mā nēn ahnictlātih.

10F. 1. Nominative case.
2. It is the carrier for the number-connector morph.
3. Nonpast tense. Class A requires *h*; Classes B, C, and D require ∅.

EXERCISE 11

11A.
1. nicah; □-∅ = sg; "I am"
2. ticateh; □-eh = qu-eh = pl; "we are"
3. ōtihuītzah; ∅-h = pl; "we came/have come/used to come/had come"
4. ōticmah; □-∅ = sg; "you (sg) have found out about it"
5. nonoc; c-∅ = sg; "I am recumbent"
6. tihuītzeh; □-eh = qu-eh = pl; "we come"
7. nihuia; ∅-∅ = sg; "I went/have gone/used to go/had gone"
8. nicahcoc; □-∅ = sg; "I lifted it"
9. tihcac; c-∅ = sg; "you are standing"

Note: In 1, 4, and 8 the irregularity accompanies an irregularity in the stem. In 1 and 4 the □-∅ would be *qui-∅* in *nicatqui* and *ōticmatqui*. In 8 it would be *c-∅* in *nicahcocuic*.

11B.
1. ōcatca; ca = distant-past-as-past tense; "he/she was; he/she has been; he/she used to be; he/she had been"
2. anhuih; ∅ = present; "you (pl) are going"
3. ōyahqueh; ∅ = preterit; "they went/have gone"
4. onoz; z = future; "he/she will be recumbent"
5. tihuālhuia; a = ca = distant-past-as-past; "you (sg) came; you have come; you used to come; you had come"
6. ayāc; ∅ = preterit-as-present; "he/she is not present; he/she is absent"
7. cateh; ∅ = preterit-as-present; "they are"
8. huītzah; a = ca = distant-past-as-past; "they came/have come/used to come/had come"
9. niyeni; ni = customary present; "I usually am"
10. tiyāyah; ya = imperfect; "we used to go; we were going"
11. cahcocqueh; ∅ = preterit; "they lifted it"

11C.
1. mā capilcani; ∅-∅ = sg; "if only it were not hanging"
2. mā tiyecān; c-ān = pl; "let's be"
3. mā caxono; □-∅ = sg; "if only you were not recumbent"
4. mā ōxihcanih; ∅-h = pl; "if only you (pl) had been standing"
5. mā caxihuiān; □-ān = c-ān = pl; "I wish you (pl) weren't going; I wish you had not gone"

11D.
1. #ti-∅(yah)∅+t-in# = let's beware of going
2. ah#∅-∅+qui-∅(mah)∅+□-∅# = let him beware of not knowing it; let him be sure to know it
3. #∅-∅(on-o)h+t-in# = let them beware of being recumbent
4. ah#ti-∅(yah)∅+□-∅# = beware of not going; be sure to go
5. #∅-∅(ca-t)∅+t-in# = let them beware of being
6. #n-∅(ih-ca)h+□-∅# = let me beware of being standing

11E.
1. Are they still there? Are there still some?
2. They have not yet come. They had not yet come.
3. Has he already gone?
4. I have just now come.
5. Please go away.
6. Will you go?
7. He just now found out about it.

8. He only lifted it.
9. Don't go (pl) yet.
10. Perhaps he will hang.

11F. When translated as in (1), the VNCs are formed on the irregular perfective stem of the Class B verb *tla-(mati)*, "to know s.th.," in which vocable-final /t/ has become [h]. When translated as in (2), the VNCs are formed on the regular perfective stem of the Class D verb *tla-(mā)*, "to hunt/capture s.th."

EXERCISE 12

12A.

#pers^1-pers^2(...)num^1-num^2#	Subject
(STEM)	Predicate

12B. 1st sg = "I": #n-Ø(...)tl-Ø#
 #n-Ø(...)tli-Ø# ~ #n-Ø(...)li-Ø#
 #n-Ø(...)in-Ø#
 #n-Ø(...)Ø-Ø#
 1st pl = "we": #t-Ø(...)t-in#
 #t-Ø(...)m-eh#
 #t-Ø(...)Ø-h#

12C. In English nounwords the category of number is an inflection that affects a *nounstem*: the regular nounword formula is "(STEM)number." For example, on the morphic level we have "(BOAT)Ø, 'boat-singular,'" versus "(BOAT)s, 'boat-plural,'" which on the instance level is "boat" versus "boats." In English it is that which is named by the *nounstem* that is thought of as a single entity or more than one entity.

Nahuatl is completely different. It is the *subject personal pronoun* that is affected by the inflection for number, NOT the nounstem (the virtue of the diagrammatic formula for NNCs is that it makes this fact patently clear). The number position cooperates with the person position to constitute the subject personal pronoun, exactly as in VNCs.

Another difference between the two languages is that English nounwords are indifferent to the category of animacy in regard to number (that is, animacy, like number, belongs to the Nahuatl subject pronoun, not to the nounstem). In Nahuatl NNCs only animate subject pronouns distinguish singular from plural number; nonanimate subject pronouns show only common number. A so-called "animate nounstem" is one that is prone to (i.e., normally takes) an animate subject-pronoun; a so-called "nonanimate nounstem" is one that is prone to (i.e., normally takes) a nonanimate subject pronoun.

EXERCISE 13

13A.

#pers^1-pers^2+...)num^1-num^2#	Subject
+st(STEM)	Predicate

13B.

#pers^1-pers^2+...)num^1-num^2#	Subject
+st^1-st^2(STEM)	Predicate

Key to the Exercises

13C. 2nd sg = "you (sg)": #t-Ø+ . . .)uh-Ø#
　　　　　　　　　　　　　　#t-Ø+ . . .)hui-Ø#
　　　　　　　　　　　　　　#t-Ø+ . . .)Ø-Ø
　　　2nd pl = "you (pl)": #am-Ø+ . . .)hu-ān#

13D. 1. t-o ~ t-☐　　　　5. n-o ~ n-☐
　　　2. m-o ~ m-☐　　　6. ī-m ~ ī-n
　　　3. ī-Ø　　　　　　　7. tla
　　　4. tē　　　　　　　　8. am-o ~ am-☐

13E. 1. possessive case; 2. singular number

13F. 1. 1st-person singular-number; 2. 3rd-person possessive-case

EXERCISE 14

14A. 1. *a.*

#ni-Ø(. . .)tl-Ø#	Subject
(cihuā)	Predicate

"I am a/the woman"

b.

#Ø-Ø+ . . .)uh-Ø#	Subject
+ī-Ø(cihuā)	Predicate

"she is his woman/wife"

c.

#ti-Ø(. . .)Ø-h#	Subject
(cihua)	Predicate

"we are women"

d.

#am-Ø+ . . .)hu-ān#	Subject
+ī-n(cihuā)	Predicate

"you are their women/wives"

2. *a.*

#n-Ø(. . .)tli-Ø#	Subject
(oquich)	Predicate

"I am a/the man"

b.

#Ø-Ø+ . . .)hui-Ø#	Subject
+n-☐(oquich)	Predicate

"he is my man/husband"

c.

#am-Ø(. . .)t-in#	Subject
(oquich)	Predicate

"you are men"

d.

#Ø-Ø+. . .)hu-ān#	Subject
+am-☐(oquich)	Predicate

"they are your (pl) men"

3. *a.*

#Ø-Ø+ . . .)Ø-Ø#	Subject
+am-o(cax)	Predicate

"it is your (pl) bowl; they are your (pl) bowls"

b.

#Ø-Ø(. . .)tl-Ø#	Subject
(caxi)	Predicate

"it is a/the bowl; they are (some)/the bowls"

4. a.

#Ø-Ø(...)tl-Ø#	Subject
(tōcāi)	Predicate

"it is a/the name; they are (some)/the names"

b.

#Ø-Ø+...)Ø-Ø#	Subject
+ī-Ø(tōcā)	Predicate

"it is his/her name; they are his/her names"

5. a.

#Ø-Ø(...)in-Ø#	Subject
(mich)	Predicate

"it is a/the fish"

b.

#Ø-Ø+...)Ø-Ø#	Subject
+n-o(mich)	Predicate

"it is my fish"

c.

#Ø-Ø(...)t-in#	Subject
(mī-mich)	Predicate

"they are fish/fishes"

d.

#Ø-Ø+...)hu-ān#	Subject
+m-o(mich)	Predicate

"they are your (sg) fish/fishes"

14B. 1. a. #Ø-Ø(...)tl-Ø# = it; it is a/the crow
   b. #Ø-Ø(...)m-eh# = they; they are crows
   c. #Ø-Ø(...)uh-Ø# = it; it is their crow
   d. #Ø-Ø(...)hu-ān# = they; they are my crows
2. a. #Ø-Ø(...)tl-Ø# = it/they; it is a/the hand; they are hands
   b. #Ø-Ø(...)Ø-Ø# = it/they; it is my hand; they are my hands
3. a. #n-Ø+...)Ø-Ø# = I; I am his/her grandmother
   b. #ni-Ø(...)tli-Ø# = I; I am a grandmother
   c. #ti-Ø(...)t-in# = we; we are grandmothers
   d. #Ø-Ø+...)hu-ān# = they; they are our grandmothers
4. a. #Ø-Ø+...)Ø-Ø# = it; it is your nose
   b. #Ø-Ø(...)tl-Ø# = it/they; it is a nose/point; they are noses/points
5. a. #Ø-Ø(...)Ø-Ø# = it; it is a/the dog
   b. #Ø-Ø+...)Ø-Ø# = it; it is your (sg) dog
   c. #Ø-Ø(...)m-eh# = they; they are (some)/the dogs
   d. #Ø-Ø+...)hu-ān# = they; they are your (pl) dogs
6. a. #Ø-Ø(...)in-Ø# = it; it is a/the star
   b. #Ø-Ø(...)t-in# = they; they are (some)/the stars

14C. 1. a.

#Ø-Ø(...)li-Ø#	Subject
+_(cal)	Predicate

"it is a/the house; they are (some)/the houses"

b.

#Ø-Ø+...)Ø-Ø#	Subject
+n-o(cal)	Predicate

"it is my house; they are my houses"

Key to the Exercises

2. *a.*

#Ø-Ø+ . . .)Ø-Ø#	Subject
+ī-Ø(cac)	Predicate

"it is his/her sandal; they are his/her sandals"

b.

#Ø-Ø+ . . .)tli-Ø#	Subject
+_(cac)	Predicate

"it is a/the sandal; they are (some)/the sandals"

3. *a.*

#Ø-Ø(. . .)li-Ø#	Subject
+_(cōl)	Predicate

"he is a/the grandfather"

b.

#Ø-Ø+ . . .)Ø-Ø#	Subject
+n-o(cōl)	Predicate

"he is my grandfather"

c.

#Ø-Ø(. . .)t-in#	Subject
+_(cōl)	Predicate

"they are grandfathers"

d.

#an-Ø+ . . .)hu-ān#	Subject
+t-o(cōl)	Predicate

"you are our grandfathers"

4. *a.*

#Ø-Ø+ . . .)Ø-Ø#	Subject
+tē(āhui)	Predicate

"she is s.o.'s aunt; she is an aunt"

b.

#Ø-Ø(. . .)tl-Ø#	Subject
+_(āhui)	Predicate

"she is an/the aunt"

c.

#Ø-Ø(. . .)m-eh#	Subject
+_(āhui)	Predicate

"they are aunts"

d.

#ti-Ø+ . . .)hu-ān#	Subject
+m-☐(āhui)	Predicate

"we are your (sg) aunts"

5. *a.*

#Ø-Ø+ . . .)hui-Ø#	Subject
+am-☐(oh)	Predicate

"it is your (pl) path/road; they are your (pl) paths/roads"

b.

#Ø-Ø(. . .)tli-Ø#	Subject
+_(oh)	Predicate

"it is a/the path/road; they are (some)/the paths/roads"

14D. 1. *a.* +ī-Ø(ma-l) = his captive; he is his captive
   b. +tē(ma-l) = s.o.'s captive; we are s.o.'s captives
   c. +_(ma-l) = a/the captive; I am a/the captive
   d. +_(mā-ma-l) = (affinal) captives; they are captives
2. *a.* +_(iy-e) = tobacco smoke/tobacco; it is tobacco smoke/tobacco
   b. +m-☐(iy-e) = your tobacco smoke/tobacco; it is your (sg) tobacco smoke/tobacco

3. *a.* +_(me) = a/the maguey plant; it is a/the maguey plant; they are maguey plants
   b. +m-o(me) = your maguey plant; it is your maguey plant; they are your maguey plants
4. *a.* +_(e) = a/the bean; it is a/the bean; they are (some)/the beans
   b. +m-∅(e) = your bean; it is your bean; they are your beans
5. *a.* +_(cihuā) = a/the woman; you are a/the woman
   b. +ī-∅(cihuā) = his woman/wife; you are his woman/wife
   c. +_(cihua) = a/the woman/wife; you are (some)/the women
   d. +am-o(cihuā) = your (pl) woman/wife; they are your (pl) women/wives

14E. 1. #t-∅(ō-ōtz)t-in# = we are prenant women [< (ōtz)-tli-]
   2. #∅-∅+ī-n(coh-conē)hu-ān# = they are their (individually possessed) children [< (conē)-tl-. "Their" refers only to women here.]
   3. #∅-∅+t-o(cah-cax)∅-∅# = they are our varied/separate bowls [< (caxi)-tl-]
   4. #an-∅(tī-tīci)∅-h# = you are healers/midwives/doctors [< (tīci)-tl-]
   5. #∅-∅+ī-∅(cueh-cuē)∅-∅# = they re her varied skirts [< (cuēi)-tl-]

14F. 1. amiyeuh
   2. mōmōyoh
   3. tocahcac
   4. mihītzhui
   5. ihiyetl
   6. nomōyōhuān
   7. mocac ~ amocac
   8. īyac

EXERCISE 15

15A. 1. +t-o(cuāuh) = our eagle; NNC = it is our eagle
   2. +am-o(nā) = +am-o(nān) = your (pl) mother; NNC = they are your mothers
   3. +n-o(tlāca) = my slave; NNC = they are my slaves
   4. +t-o(cn-ī) = +t-o(cn-īuh) = our friend; NNC = you are our friends
   5. +ī-∅(pil-lo) = his nobleman; NNC = he is his nobleman
   6. +ī-∅(tēuc-yō) = his lord; NNC = we are his courtiers/liege lords
   7. +n-o(nān) = my mother; NNC = you are my mother
   8. +t-o(cuā) = +t-o(cuāuh) = our eagle; NNC = they are our eagles
   9. +n-o(cn-īuh) = my friend; NNC = you are my friend
   10. (tlā-tlācoh) = (affinity) slaves; NNC = they are slaves
   11. +ī-∅(tēuc-yo) = his lord; NNC = I am his lord
   12. +n-o(pil-lo) = my noble; NNC = you are my noblemen

15B. 1. #∅-∅+t-∅(āxcā)∅-∅# = it is our property, it is ours
   2. #∅-∅+am-o(tē-tah)hu-ān# = they are your (pl) fathers
   3. #∅-∅+m-o(chān)∅-∅# = it is your (sg) home
   4. #∅-∅+ī-∅(tē-ic-cā)hu-ān# = they are his younger brothers
   5. #∅-∅+t-o(tla-mā)∅-∅# = they are our sleeves
   6. #∅-∅+m-o(tle-mā)uh-∅# = it is your (sg) incense ladle
   7. #t-∅+ī-∅(ic-cāuh)∅-∅# = you are his younger brother
   8. #∅-∅+m-o(tlā-tla-ht-ō-l)∅-∅# = they are your prolix words
   9. #an-∅+t-o(tē-āch-cā)hu-ān# = you are our older brothers
   10. #∅-∅+ī-∅(tla-nacaz)∅-∅# = it is its corner, they are its corners; they are their corners

Key to the Exercises 123

      11. #ti-Ø+n-o(yāō)uh-Ø# = you are my enemy
      12. #t-Ø+ī-Ø(poh)hu-ān# = we are his peers, we are like him

15C. 1. It is an (outside) corner. They are corners.
     2. They are our ears. It is the ear of one of us. It is an ear.
     3. Are we not your (pl) mothers?
     4. He is not their older brother.
     5. Perhaps it is their property. Perhaps it is theirs.
     6. They are still our enemies.

15D. 1. Ca titotēucyo.
     2. Cuix ahtimotēucyōhuān.
     3. Zan notlācauh.
     4. Ahoc tocnīhuān
     5. Mā catīyāōuh.
     6. Ahtinopoh.

EXERCISE 16

16A. 1. #t-Ø(a-c-ah)Ø-Ø# = you (sg) are s. o.
     2. #an-Ø(tl-eh)m-eh# = what are you (pl)?
     3. #Ø-Ø(quē-x-qui-ch)Ø-Ø# = how much is it? how much is there? how many are there?
     4. #ti-Ø(miye-quī-n)t-in# = we are many
     5. #n-Ø(itl-ah)Ø-Ø# = I am s.th.
     6. #Ø-Ø(iz-quī-n)☐-☐# = they are as many, they are an equal number
     7. #Ø-Ø(yeh-yeh-huā)tl-Ø# = they are various kinds of things
     8. #Ø-Ø(a-chi)Ø-Ø# = it is a small amount
     9. #am-Ø(eh-huā-n)t-in# = you are entities
    10. #Ø-Ø(cā-tl-e-in)Ø-Ø# = which one is it?
    11. #Ø-Ø(ix-a-chī-n)☐-☐# = they are many/numerous
    12. #Ø-Ø(yeh-huā-n)☐-☐# = they are entities
    13. #am-Ø(mo-chī-n)☐-☐# = you (pl) are all
    14. #ti-Ø(quē-x-qui-ch)t-in# = how many are we? how many are there of us?
    15. #az-Ø(ce-quī-n)t-in# = you (pl) are some (people)
    16. #ti-Ø(tl-eh)Ø-Ø# = what are you (sg)?

16B. 1. It is the very same one.
     2. They are as many again.
     3. Perhaps you (pl) are some people.
     4. Are they the ones?
     5. We are only a few. We are not many.
     6. Are we nothing?
     7. Already you (pl) are a full amount. Already you are a sufficient number.
     8. Are you (pl) something? Are you (pl) anything?
     9. It is still just a little. There is still a small amount.
    10. I am indeed the one.

16C. 1. #no-Ø+c-Ø+on(... = #1sg-nom+3obj-sg+thither(...
2. #n-Ø+on+n-o(... = #1sg-nom+thither+1sg-reflex(...
3. #an-Ø+c-Ø+om+m-o(... = #2pl-nom+3obj-sg+thither+2pl-reflex(...
4. #am-Ø+on+tē(... = #2pl-nom+thither+s.o.(...
5. #ni-Ø+qu-im+on+n-o(... = #1sg-nom+3obj-pl+thither+1sg-reflex(...
6. #n-Ø+on+tla(... = #1sg-nom+thither+s.th.(...

EXERCISE 17

1. ō#<u>Ø-Ø</u>+qui-Ø(chīuh)Ø+□-Ø# #Ø-Ø+n-o(cōl)Ø-Ø# = <u>He</u>-made-it <u>he-is-my-grandfather</u>; i.e., My grandfather made it.
2. #<u>Ø-Ø</u>(tzahtzi)Ø+<u>Ø-h</u># #Ø+Ø(mo-chī-n)t-in# = <u>They</u>-shout <u>they are all</u>; i.e., All shout.
3. ah#<u>Ø-Ø</u>+on(ca-h)Ø+□-Ø# #Ø-Ø(cin)tli-Ø# = <u>It</u>-is-not-there <u>it-is-a-dried-ear-of-maize</u>; i.e., There is no dried ear of maize./There are no dried ears of maize. There is no maize.
4. ō#<u>t-Ø</u>(on-o)ca+<u>Ø-h</u># #ti-Ø(miye-quī-n)t-in# = <u>We</u>-were-recumbent-there <u>we-are-many</u>; i.e., Many of us were recumbent there.
5. #<u>Ø-Ø</u>+tē(ihtlac-o-a)Ø+<u>Ø-Ø</u># #Ø-Ø(pey-ō)tl-Ø# = <u>It</u>-damages-people <u>it-is-peyote</u>; i.e., Peyote harms people.
6. #<u>Ø-Ø</u>(huī-tz)Ø+□-eh# #Ø-Ø(cal-pōl)t-in# = Already <u>they</u>-come <u>they-are-members-of-a-town-quarter</u>; i.e., Members of a town quarter are already coming.

17B. 1. ō#to-Ø+c-<u>Ø</u>+on(cui)Ø+c-Ø# #<u>Ø-Ø</u>+n-□(ayoh)Ø-Ø# = Perchance you-have-taken-it-thither <u>it-is-my squash</u>? i.e., Have you taken my squash?
2. #Ø-Ø+<u>qu-im</u>(itt-a)Ø+c-Ø# #Ø-Ø(cī-cītlal)t-in# = He/She-saw-<u>them</u> <u>they-are-stars</u>; i.e., He/She saw the stars.
3. #Ø-Ø+qui-Ø(chīuh)Ø+qu-eh# #Ø-Ø+ī-n(huīpil)Ø-Ø# = They-made-<u>them</u> <u>they-are-their blouses</u>; i.e., They made their blouses.
4. ō#Ø-Ø+<u>qu-im</u>(pēuh)Ø+□-Ø# oc #Ø-Ø(ce-quī-n)t-in# = He-has-conquered-<u>them</u> still <u>they-are-some</u>; i.e., He has conquered some others. He has conquered others.
5. #ni-Ø+<u>c-Ø</u>(namaca)Ø+Ø-Ø# #Ø-Ø(cac)tli-Ø# = I-sell-<u>it/them</u> <u>it-is-a-sandal/they-are-sandals</u>; i.e., I sell the sandal/sandals.
6. #Ø-Ø+<u>c-Ø</u>(ōya)Ø+Ø-h# #Ø-Ø(cin)tli-Ø# = They-shell-<u>it</u> <u>it-is-maize</u>; i.e., They shell maize.

17C. 1. #Ø-Ø+<u>n-o</u>(tōpīl)Ø-Ø# #<u>n-Ø</u>(eh-huā)tl-Ø# = It-is-<u>my</u>-staff-of-office <u>I-am-the-entity</u>; i.e., It is <u>my</u> staff [The underlined "my" in the final translation indicates vocal stress.]
2. #Ø-Ø+<u>ī-Ø</u>(te)uh-Ø# #Ø-Ø(tōtō)tl-Ø# = It-is-<u>its</u>-egg <u>it-is-a/the-bird</u>; i.e., It is a/the bird's egg. They are a/the bird's eggs.
3. #Ø-Ø+<u>ī-Ø</u>(ocuil)hu-ān# #Ø-Ø(cuahui)tl-Ø# = They-are-<u>its</u>-worms <u>it-is-a/the-tree</u>; i.e., They are the tree's worms. The tree has worms. They are the trees' worms. The trees have worms.
4. #Ø-Ø+<u>ī-Ø</u>(cōn)Ø-Ø# #Ø-Ø+n-o(cih)Ø-Ø# = It-is-<u>her</u>-pot <u>she-is-my-grandmother</u>; i.e., It is my grandmother's pot. They are my grandmother's pots.
5. #Ø-Ø+<u>m-□</u>(āxcā)Ø-Ø# #ti-Ø+t-o(cn-īuh)Ø-Ø# = It-is-<u>your</u>-property <u>you-are-our-friend</u>; i.e., It is the property of you our friend.

Key to the Exercises

6. #Ø-Ø+ī-m(pil)hu-ān# #Ø-Ø(mā-cē-hua-l)t-in# = They-are-<u>their</u>-children <u>they-are-commoners</u>; i.e., They are the children of commoners.

17D. 1. ītah = *suppl subj*; octli = *suppl obj*; SEN = His/Her father did not drink the pulque.
2. nocuē = *suppl obj*; nonān = *suppl subj*; SEN = My mother is looking for my skirt.
3. ītōcā = *suppl subj*; īconēuh = *suppl poss*; īcnīuh = *suppl poss*; nocihuāuh = *suppl poss*; SEN = My wife's friend's child's name is nothing. My wife's friend's child has no name.
4. īncihuāhuān = *suppl poss*; tocnīhuān = *suppl poss*; SEN = They are the blouses of our friends' wives.
5. īmohhui = *suppl obj*; toyāōhuān = *supp poss*; SEN = We have seen our enemies' path.
6. īmahmā = *suppl obj*; cuahuitl = *suppl poss*; nehhuātl = *suppl subj*; SEN = I gathered the (varied) branches of the tree/trees.

17E. 1. *a.* mochīntin = *suppl subj*; SEN = All leave.
   b. mochīntin = *suppl subj as topic*; SEN = As for all, they leave.
2. *a.* nochīmal = *suppl obj*; SEN = Did he seize my shield?
   b. nochīmal = *suppl obj as topic*; SEN = As for my shield, did he seize it?
3. *a.* yehhuātl = *suppl subj*; SEN = Let <u>him/her</u> beware of standing up. [for emphasis]
   b. yehhuātl = *suppl subj as topic*; SEN = As for him/her, let him/her beware of standing up.
4. *a.* mocnīuh = *suppl poss*; SEN = I am your friend's enemy.
   b. mocnīuh = *suppl poss as topic*; SEN = As for your friend, I am his enemy.
5. *a.* cōmitl = *suppl obj*; SEN = Buy the bowl/bowls.
   b. cōmitl = *suppl obj as topic*; SEN = As for the bowl/bowls, buy it/them.

17F. 1. He/She wants it all. How much does he/she want?
2. You will buy sandals. What will you buy?
3. They seize everything. How many do they seize?
4. He/She will gather pine torchwood. What will he/she gather?
5. It is <u>his/her</u> property. Whose property is it? ~ Whose is it?

17G. 1. His children are many.
2. What did you say?
3. Beware of ruining my necklace.
4. As for their house, let's make it.
5. Did they all fall down?
6. They no longer said anything.
7. Is your father your father? Is your mother your mother?
8. Bring fire.

EXERCISE 18

18A. 1. [In notōcā = *suppl obj*.] = I shall set down my name; i.e., I shall sign my name.
2. [In ocuiltin = *suppl obj*.] = It catches the worms.
3. [In xōchitl = *suppl obj*.] = Did you smell the flowers?
4. [In ītlācahuān = *suppl subj*.] = His slaves will die (i.e., will be sacrificed).

5. [In ōn = *suppl obj*.] = Don't (sg) buy that one.
6. [In amoyāōhuān = *suppl subj*.] = Your enemies are leaving!
7. [In māxcā = *suppl subj*.] = Your property is my property. Yours is mine. What is yours is mine.
8. [In notōtolhuān = *suppl obj*.] = Your dog killed my turkey hens.
9. [In īpetl = *suppl obj*; in nonān = *suppl poss*.] = Beware of ruining my mother's mat(s).
10. [In īn = *suppl obj*.] = Take this one.
11. [In īyōllo = *suppl subj*; cayāc = *suppl poss*. This is a discontinuous structure of supplementation; see § 18.4.] = Let no one's heart be sad.
12. [In octli = *suppl subj*.] = The pulque is abandoning me; i.e., I am becoming sober.

18B
1. [In nehhuātl = *suppl subj* (for emphasis).] = I shall climb up there.
2. [In miztli = *suppl subj*.] The puma eats meat.
3. [In tōtōtl = *suppl poss* (in a discontinuous structure of supplementation.] = I heard the bird's song.
4. [In tōtōchtin = *suppl subj*.] The rabbits became afraid.
5. [In yehhuāntin = *suppl subj* (for emphasis)] They are our grandfathers.
6. [In īcal = *suppl subj*.] Their god's house was burning [*In īnteōuh* is functioning as a supplementary possessor (in a discontinuous structure of supplementation).].
7. [In zacatl = *suppl obj*.] They carry bunchgrass.
8. [In nehhuātl = *suppl obj* (for emphasis).] They are waiting for me.

18C.
1. The jaguar sees the deer. The deer sees the jaguar.
2. The man summoned the woman. The woman summoned the man.
3. My friend respects his/her uncle. His/Her uncle respects my friend. He/She respects my friend's uncle.
4. Their enemies had deceived them. They had deceived their enemies.

18D.
1. What have you (pl) done? [The personal-pronoun object serving as head of the structure of supplementation is present only silently.]
2. Where is his home? [The principle clause has been deleted.]
3. The men were setting the blankets down. [The supplementary subject (1st plural = we are men) disagrees in person with its basic subject (3rd plural).]
4. Did you steal? Did you steal the necklace? [When there is a supplementary object, the VNC is transitive; when there is none, it is intransitive.]
5. Have you and the merchant hidden something? [The "named partner" construction.]
6. They all crossed over. [Apparent disagreement in number between the supplement and its head.]

18E.
1. What are you doing, buddy?
2. Don't say it, my friend.
3. I see you, my children.
4. Drink it, my husband.
5. Beware of taking it, my little brother.
6. My young man, listen to the words. [What in English is a vocative here is merely a supplementary subject in the role of topic in Nahuatl.]

Key to the Exercises 127

EXERCISE 19

19A.
1. [ōyahqueh = *suppl obj.*] = I sent the ones who went.
2. [ōtiquihtoh = *suppl obj.*] = I did not hear what you said.
3. [moyāhuacah = *suppl subj.*] = The ones who had dispersed came back together.
4. [ōteciya = *suppl subj.*] = The one who was grinding would soon die. [The future tense VNC in the principal clause is translated as English future-in-the-past, because in the adjunct clause the VNC is in the imperfect tense.]
5. [ōticchīuh = *suppl obj.*] = I saw what you did/made.
6. [ōquināmoyāqueh = *suppl subj.*] = The ones who abducted him/her are there. [Context may force the preterit-as-present tense VNC in the principal clause to be translated as the past tense "were."]
7. [ōompanōqueh = *suppl subj* ~ *suppl obj* (depending on context).] = The ones who crossed over overtook them. They overtook the ones who crossed over. [In *ōompanōqueh* is the topic.]
8. [quitquih = *suppl obj.*] = Seize (pl) what they are carrying. [The bridge between the two clauses lies between the object pronoun in the supplement and its object-pronoun head in the principal clause.]
9. [quipiyazqueh in teōtl = *suppl obj.*] = He selected the ones who guarded the god (i.e., the idol or image representing the god).
10. [tictēmoa = *suppl subj.*] = Here is what you are seeking.
11. [tiquihtoa = *suppl obj.*] = I shall do what you say.
12. [huītecoh = *suppl subj.*] = The ones who are struck by lightning go there. [*(huī-tec-ō)* is the nonactive stem of *tē-(huī-tequi)*, "to thrash/beat/whip s.o." The passive VNC is here used in the sense "they are struck by lightning."]

19B.
1. Those are wealthy and happy. ~ Those are enjoying life.
2. As for these, their lord deceived them.
3. Who notably were the ones to whom she/he shouted?
4. Those speak a foreign language.
5. These are reviving/coming to their senses.
6. Who were the ones who set it down?

19C.
1. [cuix quinamacaz = *suppl obj*; referent for the personal-pronoun object *qui-Ø.*] = We do not know whether he will sell it/them.
2. [in ōquihcuiloh in āmoxtli = *suppl subj*; referent for the personal-pronoun subject *Ø-Ø*(... +□-*Ø*] = Is it true that he wrote the book?
3. [ye miquiz in ōteciya = *suppl subj*; referent for the personal-pronoun subject *Ø-Ø*(... +*Ø-Ø*] = It seemed/used to seem that the one who was grinding would soon die. [The supplement is itself a structure of subject supplementation (of the shared-referent type).]
4. [in quimāmāzqueh in ixquich = *suppl subj*; referent for the personal-pronoun subject *Ø-Ø*(... +□-*Ø*] = Will it be possible for them to carry so much?
5. [in ca ye huālahcizqueh = *suppl obj*; referent for the personal-pronoun object *qu-Ø.*] = He said that they would soon arrive hither.
6. [octli qui = *suppl subj*; referent for the personal-pronoun subject *Ø-Ø*(... +*Ø-Ø*] = It seems he is drinking pulque.

7. [in mā tiquīnāyacān = *suppl subj*; referent for the personal-pronoun subject ∅-∅+ ... +∅-∅] = It wants itself (i.e., it is necessary) that we hide it/them.
8. [in mā monāmicti in nochpōch = *suppl subj*; referent for the personal-pronoun object *qu-∅.*] = I yearn for my daughter to get married. [The supplement is itself a structure of subject supplementation (of the shared-referent type).]
9. [in mā caxictlati = *suppl obj*; referent for the personal-pronoun object *qu-∅.*] = I request that you (sg) not burn it/them.
10. [in ōmpa tiyāzqueh = *suppl subj*; referent for the personal-pronoun subject ∅-∅+ ... +□-∅.] = It will not be possible for us to go there.
11. [in titēlpōchtli = *suppl subj*; referent for the personal-pronoun subject ∅-∅(... + ∅-∅.] = appears that you are a youth; i.e., You look young. [Contrast the subject complement construction in § 51.3.]
12. [in niccuāz = *suppl subj*; referent for the personal-pronoun subject ∅-∅(... + □-∅.] = It will not be possible for me to eat it.
13. [in mā caniquitta = *suppl obj*; referent for the personal-pronoun object *c-∅.*] = I want not to see him/her/it.

19D. 1. [tichuīcaz in ēhuatl = *suppl obj*; head = *qu-∅.*] = Remember to carry the hide(s)/skin(s).
2. [titlahtzomaz = *suppl obj*; head = *c-∅.*] = Do you know how to sew?
3. [māltīz = *suppl obj*; head = *c-∅.*] = He/She doesn't want to bathe.
4. [niquīz in pahtli = *suppl obj*; head = *qu-∅.*] = I forgot to drink (i.e., take) the medicine. [The supplementt is itself a structure of object supplementation (but of the shared-referent type).]
5. [in nicchīhuaz in ōn = *suppl obj*; head = *c-∅.*] = I don't know how to do/make that. [The supplement is itself a structure of object supplementation.]
6. [ancontēmōzqueh = *suppl obj*; head = *qui-∅.*] = Do you (pl) want to look for him/her/it?

19E. 1. It is said (notably) that he burned it all ~ that he burned everything.
2. Did you say that they will go?
3. There is told (*lit.*, it says itself) how they gave shape to their dugouts. [*tla-(xīma)*, "to cut away s.th. (here, excess wood)."]
4. It is said their god summoned them
5. He said, "Beware (sg) of not doing it." I.e., He said, "Be sure to do it."
6. Will you (sg) still say, "Send me thither"?
7. It is said that he is/was a sorcerer. [*lit.*, a sorcerer is/was he.]

19F. In shared referent supplementation the personal pronoun that is the head and some personal pronoun in the supplement refer to the same entity in the nonlinguistic reality, and the supplement names or identifies the entity referred to by the pronoun functioning as head.

In included-referent supplementation some stretch of linguistic matter (a nuclear clause, a clause group, or an entire sentence) is treated as a nominal unit (with a 3rd-person singular value), so that it can serve as the referent for a 3rd-person singular pronoun that serves as the head in the principal clause.

Key to the Exercises

EXERCISE 20

20A.
1. to tread on s.th.; (*i*cx-ō) ~ (*i*cza-lō)
2. to return; (īlō-ch-ō)
3. to make/do s.th.; (āyī-hua)
4. to take s.th.; (cuī-hua)
5. to throw rocks at s.th.; (mōtla-lō)
6. to get up; (ē-ō-hua)
7. to grind (grain); (tecī-hua)
8. to live; (yōlī-hua)
9. to know s.th.; (mach-ō)
10. to cut s.th.; (tec-ō)
11. to smell s.th.; (*i*hnec-ō) ~ (*i*hnecu-ō)
12. to carry s.th. on one's back; (māma-lō)
13. to be; (ye-lo-hua)
14. to throw s.th.; (tlāza-lō) ~ (tlāx-ō)
15. to take hold of s.th.; (ān-ō) > (āna-lō)
16. to fall; (huech-o-hua)
17. to arrive; (ahxī-hua)
18. to burn s.th.; (tla-tī-lō)
19. to cry; (chōc-o-hua)
20. to become tired; (ciy-a-ō-hua)
21. to come; (huī-lo–hua-tz)

20B.
1. (ihcuil-i-ō-hua)
2. (cāhu-a-lō)
3. (quimil-ō-lō)
4. (tzacu-a-lō)
5. (tlal-i-ō-hua)
6. (pa-lō)
7. (pol-i-ō-hua)
8. (tlam-o-hua)

EXERCISE 21

21A.
1. #ni-∅+c-∅(āna)∅+∅-∅# = I seize it/them
   #∅-∅(ān-o)∅+∅-∅# = it is seized ~ they are seized
   #∅-∅(āna-lo)∅+∅-∅# = it is seized ~ they are seized
2. #∅-∅+am-ēch(toca)ya+∅-h# = they used to follow/pursue you (pl)
   #an-∅(toc-ō)ya+∅-h# = you (pl) used to be followed/pursued
3. #ni-∅+qu-im(ihcal)∅+☐-∅# = I fought them
   #∅-∅(ihcalī-lō)∅+qu-eh# = they were fought
4. #∅-∅+m-itz(īmacaci)z+☐-∅# = he will respect your (sg)
   #t-∅(īmacax-ō)z+☐-∅# = you will be respected
5. #t-∅+☐-∅(āyi)z+qu-eh# = we shall make/do it
   #∅-∅(āyī-hua)z+☐-∅# = it will be made/done
6. #an-∅+n-ēch(nāmiqui)∅+∅-h# = you (pl) encounter me
   #ni-∅(nāmic-o)∅+∅-∅# = I am encountered

21B. 1. it used to be wanted; Ø-Ø(. . . +Ø-Ø = "it" < qui-Ø = "it"
2. you (sg) were seized; t-Ø(. . . +c-Ø = "you (sg)" < m-itz = "you (sg)"
3. they are accompanied; Ø-Ø(. . . +Ø-h = "they" < qu-in = "them"
4. I had been respected; n-Ø(. . . +Ø-Ø = "I" < n-ēch = "me"
5. we were destroyed; ti-Ø(. . . +qu-eh = "we" < t-ēch = "us"
6. you (pl) will be abandoned; an-Ø(. . . +qu-eh = "you (pl)" < am-ēch = "you (pl)"

21C. 1. he will accompany you (pl); am-ēch = "you (pl)" > an-Ø(. . . +qu-eh = "you (pl)"
2. you (sg) drank it; qu-Ø = "it" > Ø-Ø(. . . +c-Ø = "it"
3. we shall destroy them; qu-im = "them" > Ø-Ø(. . . +qu-eh = "they"
4. he will seize me; n-ēch = "me" > n-Ø(. . . ☐-Ø = "I"
5. he sent you as a messenger; m-itz = "you (sg)" > ti-Ø(. . . ☐-Ø = "you (sg)"
6. he had captured us; t-ēch = "us" > ti-Ø(. . . +Ø-h = "we"

21D. 1. *a.* they accompany us
   b. (1) #Ø-Ø+t-ēch(huīca)Ø+Ø-h#
       (2) ⌄+t-ēch(huīca)Ø+⌄
       (3) . . . +t-ēch(huīc-ō)Ø+ . . .
       (4) #ti-Ø(huīc-o)Ø+Ø-h#
   c. tihuīcoh = we are accompanied
2. *a.* I encounter them
   b. (1) #ni-Ø+qu-in(nāmiqui)Ø+Ø-Ø#
       (2) ⌄+qu-in(nāmiqui)Ø+⌄
       (3) . . . +qu-in(nāmic-ō)Ø+ . . .
       (4) #Ø-Ø(nāmic-o)Ø+Ø-h#
   c. nāmicoh = they are encountered
3. *a.* they had fought you (pl)
   b. (1) #Ø-Ø+am-ēch(ihcal)ca+Ø-h#
       (2) ⌄+am-ēch(ihcal)ca+⌄
       (3) . . . +am-ēch(ihcalī-hua)ca+ . . .
       (4) #am-Ø(ihcalī-hua)ca+Ø-h#
   c. amihcalīhuacah = you (pl) had been fought
4. *a.* we shall bleed ourselves
   b. (1) #ti-Ø+t-o(zō)z+qu-eh#
       (2) ⌄+t-o(zō)z+⌄
       (3) . . . +t-o(zō-hua)z+ . . .
       (4) #ti-Ø+ne(zō-hua)z+qu-eh#
   c. tinezōhuazqueh = we shall be self-bled
5. *a.* we hid you (sg)
   b. (1) #ti-Ø+m-itz(tlā-ti-h)Ø+qu-eh#
       (2) ⌄+m-itz(tlā-ti-h)Ø+⌄
       (3) . . . +m-itz(tlā-ti-lō)Ø+ . . .
       (4) #ti-Ø(tlā-ti-lō)Ø+c-Ø#
   c. titlātilōc = you (sg) were hidden

Key to the Exercises 131

21E.
1. Were you (sg) not created? [tē-(yōco-ya)]
2. As for this one/these, let it/them not be worn. [tla-(quēmi)]
3. The jadeite will no longer be drilled. [tla-(mamali)]
4. Perhaps the tribute has been seized. [tla-(āna)]
5. Everything will be moved. [tla-(*i*hcuani-ā)]
6. Let's beware of being captured. [tē-(mā)]
7. The moon has been eaten (i.e., eclipsed). [tla-(cuā)]
8. Then we were sent thither as messengers. [tē-(tītlani)]
9. Others have been seen. [tē- ~ tla-(*i*tt-a)]
10. Was their book destroyed/lost? ~ Were their books destroyed/lost? [tla-(pol-o-ā)]
11. How many will be written/painted? [tla-(*i*hcuil-o-ā)]
12. All of you will be captured. [tē-(mā)]
13. I am summoned. The Sun summons me. [tē-(nōtza)]

21F.
1. [ahmihtoa = it does not say itself] = From where they came is not told.
2. [mocōhuaz = it will buy itself] = The bowl(s) will be bought.
3. [ahmomati = it does not know itself] = It is not known whether it was destroyed.
4. [ōmocuic = it has taken itself] = Their property has been taken.
5. [monequiz = it will want itself] = How much is still needed?
6. [monamaca = it sells itself] = There sandals/shoes are sold.
7. [ōmottaca = it had seen itself] = The flag(s) had been seen.
8. [mopāhuaci = it cooks itself in a pot] = The sweet potato is cooked in a pot. Sweet potatoes are cooked in a pot.
9. [moxca = it bakes itself] = It is also baked. They are also baked.
10. [mohotqui = they carry themselves individually/separately] = Reeds are carried individually/separately.
11. [mochīhuaya = it/they used to make itself/themselves] = Arrows used to be made. None were unequal in length.

EXERCISE 22.

22A.
1. #Ø-Ø(cē-hua)Ø+Ø-Ø# = it becomes cold [not supplementable]
2. #Ø-Ø(pix-a-hui)ya+Ø-Ø# = it was drizzling [not supplementable]
3. #Ø-Ø(til-ā-hua)Ø+Ø-Ø# = it rains hard [not supplementable]
4. #Ø-Ø(til-ā-hua)Ø+Ø-Ø# = it becomes thickly woven [supplementable]
5. ō#Ø-Ø(tēn)Ø+☐-Ø# = it became brimming full [supplementable]
6. #Ø-Ø(moy-ā-hua)Ø+c-Ø# = it/they became dispersed/disseminated [supplementable]
7. #Ø-Ø(yohua)ya+Ø-Ø# = it was becoming night [not supplementable]
8. #Ø-Ø(chip-ī-ni)Ø+Ø-Ø# = it drips [supplementable]
9. #Ø-Ø(mani)Ø+Ø-Ø# = it covers a flat surface [supplementable]
10. #Ø-Ø(quiy-a-hui)Ø+Ø-Ø# = it is raining [not supplementable]
11. #Ø-Ø(tlami)z+☐-Ø# = it will end [supplementable]
12. #Ø-Ø(te-c-i-hui)ya+Ø-Ø# = it was hailing [not supplementable]
13. #Ø-Ø(tōna)ya+Ø-Ø# = it was sunshining [not supplementable]
14. #Ø-Ø+m-o(chīhua)z+☐-Ø# = it will be done/made [supplementable]
15. ō#Ø-Ø(chal-ā-n)Ø+☐-Ø# = it became cracked [supplementable]

22B. 1. *a.* #t-Ø(ahci)Ø+Ø-h# = we arrive
      b. #Ø-Ø(ahxī-hua)Ø+Ø-Ø# = people arrive, everyone arrives
   2. *a.* #az-Ø(cia-hui)Ø+Ø-h# = you (pl) become tired
      b. #Ø-Ø(cia-ō-hua)Ø+Ø-Ø# = people become tired, everyone becomes tired
   3. *a.* #ti-Ø(teci)z+☐-Ø# = you (sg) will grind
      b. #Ø-Ø(tex-o-hua)z+☐-Ø# = people/everyone will grind
   4. *a.* #ti-Ø+t-o(zahua)Ø+Ø-h# = we fast
      b. #Ø-Ø+ne(zahua-lo)Ø+Ø-Ø# = people fast/everyone fasts
   5. *a.* #Ø-Ø(ē-hua)Ø+qu-eh# = they got up, they took off (in flight)
      b. #Ø-Ø(ē-ō-hua)Ø+c-Ø# = everyone got up, all took off
   6. *a.* #ni-Ø+tla(caqui)Ø+Ø-Ø# = I hear s.th./things
      b. #Ø-Ø+tla(cac-o)Ø+Ø-Ø# = people hear things, things are heard
   7. *a.* #an-Ø+tē(chiya)Ø+Ø-h# = you (pl) wait for s.o.
      b. #Ø-Ø+tē(chiya-lo)Ø+Ø-Ø# = people wait for people
   8. *a.* #Ø-Ø(pēhua)z+☐-Ø# = it will begin
      b. #Ø-Ø(pē-ō-hua)z+☐-Ø# = things (in general) will begin

22C. 1. *a.* you (pl) seek s.th./things
      b. (1) #an-Ø+tla(tēm-o-a)Ø+Ø-h#
           (2) ⌄+tla(tēm-o-a)Ø+ ⌄
           (3) . . . +tla(tēm-ō-lō)Ø+ . . .
           (4) #Ø-Ø+tla(tēm-ō-lo)Ø+Ø-Ø#
      c. tlatēmōlo = s.o. is seeking s.th., people are seeking things
   2. *a.* you (sg) slept
      b. (1) ō#ti-Ø(coch)Ø+☐-Ø#
           (2) ō# ⌄(coch)Ø+ ⌄
           (3) ō# . . . (cochī-hua)Ø+ . . .
           (4) ō#Ø-Ø(cochī-hua)Ø+c-Ø#
      c. ōcochīhuac = people slept
   3. *a.* we are astonished
      b (1) #ti-Ø+t-☐(īz-a-hui-a)Ø+Ø-h#
          (2) ⌄+t-☐(īz-a-hui-a)Ø+ ⌄
          (3) . . . +t-☐(īz-a-huī-lō)Ø+ . . .
          (4) #Ø-Ø+ne(īz-a-huī-lo)Ø+Ø-Ø#
      c. neīzahuīlo = people are astonished, everyone is astonished
   4. *a.* they follow s.o./people
      b (1) #Ø-Ø+tē(toca)Ø+Ø-h#
          (2) ⌄+tē(toca)Ø+ ⌄
          (3) . . . +tē(toc-ō)Ø+ . . .
          (4) #Ø-Ø+tē(toc-o)Ø+Ø-Ø#
      c. tētoco = people follow s.o./people
   5. *a.* they will die
      b (1) #Ø-Ø(miqui)z+qu-eh#
          (2) ⌄(miqui)z+ ⌄
          (3) . . . (mic-o-hua)z+ . . .
          (4) #Ø-Ø(mic-o-hua)z+☐-Ø#
      c. micohuaz = people/everyone will die

Key to the Exercises

22D. 1. *a.* #∅-∅(cōhua-lo)∅+∅-∅# = it is being bought ~ they are being bought
     b. #∅-∅+tla(cōhua-lo)∅+∅-∅# = people buy things
  2. *a.* #∅-∅(tōc-o)∅+∅-h# = they are being buried
     b. #∅-∅+tē(tōc-o)∅+∅-∅# = people are burying people
  3. *a.* #∅-∅(tlāx-ō)∅+c-∅# = it was thrown
     b. #∅-∅+tla(tlāx-ō)∅+c-∅# = people threw things
  4. *a.* #∅-∅(pītza-lō)∅+c-∅# = it was blown on ~ they were blown on
     b. #∅-∅+tla(pītza-lō)∅+c-∅# = people blew on things
  5. *a.* #∅-∅(cuī-hua)z+☐-∅# = it will be taken ~ they will be taken
     b. #∅-∅+tla(cuī-hua)z+☐-∅# = people will take things
  6. *a.* #an-∅(tzacu-a-lō)z-qu-eh# = you (pl) will be locked up
     b. #∅-∅+tē(tzacu-a-lō)z+☐-∅# = people will lock up people

22E. 1. *a.* #∅-∅(nēci)∅+∅-∅# = it appears ~ they appear
     b. #∅-∅(tla-nēci)∅+∅-∅# = things (in general) appear; i.e., it becomes light, day breaks
  2. *a.* #∅-∅(pol-i-hui)∅+∅-∅# = it becomes lost/destroyed
     b. #∅-∅(tla-pol-i-hui)∅+∅-∅# = things (in general) become lost/destroyed
  3. *a.* #∅-∅(yohua)∅+∅-∅# = it becomes night, night falls
     b. #∅-∅(tla-yohua)∅+∅-∅# = it becomes dark, night falls
  4. *a.* #∅-∅(on-o)∅+c-∅# = he/she/it is recumbent there
     b. #∅-∅(tla-on-o)∅+c-∅# = people (in general) are recumbent there; everything is in place (for a social gathering)
  5. *a.* #∅-∅(com-ō-ni)∅+∅-∅# = it (e.g., a fire) crackles
     b. #∅-∅ (tla-com-ō-ni)∅+∅-∅# = there is a crackling sound
  6. *a.* #ni-∅(ce-ce-ya)∅+∅-∅# = I become/am cold
     b. #∅-∅(tla-ce-ce-ya)∅+∅-∅# = it (i.e., the weather) is cold

22F. 1. If only everyone soon returns. I hope everyone soon returns.
  2. People will presently cross over.
  3. Did all fall down?
  4. Let people not destroy things.
  5. It had not yet become dawn.
  6. Will people soon come?
  7. Perhaps everyone/people had eaten their fill.
  8. Just now it (i.e., the weather) became warm.
  9. Let people/everyone beware of going out.
  10. Won't it (i.e., the weather) become cold?

22G. 1. *a.* Will it/they be sold?
     b. Will people sell things?
  2. *a.* Let's not be captured.
     b. May people not capture people
  3. *a.* Just now you (pl) have been abandoned.
     b. Just now people have abandoned things.
  4. *a.* Perhaps people will destroy things.
     b. Perhaps I shall be destroyed.
  5. *a.* Let people beware of not accompanying people; i.e., Let people be sure to accompany people.

b. Let him beware of not being accompanied; i.e., Let him be sure to be accompanied.
6. *a.* Will it soon be eaten?
   b. Will people soon eat (something)?

EXERCISE 23

23A. Transitive verbstems are either directive, causative, or applicative stems. A directive stem is one that is intrinsically transitive (that is, it is transitive without the addition of a suffix to give it that value); examples are *tē-(ihxili)*, "to give s.o. a puncture wound, to spear s.o."; *tla-(pā)*, "to dye s.th."; *m-o-(zō)*, "to bleed o.s." The directive stem requires a direct object (which from an English perspective should be differentiated as either a direct or an indirect object).

A causative stem is one derived by means of a causative suffix. This suffix requires a causative object pronoun that is at one and the same time the object of the suffix and the agent of the action reported by the stem; examples are: *tla-(iht-o-ā)*, "to cause s.th. to become uttered"; *tla-(tēm-a)*, "to cause s.th. to become full."

An applicative stem is one derived by means of an applicative suffix. This suffix requires an applicative object pronoun that refers to an entity that is only tangentially involved in the action reported by the verbstem (the suffix conveys a meaning usually expressed in English by such prepositions as "to," "for," "from," "belonging to").

23B. A mainline object is either a direct object (when it is the only object) or the last added causative or applicative object. A shuntline object is one that has been superseded by a later added object. For example, if the Nahuatl situation held in English, a sentence such as "I mailed it" would have "it" as a mainline direct object. But in "I mailed it to her" the direct object "it" becomes a shuntline object, because the applicative object "to her" takes on the mainline status. And in "I mailed it to her for him" the direct object "it" is further demoted to a first-level shuntline status, while the applicative object "to her" is downgraded to a second-level shuntline status by the applicative object "for him," which has now assumed mainline status. While these distinctions have no place in English, they are of great importance in Nahuatl.

23C. 1. Specific projective before reflexive; e.g., "n-ēch+m-o."
   2. Specific projective before nonspecific projective; e.g., "n-ēch+tla" or "n-ēch+tē."
   3. Reflexive before nonspecific projective; e.g., "m-o+tla" or "m-o+tē."
   4. Human before nonhuman; i.e., "tē+tla."

EXERCISE 24

24A. 1. *a.* #n-∅(ahci)∅+∅-∅# = I arrive
   b. #ni-∅+c-∅(ahci)∅+∅-∅# = I overtake him/her/it [unsponsored applicative object pronoun]
2. *a.* #∅-∅(ac)∅+□-∅# = it entered
   b. #∅-∅+c-∅(aqui-h)∅+□-∅# = he caused it to enter; he transplanted it; he put it in a hole, he drove it (e.g., a stake) in
3. *a.* #∅-∅(mani)∅+∅-∅# = it extends (upon an area), it lies/sits/rests (covering an area of any size)

Key to the Exercises 135

       b. #∅-∅+qui-∅(man-a)∅+∅-∅# = he causes it to extend (upon a surface), i.e., he sets it down

  4. *a.* #∅-∅(cuepi)∅+∅-∅# = it is turning around

     b. #∅-∅+m-o(cuep-a)∅+∅-∅# = he is causing himself to turn around; i.e., he is returning

  5. *a.* #∅-∅(tōca)∅+∅-∅# = he is doing the planting

     b. #∅-∅+qui-∅(tōca)∅+∅-∅# = he is planting it/them [unsponsored applicative object pronoun]

  6. *a.* #∅-∅(chihcha)∅+∅-∅# = he is spitting

     b. #∅-∅+qui-∅(chihcha)∅+∅-∅# = he is spitting on it/him/her [unsponsored applicative object pronoun]

  7. *a.* #∅-∅(tlan)∅+☐-∅# = it came to an end

     b. #∅-∅+qui-∅(tlami-h)∅+☐-∅# = he brought it to an end, he finished/concluded it

  8. *a.* ō#ni-∅(tēmic)∅+☐-∅# = I dreamed, I had a dream

     b. ō#ni-∅+c-∅(tēmic)∅+☐-∅# = I dreamed about it/him/her [unsponsored applicative object pronoun]

  9. *a.* #∅-∅(ce-hui)∅+∅-h# = they are cooling off, they are calming down

     b. #∅-∅+m-o(ce-hui-a)∅+∅-h# = they are causing themselves to cool off, i.e., they are resting

 10. *a.* ō#n-∅(ihuin-ti)∅+c-∅# = I became tipsy/drunk

     b. ō#ti-∅+n-ēch(ihuin-ti-h)∅+☐-∅# = you (sg) got me tipsy/drunk

24B. 1. *a.* #∅-∅(chip-ī-ni)∅+∅-∅# = it is dripping

     b. #∅-∅+qui-∅(chip-ī-ni-a)∅+∅-∅# = he is sprinkling it/them, he is besprinkling it/them [An unusual meaning shift; the causative object seems to be merely implied beneath an overriding applicative meaning. It may be that the VNC should be analyzed as an applicative, i.e., #∅-∅+qui-∅(chip-ī-n-ia)∅+∅-∅#, but this does not really explain away the peculiarity.]

  2. *a.* ō#∅-∅(chit-ō-n)∅+☐-∅# = it popped off

     b. ō#ni-∅+c-∅(chit-ō-ni-h)∅+☐-∅# = I popped it off

  3. *a.* #∅-∅(tom-ā-hua)∅+∅-h# = they are becoming plump

     b. #∅-∅+qu-in(tom-ā-hu-a)∅+∅-∅# = he is fattening them

  4. *a.* #∅-∅(com-ō-ni)ya+∅-∅# = it was flaring up

     b. #∅-∅+m-o(com-ō-ni-ā)ya+∅-h# = they were rioting

  5. *a.* ō#∅-∅(chal-ā-n)∅+☐-∅# = it made a grating sound

     b. ō#ti-∅+t-o(chal-ā-ni-h)∅+qu-eh# = we clashed with one another

  6. *a.* #∅-∅(zāl-i-hui)∅+∅-∅# = it is becoming stuck on

     b. #ni-∅+c-∅(zāl-o-a)∅+∅-∅# = I am pasting it on

  7. *a.* ō#∅-∅(mel-ā-hua)∅+c-∅# = it became straight

     b. ō#ti-∅+c-∅(mel-ā-uh)∅+qu-eh# = we straightened it

  8. *a.* #∅-∅(pix-a-hui)∅+∅-∅# = it is drizzling

     b. #an-∅+qui-∅(pix-o-a)∅+∅-h# = you (pl) are broadcasting them (i.e., the seeds)

24C. 1. Their way of living has already become ruined. They have already ruined their way of living.

  2. Let's beware of not overtaking them; i.e., Let's be sure to overtake them. Let's beware of not arriving; i.e., Let's be sure to arrive.

3. Have you already repaid it (i.e., a debt)? Has it already become restored?
4. Give me a rest. Would that I may rest/calm down.
5. Things just now became stuck on. It has just now been pasted on. ~ They have just now been pasted on.
6. The rope/cord has not yet broken. They have not yet broken the rope/cord.
7. Did the fire flare up? ~ Has the fire flared up?
8. Let's not stumble; let's not fall.
9. My children have already become ashamed.
10. It was just dripping. Perhaps they were besprinkling it.
11. Will it soon become destroyed? Will it soon be destroyed?
12. Perhaps the water will become clean. Perhaps I shall become purified.
13. The stick has become curved/bent. I have curved/bent the stick.
14. The wall has collapsed. The bird sat on its eggs.
15. My shoe is becoming untied. I untie my shoe(s).

EXERCISE 25

25A. 1. *a.* #Ø-Ø(temo)Ø+Ø-Ø# = it is descending
 b. #ni-Ø+c-Ø(temo-huia)Ø+Ø-Ø# = I am causing it to descend; i.e., I am lowering it. [*Also*, I am digesting it.]
 2. *a.* #ti-Ø(pano)Ø+Ø-Ø# = you (sg) are crossing the river
 b. #Ø-Ø+m-itz(pana-huia)Ø+Ø-Ø# = he is carrying you across the river [*Also applic*, he is surpassing you; he is overtaking and passing beyond you.]
 3. *a.* #Ø-Ø(pēhua)Ø+Ø-Ø# = it is beginning
 b. #ni-Ø+c-Ø(pēhua-l-tia)Ø+Ø-Ø# = I am causing it to begin; I am starting it
 4. *a.* #ti-Ø(mahui)Ø+Ø-Ø# = you (sg) are afraid
 b. #ni-Ø+m-itz(mauh-tia)Ø+Ø-Ø# = I am frightening you
 5. *a.* #ni-Ø(nēci)Ø+Ø-Ø# = I am appearing
 b. #ni-Ø+n-o(nēx-tia)Ø+Ø-Ø# = I am revealing myself
 6. *a.* #Ø-Ø(nel-ti)Ø+Ø-Ø# = it is becoming true; it is proving true; it is becoming verified
 b. #ni-Ø+c-Ø(nel-ti-lia)Ø+Ø-Ø# = I am proving it to be true; I am verifying it
 7. *a.* #ti-Ø(quīza)Ø+Ø-h# = we are going out/exiting
 b. #Ø-Ø+t-ēch(quīx-tia)Ø+Ø-Ø# = he is causing us to go out/exit; he is dismissing us
 8. *a.* #Ø-Ø(quīx-o-hua)Ø+Ø-Ø# = things are going out/getting out
 b. #ni-Ø+tla(quīx-tia)Ø+Ø-Ø# = I am letting things out/putting things out
 9. *a.* #ni-Ø(huetzca)Ø+Ø-Ø# = I am laughing
 b. #ti-Ø+n-ēch(huetzquī-tia)Ø+Ø-Ø# = you (sg) are making me laugh
 10. *a.* #Ø-Ø(ehco)Ø+Ø-Ø# = he/she arrives
 b. #ti-Ø+qu-Ø(ehca-huia)Ø+Ø-h# = we are causing him/her to arrive

25B. 1. *a.* #ni-Ø+qu-Ø(itt-a)Ø+Ø-Ø# = I see it/them
 b. #ti-Ø+n-ēch+☐-Ø(itt-ī-tia)Ø+Ø-Ø# = you cause me to see it/them; i.e., you (sg) show it/them to me
 2. *a.* #ni-Ø+n-o(piya)Ø+Ø-Ø# = I guard myself; i.e., I remain aloof
 b. #ni-Ø+c-Ø+n-o(piya-l-tia)Ø+Ø-Ø# = I cause him to guard me; i.e., I entrust myself to his keeping

Key to the Exercises 137

   3. *a.* #∅-∅+qui-∅(mati)∅+∅-h# = they know it
      b. #ni-∅+qu-im+□-∅(machī-l-tia)∅+∅-∅# = I cause them to know it; I inform them of it
   4. *a.* #ni-∅+c-∅(nāmiqui)∅+∅-∅# = I meet it, I encounter it
      b #ni-∅+c-∅+n-o(nāmic-tia)∅+∅-∅# = I cause myself to meet it; i.e., I bring it upon myself
   5. *a.* #ni-∅+c-∅(tep-ē-hu-a)∅+∅-∅# = I cause it/them to spill/fall to the ground
      b. #∅-∅+n-ēch+□-∅(tep-ē-hu-a-l-tia)∅+∅-∅# = they cause me to scatter it/them; i.e., they rip it/them from me
   6. *a.* #an-∅+qui-∅(pol-o-a)∅+∅-h# = you (pl) are causing it/them to become lost; i.e., you are losing it/them
      b. #n-∅+am-ēch+□-∅(pol-o-l-tia)∅+∅-∅# = I am causing you (pl) to lose it/them; i.e., I am ridding you of it/them

25C. 1. (1.a) #∅-∅(pēhua)∅+∅-∅# = it is beginning; (b) . . . +c-∅ . . . tia) . . . ; (c) . . . +c-∅(pēhua-l-tia) . . . ; (d) #ti-∅+c-∅(pēhua-l-tia)∅+∅-∅#; (2) ticpēhualtia = you are causing it to begin, you are starting it
   2. (1.a) #t-∅(ahci)∅+∅-∅# = you (sg) are arriving; (b) . . . +m-itz . . . tia) . . . ; (c) . . . +m-itz(ahxī-tia) . . . ; (d) #ti-∅+m-itz(ahxī-tia)∅+∅-h#; (2) timitzahxītiah = we are taking you (to a place)
   3. (1.a) #∅-∅(temo-hua)∅+∅-∅# = everything is descending; (b) . . . +tla . . . huia) . . . ; (c) . . . +tla(temo-huia) . . . ; (d) #∅-∅+tla(temo-huia)∅+∅-∅#; (2) tlatemohuia = he is lowering things
   4. (1.a) #∅-∅(ce-ce-ya)∅+∅-∅# = it becomes cold, they become cold; (b) . . . +qui-∅ . . . lia) . . . ; (c) . . . +qui-∅(ce-ce-lia) . . . ; (d) #∅-∅+qui-∅(ce-ce-lia)∅+∅-h#; (2) quiceceliah = they are chilling it/them
   5. (1.a) #ti-∅(nēci)∅+∅-∅# = you (sg) are appearing; (b) . . . +m-o . . . tia) . . . ; (c) . . . +m-o(nēx-tia) . . . ; (d) #ti-∅+m-o(nēx-tia)∅+∅-∅#; (2) timonēxtia = you are causing yourself to appear; i.e., you are revealing yourself

25D. 1. (1.a) #ni-∅+qu-in(caqui)∅+∅-∅# = I hear them; (b) . . . +n-ēch . . . tia) . . . ; (c) . . . +n-ēch+□-in(caquī-tia) . . . ; (d) #an-∅+n-ēch+□-in(caquī-tia)∅+∅-h#; (2) annēchincaquītiah = you (pl) are making me hear them
   2. (1.a) #∅-∅+tla(tep-ē-hu-a-lo)∅+∅-∅# = people are scattering things on the ground; (b) . . . +tē . . . tia) . . . ; (c) . . . +tē+tla(tep-ē-hu-a-l-tia) . . . ; (d) #ni-∅+tē+tla(tep-ē-hu-a-l-tia)∅+∅-∅#; (2) nitētlatepēhualtia = I am causing people to scatter things on the ground
   3. (1.a) #an-∅+qui-∅(māma)∅+∅-h# = you carry it/them on your backs; (b) . . . +m-o . . . tia) . . . ; (c) . . . +qui-∅+m-o(māma-l-tia) . . . ; (d) #an-∅+qui-∅+m-o (māma-l-tia) ∅+∅-h; (2) anquimomāmaltiah = you (pl) take it/them upon your backs
   4. (1.a) #ti-∅+c-∅(cua)∅+∅-∅# = you (sg) eat it; (b) . . . +m-itz . . . tia) . . . (c) . . . +m-itz+□-∅(cua-l-tia) . . . ; (d) #ti-∅+m-itz+□-∅(cua-l-tia)∅+∅-h#; (2) timitzcualtiah = we cause you to eat it; i.e., we feed it to you
   5. (1.a) #∅-∅+m-o(zōma)∅+∅-∅# = he/she frowns in anger; (b) . . . +qui-∅ . . . tia) . . . ; (c) . . . +qui-∅+ne(zōma-l-tia) . . . ; (d) #∅-∅+qui-∅+ne(zōma-l-tia)∅+∅-h#; (2) quinezōmaltiah = they make him/her frown in anger

25E. 1. I wish you (sg) had not killed the messenger.
  2. He has already been made to do it/make it/them.
  3. I am not digesting the food.
  4. Has he readied himself? Has he gotten ready?
  5. The songs are no longer being taught to people.
  6. Have they already shown him the shield(s)?
  7. Perhaps he will cause himself to encounter something; i.e., Perhaps he will bring something upon himself. Perhaps something will befall him.
  8. I hope they are causing them to lose things; i.e., I hope they are causing them to throw off/get rid of their anger/bad habits.
  9. Beware of making people frown in anger.
  10. He/She will get him/her to eat a little more.
  11. Did he/she make him/her drink the medicine? Did he/she get him/her to drink the medicine?
  12. It does not eat them; it just kills the turkeys. [English prefers: It does not eat the turkeys; it just kills them.]
  13. The omen frightened him.
  14. Has she (i.e., the midwife) already caused (i.e., helped) it to be born?
  15. I was caused to see her necklace; i.e., I was shown her necklace.
  16. Let them cause themselves to abandon things . . . let everyone cause himself to abandon things; i.e., Let them abstain . . . let everyone abstain.
  17. As for their boats, let's sink them.
  18. You cause his face to come out; i.e., You resemble him in the face.
  19. Then people make people go up; i.e., Then all (of those to be sacrificed) are taken up (to the top of the pyramid).
  20. They caused everything to emerge; i.e., They took out everything.
  21. She makes everyone cry; she makes everyone sad.

EXERCISE 26

26A. 1. *a.* #∅-∅+c-∅+on(itt-a)∅+∅-∅# = he/she goes to see him/her/it
  b. #∅-∅+qu-im+☐-∅+on(itt-i-lia)∅+∅-∅# = he/she goes to see him/her/it for them
 2. *a.* #ni-∅(nāhua-ti)∅+∅-∅# = I am clear sounding; i.e., I speak clearly
  b. #ni-∅+m-itz(nāhua-t-ia)∅+∅-∅# = I speak clearly to you; i.e., I give you a command/order
 3. *a.* #ti-∅+m-☐(ihyān-a)∅+∅-∅# = you hide (yourself); you take shelter from the rain
  b. #ti-∅+n-ēch+ne(hyān-i-lia)∅+∅-∅# = you hide from me
 4. *a.* #ni-∅(chōca)∅+∅-∅# = I weep
  b. #ni-∅+c-∅(chōca)∅+∅-∅# = I weep for him/her [unsponsored applicative object pronoun]
 5. *a.* #ni-∅+tla(h-tlani)∅+∅-∅# = you (sg) request s.th.
  b. #ti-∅+n-ēch+tla(h-tlani-lia)∅+∅-∅# = you request s.th. from me
 6. *a.* #∅-∅(ēl-ci-hci-hui)∅+∅-∅# = they are sighing
  b. #∅-∅+qu-∅(ēl-ci-hci-hui)∅+∅-∅# = they are sighing for him/her/it [unsponsored applicative object pronoun]
 7. *a.* #ni-∅+c-∅(cōhua)∅+∅-∅# = I buy it

Key to the Exercises

        b. #ni-∅+c-∅+n-o(cōhu-ia)∅+∅-∅# = I buy it for myself
    8. *a*. #ti-∅(tēmiqui)∅+∅-h# = we dream
        b. #ti-∅+c-∅(tēmiqui)∅+∅-h# = we dream about him/her/it [unsponsored applicative object pronoun]

26B. 1. (1.a) #ti-∅+c-∅(cōhua)∅+∅-∅# = you buy it; (b) . . . +n-ēch . . . lia) . . . (c) . . . +n-ēch+☐-∅(cōhui-lia) . . . ; (2) tinēchcōhuilia = you buy it for me
    2. (1.a) #ni-∅+qu-∅(iht-o-a)∅+∅-∅# = I say it; (b) . . . +qu-im . . . huia) . . . ; (c) . . . +qu-im+☐-∅(iht-a-l-huia) . . . ; (2) niquimihtalhuia = I say it about them
    3. (1.a) #ti-∅+t-o(tlā-ti-a)∅+∅-h# = we hide (ourselves); (b) . . . +am-ēch . . . lia) . . . ; (c) . . . +am-ēch+ne(tlā-ti-lia) . . . ; (2) tamēchnetlātiliah = we hide from you (pl)
    4. (1.a) #an-∅+qui-∅(caqui)∅+∅-h# = you (pl) hear it; (b) . . . +tē . . . lia) . . . ; (c) . . . +qui-∅+tē(caqui-lia) . . . ; (2) anquitēcaquiliah = you (pl) hear it from people
    5. (1.a) #∅-∅+t-ēch(nōtza)∅+∅-∅# = he/she summons us; (b) . . . +m-itz . . . lia) . . . ; (c) . . . +m-itz+☐-☐(nōchi-lia) . . . ; (2) mitznōchilia = he/she summons us for you

26C. 1. #∅-∅+m-o(coco-lia)∅+∅-h# = they are sick in relation to one another; i.e., they hate one another; cocoyah = they are sick
    2. #∅-∅+qu-in(tla-quechi-lia)∅+∅-∅# = he is telling them stories; tlaquetza = he is telling a story/stories
    3. #∅-∅+qui-∅+☐-∅(tlāxi-lia)∅+∅-∅# = he/she is throwing it from her; i.e., he/she is causing her to have an abortion; quitlāza = he/she is throwing it
    4. #ni-∅+c-∅+☐-∅(tēqui-lia)∅+∅-∅# = I am stretching it/them out lengthwise for him/her; nictēca = I am stretching it/them out
    5. #ni-∅+m-itz(tla-chīhu-ia)∅+∅-∅# = I am putting a spell on you; nitlachīhua = I am doing s.th.
    6. #n-∅+am-ēch+☐-∅(chīhui-lia)∅+∅-∅# = I am doing s.th. for you; nicchīhua = I am doing/making it
    7. #ti-∅+m-o+tla(h-tlan-ia)∅+∅-∅# = you are asking s.th. about yourself, you are examining your conscience; titlahtlani = you are asking/requesting s.th.

26D. 1. I hope our field(s) won't be hailed on.
    2. Perhaps they will answer him.
    3. Think about it for a minute.
    4. Our enemies did not hear it from me.
    5. Did they not use to hate one another?
    6. Have you already done/made it for them?
    7. I shall receive nothing from you.
    8. My grandfather went to see it for himself.
    9. Beware (sg) of opening it/them for them.
    10. They used to give food to him/her. [The *-huāl-* indicates that the speaker allies himself with the receiver.]
    11. Let's beware of not paying it to him; i.e., Let's be sure to pay it to him.
    12. Did people shout to people? ~ Were people shouted to?
    13. What is it that you will give to me? ~ What will you give me?
    14. They took all/everything from them.
    15. He informed them of what the god said to him.

16. Did the youths help?
17. They used to fast for the deer (before hunting them).

EXERCISE 27

27A. 1. *a.* #∅-∅(tzel-i-hui)∅+∅-∅# = it is sifting down
  b. #∅-∅(tze-tzel-i-hui)∅+∅-∅# = it is drizzling
 2. *a.* #ni-∅+tla(cua)∅+∅-∅# = I am eating
  b. #ni-∅+tla(cua-cua)∅+∅-∅# = I am chewing
 3. *a.* #∅-∅(pol-ō-ni)∅+∅-∅# = he is stuttering
  b. #∅-∅(po-pol-o-ca)∅+∅-∅# = he is speaking a foreign language
 4. *a.* #ti-∅+qu-∅(ihxili)∅+∅-∅# = you spear him
  b. #ti-∅+c-∅(xi-hxili)∅+∅-∅# = you spear him repeatedly
 5. *a.* #∅-∅(chihcha)∅+∅-∅# = he is spitting
  b. #∅-∅(chih-chihcha)∅+∅-∅# = he is sputtering
 6. *a.* #ti-∅+c-∅(te-ī-ni-a)∅+∅-∅# = you are smashing it/them
  b. #ti-∅+c-∅(te-te-i-tz-a)∅+∅-∅# = you are gnawing/crunching it/them (e.g., a bone/bones)
 7. *a.* #ni-∅+m-itz(nōtza)∅+∅-∅# = I call you (sg)
  b. #ni-∅+m-itz(noh-nōtza)∅+∅-∅# = I am conversing with you
 8. *a.* #∅-∅+m-itz+☐-∅(nōchi-lia)∅+∅-∅# = he is calling him/her for you
  b. #∅-∅+m-itz+☐-∅(nō-nōchi-lia)∅+∅-∅# = he is advising him/her for you

27B. 1. Have people made oblations severally? I.e., Has each person made an oblation?
 2. The men (of our group) come pursuing/chasing things.
 3. The men (of our group) come running.
 4. Walk (pl) over here.
 5. They are singing for each of their gods.
 6. Let them beware of closing them.
 7. Shake (pl) the tree(s). [a command to inferiors]
 8. Let them beat the drum(s) for them.
 9. Is it true that he hastened him away?
 10. He said that they gave each of them commands regarding people.
 11. Then there was repeated spearing of people.
 12. The mountain was still smoking.
 13. The maidens each used to take it upon themselves to bear dried ears of maize on their backs.
 14. They caused her sorrows to become lost; i.e., They banished her sorrows.
 15. The mosquitoes were whining/buzzing.
 16. They indeed used to make him/it run.
 17. The people were fishing/seining.
 18. Everyone ran.
 19. We each have already rested. ~ We formerly rested from time to time.
 20. Then there was resting on the part of each.
 21. The lord gave a blanket to each of them.
 22. I untie his shoes. ~ I undo his sandals.

Key to the Exercises 141

23. Someone did not burn his own various belongings. [English would prefer: "Some did not burn their own various belongings."]
24. "Is the rain falling repeatedly in big drops?"—"No, it is only falling in small drops." I.e., "Is is raining heavily?—"No, it is only drizzling."
25. O Mexihcas, let everyone hurry hither. [This optative VNC contains an impersonal *tla.*]
26. The merchants are causing him to see various things; i.e., The merchants are showing him various things.
27. We were causing the youths to look and look; i.e., We were teaching the youths to be observant.

EXERCISE 28

28A. 1. #∅-∅+m-o(mi-mil-o-h-∅-ti-yah)∅+□-∅# = it went rolling along [*Momimiloh*, "it rolled on the ground"; *yah*, "it went."]
2. #∅-∅(quiy-a-uh-∅-ti-mani)∅+∅-∅# = it is raining all around [*Quiyauh*, "it rained"; *mani*, "it lies/spreads (over a surface)."]
3. #ti-∅+t-o(pix-∅-t-o)∅+qu-eh# = we sit/lie aloof [*Titopixqueh*, "we remained aloof"; *tonoqueh*, "we are recumbent."]
4. #∅-∅(qui-quin-a-ca-∅-ti-uh)∅+∅-∅# = it goes whining along [*Quiquinacac*, "it whined"; *yauh*, "it goes."]
5. ō#∅-∅+qui-∅(cui-∅-ti-huetz)∅+□-∅# = he abruptly/quickly took it/them [*Quicuic*, "he took it/them"; *ōhuetz*, "he fell."]
6. #an-∅+qui-∅(quetz-∅-ti-huī-tz)∅+□-eh# = you (pl) come along setting them upright [*Anquiquetzqueh*, "you (pl) set it/them upright"; *anhuītzeh*, "you (pl) come."]
7. ō#∅-∅(tla-nēz-∅-ti-man)ca+∅-∅# = it had become bright and clear all around [*Tlanēz*, "it became bright and clear" (a tla impersonal VNC); *ōmanca*, "it had lain/spread (over a surface—here, the land)."]
8. #∅-∅(ih-ih-cī-ca-∅-ti-huī-tz)a+∅-h# = they came along continually panting [*Ihih-cīcaqueh*, "they continually panted"; *huītzah*, "they came."]
9. #∅-∅+m-o(man-∅-ti-quīz)∅+□-∅# = it quickly set itself down; i.e., it was quickly set down [*Moman*, "it set itself down"; i.e., "it was set down"; *quīz*, "it exited."]
10. #∅-∅+qu-im+on(itz-∅-t-o)∅+qu-eh# = they lie/sit looking thither at them [*Quimonittaqueh*, "they looked thither at them"; *onoqueh*, "they are recumbent."]
11. #to-∅+c-∅+on(tēn-∅-ti-hui)∅+∅-h# = we go along filling them [*Tocontēnqueh*, "we filled it/them thither"; *tihuih*, "we go."]
12. #∅-∅+on(tla-chix-∅-ti-ca-t)ca+∅-h# = they were watching thither [*Ontlachixqueh*, "they watched thither"; *catcah*, they were."]

28B. 1. ō#ni-∅(mic-∅-ti-m-o-tlāl-i-h)∅+□-∅# = I became (like) dead; i.e., my face became deathly pale, my face took on a deathly pallor [*Nimic*, "I died"; *ōninotlālih*, ''I sat down."]
2. #∅-∅(tlīl-i-uh-∅-ti-m-o-quetza)z+□-∅# = it will gradually become black [*Tlīliuh*, "it became/turned black"; *moquetzaz*, "it will erect itself," i.e., "it will be erected."]
3. #∅-∅(xel-i-uh-∅-ti-m-o-cāhua)∅+∅-∅# = it remains split, they remain split [*Xeliuh*, "it became split"; *mocāhua*, "it abandons itself," i.e., "it ceases, it remains behind."]

4. ō#Ø-Ø(ihyā-ya-Ø-ti-m-o-tēca)Ø+c-Ø# = it began to stink [*Ihyāyac*, "it stank"; *ōmotēcac*, "it stretched itself out," i.e., "it was stretched out."]
5. #Ø-Ø(tla-nēz-Ø-ti-m-o-quetz)Ø+☐-Ø# = it gradually became bright and clear all around [*Tlanēz*, "it became bright and clear"; *moquetz*, "it erected itself," i.e., "it was erected/set upright."
6. ō#Ø-Ø(tla-mat-Ø-ti-m-o-man)Ø+☐-Ø# = it (i.e., the wind) gradually became calm [*Tlamah*, "it became prudent/patient"; *moman*, "it set itself down."]
7. #Ø-Ø(tom-ā-hua-Ø-ti-m-o-quetza)Ø+Ø-Ø# = it is gradually becoming plump [*Tomāhuac*, "it became plump"; *moquetza*, "it erects itself," i.e., "it is being erected/set upright."]
8. #Ø-Ø(tla-yohua-Ø-ti-m-o-man-a)Ø+Ø-Ø# = it is slowly becoming night [*Tlayohuac*, "it became night" (a doubly impersonal VNC); *momana*, "it is setting itself down," i.e., "it is being set down."]

28C.
1. #Ø-Ø+c-Ø(olol-o-h-Ø-ti-tlāl-i-h)Ø+qu-eh# = they set him down wrapped up [*Cololohqueh*, "they wrapped him up"; *quitlālihqueh*, "they set him down."]
2. #ni-Ø+c-Ø(tzauc-Ø-ti-cāuh)Ø+☐-Ø# = I left it closed [*Nictzauc*, "I closed it"; *niccāuh*, "I left/abandoned it."]
3. ō#Ø-Ø+n-ēch(huilān-Ø-ti-quīx-tih)Ø+☐-Ø# = he dragged me out [*Ōnēchhuilān*, "he dragged me"; *ōnēchquīxtih*, "he caused me to leave."]
4. #Ø-Ø+qui-Ø(tēn-Ø-ti-māy-a-uh)ca+Ø-Ø# = he had pushed him down flat on the ground [*Quitēn*, "he put him down"; *quimāyauhca*, "he had pushed against him."]
5. #ni-Ø+n-o(zauh-Ø-ti-tēca)z+☐-Ø# = I shall stretch out having refrained from eating [*Ninozauh*, "I refrained from eating/I fasted", *ninotēcaz*, "I shall stretch out."]
6. #ti-Ø+c-Ø(tlap-o-h-Ø-ti-cāhua)z+qu-eh# = we shall leave it closed [*Tictlapohqueh*, "we closed it"; *ticcāhuazqueh*, "we shall leave/abandon it."]

28D.
1. #ti-Ø+c-Ø(chīhua-z-nequi)Ø+Ø-h# = we want to make it [*Ticchīhuazqueh*, "we shall make it"; *ticnequih*, "we want it."]
2. #ni-Ø(huel-i-ti-z-qui)ya+Ø-Ø# = I should be able [*Nihuelitiz*. "I shall be able"; *nicquiya, "I willed it."]
3. #Ø-Ø+m-☐(ihtō-tī-z-qui)ya+Ø-h# = they would dance [*Mihtōtīzqueh*, "they will dance"; *quiquiyah, "they willed it."]
4. #Ø-Ø+qui-Ø(necuil-ō-z-nec)Ø+☐-Ø# = he wanted to twist/bend it/them [*Quinecuilōz*, "he will twist/bend it/them"; *quinec*, "he wanted it."]
5. #ni-Ø+qu-Ø(ihnecui-z-nequi)Ø+Ø-Ø# = I want to smell it/them [*Niquihnecuiz*, "I shall smell it/them"; *nicnequi*, "I want it."]
6. ō#Ø-Ø(huetz-Ø-t-o-z-nec)Ø+qu-eh# = they have wanted to lie having fallen; i.e., they wanted to continue sitting [*Huetztozqueh*, "they will lie having fallen" (i.e., *huetzqueh*, "they fell," plus *onozqueh*, "they will be recumbent"); *ōquinecqueh*, "they have wanted it."]
7. #ni-Ø+c-Ø(yōco-ya-z-qui)ya+Ø-Ø# = I would invent/construct it [*Nicyōcoyaz*, "I shall invent/construct it"; *nicquiya, "I willed it."]
8. #ti-Ø+t-o(tlal-ō-z-nequi)ya+Ø-h# = we used to want to run, we were wanting to run [*Titotlalōzqueh*, "we shall run"; *ticnequiyah*, "we used to want it, we were wanting it."]

Key to the Exercises 143

28E.
1. People went along dying on both sides.
2. The nobles abruptly came back.
3. Doesn't he/she want to tell him/her what he/she did?
4. Their fathers are calling out to them.
5. Would you answer him?
6. The Mexihcas would help us.
7. They go along taking everyone.
8. Their friends lay watching them.
9. It already wants to become dawn; i.e., Day is about to break.
10. The road stands directly hither; i.e., The road leads directly hither.
11. Our enemies come beating things (i.e., drums).
12. The road gradually became slippery. People are just slipping and sliding.
13. They go rounding up the captives.
14. Our enemies lie surrounding us.
15. His arrows are being with him; i.e., He has his arrows with him.
16. Some others came to help him.
17. The coals go along (i.e., continue) bursting into pieces.
18. The doctors sat taking counsel among themselves.
19. He quickly accepted the words/speech (i.e., the decision).
20. The gods spread in a circle around the fire pit.
21. The road became clear.

EXERCISE 29

29A.
1. #∅-∅+qu-∅+□-∅(itt-ī-tī-□-t-o)∅+∅-∅# = he/she went in order to show it to him/her [*Quittītīz*, "he/she will cause him/her to see it; he/she will show it to him/her."]
2. #∅-∅+qu-∅(itt-a-□-t-o)∅+∅-∅# = he/she went in order to see it [*Quittaz*, "he/she will see it."]
3. #∅-∅+qu-∅+□-∅(il-huī-□-qu-ī-uh)∅+∅-∅# = he/she will come in order to say it to him/her [*Quilhuīz*, "he/she will say it to him/her."]
4. ō#∅-∅+c-∅+on(tzah-tzacu-a-□-c-o)∅+∅-h# = they have come in order to block/close them each (i.e., the exits) up [*Contzahtzacuazqueh*, "they will block/close them each thither."]
5. #∅-∅+huāl+m-o(cuep-a-□-t-ī-hui)∅+∅-h# = they go/will go in order to return hither [*Huālmocuepazqueh*, "they will return hither."]
6. #∅-∅+tla(cōhua-lō-□-c-o)∅+∅-∅# = all came to buy things, people came to buy things [*Tlacōhualōz*, "people will buy things."]
7. ō#ti-∅(tlehcō-□-t-o)∅+∅-h# = we went in order to ascend [*Titlehcōzqueh*, "we shall ascend."]
8. #∅-∅+on(ahci-□-qu-ī-hui)∅+∅-h# = they will come in order to arrive there [*Onahcizqueh*, "they will arrive there."]
9. #ni-∅+c-∅+□-∅(caquī-tī-□-c-o)∅+∅-∅# = I came/have come in order to inform him/her of it [*Niccaquītīz*, "I shall inform him/her of it."]
10. #ti-∅+qu-im(pal-ē-huī-□-c-o)∅+∅-h# = we came/have come in order to help them [*Tiquimpalēhuīzqueh*, "we shall help them."]

11. #∅-∅(tlah-tla-mā-☐-t-ī-uh)∅+∅-∅# = he goes/will go in order to fish [*Tlahtlamāz*, "he will fish."]
12. #∅-∅(quīx-o-hua-☐-t-o)∅+∅-∅# = all went in order to exit [*Quīxohuaz*, "all will exit."]

29B.
1. mā #∅-∅+qu-im+on(tep-ē-hu-a-☐-t-ī)∅+∅-n# = if only they would go in order to disperse/scatter them thither [*Quimontepēhuazqueh*, "they will disperse/scatter them thither."]
2. mā #∅-∅+qui-∅(nāpal-ō-☐-qu-i)∅+∅-∅# = if only he would come in order to carry it in his arms [*Quināpalōz*, "he will carry it in his arms."]
3. tlā #xi-∅+c-∅(nāmiqui-☐-t-ī)∅+∅-n# = please go (pl) in order to meet him/her [*Anquināmiquizqueh*, "you (pl) will meet him/her."]
4. mā ca#ti-∅+c-∅+☐-∅(mah-maca-☐-t-ī)∅+∅-n# = let's not go in order to give them to him/her [*Ticmahmacazqueh*, "we shall give them (i.e., various things) to him/her."]
5. mā #∅-∅+qui-∅(nō-nōtz-∅-ti-huetzi-☐-qu-ī)∅+∅-n# = if only they would come to counsel him quickly [*Quinōnōtztihuetzizqueh*, "they will quickly counsel him."]
6. mā #xi-∅(pah-ti-☐-t-i)∅+∅-∅# = go (sg) in order to get well [*Tipahtiz*, "you (sg) will get well."]

29C.
1. They went in order to get stalks of green maize.
2. They came in order to cross the river.
3. He will come in order to leave food.
4. Our enemies came in order to contend against us.
5. The messengers went in order to see the boat(s).
6. We shall come in order to give you (pl) his blankets.
7. It has come to be known that the nobles are already coming.
8. They went in order to catch their breath.
9. They came in order to seize our equipment.
10. They went in order to show it to the lord.
11. They came in order to drag the captive away.
12. I have come in order to say to you (sg) the words of our lord.
13. Go in order to see your father.
14. Will they soon come to shell the dried ears of maize?
15. I indeed did not come to hurt/harm you (sg).
16. Come (pl) in order to help me.
17. Is it true that they did not go in order to disperse their enemies?
18. Perhaps he will go in order to get the medicine for you (sg).
19. It will not be possible for us to go in order to beg things. Let us just beware of angering them with that.

EXERCISE 30

30A.
1. #∅-∅+qu-∅(ilhui-quīx-ti-lia)∅+∅-h# = they cause a day to come out/pass for him; i.e., they celebrate a festival day in his honor [< (ilhui)-tl-, "festival day; day"]
2. #ti-∅(tlāca-mic-tih)∅+qu-eh# = we killed a human being; i.e., we performed a human sacrifice [< (tlāca)-tl-, "person, human being"]
3. #ni-∅(tequi-cāhua)z+☐-∅# = I shall leave work; i.e., I shall retire [< (tequi)-tl-, "work, job"]

Key to the Exercises

    4. #an-∅+qu-im(oh-tlāxi-lia)∅+∅-h# = you (pl) are hurling a road from them; i.e., you (pl) are blocking a road to them, you (pl) are misdirecting them [< (oh)-tli-, "path, road"]

    5. #∅-∅(tlahu-ēl-cui)∅+∅-∅# = he is taking anger; i.e., he is getting angry [< (tlahu-ēl)-li-, "anger"]

    6. #ni-∅+c-∅(cuitla-chīhu-ia)∅+∅-∅# = I am making excrement on him; i.e., I am accusing him undeservedly [< (cuitla)-tl-, "excrement"]

    7. #∅-∅+t-ēch(oh-quechi-lia)∅+∅-h# = they are erecting a road for us; i.e., they are opening up a road for us [< (oh)-tli-, "path, road"]

    8. #ti-∅(cuauh-aqui-ā)ya+∅-∅# = you (sg) were causing trees to enter; i.e., you were planting trees [< (cuahui)-tl-, "tree; stake; wood"]

30B. 1. #∅-∅+qui-∅(te-ilpi-h)∅+☐-∅# = he tied it like a rock; i.e., he tied it firmly [< (te)-tl-, "rock"]

    2. #∅-∅(ā-pano)∅+∅-h# = they cross on water; i.e., they are crossing a river [< (ā)-tl-, "water"]

    3. #ti-∅+c-∅(ōl-chip-ī-ni-a)∅+∅-∅# = you (sg) are sprinkling it with (liquid) rubber [< (ōl)-li-, "latex, rubber"]

    4. #ni-∅+qu-∅(icxi-pol-ac-tia)∅+∅-∅# = I am causing it to enter under water with my foot; i.e., I am pushing it under water with my foot [< (icxi)-tl-, "foot"]

    5. #ti-∅+c-∅(me-ca-pā-tz-ca)∅+∅-h# = we are squeezing liquid from it with cords/ropes; i.e., we are squeezing it with cords/ropes [< (me-ca)-tl-, "a cord/rope"]

    6. #ti-∅+m-o(tequi-pach-o-a)∅+∅-∅# = you are pressing yourself down with work; i.e., you are worrying [< (tequi)-tl-, "work, job"]

    7. #ni-∅+qu-in(yac-āna)∅+∅-∅# = I am seizing/taking them by the nose; i.e., I am leading them [< (yaca)-tl-, "nose, point"]

    8. #an-∅(cal-aqui)∅+∅-h# = you (pl) are entering into a house; i.e., you are entering [< (cal)-li-, "house"]

30C. 1. ō#∅-∅(izte-hueh-huē-i-ya)∅+c-∅# = he/she has become long at the nails; i.e., he/she has long fingernails [Īzte, "they are his/her nails."]

    2. #ni-∅+n-o(metz-poz-tec)ca+∅-∅# = I had broken myself at the thigh; i.e., I had broken my thigh [Nometz, "it is my thigh."]

    3. #ti-∅+c-∅(cuā-tzay-ā-n-a)∅+∅-∅# = you tear/rip/cleave him at the head; i.e., you wound him in the head (e.g., with a knife) [Īcuā, "it is his head."]

    4. #∅-∅+qu-in(mīl-chīhua)∅+∅-∅# = they work them at the field(s); i.e., they work their (i.e., other people's) fields [Īmmīl, "they are their cultivated fields."]

    5. #∅-∅+m-o(nān-mic-tih)∅+☐-∅# = he killed himself by means of his mother; i.e., he killed his mother [Īnān, "she is his mother."]

    6. #∅-∅+qui-∅(quimil-pa-tla)∅+∅-∅# = he exchanged him at his bundle; i.e., he took over his bundle [Īquimil, "it is his bundle."]

    7. #ti-∅+m-o(cxi-pāca)∅+∅-∅# = you (sg) wash yourself at the feet; i.e., you wash your feet [Mocxi, "they are your feet."]

    8. #ti-∅+t-o(cac-cop-ī-n-a)∅+∅-h# = we pull ourselves off from the sandals/shoes; i.e., we remove our sandals/shoes [Tocac, "they are our sandals/shoes."]

30D. 1. #ni-∅+n-o(tlācoh-cuep-a)z+□-∅# = I shall turn myself a slave; i.e., I shall become a slave [< (tlācoh)-tli-, "slave"]
2. #∅-∅+qui-∅(pil-quīx-tia)∅+∅-∅# = it causes them (e.g., antlers) to come out a child; i.e., it rejuvenates/regenerates them [< (pil)-li-, "child"]
3. #ti-∅+qu-in(yāō-chīhua)∅+∅-h# = we make them be enemies; i.e., we make war on them [< (yāō)-tl-, "enemy"]
4. #ti-∅+m-o(xolo-pih-cuep-a)∅+∅-∅# = you turn yourself a fool; i.e., you become a fool [< (xolo-pih)-tli-, "fool"]
5. #an-∅+qui-∅(tētzām-mati)∅+∅-h# = you (pl) know it to be a bad omen; i.e., you (pl) consider it a bad omen [< (tētzāhui)-tl-, "bad omen, evil omen"]
6. #∅-∅+m-o(zōl-neh-nequi)∅+∅-∅# = it pretends itself a quail; i.e., it resembles a quail [< (zōl)-in-, "quail"]
7. #n-∅+am-ēch(icn-īuh-toca)ya+∅-∅# = I used to believe you to be my friends; i.e., I used to consider you my friends [< (icn-īuh)-tli-, "friend"]
8. #ti-∅+c-∅(teō-mati)∅+∅-h# = we know him to be a god; i.e., we worship him [< (teō)-tl-, "god"]

30E. 1. The captive had just gone along continually sighing.
2. He still looks like a young man.
3. The men forced him to retreat.
4. It just busily eats the meat.
5. He just came readying himself for war.
6. Let them not cause you (pl) distress.
7. We commoners go along yelling at them.
8. Take courage, my friend.
9. They would intercept their enemies. ~ Their enemies would intercept them.
10. They stood facing toward the fire pit.
11. The lord sees people to be orphans; i.e., The lord looks kindly upon people.
12. Here people came in order to merit/acquire land.
13. Beware of looking to this side.
14. The snake shot him with venom; i.e., The poisonous snake bit him.
15. Did they invite you?
16. I have already fed the deer (i.e., the horses).
17. My father set down my name; i.e., My father enrolled me.
18. The water goes roaring along.
19. The Mexihcas went in order to seek land.
20. The snake was hissing.
21. I shall just stretch out under covers.

EXERCISE 31

31A. I. 1. *a.* hard-metal-piece at-the-butt/base; *b.* ferrule (i.e., cap attached at the end of a pole, lance, staff, etc., prevent splitting)
2. *a.* arrow made-of-hard-metal; *b.* bolt (as used in a crossbow)
3. *a.* pot for-arrows; *b.* quiver
4. *a.* black-ink from-on-the-bottom-of-a-pot; *b.* pot soot

Key to the Exercises 147

        5. *a.* water like-black-ink; *b.* murky depths of deep water
        6. *a.* turkey on-water; *b.* pelican
        7. *a.* egg from-a-turkey; *b.* turkey egg
        8. *a.* house made-of-rock; *b.* vaulted chamber
        9. *a.* path leading-to-a-house; *b.* walk (leading to a house)
      10. *a.* edge of-a-road/path; *b.* roadside
      11. *a.* hair around-the-lips; *b.* beard
      12. *a.* structure made-of-hair; *b.* wig
      13. *a.* head of-a-house; *b.* roof
      14. *a.* tree growing-on-the-head; *b.* antler, horn
      15. *a.* crotch of-a-tree; *b.* tree crotch
      16. *a.* strip-of-cloth for-the-crotch; *b.* breechcloth

   II. 1. *a.* down-below-part that-serves-as-a-foundation; *b.* buttock
        2. *a.* head that-is-down-below; *b.* knee
        3. *a.* flesh on-the-head; *b.* fleshy-crest on-the-crown-of-a-chicken's head; i.e., chicken's comb
        4. *a.* sauce made-from-meat; *b.* meat stew
        5. *a.* bowl for-making-sauce; *b.* (stone) mortar (used with a pestle)
        6. *a.* platform serving-for-a-bowl; *b.* plate

31B. I. 1. *a.* structure made-of-mats; *b.* wickerwork chest/coffer
        2. *a.* structure for-a-god; *b.* temple
        3. *a.* structure made-for-on-water; *b.* dugout canoe; boat
        4. *a.* house made-of-thatch (?); *b.* pole-and-thatch hut
        5. *a.* housing made-of-wood; *b.* large wooden cage (serving as a prison)
        6. *a.* house for-turkeys/hens; *b.* turkey/hen coop

   II. 1. *a.* rock made-of-sand; *b.* sandstone
        2. *a.* rock related-to-god, *b.* jet
        3. *a.* rock at-the-foundation/base; *b.* foundation stone
        4. *a.* egg from-a-bird; *b.* bird egg
        5. *a.* egg from-a-snake; *b.* snake egg
        6. *a.* stone for-beneath-the-lower-lip; *b.* lip plug/labret
        7. *a.* rock/egg of-water/urine; *b.* testicle
        8. *a.* egg of-the-face; *b.* eyeball

31C. I. 1. *a.* housing over-fire; *b.* chimney
        2. *a.* pot for-over-fire; *b.* crucible
        3. *a.* bowl to-contain-fire; *b.* clay censer
        4. *a.* hand for-fire; *b.* fire shovel
        5. *a.* mosquito made-of-fire; *b.* spark
        6. *a.* tassel made-of-fire; *b.* flame
        7. *a.* flower made-by-fire; *b.* live coal, red-hot coal
        8. *a.* snake as-painful-as-fire; *b.* snake with a deadly bite
        9. *a.* trumpet producing-fire; *b.* cannon/firearm
      10. *a.* stick for-producing-fire; *b.* fire drill

   II. 1. *a.* face of-a-house; *b.* house front, entryway

2. *a.* land of-a-house; *b.* land on which a house sits
3. *a.* field of-a-house; *b.* land around a house
4. *a.* ear of-a-house; *b.* (outside) corner of a house
5. *a.* manifoldly-curved-thing in-the-form-of-a-house; *b.* maze, labyrinth [Notice reduplication on matrix.]
6. *a.* soot of-a-house; *b.* soot

31D. 1. *a.* (ā)-tl- = water; (cal)-li- = structure; (oh)-tli- = road; *b.* (a + b) + c [i.e., (ā-cal)-li-, "dugout canoe" + (oh)-tli-]; *c.* road for canoes; i.e., canal
2. *a.* (te)-tl- = rock; (māi)-tl- = hand; (tla)-tl- = strip(s) of cloth; *b.* a + (b + c) [i.e., (te)-tl- + (mā-tla)-tl, "net"]; *c.* net for a rock; i.e., sling
3. *a.* (xāmi)-tl- = adobe brick; (ā)-tl- = water; (cal)-li- = structure; *b.* a + (b + c) [i.e., (xāmi)-tl- + (ā-cal)-li-, "(small) dugout canoe"]; *c.* dugout-like-thing for forming a brick; i.e., adobe-brick mold
4. *a.* (xō-chi)-tl- = flower; (chi-nāmi)-tl- = hedge/cane fence; (cal)-li- = enclosed area; *b.* a + (b + c) [i.e., (xō-chi)-tl- + (chi-nān-cal)-li-, "area enclosed by a fence"]; *c.* flower garden
5. *a.* (ilhui)-tl- = day; (ca)-tl- = associated entity; (ā)-tl- = water; (tēn)-tli- = lip, edge; *b.* ((a + b) + c) + d [i.e., (ilhui-ca-ā)-tl-, "sky water, sea, ocean" + (tēn)-tli-]; *c.* edge/shore of the ocean, seashore
6. *a.* (īx)-tli- = surface/face/eye; (tez)-tli- = abraded thing; (ca)-tl- = associated entity; *b.* a + (b + c) [i.e., (īx)-tli- + (tez-ca)-tl-, "mirror"]; *c.* mirrors in front of the eyes; i.e., eyeglasses
7. *a.* (ā)-tl- = water; (tepē)-tl- = hill, mountain; (te-nāmi)-tl- = stone barrier/wall; *b.* (a + b) + c [i.e., (ā-l-tepē)-tl, "water-and-hill," i.e., town/city + (te-nāmi)-tl-]; *c.* wall of a town/city
8. *a.* (māi)-tl- = hand; (tle)-tl- = fire; (quiquiz)-tli- = conch-shell trumpet/horn; *b.* a + (b + c) [i.e., (māi)-tl- + (tle-quiquiz)-tli-, "fire trumpet; i.e., cannon/gun"]; *c.* a firearm, an harquebus, a shotgun

Note: In 4 above the formula is really a + ((b + c) + d) and in 7 it is really (a + b) + (c + d), but since the stems *(chi)-tl-*, "hedge?" and *(nāmi)-tl-*, "barrier," are not listed in dictionaries and apparently do not occur outside of *(chi-nāmi)-tl-* and *(te-nāmi)-tl-*, these compound stems have been treated in the formulas in the Key as if they were simple stems.

31E. 1. Is this your (pl) noble metal (i.e., gold or silver)?
2. Only some crossed the canal.
3. They hurried. They paddled diligently. They bumped into one another with their dugouts.
4. The quiver of each of them went along having become filled; i.e., They each had their full quivers with them.
5. They shoot the temple with fire arrows.
6. We filled/loaded the equipment into dugout canoes.
7. He immediately cut off her head.
8. She gave her a mortar.
9. He goes around drilling his fire stick here and there [i.e., practicing starting fires].
10. They went following the edge of the road.

Key to the Exercises 149

11. The tongues of fire repeatedly rise up.
12. The pelican summons the wind.
13. Punishment (*lit.*, sticks and stones) will move continually against you (sg); i.e., You (sg) will continually suffer punishment.
14. They quickly abandoned the cannon.

EXERCISE 32

32A. 1. *a.* #∅-∅(ā-l-tepē)tl-∅# = it is a city/town
 b. #∅-∅(ā-l-tepē-tōn)tli-∅# = it is a small city/town
 2. *a.* #∅-∅+n-o(nān)∅-∅# = she is my mother
 b. #∅-∅+n-o(nān-tzin)∅-∅# = she is my mother (H) ~ she is my dear mother [H = honorific status.]
 3. *a.* #∅-∅+t-o(chichi-conē)hu-ān# = they are our puppies
 b. #∅-∅+t-o(chichi-conē-pi-pīl)hu-ān# = they are our dear little puppies
 4. *a.* #∅-∅(ā-cal)-li-∅# = it is a dugout canoe
 b. #∅-∅(ā-cal-zol)li-∅# = it is a dilapidated dugout canoe
 5. *a.* #∅-∅+m-o(tah)∅-∅# = he is your father
 b. #∅-∅+m-o(tah-tzin)∅-∅# = he is your father (H) ~ he is your dear father
 6. *a.* #∅-∅(cuā-cuahui)tl-∅# = it is an antler/a horn; they are antlers/horns
 b. #∅-∅(cuā-cuahui-tōn)tli-∅# = it is a small antler/horn
 7. *a.* #∅-∅+ī-∅(conē)uh-∅# = he/she is her child
 b. #∅-∅+ī-∅(conē-tzin)∅-∅# = he/she is her dear child
 8. *a.* #∅-∅(tōtol)in-∅# = it is a turkey hen
 b. #∅-∅(tōtol-pōl)∅-∅# = it is a big old turkey hen
 9. *a.* #∅-∅(cuitla-pil)li-∅# = it is a tail
 b. #∅-∅(cuitla-pil-tōn)tli-∅# = it is a little tail
 10. *a.* #∅-∅(tēl-pōch)tli-∅# = he is a youth
 b. #∅-∅(tēl-pōch-tzin)tli-∅# = he is a fine young man
 11. *a.* #∅-∅(cōā)tl-∅# = it is a snake
 b. #∅-∅(cōā-tōn)tli-∅# = it is a little snake
 12. *a.* #∅-∅(yōl-ca)tl-∅# = it is a bug/insect
 b. #∅-☐(yōl-ca-tōn)tli-∅# = it is a little bug/insect

32B. 1. The little creature just lies having caused itself to fall.
 2. The *tlālomitl* [i.e., earth-bone] is a small worm.
 3. It eats little flies.
 4. A dwarf used to dispel their afflictions. ~ A dwarf used to entertain them.
 5. Some are quite small.
 6. The boys went carrying slings.
 7. It is said, "Are you a loutish Otomi?"
 8. The deaf person did not hear his words.
 9. They prepare her little skirt for the little girl.
 10. The little child laughs and laughs.
 11. They used to make an offering of small tamales to him.
 12. A road no one any longer follows is a road in disrepair. [*Also*, It is a road in disrepair that no one any longer follows.]

13. They make a little shield for the little boy.
14. May your (pl) honorable hearts abandon things; i.e., May you (H pl) yield assent/give your blessing/grant the boon.

EXERCISE 33

33A. 1. *a.* #∅-∅+qui-∅+m-o(tlā-ti-lia)∅+∅-∅# = he is hiding it/them for himself; i.e., he (H) is hiding it/them ~ he is hiding it/them (H)
 b. quitlātia = he is hiding it/them
2. *a.* #ti-∅+t-ēch+☐-∅+m-o(piya-li-lia)∅+∅-∅# = you guard it/them for us for yourself; i.e., you (H sg) guard it/them for us ~ you guard it/them (H) for us
 b. titēchpiyalia = you (sg) guard it/them for us
3. *a.* ō#∅-∅+qui-∅+m-o(cua-l-tih)∅+☐-∅# = he/she caused himself/herself to eat it; i.e., he/she (H) ate it
 b. ōquicuah = he/she ate it
4. *a.* #∅-∅+m-o+tla(mauh-ti-lia)∅+∅-∅# = he is frightening things for himself; i.e., he (H) is frightening things
 b. tlamauhtia = he is frightening things
5. *a.* #∅-∅+m-o(huap-ā-hu-i-l-tia)∅+∅-h# = they are causing themselves to get cramps; i.e., they (H) are getting cramps
 b. huapāhuah = they are getting cramps
6. *a.* #ni-∅+c-∅+n-o(ce-li-lia)∅+∅-∅# = I am being willing toward it/them for myself; i.e., I am receiving it/them for myself; i.e., I am receiving it/them (H)
 b. niccelia = I am receiving it/them
7. *a.* #an-∅+m-☐(ahxi-l-tih)∅+qu-eh# = you caused yourselves to arrive; i.e., you (H pl) arrived
 b. amahciqueh = you (pl) arrived
8. *a.* mā #xi-∅+n-ēch+m-o(pal-ē-hui-lī)∅+c-ān# = if only you may help me for yourselves; i.e., would that you (H pl) help me
 b. mā xinēchpalēhuīcān = would that you (pl) help me
9. *a.* #an-∅+m-o(cual-ā-ni-l-tia)∅+∅-h# = you cause yourselves to become angry; i.e., you (H pl) become angry
 b. ancualānih = you (pl) become angry
10. *a.* #∅-∅+m-o+tla(mōchi-lī)z+☐-∅# = he will throw stones at s.th. for himself; i.e., he (H) will throw stones at s.th.
 b. tlamōtlaz = he will throw stones at s.th.
11. *a.* #ti-∅+qu-im+m-☐(ihua-l-tiā)ya+∅-∅# = you used to cause yourself to send them as messengers; i.e., you (H sg) used to send them as messengers
 b. tiquimihuāya = you used to send them as messengers
12. *a.* #∅-∅+n-ēch+m-o(xōxi-lih)∅+☐-∅# = he/she bewitched me for himself/herself; he/she (H) bewitched me
 b. nēchxōx = he/she bewitched me

33B. 1. *a.* #∅-∅+m-o(lpi-h-∅-tzin-o-a)∅+∅-∅# = he (H) is girding himself
 b. molpia = he is girding himself
2. *a.* #ti-∅+m-o(pix-∅-tzin-o-ā)ni+∅-∅# = you (H sg) customarily remain aloof
 b. timopiyani = you (sg) customarily remain aloof

Key to the Exercises

3. *a.* #am-∅+m-o(tol-ī-ni-h-∅-tzin-o-a)∅+∅-h# = you (H pl) are poor
   b. ammotolīniah = you (pl) are poor
4. *a.* #∅-∅+m-o(zōmah-∅-tzin-o-a)∅+∅-∅# = he/she (H) frowns in anger
   b. mozōma = he/she frowns in anger
5. *a.* #ti-∅+m-o(zcal-i-h-∅-tzin-o-a)∅+∅-∅# = you (H sg) are reviving
   b. timozcalia = you (sg) are reviving
6. *a.* #am-∅+m-o(tēca-∅-tzin-ō)z+qu-eh# = you (H pl) will be stretching out
   b. ammotēcazqueh = you (pl) will be stretching out

33C. 1. *a.* #ni-∅(pol-ō-n-∅-pōl-o-a)∅+∅-∅# = I (P) am stuttering
     b. nipolōni = I am stuttering
2. *a.* #∅-∅+n-ēch(pol-ō-ni-h-∅-pōl-o-h)∅+☐-∅# = he (P) caused me to stutter ~ he caused me (P) to stutter
   b. nēchpolōnih = he caused me to stutter
3. *a.* #ti-∅+m-itz(mōtla-∅-pōl-ō)z+qu-eh# = we shall throw rocks at you (P sg)
   b. timitzmōtlazqueh = we shall throw rocks at you (sg)
4. *a.* #ti-∅+tla(cuah-∅-pōl-o-a)∅+∅-∅# = you (P sg) are eating s.th.
   b. titlacua = you (sg) are eating s.th.
5. *a.* #∅-∅+qu-im(ihxil-∅-pōl-o-h)∅+☐-∅# = he (P) speared them ~ he speared them (P)
   b. quimihxil = he speared them
6. *a.* #ti-∅+c-∅(tzom-ō-ni-h-∅-pōl-o-a)∅+∅-h# = we (P) are tearing it/them ~ we are tearing it/them (P)
   b. tictzomōniah = we are tearing it/them

33D. 1. O our lord, O my young man (H), utterly kill (H) us. [*Lit.*, thoroughly hide (H) us.]
2. There your grandfathers guard things for you (H).
3. Hear (H) for a while my words, O my grandchild.
4. Let us for yet a while provide laughter for our lord (H).
5. Perhaps he (H) will move his (H) mat.
6. What do you (H) know? [This means: "Listen to what I have to say (since you know nothing about the matter)."]
7. Will you (H) give to your child the property/possessions of the lords?
8. Rest (R) your (H) body.
9. The nobleman had gone (H) around constantly inebriated. He was hanged.
10. Guard/Keep (H) my words.
11. O my son, our lord places (H) you here.
12. As for this one, please take (H) hold of it.
13. Look (H) upon me with compassion. Consider (H) me who am your indigent one with compassion. Do I perchance do nothing for you (H)? I sweep. I pick up litter. I lay fires there where I await your (H) word. [See § 30.14.2.]
14. Do not let yourselves be afraid. Do not become fainthearted. I know that all of you will take captives. We shall kill them somehow every single one. [Despite appearances, *ximomauhtīcān* is not an honorific VNC. Also, notice the reduplication inside *quēxixquichtin*.]

15. Scram! Get out of here!
16. Have you (P pl) lost my papers/book?

EXERCISE 34

34A.
1. #∅-∅(cax-tōl-te)tl-∅# #∅-∅(om-ōme)∅-∅# = they are 15 + 2 (i.e., 17) in number
2. #∅-∅(ōm-pōhua-l)li-∅# #∅-∅(on-chiuc-nāhui)∅-∅# = they are 2 x 20 + 5 + 4 (i.e., 49) in number
3. #∅-∅(mah-tlāc-pān)tli-∅# #∅-∅(on-cē)∅-∅# = they are 10 + 1 (i.e., 11) rows in number
4. #∅-∅(chiuc-nāuh-ōlō)tl-∅# = they are 5 + 4 (i.e., 9) in number
5. #∅-∅(yē-pōhua-l-te)tl-∅# #∅-∅(om-ēi)∅-∅# = they are 3 x 20 + 3 (i.e., 63) in number
6. #∅-∅(chicua-cen-tla-man)tli-∅# = they are 5 + 1 (i.e., 6) in number
7. #∅-∅(tlami-∅)c-∅# #∅-∅(om-mah-tlāc)tli-∅# #∅-∅(om-ōme)∅-∅# = they are 20 + 10 + 2 (i.e., 32) in number
8. #∅-∅(mah-tlāc-pōhua-l)li-∅# #∅-∅(on-cax-tōl)li-∅# #∅-∅(om-ēi)∅-∅# = they are 10 x 20 + 15 + 3 (i.e., 218) in number
9. #∅-∅(cem-pōhua-l)li-∅# #∅-∅(om-mah-tlāc)tli-∅# #∅-∅(on-nāhui)∅-∅# = they are 1 x 20 + 10 + 4 (i.e., 34) in number
10. #∅-∅(nāuh-pōhua-l-te)tl-∅# #∅-∅(om-mā-cu-ī-l)li-∅# = they are 4 x 20 + 5 (i.e., 85) in number
11. #∅-∅(∅-∅-cax-tōl-li-∅+∅-∅-on-nāuh-pōhua-l)li-∅# = they are (15 + 4) x 20 in number; i.e., they are 380 in number

34B.
1. I want only twelve (10 + 2).
2. Are there still three?
3. I have already lost fifteen.
4. How many are you?—We are four.
5. They are not eighteen (15 + 3); they are only fifteen.
6. Give me six (5 + 1).
7. Have three rows become lost? [I.e., sixty.]
8. It is only four fingers [of it] that she is to drink.
9. The ones whom he killed were also four in number. [Notice the common number of the object pronoun *c-∅* and the common number form of *nāhui*, despite the fact that he killed humans.]
10. A comet fell. It went along being in three segments.
11. Look for two more for me.
12. How much is the price of four half-fanegas? [A fanega is a Spanish measure equivalent to 1.6 bushels.]
13. Let's yet await the ones who will come in order to destroy us. Those who are already coming are two (groups) in number.
14. The value of one small cotton blanket was one hundred cacao beans.
15. Perhaps they are four that they rolled into balls.
16. There are five. ~ Five stand/sit/rest/spread out there.
17. Both fasted.

34C.
1. caxtōlli, cempōhualli, cempōhualli ommācuīlli, cempōhualli ommahtlāctli, cempōhualli oncaxtōlli

Key to the Exercises

2. mahtlāctli, cempōhualli, cempōhualli ommahtlāctli, ōmpōhualli, ōmpōhualli ommahtlāctli, yēpōhualli

EXERCISE 35

35A.
1. #ni-∅(cal-pix-∅)qui-∅# = I am a house guarder; i.e., I am a steward/majordomo [< ōnicalpix, "I have guarded a house"]
2. #ti-∅(temō-∅)c-∅# = you are a descender [< ōtitemōc, "you have descended"]
3. #ti-∅(tla-namaca-∅)qu-eh# = we are venders/sellers [< ōtitlanamacaqueh, "we have sold things"]
4. #∅-∅(tla-māmah-∅)☐-∅# = he is a carrier [< ōtlamāmah, "he has carried things on his back"]
5. #∅-∅(mī-mic-∅)qu-eh# = they are dead people [< ōmicqueh, "they have died"]
6. #ti-∅(tla-nel-o-h-∅)☐-∅# = you are a paddler/rower [< ōtitlaneloh, "you have paddled/rowed"; i.e., ō#ti-∅(tla-nel-o-h)∅+☐-∅#, with *tla* fusion, from *tla-(nel-o-ā)*, "to stir s.th."]
7. #∅-∅(tla-pah-∅)qu-eh# = they are dyers [< ōtlapahqueh, "they have dyed things"]
8. #an-∅(te-pān-tlehcō-∅)qu-eh# = you are ones who have gone up walls, you are wall climbers [< ōantepāntlehcōqueh, "you (pl) have climbed walls"]
9. #ti-∅(tlahu-ēl-ī-lō-∅)c-∅# = you are a scoundrel/villain [< ōtitlahuēlīlōc, "you (sg) have been detested"]
10. #∅-∅(tla-mī-n-∅)qui-∅# = he is an archer/bowman [< ōtlamīn, "he has pierced s.th. with an arrow"]
11. #∅-∅(m-o-tol-ī-ni-h-∅)qui-∅# = he is a pauper/poor person [< ōmotolīnih, "he has become impoverished"]
12. #∅-∅(tē-tla-cua-l-tih-∅)qu-eh# = they are waiters/food servers [< ōtētlacualtihqueh, "they have caused people to eat s.th., they have served people food"]
13. #ni-∅(tla-pix-o-h-∅)☐-∅# = I am a sower/broadcaster [< ōnitlapixoh, "I have sown/broadcast things (i.e., seeds)"]
14. #ti-∅(t-o-tla-cu-ih-∅)qu-eh# = we are indebted ones [< ōtitotlacuihqueh, "we have taken things for ourselves," i.e., "we have borrowed things"]

35B.
1. #t-∅+ī-∅(cal-pix-∅-cā)hu-ān# = we are his stewards [ticalpixqueh, "we are stewards"]
2. #ni-∅+ti(yah-∅-cā)uh-∅# = I am s.o.'s goer; i.e., I am a warrior [ti = tē. Abs. state NNC: niyahqui, "I am a goer"]
3. #ti-∅+n-o(tla-ht-o-h-∅-cā)uh-∅# = you are my ruler [titlahtohqui, "you are a speaker/chief/ruler"]
4. #n-∅+ī-∅(ne-mach-tih-∅-cā)uh-∅# = I am his/her student [ninomachtihqui, "I am a student"]
5. #an-∅+t-o(tla-māmah-∅-cā)hu-ān# = you are our carriers (i.e., carriers in our employ) [Antlamāmahqueh, "you are carriers"]
6. #∅-∅+ī-∅(ne-izcal-i-h-∅-cā)hu-ān# = they are his proficient/able ones [mozcalihqueh, "they are self-resurrected/self-revived ones"]
7. #ti-∅+t-o(tē-yac-ān-∅-cā)uh-∅# = you are our leader/guide [titēyacānqui, "you are a leader/guide"]

8. #ni-∅+m-o(tla-mel-ā-uh-∅-cā)uh-∅# = I am your straightener (of things) [ni-tlamelāuhqui, "I am a straightener (of things)"]
9. #∅-∅+ī-∅(tōpīl-eh-∅-cā)uh-∅# = he is his constable [tōpīleh, "he is a staff owner," i.e., "he is a constable"]
10. #am-∅+ī-n(ne-ihtō-tih-∅-cā)hu-ān# = you are their dancers [ammihtōtihqueh, "you are dancers"]

35C.
1. #∅-∅(ez-zo-h-∅)☐-∅# = it is a thing that has owned blood in abundance; i.e., it is a thing covered with blood [< (ez)-tli, "blood"]
2. #∅-∅(xoco-huah-∅)☐-∅# = he/she is one who has owned fruit; i.e., he/she is a fruit owner [< (xoco)-tl-, "plum/fruit"]
3. #∅-∅+n-o(chīl-lo-h-∅-cā)uh-∅# = it is my thing that has owned abundant chili peppers; i.e., it is my thing that is highly seasoned with chili peppers [< (chīl)-li-, "chili pepper"]
4. #am-∅+ī-∅(mī-huah-∅-cā)hu-ān# = you are his ones who have owned arrows; i.e., you are his arrow owners [< (mī)-tl-, "arrow"]
5. #ti-∅(tēn-yo-h-∅)☐-∅# = you are one who has owned lips in abundance (because you are on everyone's lips, everyone is talking about you); i.e., you are famous [< (tēn)-tli-, "lip"]
6. #∅-∅+n-o(yaqu-eh-∅-cā)uh-∅# = it is my thing that has owned a point; i.e., it is my pointed thing [< (yaca)-tl-, "nose, point"]
7. #an-∅(tequi-huah-∅)qu-eh# = you are ones who have owned tribute; i.e., you are tribute owners, you are veteran warriors [< (tequi)-tl-, "tribute/work"]
8. #∅-∅(te-mā-tl-eh-∅)☐-∅# = he is one who has owned a sling; i.e., he is a sling owner [< (te-mā-tla)-tl-, "sling"]
9. #∅-∅+ī-∅(māy-eh-∅-cā)uh-∅# = he is his one who has owned hands; i.e., he is his farm laborer/field hand [< (māi)-tl-, "hand"]
10. #ti-∅(caqu-eh-∅)qu-eh# = we are ones who have owned shoes/sandals; i.e., we are shoe/sandal owners; we have shoes/sandals [< (cac)-tli-, "shoe/sandal"]

35D.
1. #ti-∅(tlahu-ēl-ī-lō-∅-cā-pōl)∅-∅# = you are a despicable scoundrel
2. #∅-∅(mic-∅-cā-tōn)tli-∅# = he/she is a small dead person
3. #an-∅(teō-pix-∅-cā-tzi-tzin)☐-☐# = you are honorable priests
4. #ni-∅(mīl-eh-∅-cā-tōn)tli-∅# = I am an unimportant/insignificant field owner
5. #∅-∅+ī-∅(ne-mach-tih-∅-cā-pi-pīl)hu-ān# = they are his beloved students
6. #∅-∅(ne-tla-cu-ih-∅-cā-pōl)∅-∅# = he is a pathetic debtor

35E.
1. #ni-∅(mauh-∅-cā-tlāca)tl-∅# = I am a coward
2. #ti-∅+m-o(tla-mel-ā-uh-∅-cā-quetza)z+☐-∅# = you will stand up in the manner of one who has straightened things; i.e., you (sg) will stand up erect and straight
3. #∅-∅+qu-im(pāc-∅-cā-tlahpal-ō-☐-t-o)∅+∅-h# = they went in order to greet them in the manner of one who has become happy; i.e., they went to greet them happily
4. #∅-∅+n-o(mīl-eh-∅-cā-poh)∅-∅# = he is my fellow field owner, he is a field owner like me
5. #∅-∅+am-ēch(mauh-∅-cā-itt-a)∅+∅-h# = they look at you (pl) in the manner of one who has become afraid; i.e., they look at you (pl) fearfully
6. #ti-∅+n-ēch(tlahu-ēl-ī-lō-∅-cā-mati)∅+∅-∅# = you (sg) consider me a scoundrel

Key to the Exercises 155

7. ō#an-∅+qui-∅(nāl-quīz-∅-cā-cac)∅+qu-eh# = you (pl) have apprehended it thoroughly
8. #∅-∅+ī-n(naca-yo-h-∅-cā-poh-tzin)∅-∅# = he is their fellow person (H) who has owned flesh in abundance; i.e., he is a bodily being like them; he is a fleshy person like them
9. #ni-∅+n-o(coco-x-∅-cā-neh-nequi)∅+∅-∅# = I pretend to be sick
10. #∅-∅+n-o(mic-∅-cā-tēx)∅-∅# = he is my widowed brother-in-law
11. #∅-∅(chān-eh-∅-cā-conē)tl-∅# = he/she is a home owner's child; i.e., he/she is a legitimate child
12. #ti-∅+m-o(mich-huah-∅-cā-poh)hu-ān# = we are your fellow fishermen; i.e., we are fish owners like you (sg)

35F.
1. What is his kingly name? ~ What is his name as a king?
2. The old men are not dancing. ~ The old men do not dance.
3. The god(-image) carriers went/traveled.
4. The war-canoe owners ran.
5. The blanket is one that has owned abundant snake masks; i.e., The blanket is covered/decorated with the snake mask (design).
6. A turkey vender is a turkey owner.
7. He carried the stewards (with him). He accompanied the stewards.
8. It is said that he was a malevolent/vicious person.
9. The rulers' labrets were gold labrets.
10. His blanket is one that has owned abundant red color on the edges; i.e., His blanket has a red border.
11. As for these, they are cultivated-field owners.
12. The maguey-fiber blanket is one that has owned abundant edges of various flowers; i.e., The maguey-fiber blanket has flowered borders.
13. A child is one who has a mother.
14. Someone envisions that he will be a slave owner.
15. It lies owning a wooden wall. It lies owning a wooden wall in every part; i.e., It is surrounded by a palisade. It is completely ringed by a palisade. [In both sentences the VNCs are formed on connective-t compound verbstems in which the embed subposition is filled by a preterit predicate built on a compound verbstem of ownerhood. The embedded predicate has not undergone nominalization, since the embed of a connective-t verbstem has to be verbal.]

EXERCISE 36

36A.
1. *a.* #ni-∅(tla-ht-o-ā)ni+∅-∅# = I customarily speak
   b. #ni-∅(tla-ht-o-ā-ni)∅-∅# = I am one who customarily speaks; i.e., I am a speaker, I am a ruler/chief/king
2. *a.* #∅-∅(itz-cuin-cuā)ni+∅-∅# = it customarily eats dogs
   b. #∅-∅(itz-cuin-cuā-ni)∅-∅# = it is one that customarily eats dogs; i.e., it is a dog eater (i.e., it is a ringtail)
3. *a.* #an-∅+tla(mati)ni+∅-h# = you (pl) customarily know things
   b. #an-∅(tla-mati-ni)∅-h# = you are ones who customarily know things; i.e., you are savants/sages

4. a. #∅-∅+tē(cuā)ni+∅-h# = they customarily eat people
   b. #∅-∅(tē-cuā-ni)m-eh# = they are ones that customarily eat people; i.e., they are wild beasts, they are cannibals
5. a. #ti-∅+t-o(zcal-i-ā)ni+∅-h# = we customarily revive/come to our senses
   b. #ti-∅(t-o-zcal-i-ā-ni)∅-h# = we are ones who customarily revive/come to our senses; i.e., we are able/capable persons
6. a. #∅-∅(mā-neh-nemi)ni+∅-h# = they customarily walk on their hands (and feet), they customarily walk on all fours
   b. #∅-∅(mā-neh-nemi-ni)∅-h# = they are ones that customarily walk on all fours; i.e., they are four-legged animals
7. a. #ti-∅+tla(mati)ni+∅-∅# = you (sg) customarily know things
   b. #ti-∅(tla-mati-ni-tōn)□-∅# = you are a small one who customarily knows things; i.e., you are a minor/unimpressive/low-quality savant
8. a. #∅-∅(tlāhu-āna)ni+∅-∅# = he customarily becomes tipsy
   b. #∅-∅(tlāhu-āna-ni-pōl)∅-∅# = he is a (miserable) drunkard
9. a. #ti-∅+tē(cuā)ni+∅-∅# = you (sg) customarily eat people
   b. #t-∅+ī-∅(tē-cuā-ni)uh-∅# = you are his thug

36B. 1. a. #∅-∅(tlāl-pōhua-lō)ni+∅-∅# = all customarily measure land
   b. #∅-∅(tlāl-pōhua-lō-ni)∅-∅# = it is an instrument for surveying, they are instruments for surveying
2. a. #∅-∅(tex-ō)ni+∅-∅# = all customarily grind
   b. #∅-∅(tex-ō-ni)∅-∅# = it is an instrument for grinding; i.e., it is a pestle/a pounder; they are pestles/pounders
3. a. #∅-∅+tla(cōhua-lō)ni+∅-∅# = all customarily buy things
   b. #∅-∅(tla-cōhua-lō-ni)∅-∅# = it is a means for buying things; i.e., it is a coin, they are coins
4. a. #∅-∅+ne(mach-tī-lō)ni+∅-∅# = all customarily learn
   b. #∅-∅(ne-mach-tī-lō-ni)∅-∅# = it is a means for learning; i.e., it is a textbook, they are textbooks
5. a. #∅-∅+ne(lpī-lō)ni+∅-∅# = all gird themselves [< m-o-(ilpi-ā), "to cause o.s. to become tied," i.e., "to gird o.s."]
   b. #∅-∅(ne-lpī-lō-ni)∅-∅ # = it is a belt, they are belts
6. a. #∅-∅+tla(tlap-ō-lō)ni+∅-∅# = all customarily open things
   b. #∅-∅(tla-tlap-ō-lō-ni-tōn)□-∅# = it is a small key, they are small keys
7. a. #∅-∅+ne(tlāl-ī-lō)ni+∅-∅# = all customarily sit down
   b. #∅-∅(ne-tlāl-ī-lō-ni)∅-∅# = it is a seat, they are seats
8. a. #∅-∅+tla(pā-tz-c-ō)ni+∅-∅# = all customarily squeeze liquid out of s.th.
   b. #∅-∅(tla-pā-tz-c-ō-ni)∅-∅# = it is a juice press/a milk pail, they are juice presses/milk pails
9. a. #∅-∅+tla(pā-tz-ca-lō)ni+∅-∅# = all customarily squeeze liquid out of s.th.
   b. #∅-∅(tla-pā-tz-ca-lō-ni)∅-∅# = it is a juice press/a milk pail; they are juice presses/milk pails
10. a. #∅-∅+tla(tlāx-ō)ni+∅-∅# = all customarily hurl s.th.
    b. #∅-∅(tla-tlāx-ō-ni)∅-∅# = it is a catapult, they are catapults

Key to the Exercises 157

36C. 1. *a.* #ni-∅+tla(nequi)ya+∅-∅# = I used to want s.th.
  b. #∅-∅+n-o(tla-nequi-ya)∅-∅# = it is my will/intention
 2. *a.* #ti-∅+tla(cuā)ya+∅-∅# = you (sg) used to eat s.th.
  b. #∅-∅+m-o(tla-cuā-ya)∅-∅# = it is your (sg) eating utensil, they are your (sg) eating utensils
 3. *a.* #∅-∅(ce-ya)ya+∅-∅# = he used to be willing
  b. #∅-∅+ī-∅(ce-ya-ya)∅-∅# = it is his will/volition
 4. *a.* #ti-∅+tla(mā-toca)ya+∅-h# = we used to follow s.th. by the hand, i.e., we used to examine s.th. by touch
  b. #∅-∅+t-o(tla-mā-toca-ya)∅-∅# = it is our sense of touch
 5. *a.* #∅-∅+tē(mī-n-a)ya+∅-∅# = it used to sting people
  b. #∅-∅+ī-∅(tē-mī-n-a-ya)∅-∅# = it is its stinger
 6. *a.* #am-∅+m-o(mā-na-huiā)ya+∅-h# = you used to defend yourselves
  b. #∅-∅+am-o(ne-mā-na-huiā-ya)∅-∅# = it is your (pl) means of defending yourselves; it is your defense, they are your defenses
 7. *a.* #∅-∅+tla(hnecui)ya+∅-h# = they were smelling s.th.
  b. #∅-∅+ī-n(tla-hnecui-ya)∅-∅# = it is their sense of smell
 8. *a.* #ni-∅(yōli)ya+∅-∅# = I was living
  b. #∅-∅+n-o(yōli-ya)∅-∅# = it is my instrument for living; i.e., it is my soul

36D. 1. *a.* ō#∅-∅(pal-ē-hu-ī-lō)ca+∅-∅# = it had been helped
  b. #∅-∅+ī-∅(pal-ē-hu-ī-lō-ca)∅-∅# = it is its action of being helped; i.e., it is its alleviation, it is the alleviation of it
 2. *a.* ō#ni-∅(tlap-ō-lō)ca+∅-∅# = I had been opened
  b. #∅-∅+n-o(tlap-ō-lō-ca)∅-∅# = it is my action of being opened; i.e., it is my openness
 3. *a.* ō#t-∅(īxi-mach-ō)ca+∅-h# = we had been recognized
  b. #∅-∅+t-□(īxi-mach-ō-ca)∅-∅# = it is our action of being recognized; i.e., it is our recognition (by others), it is the recognition of us
 4. *a.* ō#∅-∅(mic-tī-lō)ca+∅-∅# = he had been murdered
  b. #∅-∅+ī-∅(mic-tī-lō-ca)∅-∅# = it is his being murdered; i.e., it is his murder, it is the murder of him
 5. *a.* ō#∅-∅+ne(mic-tī-lō)ca+∅-h# = they had killed themselves
  b. #∅-∅+ī-n(ne-mic-tī-lō-ca)∅-∅# = it is their action of being self-killed; i.e., it is their suicide

36E. 1. *a.* ō#∅-∅(ihtlac-a-uh)ca+∅-h# = they had become spoiled/ruined
  b. #∅-∅+ī-m(ihtlac-a-uh-ca)∅-∅# = it is their defect, they are their defects
 2. *a.* ō#∅-∅+m-o(cuep)ca+∅-∅# = he had returned
  b. #∅-∅+ī-∅(ne-cuep-ca)∅-∅# = it is his action of returning; i.e., it is his return
 3. *a.* ō#ni-∅(yōl)ca+∅-∅# = I had lived
  b. #∅-∅+n-o(yōl-ca)∅-∅# = it is my means of living; i.e., it is my sustenance
 4. *a.* ō#ti-∅(nēz)ca+∅-h# = we had appeared
  b. #∅-∅+t-o(nēz-ca)∅-∅# = it is the means by which we (continue to) appear; i.e., it is our trace, they are our traces; it is the trace of us, they are the traces of us
 5. *a.* ō#ti-∅(huel-nēz)ca+∅-∅# = you (sg) had appeared pleasing
  b. #∅-∅+m-o(huel-nēz-ca)∅-∅# = it is your action of appearing pleasing; i.e., it is your (sg) good/pleasing/attractive appearance

36F. 1. Their traces are many.
2. The woman received the curative.
3. The metal ax is not left out/omitted.
4. Do you (pl) wish to be the ruler's/king's warriors?
5. Its/Their use is nothing; i.e., It is useless. They are useless. There is no need for it/them.
6. The hawk is a continual hunter/pursuer.
7. Here are the defects of the Otomis.
8. The tree squirrel eats the new growth/fresh sprouts of the tree(s).
9. The god is a war commander.
10. The/A monkey sits like a man.
11. The eclipse of the sun frightened them.
12. Is there a drinking vessel? Are there any drinking vessels?

EXERCISE 37

37A. 1. a. #Ø-Ø(tzahtzi)Ø+Ø-Ø# = he is shouting
   b. #Ø-Ø+ī-Ø(tzahtzi-liz)Ø-Ø# = it is his act of shouting
   c. #Ø-Ø(tzahtzi-liz)tli-Ø# = it is an act of shouting
2. a. #ti-Ø+tē(tlahpal-o-a)Ø+Ø-Ø# = you (sg) urge people to be healthy/vigorous; i.e., you greet people
   b. #Ø-Ø+m-o(tē-tlahpal-ō-liz)Ø-Ø# = it is your act of greeting people
   c. #Ø-Ø(tē-tlahpal-ō-liz)tli-Ø# = it is an act of greeting people
3. a. #ti-Ø+t-o(nēx-tia)Ø+Ø-h# = we are causing ourselves to appear
   b. #Ø-Ø+t-o(ne-nēx-tī-liz)Ø-Ø# = it is our self-revelation
   c. #Ø-Ø(ne-nēx-tī-liz)tli-Ø# = it is an act of self-revelation
4. a. #an-Ø+tē(xōxa)Ø+Ø-h# = you (pl) are bewitching people
   b. #Ø-Ø+am-o(tē-xōxa-liz)Ø-Ø# = it is your (pl) act of bewitching people
   c. #Ø-Ø(tē-xōxa-liz)tli-Ø# = it is the/an act of bewitching s.o.
5. a. #Ø-Ø+m-o(cuep-a)Ø+Ø-Ø# = he is returning
   b. #Ø-Ø+ī-Ø(ne-cuep-a-liz)Ø-Ø# = it is his act of returning
   c. #Ø-Ø(ne-cuep-a-liz)tli-Ø# = it is an act of returning
6. a. #Ø-Ø+qu-Ø(ēl-ē-hu-ia)Ø+Ø-Ø# = he desires it/them
   b. #Ø-Ø(ēl-ē-hu-ī-z)tli-Ø# = it is/they are worthy of being desired; it is/they are desirable
7. a. #Ø-Ø(chichi-ya)Ø+Ø-Ø# = it becomes bitter
   b. #Ø-Ø+ī-Ø(chichi-liz)Ø-Ø# = it is its action of becoming bitter; it is its bitterness
   c. #Ø-Ø(chichi-liz)tli-Ø# = it is the action of becoming bitter; it is bitterness
8. a. #ni-Ø+n-o(cāuh-Ø-ti-quīza)Ø+Ø-Ø# = I abruptly stop off (somewhere)
   b. #Ø-Ø+n-o(ne-cāuh-Ø-ti-quīza-liz)Ø-Ø# = it is my act of abruptly stopping off
   c. #Ø-Ø(ne-cāuh-Ø-ti-quīza-liz)tli-Ø# = it is an act of abruptly stopping off
9. a. #Ø-Ø+qui-Ø(nequi)Ø+Ø-Ø# = he wants it/them
   b. #Ø-Ø(nequi-z)tli-Ø# = it is/they are worthy of being wanted; it is/they are desirable

37B. 1. a. #an-Ø+n-ēch(tītlani)Ø+Ø-h# = you (pl) are sending me as a messenger
   b. #ni-Ø(tītlan-o)Ø+Ø-Ø# = I am being sent as a messenger

Key to the Exercises 159

        c. #ni-∅(tītlan)tli-∅# = I am one who is being sent as a messenger; i.e., I am a messenger
   2. *a.* #∅-∅+qui-∅(piya)∅+∅-h# = they are guarding it
      b. #∅-∅(piya-lo)∅+∅-∅# = it is being guarded
      c. #∅-∅(piya-l)li-∅# = it is a guarded thing; it is a cache/a store of goods
   3. *a.* #ti-∅+c-∅(nāhua-t-ia)∅+∅-h# = we are commanding it
      b. #∅-∅(nāhua-t-ī-lo)∅+∅-∅# = it is being commanded
      c. #∅-∅+t-o(nāhua-t-ī-l)∅-∅# = it is our command [*Also*, it is a thing commanded of us, i.e., it is our obligation.]
   4. *a.* #∅-∅+qui-∅(tzacu-a)∅+∅-∅# = he is closing it
      b. #∅-∅(tzacu-a-lo)∅+∅-∅# = it is being closed
      c. #∅-∅(tzacu-a-l)li-∅# = it is a thing that has been closed; i.e., it is a pyramid
   5. *a.* #∅-∅+qui-∅(mah-cē-hu-a)∅+∅-∅# = he deservedly attained it
      b. #∅-∅(mah-cē-hu-a-lo)∅+∅-∅# = it is being deservedly attained
      c. #∅-∅(mah-cē-hu-a-l)li-∅# = it is a deserved thing/a merited thing
   6. *a.* #ti-∅+c-∅(poz-ō-n-a)∅+∅-h# = we are boiling it
      b. #∅-∅(poz-ō-n-a-lo)∅+∅-∅# = it is being boiled
      c. #∅-∅(poz-ō-n-a-l)li-∅# = it is the result of being boiled; i.e., it is foam
   7. *a.* #ni-∅+c-∅(pa)∅+∅-∅# = I am dyeing it
      b. #∅-∅(pa-lo)∅+∅-∅# = it is being dyed
      c. #∅-∅(pa-l)li-∅# = it is a thing that can be used for dyeing; i.e., it is black clay
   8. *a.* #ni-∅+c-∅+tē(maca)∅+∅-∅# = I am giving it to s.o.
      b. #∅-∅+tē(mac-o)∅+∅-∅# = it is being given to s.o.
      c. #∅-∅+n-o(tē-mac)∅-∅# = it is my gift

37C. 1. The courtyard lies owning a wooden wall; i.e., The courtyard is encircled by a palisade.
   2. The messengers did this.
   3. He is sending the shamans.
   4. The merchants survive their captives. All survive their captives; i.e., The merchants sacrifice their captives. All sacrifice captives.
   5. They busy themselves with the act of blowing on people; i.e., They busy themselves with casting spells on people.
   6. He will request from him his favor.
   7. Perhaps they will take sick.
   8. Already your enemies are leaving in disguise (i.e., stealthily).
   9. They also amuse themselves with bewitching people.
  10. Are we not a match? ~ Are we not equals?
  11. "I shall indeed thoroughly hide (i.e., kill) you."—"Fine [*lit.*, Indeed, it is already good]. Come on [i.e., you are welcome to try]."
  12. Some climbed the pyramid.

EXERCISE 38

38A. 1. *a.* #∅-∅(chihcha-lo)∅+∅-∅# = people spit [< (chihcha)]
      b. #∅-∅(chihcha-l)li-∅# = it is spit/spittle

2. *a.* #∅-∅+tla(tatac-o)∅+∅-∅# = people dig s.th. [< tla-(tataca)]
   b. #∅-∅(tla-tatac)tli-∅# = it is a pit
3. *a.* #∅-∅+tla(lpī-lo)∅+∅-∅# = people are tying s.th. [< tla-(*i*lpi-ā), "to cause s.th. to become tied"]
   b. #∅-∅(tla-lpī-l)li-∅# = it is a knot/a knotted/tied thing
4. *a.* #∅-∅+tla(xca-lo)∅+∅-∅# = people are baking s.th. [< tla-(*i*xca).]
   b. #∅-∅(tla-xca-l)li-∅# = it is a tortilla/bread
5. *a.* #∅-∅+ne(cuil-tōn-ō-lo)∅+∅-∅# = people are rich [< m-o-(cuil-tōn-o-ā)]
   b. #∅-∅(ne-cuil-tōn-ō-l)li-∅# = it is wealth

38B. 1. *a.* #∅-∅(cuauh-huā-tz-a-lo)∅+∅-∅# = people dry out wood, wood is being dried [< (cuauh-huā-tz-a), "to cause wood to become dry"]
   b. #∅-∅(cuauh-huā-tz-a-l)li-∅# = it is wood that has been dried, it is dry wood, it is deadwood
2. *a.* #∅-∅+ne(īx-cāhu-ī-lo)∅+∅-∅# = people are minding their own business [< m-☐-(īx-cāhu-iā)]
   b. #∅-∅(ne-īx-cāhu-ī-l)li-∅# = it is a private thing
3. *a.* #∅-∅(nāhua-t-ī-lo)∅+∅-∅# = it is being commanded [< tla-(nāhua-t-iā)]
   b. #∅-∅(teō)tl-∅# #∅-∅+ī-∅(nāhua-t-ī-l)∅+∅-∅# = it is a/the god's command; #∅-∅(teō-nāhua-t-ī-l)li-∅# = it is a divine command
4. *a.* #∅-∅(cua-hchic-o)∅+∅-∅# = people are scraping heads (clean of hair) [The embed is *(cuāi)-tl-*, "head," and the matrix is *tla-(ihchiqui)*, "to scrape s.th. clean."]
   b. #∅-∅(cua-hchic)tli-∅# = it is a head that has been shaved, he is a shaved head; i.e., he is a high-ranking warrior
5. *a.* #∅-∅(tla-quetza-lo)∅+∅-∅# = people set s.th. upright [< tla-(quetza)]
   b. #∅-∅(tla-quetza-l)li-∅# #∅-∅(te)tl-∅# = it is a column that is of stone; #∅-∅(te-tla-quetza-l)li-∅# = it is a stone column

38C. 1. Have people already filled the temple courtyard?
2. This resembles amber/foam.
3. Who is a/the baker?
4. Do you want to make tortillas?
5. People used to survive their (ceremonially) bathed ones. The merchants used to bathe people (ceremonially), [i.e., in preparation for their sacrifice].
6. He is sending an ambassador. [*Lit.*, a word-carrier.]
7. They used to inform him of his words. [The *-huāl-* indicates that the speaker of this sentence allies himself with the individual referred to by the *-qui-*.]
8. The shaved-heads (i.e., high-ranking warriors) come out.
9. They are giving them an equal number of things.
10. It is only the ruler's/king's private matter.
11. Beans are the food of these.
12. They simply put shelled maize into nets.
13. The deadwood lies fallen.
14. A grasshopper has spittle.
15. Soon they will be eaten by means of wild animals (i.e., soon wild animals will eat them); they will be wild-animal food; they will be the food of wild animals.

Key to the Exercises

16. They caused the Sun to be enclosed; i.e., They built a pyramid to/for the Sun.
17. It was said that this day-sign was not good; it was a vicious day sign.
18. All the gods stood around the fire pit.

EXERCISE 39

39A. 1. *a.* ō#∅-∅+tla(quēn)∅+☐-∅# = he wore s.th.
    b. #∅-∅(tla-quēn)tli-∅# = it is clothing
2. *a.* ō#∅-∅(tle-quiquiz)∅+☐-∅# = it resounded with fire, it (e.g., a cannon) discharged/went off
    b. #∅-∅(tle-quiquiz)tli-∅# = it is a firearm/gun/cannon
3. *a.* ō#∅-∅+tē(nōtz)∅+☐-∅# = he summoned people
    b. #∅-∅(tla-nōtz)tli-∅# = he is one who has been summoned
4. *a.* ō#∅-∅+tla(quetz)∅+☐-∅# = he/she set s.th. upright
    b. #∅-∅(tla-quetz)tli-∅# = it is a neatly stacked pile of firewood
5. *a.* ō#ni-∅+tla(chīuh)∅+☐-∅# = I made s.th.
    b. #∅-∅+n-o(tla-chīuh)∅-∅# = it is my artifact/worked land
6. *a.* ō#∅-∅(yōl)∅+☐-∅# = it lived
    b. #∅-∅(yōl)li-∅# = it is a thing that results from living, it is life
7. *a.* *ō#∅-∅(yōl-lo-h)∅+☐-∅# = *it has owned life in every part
    b. #∅-∅(yōl-lo-h)tli-∅# = it is a heart
8. *a.* *ō#∅-∅+tla(zo-h)∅+☐-∅# = *he prized s.th.
    b. #∅-∅(tla-zo-h)tli-∅# = it is a thing that is cherished; it is a precious thing
9. *a.* ō#∅-∅(nen)∅+☐-∅# = he has lived
    b. #∅-∅+ī-∅(nen)∅-∅# = it is what has been lived by him/her; it is his/her life
10. *a.* ō#ni-∅+tla(l-cāuh)∅+☐-∅# = I forgot s.th.
    b. #∅-∅(tla-l-cāuh)tli-∅# = it is a forgotten thing

39B. 1. *a.* #ti-∅(t-o-nōtz-∅)qu-eh# = we are mutual summoners
    b. #∅-∅(ne-nōtz)tli-∅# = it is an accord/compact/mutual agreement/mutual decision
2. *a.* #∅-∅(tla-mel-ā-uh-∅)qui-∅# = he is an explicator
    b. #∅-∅(tla-mel-ā-uh)tli-∅# = it is an explicated thing
3. *a.* #∅-∅(tla-chīuh-∅)qui-∅# = he is a maker
    b. #∅-∅(tla-chīuh)tli-∅# = it is an artifact/worked land
4. *a.* #∅-∅(poz-tec-∅)qui-∅# = it is a thing (e.g., leg, stick) that becomes broken
    b. #∅-∅(poz-tec)tli-∅# = it is a broken thing (e.g., leg, stick)
5. *a.* #∅-∅(tlah-tla-l-pītz-∅)qui-∅# = he is one who repeatedly/in various places blows on s.th
    b. #∅-∅(tlah-tla-l-pītz)tli-∅# = it is a thing that is repeatedly blown on/blown on in various places
6. *a.* #∅-∅(tla-namaca-∅)c-∅# = he/she is one who sells things; he/she is a shopkeeper/salesperson
    b. #∅-∅(tla-namac)tli-∅# = it is a thing that has been sold
7. *a.* #∅-∅(tē-ih-xil-∅)qui-∅# = he is a spearer/stabber
    b. #∅-∅(tla-h-xil)li-∅# = he/it is one that has been speared/stabbed
8. *a.* #∅-∅(tla-cāuh-∅)qui-∅# = he is a discarder/abandoner/leaver
    b. #∅-∅(tla-cāuh)tli-∅# = it is an empty space/s.th. left behind; they are leftovers

39C. 1. *a.* #ni-∅+tla(tqui)∅+∅-∅# = I carry s.th.
      b. #∅-∅+n-o(tla-tqui)∅-∅# = it is my property; they are my belongings
   2. *a.* #∅-∅+tla(zo)∅+∅-∅# = he/she is piercing/puncturing s.th.
      b. #∅-∅(tla-zō)tl-∅# = it (e.g., a bead) is a thing strung on a cord/thread
   3. *a.* #∅-∅(quiy-a-hui)∅+∅-∅# = it is raining
      b. #∅-∅(quiy-a-hui)tl-∅# = it is rain
   4. *a.* #∅-∅+tla(zaca)∅+∅-∅# = he transports s.th.
      b. #∅-∅(zaca)tl-∅# = it is straw/hay
   5. *a.* #∅-∅+tla(te-chal-o-a)∅+∅-∅# = it is scolding s.th. from a rock
      b. #∅-∅(te-chal-ō)tl-∅# = it is a ground squirrel
   6. *a.* #ni-∅+tla(cuih-cui)∅+∅-∅# = I am carving s.th. (in stone or wood)
      b. #∅-∅(tla-cuih-cui)tl-∅# = it is a sculpted thing (in stone or wood)
   7. *a.* #∅-∅+tla(quēmi)∅+∅-∅# = he/she puts s.th. on
      b. #∅-∅(tla-quēmi)tl-∅# = it is clothing
   8. *a.* #∅-∅(ce-pay-a-hui)∅+∅-∅# = it is snowing
      b. #∅-∅(ce-pay-a-hui)tl-∅# = it is snow

39D. 1. *a.* #∅-∅(tla-ht-ō-l)li-∅# = it is an utterance/a word
      b. #∅-∅(tla-ht-ō-l-lō)tl-∅# = it is wordiness, i.e., it is history
   2. *a.* #∅-∅(ah-tlāca)tl-∅# = he is inhuman
      b. #∅-∅(ah-tlāca-yō)tl-∅# = it is inhumanity
   3. *a.* #∅-∅(oquich)tli-∅# = he is a man
      b. #∅-∅(oquich-yō)tl-∅# = it is a heroic deed/manliness
   4. *a.* #∅-∅(nān)tli-∅# = she is a mother
      b. #∅-∅(nān-yō)tl-∅# = it is motherhood
   5. *a.* #∅-∅(mahui-z)tli-∅# = he is a person worthy of honor
      b. #∅-∅(mahui-z-zō)tl-∅# = it is honor/dignity
   6. *a.* #∅-∅(tēn)tli-∅# = it is a lip; they are lips
      b. #∅-∅(tēn-yō)tl-∅# = it is fame
   7. *a.* #∅-∅(tla-ht-o-h-∅)qui-∅# = he is a ruler/king
      b. #∅-∅(tla-ht-o-h-∅-cā-yō)tl-∅# = it is a kingdom
   8. *a.* #∅-∅(ich-ca)tl-∅# = it is a sheep
      b. #∅-∅(ich-ca-yō)tl-∅# = it is a thing pertaining to sheep

39E. 1. *a.* #∅-∅+ī-∅(chiqu-i-uh)∅-∅# = it is his/her basket
      b. #∅-∅+ī-∅(chiqu-i-uh-yo)∅-∅# = it is his/her rib cage
   2. *a.* #∅-∅+n-o(xināch)∅-∅# = it is my seed; they are my seeds
      b. #∅-∅+n-o(xināch-yo)∅-∅# = it is my semen
   3. *a.* #∅-∅+m-o(tohmi)uh-∅# = it is your fur (which you obtained)
      b. #∅-∅+ī-∅(tohmi-yo)∅-∅# = it is its fur
   4. *a.* #∅-∅+m-o(nac)∅-∅# = it is your (sg) meat (which you obtained)
      b. #∅-∅+m-o(naca-yo)∅-∅# = it is your flesh/body
   5. *a.* #∅-∅+ī-∅(xō-chih-cua-l)∅-∅# = it is his/her fruit
      b. #∅-∅+ī-∅(xō-chih-cua-l-lo)∅-∅# = it is its fruit
   6. *a.* #∅-∅+ī-∅(nex)∅-∅# = they are his/her ashes (which he/she obtained)
      b. #∅-∅+ī-∅(nex-xo)∅-∅# = they are his/her ashes (of his/her cremated body); they are its ashes (the result of its being burned)

Key to the Exercises 163

39F. 1. *a*. #Ø-Ø(xo-xō-hui)Ø+Ø-Ø# = it is becoming green
    b. #Ø-Ø(xo-xo-c)tli-Ø# = it is a green-colored thing
 2. *a*. #Ø-Ø(cual-ā-ni)Ø+Ø-Ø# = he is becoming angry
    b. #Ø-Ø(cual-a-c)tli-Ø# = it is the result of becoming angry; i.e., it is slaver/slobber
 3. *a*. #Ø-Ø(catz-ā-hua)Ø+Ø-Ø# = it is becoming dirty
    b.#Ø-Ø(catz-a-c)tli-Ø# = it is a dirty/black thing
 4. *a*. #Ø-Ø+tla(pech-o-a)Ø+Ø-Ø# = he gives s.th. a flat foundation
    b. #Ø-Ø(tla-pech)tli-Ø# = it is a platform/litter/bier/bedstead
 5. *a*. #Ø-Ø(tzap-ī-ni)Ø+Ø-Ø# = it becomes pricked
    b. #Ø-Ø(tzap)tli-Ø# = it is a thorn
 6. *a*. #Ø-Ø+tla(comōl-o-a)Ø+Ø-Ø# = he is excavating s.th.
    b. #Ø-Ø(tla-comōl)li-Ø# = it is a pit/an excavation
 7. *a*. #Ø-Ø(malacach-i-hui)Ø+Ø-Ø# = it is revolving
    b. #Ø-Ø(malacach)tli-Ø# = it is a circle
 8. *a*. #Ø-Ø(tlahpal-i-hui)Ø+Ø-Ø# = he/she/it is becoming energetic
    b. #Ø-Ø(tlahpal)li-Ø# = it is an effort
 9. *a*. #Ø-Ø(ilacach-i-hui)Ø+Ø-Ø# = it is swirling
    b. #Ø-Ø(ilacach)tli-Ø# = it is a swirl
 10. *a*. #Ø-Ø(petz-i-hui)Ø+Ø-Ø# = it becomes polished/shiny
    b. #Ø-Ø(petz)tli-Ø# = it is pyrite (mineral used for making mirrors)

39G. 1. His flesh is sick; i.e., He is sick.
 2. The priest liked his (own) words.
 3. He has already lost his property.
 4. They are acquainted with the essence of herbs.
 5. They knew the characteristics of the stars.
 6. He is dressing him in a rich costume.
 7. The youths' labor was shared/common/communal labor.
 8. Their bows are of (hard) metal.
 9. The vital blood of the ones who were dying (*here*, "being sacrificed") came to reach all the way to there.
 10. They set the litter down.
 11. Your (pl) efforts are needed.
 12. The one who is not brave hearted just runs away.
 13. Do quickly what you are told to do.
 14. There they caught their breath. They caught their breath.
 15. They went carrying wooden platforms/litters.
 16. They went to bury the charcoal of the pinewood.
 17. They went having only one bow with them. They went carrying their quivers on their backs.
 18. He (H) is doing his commonerhood with diligence; i.e., He (H) is acting like a commoner intemperately. He is degrading himself.
 19. Call (pl) out in contriteness to our lord (H).
 20. He pretends to know s.th.
 21. You, quickly take up what you are told to take up.

22. He said to the Mexihcas, "O my children, let's cut sod. Let's erect a modest little sod-cut thing (i.e., a little thing made of cut sod)." [The reference is to an altar.]

EXERCISE 40

40A. 1. #∅-∅(cōz)tli-∅# = (a) it is a yellow thing; (b) it is yellow [< (cōz-a-hui), "to become yellow colored"]
2. #∅-∅(tla-pah-tī-l)li-∅# = (a) he is a person restored to health; (b) he is cured/healed/well again [< tē-(pah-ti-ā), "to cause s.o. to have (good) medicine; to cure s.th."]
3. #∅-∅(tzōl)li-∅# = (a) it is a narrowed/contracted thing; (b) it is narrow/compressed [< (tzōl-i-hui), "to become narrow/contracted/compressed"]
4. #∅-∅(yēc)tli-∅# = (a) it is a completed thing; (b) it is good [< (yēc-a-hui), "to become complete"]
5. #∅-∅(catz-a-c)tli-∅# = (a) it is a dirty thing; (b) it is dirty [< (catz-ā-hua), "to become dirty"]
6. #∅-∅(tla-tla-c)tli-∅# = (a) it is a red-colored thing; (b) it is red [< (tla-tlā-hui), "to become red"]
7. #∅-∅(tla-coh-cop-ī-n)tli-∅# = (a) it is an unbuttoned thing; (b) it is unbuttoned [< tla-(coh-cop-ī-n-a), "to pull thing after thing (i.e., button after button) loose (from buttonholes)"]
8. #∅-∅(mel-a-c)tli-∅# = (a) it is a thing that has become straight; (b) it is straight [< (mel-ā-hua), "to become straight"]
9. #∅-∅(tla-ān)tli-∅# = (a) it is a thing that has been taken hold of; (b) it is unsheathed/disinterred/uprooted [< tla-(āna), "to seize/take hold of s.th."]
10. #∅-∅(ne-īx-cāhu-ī-l)li-∅# = (a) it is a private thing; (b) it is private [< m-□-(īx-cāhu-iā), "to mind one's own business"]

40B. 1. #∅-∅(tlīl-i-uh-∅)qui-∅# = (a) it is a black thing; (b) it is black [< (tlīl-i-hui), "to become black"]
2. #∅-∅(catz-ā-hua-∅)c-∅# = (a) it is a dirty thing; (b) it is dirty [< (catz-ā-hua), "to become dirty"]
3. #∅-∅(ich-ti-∅)c-∅# = (a) it is a wiry thing; (b) it is wiry [< (ich-ti), "to become like maguey fiber"]
4. #∅-∅(yaca-huitz-ti-∅)c-∅# = (a) it is a thing with a pointed end; (b) it is sharp pointed [< (yaca-huitz-ti), "to become like a thorn at the nose (i.e., at the point)"]
5. #∅-∅(tlan-∅)qui-∅# = (a) it is a finished/concluded thing; (b) it is finished/concluded [< (tlami), "to come to an end; to become finished; to become used up"]
6. #∅-∅(tla-tla-c-ti-∅)c-∅# = (a) it is a bright red thing; (b) it is bright red [< (tla-tla-c-ti), "to become bright red"]
7. #∅-∅(teuh-yo-h-∅)□-∅# = (a) it is a dust-covered thing; (b) it is dusty [< *(teuh-yo-ā), "to have abundant dust"]
8. #∅-∅(til-ā-hua-∅)c-∅# = (a) it is a thick-woven thing (such as a blanket or thatched roof); (b) it is thick woven [< (til-ā-hua), "to become close woven"]
9. #∅-∅(tlap-ā-n-∅)qui-∅# = (a) it is a broken thing; (b) it is broken [< (tlap-ā-ni), "to become broken"]

Key to the Exercises 165

     10. #Ø-Ø(huē-i-ya-Ø)c-Ø# = (a) it is a long thing; (b) it is long [< (huē-i-ya), "to become long"]

40C. 1. #Ø-Ø(ihyā-Ø)c-Ø# = (a) it is a foul-smelling thing; (b) it is foul smelling [< (ihyā-ya), "to stink"]
    2. #Ø-Ø(ā-ti-Ø)c-Ø# = (a) it is a watery thing; (b) it is watery [< (ā-ti-ya), "to become water"]
    3. #Ø-Ø(chichi-Ø)c-Ø# = (a) it is a bitter thing; (b) it is bitter [< (chichi-ya), "to become bitter"]
    4. #Ø-Ø(yancui-Ø)c-Ø# = (a) it is a new/recent thing; (b) it is new/recent [< (yan-cui-ya), "to become new/recent"]
    5. #Ø-Ø(ītz-ti-Ø)c-Ø# = (a) it is a cold thing; (b) it is cold [< (ītz-ti-ya), "to become like obsidian," i.e., "to become cold"]
    6. #Ø-Ø(xoco-Ø)c-Ø# = (a) it is a tart/sour thing; (b) it is tart/sour [< (xoco-ya), "to become like a plum," i.e., "to become tart/sour"]
    7. #Ø-Ø(cōz-ti-Ø)c-Ø# = (a) it is a yellow thing; (b) it is yellow [< (cōz-ti-ya), "to become yellow"]
    8. #Ø-Ø(ce-ce-Ø)c-Ø# = (a) it is a cold thing; (b) it is cold [< (ce-ce-ya), "to become like ice," i.e., "to become cold"]

40D. 1. #Ø-Ø(chiya-lō-ni)Ø-Ø# = it is worthy of being awaited [< tla-(chiya), "to await s.th."]
    2. #Ø-Ø(pōhua-lō-ni)Ø-Ø# = it is countable [< tla-(pōhu-a), "to count s.th."]
    3. #Ø-Ø(nec-ō-ni)Ø-Ø# = it is desirable [< tla-(nequi), "to want s.th."]
    4. #Ø-Ø(chōqui-lī-lō-ni)Ø-Ø# = it is lamentable [< tla-(chōqui-liā), "to cry about s.th."]
    5. #Ø-Ø(namac-ō-ni)Ø-Ø# = it is sellable [< tla-(namaca), "to sell s.th."]
    6. #Ø-Ø(ich-tec-ō-ni)Ø-Ø# = it is susceptible to theft [< qu-Ø-(ich-tequi), "to steal a specific thing"]
    7. #Ø-Ø(cua-lō-ni)Ø-Ø# = it is edible [< tla-(cuā), "to eat s.th."]
    8. #Ø-Ø(chīhua-lō-ni)Ø-Ø# = it is feasible/doable [< tla-(chīhua), "to make/do s.th."]

40E. 1. The city is walled.
    2. The things are many.
    3. We old men are alone.
    4. Their dogs are big.
    5. They are lazy. They are lazy.
    6. The storyteller is pleasing of words/speech.
    7. The farmer is strong.
    8. The smoke is foul smelling.
    9. The hair of some is black.
    10. Their skirts are not long.
    11. Three are poor.
    12. The sandals of the men are expensive.
    13. *My* face is bloody.
    14. The scorpion is diverse; i.e., Scorpions are of various kinds.
    15. His beard is long.

16. This is not potable.
17. The fruit of the mesquite is green bean–like.
18. The commander of the troops is worthy of being respected.
19. Its wings are dull yellow [i.e., "smoke yellow"].
20. The blankets with embroidery are marvelous.

EXERCISE 41

41A. 1. *a.* #∅-∅(cham-a-c)tli-∅# = it is thick
  b. #∅-∅(cham-a-c-cal-ti-∅)c-∅# = it is very thick
 2. *a.* #∅-∅(huitz)tli-∅# = it is sharp pointed [As nonadjectival NNC, "it is a thorn."]
  b. #∅-∅(huitz-tōn)tli-∅# = it is slightly sharp pointed
 3. *a.* #∅-∅(cōz)tli-∅# = it is yellow colored
  b. #∅-∅(cōz-pōl)∅-∅# = it is quite yellow
 4. *a.* #∅-∅(huap-a-c)tli-∅# = it is stiff
  b. #∅-∅(huap-a-c-pah-ti-∅)c-∅# = it is very stiff
 5. *a.* #∅-∅(hueh-huē-i-n)t-in# = they are big
  b. #∅-∅(hueh-huē-i-po-pōl)∅-∅# = they are quite big
 6. *a.* #∅-∅(ītz-ti-∅)c-∅# = it is cold
  b. #∅-∅(ītz-ti-∅-cā-pah-ti-∅)c-∅# = it is frigid
 7. *a.* #∅-∅(tapayol-ti-∅)c-∅# = it is ball-like
  b. #∅-∅(tapayol-ti-∅-cā-tōn)tli-∅# = it is slightly ball-like
 8. *a.* #∅-∅(tlahpal-ti-∅)c-∅# = it is firm/strong
  b. ∅-∅(tlahpal-ti-∅-cā-pōl)∅-∅# = it is quite firm/strong

41B. 1. *a.* #n-∅(iztā-∅)c-∅# = I am white
  b. #ni-∅(cuā-iztā-∅)c-∅# = I am white at the head, i.e., I am white-headed
 2. *a.* #∅-∅(tlahu-ēl-ī-l-ō-∅)c-∅# = he is evil/perverse/vicious
  b. #∅-∅(tēn-tlahu-ēl-ī-lō-∅)c-∅# = he is evil at the lips, i.e., he is evil tongued
 3. *a.* #∅-∅(huitz-ti-∅)c-∅# = it is pointed
  b. #∅-∅(tzīn-huitz-ti-∅)c-∅# = it is pointed at the base
 4. *a.* #ti-∅(chic-ā-hua-∅)c-∅# = you are strong
  b. #ti-∅(yōl-lo-h-chic-ā-hua-∅)c-∅# = you are strong at the heart, i.e., you are strong hearted
 5. *a.* #ti-∅(tlahu-ēl-ī-lō-∅)qu-eh# = we are evil
  b. #ti-∅(yāō-tlahu-ēl-ī-lō-∅)qu-eh# = we are evil in war; we are war hellions [Here *(yāō)-tl-*, which normally is translated as "enemy," is standing for *(yāō-yō)-tl-*, "war."]
 6. *a.* #n-∅(izta-l)li-∅# = I am white
  b. #ni-∅(cuā-izta-l)li-∅# = I am white at the head, i.e., I am white-headed
 7. *a.* #∅-∅(huā-c)tli-∅# = it is dry
  b. #∅-∅(tlāl-huā-c)tli-∅# = it (i.e., land) is dry in the form of land, i.e., it is dry land, it is an island
 8. *a.* #∅-∅(huā-c-∅)qui-∅# = he/she/it is dry
  b. #∅-∅(cuauh-huā-c-∅)qui-∅# = he/she is dry like a piece of wood, i.e., he/she is emaciated

Key to the Exercises 167

    9. *a.* #∅-∅(huī-ya-∅)c-∅# = he is long
        b. #∅-∅(tlāca-huī-ya-∅)c-∅# = he is long in the form of a man, i.e., he is a tall man
  10. *a.* #∅-∅(ihyā-∅)c-∅# = it is foul smelling
       b. #∅-∅(xoqu-ihyā-∅)c-∅# = it is foul smelling like a stew pot [< (xoc)-tli-, "pot, stew pot"]
  11. *a.* #∅-∅(til-ā-hua-∅)c-∅# = it is thick
       b. #∅-∅(ihhui-til-ā-hua-∅)c-∅# = it is thick at the feathers, i.e., it is thickly feathered
  12. *a.* #∅-∅(til-ā-hua-∅)c-∅# = it is thick
       b. #∅-∅(ihhui-yō-til-ā-hua-∅)c-∅# = it is thick at the plumage, i.e., it is thickly plumaged
  13. *a.* #∅-∅(olol-ti-∅)c-∅# = it is round/ball shaped
       b. #∅-∅(cuitla-olol-ti-∅)c-∅# = it is round at the back, i.e., it is round backed
  14. *a.* #an-∅(catz-a-c)t-in# = you (pl) are black
       b. #an-∅(teō-catz-a-c)t-in# = you (pl) are black in the form of gods, i.e., you (pl) are sacredly black
  15. *a.* #∅-∅(te-con-ti-∅)c-∅# = it is pot shaped
       b. #∅-∅(cuā-te-con-ti-∅)c-∅# =it is pot shaped at the head; i.e., it is pot headed
  16. *a.* #∅-∅(pitz-a-c-to-tōn)t-in = they (nonanimate) are quite slender [See § 32.7.]
       b. #∅-∅(mā-pitz-a-c-to-tōn)t-in# = they (i.e., branches) are quite slender as branches go; i.e., they are quite slender branches [< (māi)-tl-, "hand, arm"; *by extension*, "branch."]

41C. 1. *a.* #∅-∅(tla-zo-h)tli-∅# = it is precious/expensive
       b. #∅-∅(tla-zo-h-cuēi)tl-∅# = it is a precious/expensive skirt
    2. *a.* #∅-∅(te-poz)tli-∅# = it is (hard) metal
       b. #∅-∅+ī-n(te-poz-tōpīl)∅-∅# = they are their iron staffs
    3. *a.* #∅-∅(tlahu-ēl-ī-lō-∅)c-∅# = he is evil
       b. #∅-∅(tlahu-ēl-ī-lō-∅-cā-tla-ht-ō-l)li-∅# = it is a word/speech of an evil one; i.e., it is an evil word/speech
    4. *a.* #∅-∅(ich)tli-∅# = it is maguey fiber
       b. #∅-∅+ī-m(ich-tilmah)∅-∅# = they are their maguey-fiber blankets/cloaks/capes
    5. *a.* #∅-∅(coco-x-∅)qui-∅# = she is sick
       b. #∅-∅+m-o(coco-x-∅-cā-nān)∅-∅# = she is your sick mother
    6. *a.* #∅-∅(mauh-∅)qui-∅# = he is fearful/afraid
       b. #∅-∅(mauh-∅-cā-mic-∅)qui-∅# = he is one who has fainted with fear

41D. 1. His friend is not stouthearted.
    2. Their cotton breechcloths go along being; i.e., They have their cotton breechcloths with them.
    3. The blanket is richly finished.
    4. Their dogs are nastily large.
    5. His important property comes forth.
    6. The youth is evil livered; i.e., The youth is evil hearted.
    7. They used to give them precious/expensive blankets.

8. They came in order to come out onto dry land; i.e., They came in order to land. [The embed is *(tlāl-huā-c-Ø)-qui-*, "dry land."]
9. I am already the owner of white at the head; i.e., I am already white-headed.
10. The one summoned is sweet of speech; i.e., pleasant speaking.

EXERCISE 42

42A. 1. *a.* Their skirts are long.
    b. They are their skirts that are long. They are their long skirts.
2. *a.* The bread is honeyed.
    b. It is bread that is honeyed. It is honeyed bread.
3. *a.* The smoke is foul smelling.
    b. It is smoke that is foul smelling. It is foul-smelling smoke.
4. *a.* The breeze is cold.
    b. It is a breeze that is cold. It is a cold breeze.
5. *a.* The mat is good./The mats are good.
    b. It is a mat that is good./They are mats that are good. It is a good mat./They are good mats.
6. *a.* The water is good.
    b. It is water that is good. It is good water.
7. *a.* You who are a farmer are strong.
    b. You are a farmer who is strong. You are a strong farmer.
8. *a.* My slaves are lazy.
    b. They are my slaves who are lazy. They are my lazy slaves.

42B. 1. *a.* You, who are prudent, are a lord.
    b. You are a person/lord who is prudent. You are a prudent person/lord.
2. *a.* What we have set is a fire.
    b. It is a fire that we have set.
3. *a.* I, who am good, am your grandson.
    b. I am your grandson who is good. I am your good grandson.
4. *a.* That which they made is a house.
    b. It is a/the house that they made. It is a/the house made by them.
5. *a.* That which is dry is land.
    b. It is land that is dry. It is dry land.
6. *a.* The women are slaves.
    b. They are slaves who are women. They are female slaves.

42C. 1. *a.* The steward who is big/important went. The big/important steward went.
    b. The big/important steward went.
2. *a.* Bread that is white is needed. White bread is needed.
    b. White bread is needed.
3. *a.* A sickness that is big occurred. A big sickness occurred. [*Lit.*, "it made itself."]
    b. A big sickness occurred.
4. *a.* He is digging noble metal that is yellow. He is digging yellow noble metal; i.e., He is digging gold.

Key to the Exercises

        b. He is digging yellow noble metal; i.e., He is digging gold.
    5. *a.* He is selling precious/expensive blankets.
        b. He is selling precious/expensive blankets.

42D. 1. The food that they used to eat used to be just made communally. [*lit.*, "it used to make itself as one."]
    2. He is selling various kinds of feathers.
    3. The snake sees the seated plebeians.
    4. Its water is cold water.
    5. They were acquainted with the stars located there.
    6. Traces of the ones who built it are indeed also many.
    7. He took along a few other stewards.
    8. They listen to the words that the old men go along saying.
    9. The peyote that grows there is <u>their</u> discovery.
    10. The tree that was standing (there) was thick.
    11. They showed them the necklace(s) that they brought. [*lit.*, "they fetched it/them hither."]
    12. The dugouts/boats that they navigated into there [*lit.*, "they caused them to enter thither."] were two in number.
    13. Every person heard it.
    14. They are giving them all the things that they carried.

42E. *Xāyacatl*, "it is a face," is an adjunct clause adjectivally modifying the principal clause *tlachihchīhualli*, "it is a counterfeit/spurious thing."

    Xāyacatlachihchīhualli = "it is a counterfeit thing in the form of a face." *Tlachihchīhualli xāyacatl* = "it is a counterfeit thing that is a face."

    The same modifier-to-head relationship holds in the concatenate structure as in the compound nounstem.

EXERCISE 43

43A. 1. *a.* Adjr they-are-women, indeed they-are-expensive/precious-things adjr they-are-blouses adjr they-made them.
        b. The blouses that the women made were expensive/precious.
    2. *a.* Indeed he-is-the-one adjr he-set-it-down adjr it-is-the-funny-anecdote/tale.
        b. He is indeed the one who composed the funny anecdote/tale.
    3. *a.* They-caused-themselves-to-be-afraid adjr they-are-the-shamans adjr they-killed-him adjr he-is-the-merchant.
        b. The shamans who killed the merchant were frightened.
    4. *a.* They-are-lazy adjr they-are-commoners adjr it-is-at-that-place they-are they-are-their-fields.
        b. The commoners whose fields are there are lazy.
    5. *a.* Adjr they-are-tamales he-sells-them, they-are-the-ones adjr they-are-turkey-egg-tamales.
        b. The tamales that he sells are those that are turkey-egg tamales.
    6. *a.* They-took-it adjr it-is-everything adjr they-saw-it.
        b. They took everything that they saw.

43B. 1. *a.* She-is-one-in-number she-fetched-water she-is-a-woman adjr she-saw-them.
   b. It was a woman fetching water who saw them. [This can also be understood as a structure of supplementation: "The one who saw them was a woman who was fetching water."]
2. *a.* Adjr it-was-this-one it-was-equipment adjr it-needed-itself they-used-to-guard-it adjr they-were nobles.
   b. The nobles used to guard this equipment that was needed; i.e., The nobles used to guard this necessary equipment.
3. *a.* He-sells-them adjr they-are-various-kinds they-are-feathers adjr they-are-precious-ones.
   b. He sells various kinds of feathers that are precious; i.e., He sells various kinds of precious feathers.
4. *a.* They-seized-him-thither he-was-one-in-number he-was-a-big-one he-was-a-warrior adjr he-was-a-strong-one.
   b. They went and captured a big warrior who was strong; i.e., They went and captured a big, strong warrior.
5. *a.* She-guards-it it-is-one-in-number it-is-a-mirror adjr it-is-a-round-one.
   b. She keeps/has a mirror that is round. ~ She keeps/has a round mirror.

43C. 1. *a.* I-give-it-to-you(sg) it-is-everything adjr it-is-wealth. It-is-everything I-give-it-to-you adjr it-is-wealth.
   b. I am giving you everything that is wealth. ~ I am giving you every wealth.
2. *a.* It-owned-abundant-breath adjr it-was-pulque adjr they-used-to-drink-it. Adjr it-was-pulque it-owned-abundant-breath adjr they-used-to-drink-it.
   b. The pulque that they used to drink was very strong.
3. *a.* He-accompanied-them-hither they-were-many they-were-Spaniards. They-were-many he-accompanied-them-hither they-were-Spaniards.
   b. He brought many Spaniards.
4. *a.* It-is-there it-is-everything adjr it-is-agricultural-produce. It-is-everything it-is-there adjr it-is-agricultural-produce.
   b. Everything that is agricultural produce is there; i.e., All agricultural produce is there.
5. *a.* They-died they-were-many adjr they-were-warriors. They-were-many they-died adjr they-were-warriors.
   b. Many warriors died.
6. *a.* They-caused-themselves-to-be-afraid they-were-all adjr they-were-our-enemies. They-were-all they-caused-themselves-to-be-afraid adjr they-were-our-enemies.
   b. All who were our enemies were frightened. I.e., All our enemies were frightened.
7. *a.* They-are-the-ones it-was-their-discovery it-is-everything adjr it-is-at-the-present-time it-lives. It-is-everything they-are-the-ones it-was-their-discovery adjr it-is-at-the-present-time it-lives.
   b. Everything that now exists was <u>their</u> discovery.
8. *a.* They-took-it-from-them it-was-all adjr it-was-their-war-equipment. It-was-all they-took-it-from-them adjr it-was-their-war-equipment.

Key to the Exercises 171

        b. They took from them everything that was their war equipment; i.e., They took all their weapons from them.

    9. *a.* He-burns-it adjr it-is-paper it-is-a-thing-splattered-with-rubber. Adjr it-is-paper he-burns-it it-is-a-thing-splattered-with-rubber.

       b. He is burning the paper that is splattered with (liquid) rubber; i.e., He is burning the paper splattered with (liquid) rubber.

  10. *a.* Indeed it-is-a-thing-that-has-become-thin adjr it-is-a-twig adjr you-guard-it. Adjr it-is-a-twig indeed it-is-a-thing-that-has-become-thin adjr you-guard-it.

      b. The twig you have is thin. The twigs you have are thin.

43D. 1. *a.* I-gave-it-to-him adjr it-is-what adjr he-wanted-it.
      b. I gave him what he wanted.

   2. *a.* Adjr he-is-who adjr he-wants-to-leave it-is-in-that-place they-stab-and-stab-him.

     b. They there repeatedly stab the one who wants to leave; i.e., They there repeatedly stab anyone who tries to leave.

   3. *a.* I-saw-him adjr he-is-who adjr he-stole-it.
     b. I saw the one who stole it.

   4. *a.* Adjr it-is-what adjr you-said-it, indeed it-is-the-truth.
     b. What you said is indeed true.

   5. *a.* He-saw-it adjr it-is-what adjr we-will-do-it.
     b. He saw what we would do.

   6. *a.* Perchance he-knows-it adjr it-is-what adjr he-studies-it.
     b. Does he learn what he studies?

43E. 1. One of us will go in order to give them the tribute.
    2. Every fruit is there.
    3. All these mushrooms are inedible raw.
    4. He who eats a lot (of it) sees many frightening things.
    5. All the different kinds of cotton are there.
    6. No longer did anyone who was a commoner leave; i.e., No longer did any commoner leave.
    7. He is acquainted with all the various kinds of precious stones.
    8. Every old person got into motion/began to move.
    9. He is selling good chili peppers.
  10. He is acquainted with the medicines that are deadly. ~ He is acquainted with deadly medicines.
  11. The gold that they carried was a large amount.
  12. The salutations that they carried, were they many? I.e., Were the salutations that they carried many?
  13. Perhaps one of our friends is already coming.
  14. One of my older brothers [~ An older brother of mine] and I had a fight. [*Lit.,* "we killed one another," a hyperbolic way of saying "we tried to kill one another," i.e., "we fought."]
  15. I am not pleased with a single one of you. None of you satisfy me.

EXERCISE 44

44A.
1. #∅-∅(cen-ca-h)∅+☐-∅# = very [adverbialized VNC]
2. ah#∅-∅(mō)☐-∅# = not at all; no [a negativized 2nd-degree adverbialized NNC]
3. #∅-∅(necoc)☐-∅# = at/to/from both sides [2nd-degree adverbialized NNC]
4. ye = already [a particle]
5. ah#∅-∅(huel)☐-∅# = unsuccessfully, badly [negativized 2nd-degree adverbialized NNC]
6. #∅-∅(mōztla)☐-∅# = tomorrow [2nd-degree adverbialized NNC]
7. #∅-∅(tlaōco-x-∅-cā)☐-∅# = sadly [2nd-degree adverbialized NNC]
8. #∅-∅(tlacu-ā-uh)☐-∅# = strongly; especially [2nd-degree adverbialized NNC]
9. #∅-∅ (yēhua)∅+∅-∅# = a little while [adverbialized VNC]
10. #∅-∅(iz)∅+☐-∅# = here, to/from/through here [adverbialized VNC]
11. oc #∅-∅(nohmah)∅+☐-∅# = still [particle plus adverbialized VNC]
12. #∅-∅(tlahcah)☐-∅# = during the day, in the daytime [2nd-degree adverbialized NNC]
13. #∅-∅(nēn)☐-∅# = in vain, uselessly, worthlessly [2nd-degree adverbialized NNC]
14. #∅-∅(nel)☐-∅# = in truth, truly, really [2nd-degree adverbialized NNC]
15. #∅-∅(cem-ilhui)tl-∅# = for/during one day [1st-degree adverbialized NNC]
16. #∅-∅+ī-∅(chān)∅-∅# = at/to/from his/her home [1st-degree adverbialized NNC]
17. #∅-∅(cuēl)☐-∅# = briefly, quickly; already [2nd-degree adverbialized NNC]
18. #∅-∅(cem-ihca)∅+c-∅# = eternally, forever [adverbialized VNC]
19. #∅-∅(cen-yohua-l)☐-∅# = for/during one night [2nd-degree adverbialized NNC]
20. #∅-∅(chico)☐-∅# = to one side; irregularly, badly [2nd-degree adverbialized NNC]
21. #∅-∅(tlāca-ē-hu-a)tl-∅# = in a human skin [1st-degree adverbialized NNC]
22. #∅-∅(tla-mel-ā-uh-∅-cā)☐-∅# = in a straight manner [2nd-degree adverbialized NNC]
23. #∅-∅(iuh)∅+☐-∅# = thus, in this way [adverbialized VNC]
24. #∅-∅(tēl-pōch-cal)li-∅# = into a young men's house [1st-degree adverbialized NNC]

44B.
1. I am unable to carry it on my back.
2. They fall on both sides.
3. Thus is my life.
4. It customarily appears during the day.
5. It truly needs itself; i.e., It is truly needed.
6. This path/road goes to their home.
7. Shall I live forever?
8. They used to cause themselves to enter into the human skins; i.e., They used to put on the human skins.
9. Let him come quickly.
10. The youths place themselves apart.
11. It is lying crosswise.
12. They enrolled him [*lit.*, "they caused him to enter"] in the young men's house.
13. Then Quetzalcoatl said, "What is this? It is very good. It has destroyed the sickness. Where did the discomfort go? I am no longer feeling sick."

Key to the Exercises 173

14. May I soon lie resting my body!
15. The ones who died first were captives.
16. It lies watching all night.

EXERCISE 45

45A. 1. #∅-∅+ī-∅(tloc)∅-∅# = it is its/his/her vicinity; in its/his/her vicinity, near it/him/her, at its/his/her side, beside it/him/her
2. #∅-∅+ī-m(pal)∅-∅# = it is their grace; by their grace, thanks to them
3. #∅-∅+m-o(huān)∅-∅# = it is your (sg) company; in your (sg) company, with you (sg)
4. #∅-∅+n-o(tloc)∅-∅# = it is my vicinity; in my vicinity, near me, at my side, beside me
5. #∅-∅+t-o(pal)∅-∅# = it is our grace; by our grace, thanks to us
6. #∅-∅+ī-n(huān)∅-∅# = it is their company; in their company, with them

45B. 1. They do not burn with the ruler/king.
2. They are rarely/seldom at our side.
3. What is it that we shall do in order for us to be able to get out? [Usually translated: "What shall we do. . . ."]
4. If only I had lived well!
5. We have come (in order) to know ourselves/one another only by the grace of our Lord.
6. Here is another. [*Lit.*, "It is indeed another one."] Drink it down. The medicine is indeed good; by means of it your flesh [i.e., your body] will become strong.
7. The one who is drowned goes [i.e., disappears] forever.
8. It is about one fathom long.
9. Live well so that you may die well.
10. How big it is!
11. For this reason are they called "deadman-fly": it is said that their lot/destiny is our dead ones; i.e., They are called "deadman-flies," because it is said that their lot/destiny is our dead.
12. I shall eat with them.
13. She goes in order to give them to her kinsman/kinswoman; thereby she makes evident/shows self-esteem/mutual affection.
14. The ones they used to take/pick were not kinsmen.
15. What a lot of noise your fire makes! ~ How noisy your fire is!
16. Your mother, along with your elder sister, prepared (H) it for you. [Notice that the VNC has a singular subject pronoun. The adverbial unit *īhuān in mohuēltīuh* is not part of the supplementary subject; i.e., *īhuān* does NOT mean "and." There is no structure of conjunction here.]

EXERCISE 46

46A. 1. #∅-∅(tē-pah-pāqui-l-tih-∅-cā-n)☐-∅# = it is a place where people are made happy [< (tē-pah-pāqui-l-tih-∅)-qui- > (tē-pah-pāqui-l-tih-∅-cā)-tl-, "one that makes people happy"]

2. #∅-∅(tōl-lo-h-∅-cā-n)☐-∅# = it is a place characterized by abundant rushes [< (tōl-lo-h-∅)-☐- > (tōl-lo-h-∅-cā)-tl-, "one that owns abundant rushes"]
3. #∅-∅(cac-namaca-∅-cā-n)☐-∅# = it is a place where one sells sandals/shoes; it is a sandal/shoe shop [< (cac-namaca-∅)-c-> (cac-namaca-∅-cā)-tl-, "one who sells sandals/shoes"]
4. #∅-∅(tē-chōc-tih-∅-cā-n)☐-∅# = it is a place of lamentation [< (tē-chōc-tih-∅)-☐- > (tē-chōc-tih-∅-cā)-tl-, "a thing that makes people cry"]
5. #∅-∅(tla-xca-l-chīuh-∅-cā-n)☐-∅# = it is a place where one makes tortillas/bread [< (tla-xca-l-chīuh-∅)-qui- > (tla-xca-l-chīuh-∅-cā)-tl-, "one who makes tortillas/bread"]
6. #∅-∅(tē-cuil-tōn-o-h-∅-cā-n)☐-∅# = it is a place of recreation [< (tē-cuil-tōn-o-h-∅)-☐- > (tē-cuil-tōn-o-h-∅-cā)-tl-, "a thing that enriches people"]

46B. *Īonocān* has a stem formed with an active-action nounstem as embed, while the locative NNCs in 46A have a stem formed with a preterit-agentive nounstem as embed. In both formations the matrix nounstem is *(-n)-tli-*.

46C.
1. #∅-∅+ī-∅(ne-ā-l-ti-ā-yā-n)∅-∅# = it is his bathing place; *also*, in his bathing place
2. #∅-∅(cal-ac-o-hua-yā-n)☐-∅# = it is a place where people customarily enter; i.e., it is an entrance; *also*, in the entrance
3. #∅-∅+ī-∅(quīza-yā-n)∅-∅# = it is his leaving place, it is the place where he leaves; *also*, in his leaving place
4. #∅-∅(tla-yohua-yā-n)☐-∅# = it is a place where things in general become night; i.e., it is a place of darkness, it is a dark place; *also*, in a place of darkness
5. #∅-∅(panō-hua-yā-n)☐-∅# = it is a place where people customarily cross a stream/river; i.e., it is a bridge; *also*, at a bridge
6. #∅-∅(tla-xca-l-namac-ō-yā-n)☐-∅# = it is a place where tortillas are customarily sold/where bread is customarily sold; *also*, at a tortilla/bread shop
7. #∅-∅(tla-piya-lō-yā-n)☐-∅# = it is a place where people customarily guard things; *also*, in a place where people guard/keep things
8. #∅-∅+m-o(ye-yā-n)∅-∅# = it is your (sg) seat; *also*, in your seat

46D.
1. #∅-∅(noh-pal-lah)☐-∅# = it is a place of abundant prickly-pear cacti ~ in a place of abundant prickly-pear cacti
2. #∅-∅(oh-ōztō-tlah)☐-∅# = it is a place of abundant caves ~ in a place of abundant caves
3. #∅-∅(cuauh-yohua-∅-cā-tlah)☐-∅# = it is a place of abundant dark due to trees, i.e., it is a dark forest ~ in a dark forest [< (cuauh-yohua-∅)-c- > (cuauh-yohua-∅-cā)-tl-, "a thing that has become dark due to trees"]
4. #∅-∅(cah-cal-lah)☐-∅# = it is a place of abundant houses of various shapes and sizes; i.e., it is a settlement ~ in a settlement
5. #∅-∅+n-☐(e-tlah)∅-∅# = it is my place of abundant beans; i.e., it is my bean patch ~ in my bean patch
6. #∅-∅(zoqui-tlah)☐-∅# = it is a place of abundant mud; i.e., it is a mudhole/quagmire/bog ~ in a mudhole/quagmire/bog

46E.
1. #∅-∅(ā-tla-comōl-co)☐-∅# = at/in a well [< (ā-tla-comōl)-li-, "a pit/hole with water"]
2. #∅-∅(quimil-co)☐-∅# = in a bundle

Key to the Exercises 175

    3. #∅-∅+ī-∅(quiy-ā-hua-tēn-yō-c)∅-∅# = at its (i.e., the house's) doorway sill, at its entry threshold [The *(-yō)-tl-* indicates integral possession.]
    4. #∅-∅(tiānqui-z-co)☐-∅# = in a/the market
    5. #∅-∅+ī-∅(xiqu-ipil-co)∅-∅# = in his bag/sack
    6. #∅-∅+n-☐(ohua-mīl-co)∅-∅# = in my green maize-stalk field
    7. #∅-∅+ī-m(īx-co)∅-∅# = on their faces
    8. #∅-∅(tlach-co)☐-∅# = at the place of the ball game; i.e., at the ball court
    9. #∅-∅+am-o(mā-c)∅-∅# = in your (pl) hands
   10. #∅-∅(ah-pil-ō-l-co)☐-∅# = in a/the pitcher [The embed *ah-* is the glottalized embed stem of *(ā)-tl-*, "water" (see § 14.2.8); the source verbstem is *(ah-pil-o-ā)*, "to cause water to hang," i.e., "to pour water."]

46F. 1. #∅-∅(tlacō-ch-cal-co-pa)☐-∅# = from/toward the arsenal [< (tlacō-ch-cal)-li-, "house for storing arrows"]
    2. #∅-∅(mā-cu-ī-l-pa)☐-∅# = on five occasions, five times
    3. #∅-∅(zaca-teuh)☐-∅# = strawlike
    4. #∅-∅+n-o(ce-ya-liz-co-pa)∅-∅# = from in my willingness, i.e., with my willingness, willingly
    5. #∅-∅(quiy-ā-hua-c-pa)☐-∅# = from out of a doorway
    6. #∅-∅(tla-xca-l-teuh)☐-∅# = tortillalike
    7. #∅-∅ (nāuh-pa)☐-∅# = on four occasions, four times
    8. #∅-∅(mā-tla-teuh)☐-∅# = netlike
    9. #∅-∅(mah-tlāc-pa)☐-∅# #∅-∅(om-ōme)☐-∅# = on twelve occasions, twelve times [Contrast *mahtlācpa ōme*, "twelve times two."]
   10. #∅-∅+ī-∅(mā-ōpōch-co-pa)∅-∅# = from within his left hand
   11. #∅-∅(ihhui-teuh)☐-∅# = featherlike
   12. #∅-∅(cax-tōl-pa)☐-∅# = on fifteen occasions, fifteen times

46G. 1. Do not be summoned twice. [I.e., Go the first time you are summoned.]
    2. They came out of the dark forest.
    3. It is becoming divided into four parts. It is divided into four parts.
    4. Its growing place is in the forest.
    5. The little animal made itself vertical hither headfirst; i.e., The little animal fell down headfirst (in my direction).
    6. Its home is in the crags. [*Lit.*, It is in the crags that its home is.]
    7. He sets it down on the fire there in the courtyard.
    8. He died in the interior of the desert region.
    9. No one will utter anything. It will be kept to yourselves. [*Lit.*, It is only in your stomachs.]
   10. Let guard be kept everywhere along the shore.
   11. It started out from there where the sun sets. [*Lit.*, from the sun's entering place.]
   12. It is indeed for a long time that we have much desired to look upon his face; i.e., For a long time we have greatly desired to see him.
   13. It is already the proper time for me to eat. [*Lit.*, It is already my eating's needed (appointed) time.]
   14. He is pouring a little water into a small bowl.

15. I looked toward the inside of the house.
16. Did you (sg) tie it firmly? [*Lit.*, like a rock.]
17. Their hearts go upward; i.e., Their hearts are gladdened.
18. Will they favor us? Will they be on our side? [*Lit.*, Will they rise to our side?]
19. They went in order to settle at a certain place in the plains.
20. Their personal/private place is indeed in their own town quarter place. [*Īncalpōllo* = it is their integrally owned *calpōlli*; it is their own *calpōlli*.]
21. I have come in order to arrive at my arriving place; i.e., I have reached my end.
22. It was the burial place of the rulers/kings.
23. Their god said to them, "It is still farther that we go." Immediately they went going to the west. [*Lit.*, "toward the sun's entering place."]
24. No longer can it be remembered (~ can one remember) how long they dwelled there.
25. For how long it was that they lived in the desert, no longer does anyone know.
26. The people who are near his house are gathering together; i.e., His neighbors are gathering together.
27. It lives there in damp places.
28. The forest is a place where trees sprout.
29. Where is my bracelet?—Is it near my eyes? [I.e., "Why do you think I know where it is? Do you see it before my eyes?" I.e., I have no idea where it is.]
30. Sit considering yourselves as parents for a moment.

46H. *The Deer* (Florentine Codex XI, 15)

The deer with antlers [*lit.*, the deer that is an antler owner] is a male. Its antlers are chalk-colored [*lit.*, it is chalk-colored at the antlers]; its antlers are tapering and branched [*lit.*, it is tapering-branched at the antlers]. When its antlers have become loose [*lit.*, lazy], it casts them off [*lit.*, it throws itself from the antlers]. It inserts its antlers in the crotch of a tree; then it tramples backwards; there it breaks its antlers like a stick. In this fashion (~ by this means) it goes causing them to come out young (again).

The deer without antlers [*lit.*, the deer that is not an antler owner] is a female.

EXERCISE 47

47A.
1. #∅-∅(tōl-tzālan)☐-∅# = among (the) rushes
2. #∅-∅+m-o(huīc-tzin-co)∅-∅# = toward you (H)
3. #∅-∅+am-o(tzālan)∅-∅# = among you (pl)
4. #∅-∅(xō-chi-tzālan)☐-∅# = among (the) flowers
5. #∅-∅(ā-tōy-a-huīc)☐-∅# = toward a/the river
6. #∅-∅+t-o(mah-pil-tzālan)∅-∅# = between our fingers, between the fingers of one of us, between the fingers

47B.
1. #∅-∅(cax-ti-ca)☐-∅# = by means of a bowl, with a bowl
2. #∅-∅+m-o(cpa-c)∅-∅# = on your head top, on top of your head
3. #∅-∅(teō-yō-ti-ca)☐-∅# = by means of spirituality, spiritually
4. #∅-∅(cuauh-ti-ca)☐-∅# = by means of a stick, with a stick
5. #∅-∅(ōztō-t-icpa-c)☐-∅# = above a/the cave
6. #∅-∅+n-o(ca)∅-∅# = by means of me, thanks to me

Key to the Exercises 177

47C. 1. #∅-∅+n-o(tech-pa)∅-∅# = about me, with regard to me
2. #∅-∅+m-o(tlan)∅-∅# = at your side, beside you
3. #∅-∅+ī-∅(cal-tech-yo)∅-∅# = it is its (i.e., a house's) house facing/wall facing [integral possession]
4. #∅-∅+t-o(pan)∅-∅# = above us, over us, down on us
5. #∅-∅+m-☐(īx-tlan)∅-∅# = beneath your eyes, i.e., in your presence
6. #∅-∅+n-o(cxi-ti-tlan)∅-∅# = at/between my feet
7. #∅-∅+tē(ne-pan-tlah)∅-∅# = in the midst of people
8. #∅-∅(te-pān-ti-tech)☐-∅# = in contact with/on a/the wall
9. #∅-∅(tle-ti-tlan)☐-∅# = on/near/next to/in a/the fire
10. #∅-∅+t-o(cama-pan)∅-∅# = on/in our mouth, on/in the mouth of one of us

47D. 1. #∅-∅(tepē-pan-ca)tl-∅# = it is a thing associated with a mountain area
2. #∅-∅(cal-lah-ca)tl-∅# = it is a person/thing associated with a village
3. #∅-∅(ā-tez-ca-tēn-☐-ca)tl-∅# = he/she is a person associated with a place on the shore of a lake [< (ā-tez-ca-tēn-co)-☐-, "a place on the shore of a lake."]
4. #∅-∅(zoqui-tlah-ca)tl-∅# = it is a thing associated with a bog
5. #∅-∅(tlāl-cāhua-l-pan-ca)tl-∅# = it is a thing associated with abandoned land
6. #∅-∅(tōna-l-☐-ca)tl-∅# = it is a thing associated with the dry season [< (tōna-l-co)-☐-, "at/in the time of heat; i.e., in the dry season"]

47E. 1. #∅-∅(tepē-pan-ca-yō)tl-∅# = it is a thing pertaining to/characteristic of a thing associated with a mountain area
2. #∅-∅(tiānqui-z-☐-ca-yō)tl-∅# = it is a thing pertaining to/characteristic of a thing associated with a marketplace [< (tiānqui-z-co)-☐-, "a marketplace"]
3. #∅-∅(tōna-l-☐-ca-yō)tl-∅# = it is a thing pertaining to/characteristic of a thing associated with the dry season
4. #∅-∅(tepē-tlah-ca-yō)tl-∅# = it is a thing pertaining to/characteristic of a thing associated with a mountainous area/a mountain chain
5. #∅-∅(ōztō-☐-ca-yō)tl-∅# = it is a thing pertaining to/characteristic of a thing associated with in a cave/mine [< (ōztō-c)-☐-, "in a cave/mine"]
6. #∅-∅(∅-∅-tlāl-li-∅+∅-∅-ī-∅-yōl-lo-h-☐-ca-yō)tl-∅# = it is a thing pertaining to/characteristic of a thing associated with a land's center/the center of a land [< (∅-∅-tlāl-li-∅+∅-∅-ī-∅-yōl-lo-h-co)-☐-, "in the land's heart," i.e., "in the land's center"]

47F. 1. The stars are very high.
2. It begins to call out first; then the other kinds of birds that live near the water answer it.
3. It grows everywhere in the mountains. [*Lit.*, "it makes itself."]
4. They threw themselves (thither) against their enemies. [The directional prefix *on*- shows that the speaker sides with the attackers against the enemies.]
5. There in front of people he threw off his breechcloth.
6. Where night comes upon them, there they seek a cave/caves. [*Lit.*, In a/the place that it goes becoming night upon them, ...]
7. He will fall down from a roof terrace.
8. It snowed upon all of them.
9. They shoot darts (at things) with a throwing slat.

10. I threw at him with a rock. I threw at him with rocks.
11. The warriors press themselves against the wall.
12. They went to arrive at their boat(s); i.e., They reached their boat(s).
13. He looked a second time at the head top of the bird.
14. Let our lords arrive (H) in the land.
15. It is on the seashore beneath the sand that it hatches.
16. He thrashed him with a stick.
17. They brought him/her before the ruler.
18. It belongs to our town quarter/barrio.
19. Fifty-two years arrive thither (i.e., pass).
20. It stood arriving right in contact with the heart of the sky. It reached the very center of the sky.
21. In the presence of all of these, Huitzilopochtli (i.e., a sacrificial victim representing him) used to die.
22. The turkey hen makes its young enter under its wings.
23. ... as soon will become evident below in the proper place. [*Lit.*, in the face of things.]
24. The captives who will cast themselves into the fire also go along dancing.
25. How is it in truth? Indeed, no longer is there anything by means of medicine; i.e., What can be done? [I.e., it is hopeless.] There is nothing that can serve as its remedy.
26. It is underground in a burrow that it bears its young.
27. The cacatl's name is taken [*lit.*, it is a taken thing] from its croak [*lit.*, it is its speech]. Its croak is unending [*lit.*, it customarily does not end]; it says "cacaca."
28. He quickly entered among the young maize plants.
29. They infected us. [*Lit.*, They left their sickness on us.]
30. Already *I* know what it is that I shall do to you.

47G. *The Tree Squirrel* (Florentine Codex XI, 10)

A tree squirrel is the one that is a forest-dwelling squirrel [*lit.*, a squirrel that lives in a forest]. It is in the treetops that it eats. It is always only in trees that it lives, and therefore it is called "tree squirrel." It eats all pinecones. It eats the tips of new growth of trees. Also it eats tree worms. It goes around continually barking the trees; there it captures the tree worms. It whistles shrilly [*lit.*, it whistles as if with its hands].

EXERCISE 48

48A. 1. #∅-∅(Ā-ca-tzin-ti-tlan)☐-∅# = In the Vicinity of Small Reeds
2. #∅-∅(Ā-mal-ī-n-a-l-pan)☐-∅# = In the Area of Twisted Water [< (ā-mal-ī-n-a-l)-li-, "a twisted thing in the form of water"]
3. #∅-∅(Necoqu-īx-eh-∅-cā-n)☐-∅# = At the Place of the Scandalmongers/Talebearers [< necoc īxehqueh, "they are owners of two-sided faces, i.e., they are scandalmongers/talebearers"]
4. #∅-∅(Yohua-l-lān)☐-∅# = At the Place in the Vicinity of Night
5. #∅-∅(Te-tamazol-co)☐-∅# = At the Place of the Stone Toad
6. #∅-∅(∅-∅-Ā-tl-∅+∅-∅-Ī-∅-chol-o-ā-yā-n)☐-∅# = At the Water's Leaping Place, i.e., At the Falls

Key to the Exercises 179

      7. #∅-∅(Tla-ō-l-lā-n-tōn-co)☐-∅# = At the Place of Little Tlaollan [< (Tla-ō-l-lā-n)-☐-, "At the Place Beside Shelled Maize"]
      8. #∅-∅(Tecpa-yo-h-∅-cā-n)☐-∅# = At the Place of the Owners of Abundant Flint
      9. #∅-∅(Eh-ca-tepē-c)☐-∅# = At the Place on Breeze Hill/Mountain
   10. #∅-∅(Pān-ti-tlan)☐-∅# = In the Place Near Flags/Banners
   11. #∅-∅(Ā-cōl-nāhua-c)☐-∅# = At the Place in Hearing Distance of the Water Bend
   12. #∅-∅(Chīmal-huah-∅-cā-n)☐-∅# = At the Place of Shield Owners

48B. 1. #∅-∅(Ā-yaca-c)☐-∅# #∅-∅(cal-∅)qu-eh# = they are dwellers in Ayacac [< Āyacac, "At the Place of the Point of Water"]
    2. #∅-∅(Itz-cuin-cuitla-pil-☐-ca)tl-∅# = he/she is a dweller in Itzcuincuitlapilco [< (Itz-cuin-cuitla-pil-co)-☐-, "At the Place of the Dog Tail(s)"]
    3. #n-∅(Ā-cal-huah-∅)☐-∅# = I am a dweller in Acalhuahcan [< (Ā-cal-huah-∅-cā-n)-☐-, "at the Place of the Owners of Dugout Canoes"]
    4. #ti-∅(Tō-ch-pan-ē-ca)∅-h# = we are dwellers in Tochpan [< (Tō-ch-pan)-☐-, "In the Area of Rabbits"]
    5. #∅-∅(Ā-māx-tē-☐-ca)tl-∅# = he/she is a dweller in Amaxtlan [< (Ā-māx-tlā-n)-☐-, "In the Vicinity of the Water Bifurcation"]
    6. #∅-∅(Nōch-tlā-n)☐-∅# #∅-∅(tlāca)∅-h# = they are dwellers in Nochtlan [< (Nōch-tlā-n)-☐-, "the Vicinity of Prickly Pear Fruit."]
    7. #∅-∅(Tla-til-ō-l-☐-ca)tl-∅# = he/she is a dweller in Tlatilolco [< (Tla-til-ō-l-co)-☐-, "At the Place of the Mounded Thing."]
    8. #ti-∅(Tla-pa-l-tē-☐-ca)tl-∅# = you are a dweller in Tlapallan [< (Tla-pa-l-lā-n)-☐-, "the Vicinity of Color/Paint/Dye"]
    9. #∅-∅(∅-∅-Tōna-∅-ti-uh-∅-∅-∅+∅-∅-Ī-∅-īx-co)☐-∅# #∅-∅(tlāca)tl-∅# = he/she is a dweller in Tonatiuh-Iixco [< (∅-∅-Tōna-∅-ti-uh-∅-∅-∅+∅-∅-Ī-∅-īx-co)-☐-, "In the Place of the Sun's Face"]
   10. #an-∅(Chol-ō-l-tē-☐-ca)∅-h# = you are dwellers in Cholollan [< (Chol-ō-l-lā-n)-☐-, "At the Place in the Vicinity of the Refugees"]

48C. 1. #∅-∅(Xīlō-tepē-☐-ca-yō)tl-∅# = it is what is characteristic of the people of Xilotepec [< (Xīlō-tepē-c)-☐-, "At the Place on Tender-Maize-Ear Mountain"]
    2. #∅-∅(Huāuh-pan-ē-ca-yō)tl-∅# = it is what is characteristic of the people of Huauhpan [< (Huāuh-pan)-☐-, "At the Place Overlooking Amaranth." Also spelled *Huāppan*.]
    3. #∅-∅(Tziuh-cōā-☐-ca-yō)tl-∅# = it is what is characteristic of the people of Tziuhcoac [< (Tziuh-cōā-c)-☐-, "At the Place of Green (?) Snakes"]
    4. #∅-∅(Cuetlax-tē-☐-ca-yō)tl-∅# = it is what is characteristic of the people of Cuetlaxtlan [< (Cuetl-a-x-tlā-n)-☐-, "At the Place in the Vicinity of Leather"]
    5. #∅-∅(Ā-zta-cal-☐-ca-yō)tl-∅# = it is what is characteristic of the people of Aztacalco [< (Ā-zta-cal-co)-☐-, "the Place of the Egret House."]
    6. #∅-∅(Ocuil-tē-☐-ca-yō)tl-∅# = it is what is characteristic of the people of Ocuillan [< (Ocuil-lā-n)-☐-, "At the Place in the Vicinity of Worms"]

48D. 1. He came in order to arrive at a certain place (called) Cuauhtitlan [i.e., "At the Place Near Trees"].
    2. He is living there at Teotl-Iixco toward the coast [i.e., "At the Place of God's (i.e., the Sun's) Face"].

3. Immediately thereupon they ascend to the top of Snake Mountain.
4. They carried them thither to Tolpetlac [i.e., "At the Place of Rush Mats"].
5. It is the one that is the large lake that extends around us here in Mexihco.
6. They went in order to show it to the ruler/king at the monastery school at Tlillan [i.e., "At the Place in the Vicinity of Ink"].
7. They entered into Teohcalhuiyacan [i.e., "At the Place of the Long Temple"—literally, "At the Place of the Long-Thing in the Form of a Temple"].
8. In the year Eight House the Mexihcas moved to Nexticpac [i.e., "At the Place on Top of Ashes/Cinders"].
9. Here [i.e., At this time] people once again went to quarry stone at Malinalco.
10. They arrived at a certain place whose name was Calacohuayan [i.e., "At the Place Where Everyone Enters"].
11. The men whom he uses as messengers will take care of him [i.e., they will serve him] in just the same way in the Region of the Dead.
12. Here is that by means of which you will pass The Place Where the Wind Blows with Pieces of Obsidian. [This place is one of the hazards that a dead person must endure in the underworld.]

48E.
1. The people of Tliliuhqui-Tepec came in order to mingle/mix there with the people of Teohcalhuiyacan.
2. The Toltecs are also said to be Chichimecs.
3. These somewhat resemble the Cuextecs (i.e., the Huaxtecs).
4. It is said that the Toltecs considered no place distant.
5. The Matlatzincas knew themselves with regard to the sling; i.e., The Matlatzincas were experienced/skillful with the sling.
6. The Tepanec is indeed our enemy.
7. The Tlaxcaltecs and the Chololtecs formerly were clashing with one another.
8. All the Tlaxcaltecs' Otomis [i.e., elite warriors] died.
9. All of the Tenochcas became very frightened.
10. Here [i.e., At this time] the people in Xochitlan perished [i.e., Xochitlan was conquered].
11. Thereby the waterfolk [i.e., lake dwellers] know that it will rain a lot when dawn comes.
12. In his time it happened that the people of Azcapotzalco were conquered. [The singular is used in a generic sense.]

48F. *A Blood-Offering Ceremony* (Florentine Codex IX, 10)
When he has bled himself upon [the paper], immediately thereupon he comes out into the middle of the courtyard. First he performs the "throwing" ceremony [*lit.*, first he throws things (~ he makes throwing gestures)]. He throws his blood toward the sky. Next there toward the sun's exit, which used to be called "From within a Box" [i.e., East], it is four times that he throws his blood. Next there toward the sun's entrance, which used to be called "Toward the Abode for Women" [i.e., West], it is also four times that he throws his blood. Next there toward the land on his left hand, which used to be called "In the Area of the Land of the Huitznahuas" [i.e., South], it is also four times that he throws his blood. Next there toward the land on his right hand, which

Key to the Exercises 181

used to be called "On the Land of the Cloud Snakes" [i.e., North], it is also four times that he throws his blood. Only then did [i.e., does] he stop, when he bleeds [i.e., has bled] himself to the four quarters.

EXERCISE 49

49A.
1. The priest came (H) to my home.
2. He stood having entered into his disguise; i.e., He stood dressed in his disguise.
3. They are staring at one another mutually; i.e., They are staring at one another.
4. They came frightenedly out of their city.
5. I just drank; i.e., I didn't do anything other than drink.
6. The cannon falls at their command; i.e., The cannon discharges/fires at their command.
7. He ruled for only eighty days.
8. We lived like a song.
9. He entered the young men's house.
10. I spread my arms like a spoonbill (spreads its wings).
11. In their homeland it is very cold.
12. They entered someone's home.
13. He ruled for four years.
14. They used to cause them to enter into their insignia; i.e., They used to put their insignia on them.
15. We walked for a full day.

49B.
1. In truth he saw it.
2. Beware of just right off hankering after things on earth. [I.e., Beware of being quick to hanker. . . .]
3. It will be cold the day after tomorrow.
4. On the other side no boat came. [*Lit.*, "on still one side."]
5. There was an earthquake in the afternoon.
6. He has been sick for a very long time. [*Lit.*, He is sick. . . .]
7. In olden times he was the one who was their god.
8. They spoke strongly.
9. It can be drunk in all three ways. [*Lit.*, It will drink itself successfully. . . .]
10. Truly Our Lord has fulfilled (H) for us our desire for a child. [*Lit.*, . . . he has caused us to make for himself our impulse of wanting a child.]
11. Will you go back tomorrow?
12. He died suddenly.
13. He came to say it to me in secret.
14. Move that rock (~ those rocks) to the side.

49C.
1. All go to the sun's home.
2. All the time they go around with their heads bound up.
3. He entered the large young men's house.
4. They rested there for only two days.
5. It is needed every month.

49D.
1. It was every day that they walked hither.
2. It was every night that they closed it.

3. When will it be that their fasting will come to an end?
4. Indeed, it is under sand that its home is.
5. Where is it that this herb grows? [*Lit.*, it makes itself.]
6. It is from Chillohcan that it comes. [*Lit.*, It is from The Place of the Owners of Abundant Chili-Peppers. . . .]
7. In what manner is it that Our Lord will want (H) it hither? I.e., How will Our Lord ordain it?
8. It is indeed here that they will dance.
9. It was gradually that it ceased.

49E.
1. It was for one full year that it was standing forth.
2. Popcorn grows well there in their homeland.
3. It is still far into the night when it comes out.
4. Peyote grows only there in the desert region.
5. It is thus for one full day that people enter.
6. It soothes one's intestines, especially at the time that nothing has yet been eaten (i.e., . . . at the time that one has not yet eaten anything).
7. It was just quietly that they left.
8. It is very slowly that they come along going.
9. The one who eats it will no longer desire food up to the time he dies.
10. Absolutely everywhere that is somewhere that it will settle on our skin surface, (i.e., one's skin surface) immediately it festers; i.e., Anywhere it touches one's skin, the place festers.
11. It was without their being aware that they were killed; i.e., They were killed unawares.
12. Some days later once more he made up his mind about us. [*Lit.*, he spoke as one about us.]

49F. *An Aztec Warrior* (Florentine Codex XII, 101)
People gave a shout. "O Mexihcas, let it be soon!" [I.e., Up and at them!] Immediately thereupon it [i.e., the shout] incited the Tlapanec Ehcatzin, an Otomi [i.e., an elite warrior]. He hurled himself against them. He said, "O warriors, O Tlatilolcas!, up and at them! Who are the ones who are the barbarians? [I.e., Who are these barbarians that we should fear them?] Get a move on!" Immediately thereupon he went to shove/contend against one Spaniard. He struck him to the ground. He [i.e., the Spaniard] was the one who came in the lead when he [i.e., Ehcatzin] went to knock him down, the one who came out in front of it [i.e., the group of Spaniards]. And when he had finished knocking him down [*lit.*, he had gone in order to knock him down], then he drug the Spaniard away.

EXERCISE 50

50A.
1. When she awoke, immediately she cried.
2. When he had come in order to reach the place he had mentioned to him, he immediately saw the tufa (*lit.*, the stone mat).
3. At the time that he (i.e., the god) will frown in anger, he will press down the heaven.

Key to the Exercises 183

    4. Nothing was difficult when they did it.
    5. When he had gone thither, immediately thereupon he says (i.e., said) to the people, "I want to see (H) the lord Quetzalcoatl."
    6. When he used to begin singing, immediately they used to answer him.
    7. It is to three places that they go at the time that they die.
    8. It is continually dark there to where he will have departed abandoning things (i.e., to where he goes when he has died).
    9. This is that place, people say, where there is much suffering.
   10. There in the Ninth Region of the Dead, there is the place where people become individually completely destroyed.
   11. When it spreads open its tail, it is at that time that the yellow shows forth.
   12. When the kings died, they buried them there; then over them they built a pyramid for them.
   13. There they waited for a short time while they prepared the guns.

50B.
    1. He thinks that perhaps it is a child who is crying.
    2. Observe well with regard to which one first considers himself.
    3. They are going to meet someone.
    4. They thought that indeed they would kill him there.
    5. They are going in order to erect their god's house.
    6. Some others came in order to help them.
    7. Already he is going in order to give himself to the gods.
    8. All the commoners sit down together in a group (*lit.*, they fall as one) in order to make tamales for themselves (~ for one another).
    9. Every single person went in order to meet people.
   10. He used to think that it was there that they would die in battle.
   11. He is going in order to bathe.
   12. They knew something regarding (i.e., they had an idea/a suspicion about) who was the one who became frightened.
   13. Let's go dig for water so that we may drink there.
   14. He is coming to look at people in secret (*lit.*, in disguise).
   15. Let's not steal lest we be stoned.
   16. Do not commit adultery, lest you be pelted with stones (i.e., lest you be stoned).

50C.
    1. If he is still a small child, the parents still carry him.
    2. If sometime it even seemed that perhaps he was drinking pulque, then they used to go locking him up.
    3. Even though they were living at a distance, they arrived swiftly.
    4. Today, although insignia are no longer much needed, they just go on being followed as made things (i.e., they continue to be made).
    5. If somewhere something is to be done, it is still deep night when all go.
    6. Even though in truth you are not strong, you will be able to carry it (on your back).
    7. They are lazy, even though they are wiry.
    8. If he still sees nothing that will make him tipsy, he sells his blanket (to buy pulque).
    9. If your offering is nothing (i.e., if you have no offering), you will not be able to enter.

10. Although he died at home (i.e., not in battle), he was indeed a man.
11. Even though they are the ones who are the hosts, they dance.
12. If he is already upsetting it when he is holding it at dawn, it says to him, "Let me go." [*Lit.*, . . . when he is causing it (i.e., the specter) to be abroad at dawn. . . .]

50D. *Assuring the Growth of a Tooth* (Florentine Codex IV/V, 195)
When the teeth of small children fall out, mothers throw them into a mouse's hole. Or else they say to their children, "Throw it in the mouse's hole." This is because, people say, if they do not do it like this, the child's tooth will not grow well. He will be just gap-toothed.

50E. *The Tree That Broke* (Codex Chimalpahin I, 70)
When they came to arrive at the base of a tree, immediately thereupon they settled down there at its base. The tree that stood there was a very thick cypress. Then there they established an earthen altar. On it they placed the awesome one, Huitzilopochtli, after they had established it [i.e., the altar] there. And a few days later, they then offered him their travel rations. Then they would have eaten, but then they heard someone who called them. He spoke down from the top of the cypress. He said to them, "Those of you who are there, move, so that it will not fall on you. Indeed tomorrow the cypress will fall." Immediately thereupon they abandoned what they were eating. It was for a very long time that they were with bowed heads. Immediately they moved; they made way for the cypress. It came true that, when it dawned, the cypress tree was uprooted when it broke upon them.

In that place the ones who were the Aztecs or Mexihs still spent four years after they had come to settle and rest there at the base of the cypress.

EXERCISE 51

51A. 1. They are becoming liege lords of the Sun.
2. All are becoming priests.
3. Who do you know yourself to be? I.e., Who do you think you are?
4. I am eating it raw.
5. They come along having become iron.
6. They are becoming butterflies.
7. He (H) will hear it quite straight; i.e., He (H) will hear a true report.
8. We are becoming fools.
9. He became *his* image. ~ *He* became his image.
10. He who becomes a priest is chosen.

51B. 1. He is coming being (*lit.*, standing) alone.
2. Their child was born a woman; i.e., Their child was born a girl.
3. The hearth was covered with ashes.
4. Perhaps they were their darts.
5. The tree stands fat; i.e., The tree is big around.
6. Does she still appear a young woman?
7. Their clothing was of maguey fiber.
8. The war boat does not seem to be of wood.
9. Already I am looking old.

Key to the Exercises 185

  10. Their clothing was of wild-animal skins.
  11. The spoon is of wood. ~ The spoons are of wood.
  12. Their god's name was Iocippa.

51C. 1. It is full of sand. (~ It is covered with sand.) It is full of sand. (~ It is covered with sand.)
  2. Immediately the archer begins to pierce it with arrows.
  3. It is beginning to run.
  4. It is filled with straw. (~ It is covered with straw.) It is covered with straw.
  5. It is beginning to spill out.
  6. We shall stop singing.
  7. You are covered with dirt. You are covered with dirt.
  8. When already rain wants to come, at that time this bird begins to sing; i.e., Just before rain comes, this bird begins to sing.
  9. They will not be long in going in order to go to war.
  10. It is beginning to drizzle.
  11. They were indeed fully covered with dirt.
  12. They are covered with dirt.
  13. His face is bloody.
  14. It is really covered with (liquid) rubber. It is covered with (liquid) rubber.

51D. *Advantage from Adversity* (<u>Codex</u> <u>Chimalpahin</u> I, 92)
And then Coxcoxtli gave orders to his counselors, who were Colhuas. He said [*lit.*, says] to them, "Where is it that they [i.e., the Mexihcas] will be?"[I.e., "Where shall we put them?"] The counselors said to him, "O Lord, O Ruler, let them go there, let them go to be there among the hills here in Tizaapan." Then they went to leave them there, they went to settle them there at Tizaapan. And then they informed the ruler, Coxcoxtli. They said, "O Lord, O Ruler, we have gone to leave the Mexihcas in Tizaapan." Then Coxcoxtli said, "It is good. They are not humans. They are great scoundrels. Perhaps they will be finished off there, eaten by snakes. It is the veritable home of snakes."

 But the Mexihcas were extremely happy when they saw the snakes. The full number of them the Mexihcas stewed or roasted; they ate them [*lit.*, they eat them].

 And then Coxcoxtli, who remembered it [i.e., the Mexihca problem], spoke [*lit.*, speaks] about it. He said to them [i.e., his counselors], "O Colhuas, you who went in order to leave them, go in order to see them, [regarding] whether they have died." Immediately they said to him, "It is good, O Lord, O Ruler. Let's go in order to see them." And when they went and saw them, they were sitting around making things smoke; smoke hung in the air [*lit.*, extends]; they were [*lit.*, are] burning things when they arrived upon them. Immediately they said to them, "Welcome [*lit.*, you have suffered hardship . . . (this is a customary greeting, but usually spoken to the visitor)], O Mexihcas. We have come in order to see you. We have come in order to greet you. How are you?" Immediately they answered them, saying, "You have done us a favor [in coming]. We indeed are happy." They said to them, "It is good. We are going now." They came to the palace. Immediately they reported to Coxcoxtli. They said [*lit.*, say] to him, "O Lord, O Ruler, we have gone to see them. They have finished off the snakes, which they have eaten. The snakes no longer exist. They have come to an end." Then Coxcoxtli said, "Ah! Look at them. They indeed are scoundrels. Let them keep on doing what they are doing [*lit.*, let them keep on doing it]. Do not have anything to do with them [lit., do not summon them]."

EXERCISE 52

(The notation "n.i.N." means "not in Nahuatl.")

52A.
1. It has hands and (n.i.N.) it has feet; i.e., It has hands and feet.
2. He takes a steam bath three times or (n.i.N.) four times; i.e., He takes a steam bath three or four times.
3. And then he summoned the astrologers.
4. He will not drink wine or (n.i.N.) pulque.
5. And the ruler/king said to them, "Rest."
6. They quickly shout, they shrill, and (n.i.N.) they whoop [*lit.*, they strike their lips].
7. Here once again I have looked upon your (pl) faces (H) and (n.i.N.) your head tops (H); i.e., Here once again I behold your persons (H).
8. When she has recovered, immediately thereupon she enters the steam bath, and there she drinks the white medicine.
9. It is very slowly that you may walk, and it is very slowly that you may go, that you may follow a road; i.e., Walk very slowly and go very slowly following the road.

52B.
1. The man is in one place, and (n.i.N.) therewith the woman is in another. [Or understanding generic reference: "The men are in one place and the women in another."]
2. All day and (n.i.N.) with it [i.e., also] all night he was just wanting [to know] where was the road that he would follow.
3. His equipment is nothing and (n.i.N.) his property is nothing, nevertheless he is a good man; i.e., He has no possessions or (n.i.N.) property, but (n.i.N.) nevertheless he is a good man.
4. Its eggs are four in number or (n.i.N.) perhaps otherwise they are five in number; i.e., It has four or (n.i.N.) five eggs.
5. Also it is only in a miserable land that they dwell, but nevertheless they are also knowers of jadeite.
6. Did you buy it, or (n.i.N.) did you perhaps make it?
7. No one knows whether it will really become true or (n.i.N.) not.
8. And when you go, when you follow a path/road, when you come upon a road, you are not to lower your head [in humility] and (n.i.N.) also you are not to lift your head [in arrogance]. Indeed, it is a lack of breeding. You are only to walk standing quite erect.

52C.
1. Here you who are a real man are. [*Lit.*, "you are an eagle and (n.i.N.) you are a jaguar." Another translation can be "you who are a warrior," but in its context the sentence is intended as flattery to a young man about to be married and might be equivalent to "you are a grown man who knows how to carry out his manly responsibilities."]
2. And here you who are a woman already sit [*lit.*, you are a skirt and (n.i.N.) you are a blouse].
3. I consider you a precious jewel [*lit.*, it is a necklace and (n.i.N.) it is a quetzal plume].

Key to the Exercises 187

    4. I look upon you as something of high worth [*lit.*, like a necklace and (n.i.N.) like a quetzal plume].
    5. The parent [*lit.*, he is a father and (n.i.N.) he is a mother] comes bringing her, comes promising her, comes making a gift of her to you (H).
    6. He who hates someone causes him/her to swallow it in a repast/meal [*lit.*, it is water and (n.i.N.) it is food] in order to make him/her become crazy.
    7. He becomes the sun's caregiver [*lit.*, he is its mother and (n.i.N.) he is its father].
    8. He gives him authority [*lit.*, adjr it is a mat and (n.i.N.) it is a seat] and governance [*lit.*, adjr it is an instrument for carrying things and (n.i.N.) it is an instrument for bearing things on the back].

52D. *The Turkey Vulture* (Florentine Codex XI, 42)
A turkey vulture is black, dirty black, with a bright red head [*lit.*, it is chili-colored at the head] and (n.i.N.) with chalk-colored feet [*lit.*, it is chalk-colored at the feet]. Its food is anything that is dead, foul smelling, and (n.i.N.) therewith filthy [*lit.*, everything that is something that is dead, that is foul smelling, that is filth is its food].

52E. *First Paragraph to the Introduction to the* Mexican Chronicle (Codex Chimalpain Vol. 1, p. 60)
Here is told and (n.i.N.) reported how they came in order to arrive and (n.i.N.) came in order to enter, those who were the old ones who were called and (n.i.N.) designated Teochichimecas [*lit.*, God-Chichimecs (possibly, "Authentic/Awesome/Original Chichimecs")], the people of Aztlan, the Mexihs, and (n.i.N.) the Chicomoztocas [i.e., those associated with Chicomoztoc (Seven Caves Place)], who came in order to seek land and (n.i.N.) who came in order to merit land here in the great city, ciudad [*Spanish*, "city"], Mexihco Tenochtitlan, its place of renown, its place of exemplariness, the location of the rock-tuna cactus in the midst of the water, the eagle's standing place, the eagle's screeching place, the place where the eagle outspreads its wings, the eagle's eating place, the snake's hissing place, the fish's jumping place [*lit.*, its flying place], the place where the blue and (n.i.N.) yellow waters converge, where there is burning on the water [Beware! The water is NOT what is burning!], there where effort [*lit.*, breath] comes to be known among the rushes and (n.i.N.) the reeds, the place where the various people from the four directions were met and (n.i.N.) awaited, the place where the thirteen Teochichimecs came to arrive and (n.i.N.) came to settle, where they came to settle in destitution when they came to arrive.

52F. *Protection from Hail* (Florentine Codex IV/V, 192)
When it rains and (n.i.N.) it is hailing a lot, one whose field is there, or (n.i.N.) perhaps his chili-pepper patch, or (n.i.N.) perhaps his bean field, or (n.i.N.) his chia, scatters ashes from the fireplace outdoors in his courtyard. People say notably that thereby his field will not be hailed on; people say that thereby the hail perishes.

52G. *The Broken Grinding Stone* (Florentine Codex IV/V, 194)
The people here used to use the grinding stone as an evil omen for themselves. When someone there sits [i.e., sat] grinding, if it breaks [i.e., broke], thereby it seemed, people said notably, that the one who had been grinding would shortly die, or (n.i.N.) perhaps he who was the homeowner, or (n.i.N.) perhaps their children, or (n.i.N.) perhaps someone of the people of her household would die.

EXERCISE 53

53A.
1. Its head is large; it is the full amount (i.e., the same size) of our turkey cock from here; i.e., Its head is as large as that of the native turkey cock.
2. The honorableness of the merchants and (n.i.N.) of the vanguard merchants was equal [lit., it was one-rock].
3. That is not good, but (n.i.N.) this is good; i.e., This is better than that.
4. You are a greater drunkard than your father.
5. I am stronger than you.
6. You are more propertied and (n.i.N.) outfitted than I; i.e., You are wealthier than I.
7. Your property and (n.i.N.) your equipment are more abundant than mine.
8. The faults of you kings are greater than the faults of your subjects.
9. The dugouts of those who came later were bigger than the dugouts of those who came first.
10. Snow is exceedingly white; still nothing is as white; i.e., Snow is whiter than any other thing.
11. If now during the summer you are dying of cold, how much colder will you be when freezing weather comes [*lit.*, at the time of freezing]?
12. It is the same as the disguise and (n.i.N.) transformation of the owl-human (human-in-the-form-of-an-owl), who is Tezcatl-Ihpoca (i.e., of the fiend, Tezcatl-Ihpoca).
13. He is taller than I am.

53B. *The Cuitlamiztli* (Florentine Codex XI, 6)

A cuitlamiztli lives in a forest. It is exactly like a mountain lion [*lit.*, it is indeed only already also the one that is a mountain lion]. It is called "cuitlamiztli" [*lit.*, it is an excrement lion] for this reason: when it has captured a deer it begins to eat it; it eats it energetically; it lies eating it; it really finishes it. It is for two or (n.i.N.) three days that it does not eat anything (else); it just eats it entirely; it just lies stretched out [*lit.*, it lies fallen]; it lies digesting. It is called "cuitlamiztli" for this reason: because it is a glutton and (n.i.N.) furthermore because it does not hide. At night it comes to eat turkeys; it eats them up, even if they are twenty in number. When it has become sated, it just kills them, and (n.i.N.) along with this [*lit.*, with it] the sheep.

53C. *The Ringtail* (Florentine Codex XI, 6)

A ringtail [*lit.*, it is a dog-eater] is just like the cuitlamiztli [*lit.*, it is indeed only already also the one which is the cuitlamiztli]. It is called "dog-eater" for this reason: at night it comes to a village. It cries. And when it has cried, then all the dogs answer it. All howl [*lit.*, they shout]. All hear its cry from it; then they go toward it. And when they have sat down together near it, when they have formed a circle around it, then it captures as many as it will be able. It eats them. Dogs are its favorite food [*lit.*, dogs are very much its very food].

53D. *Peyote* (Florentine Codex XI, 129)

This peyote is white. And it is only there that it grows toward the north [*lit.*, toward the arsenal] in the desert region, which is called Mictlan [*lit.*, Toward Dead-man Vicinity]. It affects [*lit.*, it comes out upon him] the one who eats it or (n.i.N.) drinks it, just as

Key to the Exercises

mushrooms do. He also sees many things that are frightening or (n.i.N.) that are laugh-provoking [*lit.*, it has made someone laugh]. It is perhaps for one day or (n.i.N.) two days that it affects him, but it finally leaves him [*lit.*, nonetheless only also it leaves him]. However it indeed damages his mind [*lit.*, it damages his heart]. It causes people to lose their reason [*lit.*, to destroy things]; it makes people drunk; it affects people.

EXERCISE 54

54A. 1. #∅-∅(cen-te-ti)∅+∅-∅# = it becomes a unity. *Source*: the compound nounstem *(cen-te)-tl-*, "one rock," i.e., "one in number," formed from *(cen-)-∅-*, "one," and *(te)-tl-*, "rock." *Derivation*: by means of the inceptive/stative verbstem-forming suffix *ti* (see § 54.2.1).
   2. #ni-∅+c-∅(ne-mac-ti-a)∅+∅-∅# = I cause him/her to have a gift, i.e., I make a gift to him/her. *Source*: the nounstem *(ne-mac)-tli-*, "a gift." *Derivation*: by means of the first-type causative suffix added to the *ti*-of-possession (see § 54.5).
   3. #∅-∅(ce-hui)∅+∅-∅# = he becomes calmed down (after being angry). *Source*: *(ce)-tl-*, "ice." *Derivation*: by means of the intransitive verbstem-forming suffix *hui* (see § 54.2.2).
   4. #ti-∅(zoqui-yō-hua)∅+∅-∅# = you are covered with mud. *Source*: the compound nounstem *(zoqui-yō)-tl-*, "a thing characterized by mud." *Derivation*: by means of the inceptive/stative verbstem-forming suffix *hua* (see § 54.2.5).
   5. #∅-∅+qui-∅(tōcā-yō-ti-a)∅+∅-∅# = I cause him/her/it to have a name; i.e., I give him/her/it a name; I call him/her/it by his/her/its name. *Source*: the compound nounstem *(tōcā-yō)-tl-*, "attribute of a name." *Derivation*: by means of the first-type causative suffix *ā* added to the *ti*-of-possession (see § 54.5).
   6. #∅-∅(tēl-pōch-yah-∅-cā-ti)∅+∅-∅# = he becomes a young warrior. *Source*: the compound preterit-agentive nounstem *(tēl-pōch-yah-∅)-▢-*, "a young goer," i.e., "a young warrior." *Derivation*: by means of the inceptive/stative verbstem-forming suffix *ti* (see § 54.2.1).
   7. #∅-∅(cōz-ti-ya)∅+∅-∅# = it turns yellow. *Source*: *(cōz)-tli-*, "a yellow thing" > *(cōz-ti)*, "to become yellow." *Derivation*: by means of the verbstem-forming suffix *ya* (see § 54.2.3.*b*).
   8. #∅-∅(tequi-huah-∅-cā-ti)∅+∅-∅# = he becomes a tribute owner. *Source*: the preterit-agentive nounstem of ownership *(tequi-huah-∅)-▢-*, "tribute owner." *Derivation*: the inceptive/stative verbstem-forming suffix *ti* (see § 54.2.1).
   9. #∅-∅(xīlō-ti)∅+∅-∅# = it (a maize plant) begins to put forth maize ears. *Source*: the nounstem *(xīlō)-tl-*, "immature ear of maize before the kernels ripen." *Derivation*: by means of the inceptive/stative verbstem-forming suffix *ti* (see § 54.2.1).
   10. #∅-∅+m-▢(izhua-yō-ti-a)∅+∅-∅# = it is causing itself to have foliage; i.e., it is sprouting leaves. *Source*: the compound nounstem *(izhua-yō)-tl-*, "foliage." *Derivation*: by means of the first-type causative suffix *ā* added to the *ti*-of-possession (see § 54.4).
   11. #ni-∅+c-∅+n-o(tech-ti-a)∅+∅-∅# = I cause myself to be in contact with it; i.e., I appropriate it for myself. *Source*: the possessive-state predicate -*ī*-∅(*tech*)-, "its contact," from the relational nounstem *(tech)-▢-*, "side surface; contact." *Derivation*: by means of the inceptive/stative verbstem-forming suffix *ti* plus the

causative *ā* (see § 54.5.2; the possessor pronoun *ī-Ø* has become the verb-object pronoun *c-Ø*).

12. #ni-Ø+m-itz+n-o(cihuā-poh-ti-a)Ø+Ø-Ø# = I cause myself to become your fellow woman; i.e., I take you for my friend. *Source*: the possessive-state predicate *-m-o(cihuā-poh)-*, "your fellow-woman," from the obligatorily possessed compound nounstem *(cihuā-poh)-tli-*, "(a woman's) female equal/peer/companion." *Derivation*: by means of the inceptive/stative verbstem-forming suffix *ti* plus the causative *ā* (see § 54.5.2; the possessor pronoun *m-o* has become the verb-object pronoun *m-itz*).

54B.
1. The willow duck becomes long at the legs; i.e., The black-crowned night heron is long legged.
2. The water quail is long at the bill and (n.i.N.) it is long at the legs; i.e., The Wilson snipe is long billed and long legged.
3. When the beeswax [*lit.*, large-bee excrement] has been prepared, then on a flat stone [*lit.*, a rock with the shape of a flagstone] it is made thin, rolled with a rolling pin [*lit.*, a cylindrical tree branch].
4. When it was already time, when it was the opportune moment for the Spaniards to slay people, immediately thereupon they came forth. [Notice that future- and present-tense VNCs are being used to refer to the past; see § 57.1.]
5. Perhaps something will become our due reward and (n.i.N.) it will become our merit; i.e., Perhaps we shall deserve and merit something.
6. Did that massacre happen in your time? Were you a witness to that massacre?
7. He (H) caused the quetzal-plume crest device to become his property; i.e., He (H) took over the quetzal-plume crest device.
8. They used to say, "He will cause it to become characterized by dust, he will cause it to become characterized by trash." I.e., He will turn it into perversion. [The conjoined NNC lexical item (i.e., the biclausalism) *teuhtli tlahzolli*, "it is dust and it is trash," is equivalent to "it is perversity/perversion."]

54C. *A Rabbit in the House* (<u>Florentine</u> <u>Codex</u> IV/V, 167)
Also the rabbit was regarded as an omen when it used to enter someone's home. The farmers, the people in the fields, say, "Soon his house will perish on earth. Or (n.i.N.) perhaps soon someone will run away. Soon he will follow the path of the rabbit and the deer; soon he will become a rabbit; soon he will become a deer; soon he will cause himself to be a rabbit; soon he will cause himself to become a deer." [I.e., "he will become deranged, become like a wild animal." The conjoined lexical item *tōchtli mazātl*, "he/she is a rabbit he/she is a deer," is equivalent to "he/she is deranged (because of failing to act like a human being)."]

EXERCISE 55

55A.
1. #Ø-Ø(tlan-a-hui)Ø+Ø-Ø# = he is becoming downward; i.e., he (a sick person) is getting worse. *Source*: the relational nounstem *(tlan)-Ø-*, "bottom surface, undersurface; low-down location." *Derivation*: the intransitive destockal verbstem formation using *a-hui* (see § 55.6).

Key to the Exercises 191

    2. #∅-∅+qui-∅(tīza-huia)∅+∅-h# = they are applying white varnish to it/them. *Source*: the nounstem *(tīza)-tl-*, "white clay, chalk, white varnish." *Derivation*: by means of the single-object applicative verbstem forming suffix *huiā* (see § 55.3.2).

    3. #ti-∅(mā-cu-ī-l-mētz-tih)∅+qu-eh# = we spent five months (in a place). *Source*: the compound nounstem *(mā-cu-ī-l-mētz)-tli-* "five months." *Derivation*: by means of the temporal intransitive suffix *tiā* (see § 55.1).

    4. #ni-∅+tla(izhua-huia)∅+∅-∅# = I am using leaves on s.th., i.e., I am scrubbing s.th. with leaves. *Source*: the nounstem *(izhua)-tl-*, "leaf." *Derivation*: by means of the single-object applicative verbstem-forming suffix *huiā* (see § 55.3.2).

    5. #∅-∅+m-o(tle-huia)∅+∅-∅# = he/she experiences fire in himself/herself; he/she has a fever. *Source*: *(tle)-tl-*, "fire." *Derivation*: by using the single-object applicative verbstem-forming suffix *huiā* (see § 55.3.2).

    6. #∅-∅(ōm-pōhua-l-xiuh-tia)∅+∅-∅# #∅-∅(om-ōme)∅-∅# = he/she is forty-two years old. *Source*: *ōmpōhualxihuitl omōme*, "they are forty-two years." *Derivation*: by means of the intransitive-verbstem-forming temporal suffix *tiā* (see § 55.).

    7. #∅-∅+qui-∅(neuc-huia)∅+∅-h# = they spread honey on it ~ they sweeten it with honey. *Source*: the nounstem *(neuc)-tli-*, "honey." *Derivation*: by using the single-object applicative verbstem-forming suffix *huiā* (see § 55.3.2).

    8. #ti-∅+c-∅(xō-chi-huia)∅+∅-∅# = you use flowers (i.e., pretty speech) on her; i.e., you entice her with cajolery (to misuse her). *Source*: the nounstem *(xō-chi)-tl-*, "flower." *Derivation*: by using the single-object applicative verbstem-forming suffix *huiā* (see § 55.3.2).

55B. 1. The Mexihcas spent four years in Pantitlan.
    2. I, fool that I am, brought it upon myself.
    3. The two-toned-drum singers beat (the drums) for the slaves, played the two-toned drums for them, and (n.i.N.) intoned songs for them.
    4. He has been able to acquire things of the world.
    5. You do not value your chest and (n.i.N.) your head (i.e., your physical self), when you throw them at (i.e., risk it among) the crags and gorges, the mountains, the deserts.
    6. They go shouting things, they go shrilling (while slapping the lips), they go howling. It is said that they go howling for her and (n.i.N.) that they go as in battle. [Here "they" refers to midwives and old women, and "her" refers to a woman who has died in childbirth.]
    7. O my beloved uncles, you have become exhausted because of it; you have become worn out on account of it. [Regarding *tla-(ciya-hui)*, see §24.2.2 for intransitive verbstems that can be used as applicative ones without justification by suffixation.]
    8. In order that this be finished, first a frame is bound, then it is covered over [*lit.*, one uses a large cotton blanket on its surface] in order that it become strong

55C. *Panning for Gold* (Florentine Codex XI, 233)
There where a vein of gold [*lit.*, a path of gold] crops out [*lit.*, it is falling] in a river, the river carries the gold, washes it along. Thereby, because of that, before the Spaniards came, the Mexihcas, the Anahuacas, who were clever people, used not to dig out gold and (n.i.N.) silver; they just took the river sand and (n.i.N.) panned it in wooden trays.

They saw the gold, wherever it came to settle [*lit.*, it came to fall] with the appearance and (n.i.N.) the size of maize kernels. Then at that time [i.e., after finding all the larger sized nuggets] they used to take that resembling sand. Later they melted it; they smelted it; they were clever with it; they formed [*lit.*, they used to set them down] necklaces, bracelets, ear pendants, and (n.i.N.) labrets.

55D. *Stepping Over a Child* (Florentine Codex IV/V, 184)

When if some child lies stretched out or [n.i.N.] lies flexed, if someone steps over him/her, immediately they chide the one who has stepped over someone. They say to him/her, "Why is it that you step over him/her?"

People say that thereby no longer will the child grow. He/She will be only of small stature. And in order that he/she might remedy it, in order that it will not happen to the child, he/she jumps back over him/her. Thereby it becomes remedied.

EXERCISE 56

56A. 1. #∅-∅(∅-∅-Mah-mahui-ni-∅-∅)∅-∅# = he is (named) "He Is One Who Is Customarily Afraid Again and Again" [Such a name might be an ironic reversal, meaning in fact "one who is totally fearless."]
2. #ni-∅(∅-∅-Huē-i-∅-∅+∅-∅-Ī-∅-mī-uh-∅)∅-∅# = I am (named) "His Arrows Are Big"
3. #∅-∅(∅-∅-Iztā-∅-c-∅+∅-∅-Tōtō-tl-∅)∅-∅# = he is (named) "It Is a White Bird"
4. #ti-∅(∅-∅-Necoc-☐-∅+∅-∅-Yāō-∅-∅-tzin)∅-∅# = you (H) are (named) "He Is an Enemy toward Both Sides"
5. #∅-∅(∅-∅-Xō-chi-tōna-l-☐-∅)∅-∅# = I am (named) "It Is a Flower–Day Sign"
6. #t-∅(Ay-∅-∅-ā-∅-c-∅+∅-∅-Tlāca-tl-∅)∅-∅# = you are (named) "He Is a Person who is Nobody" [~ "He Is a Person who is Absent"]
7. #∅-∅(∅-∅-Ne-zahua-l-coy-ō-tl-∅)∅-∅# = he is (named) "It Is a Coyote that is the Result of Having Fasted"
8. #ni-∅(∅-∅-T-o-tle-huīc-ō-l-∅)∅-∅# = I am (named) "It is Our Clay Censer"
9. #∅-∅(∅-∅-Itz-cuin-cua-∅-∅-∅)∅-∅# = he is (named) "It/He Eats Dogs"
10. #ti-∅(∅-∅-T-o-yāō-tzin-∅-∅)∅-∅# = you are (named) "He (H) Is Our Enemy"
11. #∅-∅(∅-∅-Ā-ca-tōna-l-eh-∅-☐-∅)∅-∅# = he is (named) "He is an Owner of a Reed–Day Sign"
12. #ni-∅(∅-∅-Zaca-ti-tech-☐-∅+∅-∅-Cochi-∅-∅-∅)∅-∅# = I Am (named) "He Sleeps on Grass/Straw"
13. #∅-∅(∅-∅-Tlacō-xīn-∅-qui-∅)∅-∅# = he is (named) "He Is a Stick Trimmer/Whittler"
14. #ni-∅(∅-∅-Xiuh-tla-ht-o-h-∅-☐-∅)∅-∅# = I am (named) "He Is One Who Has Spoken like Turquoise"
15. #∅-∅(∅-∅-Tō-ch-āmi-∅-∅-∅)∅-∅# = he is (named) "He Hunts like a Rabbit" [The verbstem *(āmi)*, "to go on a hunt, to hunt," is intransitive, so *tōch-* is an incorporated adverb, not an incorporated object.]
16. #ti-∅(∅-∅-Tlāl-tē-☐-ca-tzin-∅-∅)∅-∅# = you are (named) "He (H) Is a Dweller in Tlallan" [Here a gentilic NNC is used as a personal-name nounstem. As a gentilic NNC *tiTlāltēcatzin* is analyzed as *#ti-∅(Tlāl-tē-☐-ca-tzin)∅-∅#*, "you (H) are one associated with (~ a dweller in) Tlallan."]

Key to the Exercises 193

17. #Ø-Ø(Ø-Ø-Ilan-cuēi-tl-Ø)Ø-Ø# = she is (named) "It Is an Old-Woman's Skirt"
18. #ni-Ø(Ø-Ø-Chāl-chiuh-cua-Ø-Ø-Ø)Ø-Ø# = I Am (named) "He Eats Jadeite"

56B. 1. Cuitlahuac would have to be either #Ø-Ø(Ø-Ø-Cuitla-huā-c-Ø-Ø)Ø-Ø#, "he is (named) 'It is a Dried-out-thing in the Form of Excrement'" [where the matrix stem is the impersonal patientive nounstem *(huā-c)-tli-*, "a thing that results from becoming dry," i.e., "a dried out thing," from the intransitive verbstem *(huā-qui)*, "to become dry"] or #Ø-Ø(Ø-Ø-Cuitla-huā-c-Ø-☐-Ø)Ø-Ø#, "he is (named) 'It Is a Thing That Has Become Dry in the Form of Excrement'" [where the matrix is the preterit-agentive nounstem *(huā-c)-qui-*, "a thing that has become dry"]. The honorific NNC of the first would be either #Ø-Ø(Ø-Ø-Cuitla-huā-c-tzin-Ø-Ø)Ø-Ø# or #Ø-Ø(Ø-Ø-Cuitla-huā-c-Ø-Ø+tzin)Ø-Ø#, and that of the second would be either #Ø-Ø(Ø-Ø-Cuitla-huā-c-Ø-☐-Ø+tzin)Ø-Ø# or #Ø-Ø(Ø-Ø-Cuitla-huā-c-Ø-cā-tzin-Ø-Ø)Ø-Ø#. None of these forms are found.

2. Cuitlahuatzin contains an unwritten glottal stop. The NNC is analyzed as #Ø-Ø(#Ø-Ø-Cuitla-huah-Ø-☐-Ø+tzin)Ø-Ø#, "he (H) is (named) 'He Is an Owner of Excrement.'" The nonhonorific NNC of this is #Ø-Ø(Ø-Ø-Cuitla-huah-Ø-☐-Ø)Ø-Ø#, "he is (named) 'He Is an Excrement Owner'" [the internal predicate of which is a preterit-agentive nounstem of ownerhood]. This is the form found in Nahuatl texts, and it is the form that English and Spanish writers should use.

56C. 1. Adorn (Hsg) him, inspire (Hsg) him, you who are the overperson, you who are Duality-Lord/Lady [The conjunctive compound NNC personal name is analyzed #t-Ø(Ø-Ø-Ōme-tēuc-tli-Ø)Ø-Ø# #t-Ø(Ø-Ø-Ōme-cihuā-tl-Ø)Ø-Ø#, where the two second-person singular subject pronouns point to one and the same entity, the originating godhead (an entity that sentence 2 below shows to be female, i.e., while both the male and female principles must cooperate in the world creation, it is the female that actually produces the result). The embed *Ōme-*, literally "two in number," stands for *Ōmeyō-*, "duality, twoness," as in the place-name NNC *Ōmeyōcān* (this goddess's abode) mentioned in sentence 5 below). The translation "Duality-Lord/Lady" is infelicitous, but it is difficult to find an English word that avoids the sex-differentiation inherent in "lord" and "lady" and covers both (contrast "king" and "queen," which have the genderless matching term "monarch").]

2. Your progenitor, Duality-Lord/Lady, the celestial woman [*lit.*, she is the sky-woman], devised [and] created you.

3. In what manner has your progenitor, Duality-Lord/Lady, provided things to you?

4. Warrior [*lit.*, eagle (and) jaguar], brave, youth, my youngest one, you (H) have come in order to arrive on earth; your progenitor, Duality-Lord/Lady, has (H) sent you hither. [Notice that we know a woman is speaking by the form of the vocatives; see § 18.11.]

5. The commoner has arrived. Ah! our progenitor, Duality-Lord/Lady, has (H) sent him hither from the Place of the Ninth Layering [i.e., the ninth sky level], from the Place of Duality.

6. Know it, understand it. Your home is not here. You are a warrior [*lit.*, you are an eagle (and) you are a jaguar]. You are the prized possession of the Omnipresent God [*lit.*, you are the roseate spoonbill [feather](and) you are the troupial [feather] of the Owner of Alongsideness and Vicinity].

7. Draw near (H) to your mother (H), Her-Skirt-Is-of-Jadeite, There-Is-Sunshine-by-means-of-Jadeite. [The second personal-name NNC is standing in apposition to the first. These are names of the goddess of standing and flowing water.] Let her (H) take you. Let her (H) thoroughly wash you. Let her (H) thoroughly bathe you. Let her carry off and dispose of the filthiness which you have brought hither from contact with your parent [*lit.*, she who is your mother and your father]. [This is part of a speech of the midwife to the newborn child.]
8. I call you, I shout to you, you who are the mother of the gods, you who are There-is-Sunshine-by-means-of-the-Stars, you who are Her-Skirt-Is-of-Stars.
9. Already they sit consoling him beside, near our parent, the Lord in Deadman Vicinity.
10. Later, after they started off, on the road they came upon demons who lay having fallen [i.e., were sitting] at the base of a big barrel cactus [*lit.*, a big pot]. . . . They, whom they call "Cloud Snakes," were seven in number. One person's name was Truth-in-Turquoise (H); the second one's name was Arrow-fish (H); the third one, the woman, their elder sister's name was God-Face-paint. But the names of the other four are not successfully known.

56D. *A Fateful Name* (Florentine Codex VII, 31)

And when, at the time that Moteuczoma installed himself (as ruler) [i.e., was installed as ruler], our years became tied to one another [i.e., a fifty-two year cycle came to an end], throughout everywhere he ordered that a captive whose name was "Xihuitl" ["Year" or "Grass" or "Turquoise"] be sought. He was to be seized anywhere. And one was caught. He was a person from Huexotzinco, a well-born person. His name was "Xiuhtlamin" ["He-Has-Arrow-pierced-Things-With-Turquoise"]. He was made a captive in Tlatilolco. The captor's name was "Itzcuin" ["Dog"], but thereafter he was named, thereafter he was called "He-Is-the-One-Who-Is-the-Captor-of-Xiuhtlamin."

It was on *his* captive's breast that the fire stick fell [i.e., that the new fire was started]. All of his body ended in the fire [i.e., The fire consumed his entire body]. And [because a body was no longer available] it was merely with amaranth dough that he [the captor] made an image of him [*lit.*, he caused him to have a representational surrogate] on which he paid his respects to him. He added it to dried-maize-kernel stew, whereby he fed it to people.

56E. *After Kingship Ended in Tlatilolco* (Florentine Codex IX, 2)

When Moquihuixtzin[1] died (H), no longer was a ruler/king [*lit.*, no longer was one who was a (royal bloodline) speaker] instated in Tlatilolco. Then began merely military deputy-rulership [*lit.*, Then it began that people speak like eagles, i.e., that there is speaking/ruling by means of (appointed) elite warriors]. And here starts merely military deputy-rulers/governors [*lit.*, the ones who have spoken/ruled like eagles] who were instated in the authority left vacant by the ruler/king Moquihuixtzin [*lit.*, who settled themselves on the ruler/king Moquihuixtzin's mat-and-seat when he went having abandoned it; i.e., when he was killed]; the ones who guarded things for him [i.e., who assumed his authority] were these: the general (H) Tzihuacpopocatzin [i.e., he (H) is "It-Emits-Heat-Shimmer-from-a-Tzihuactli-Plant"], and the commanding general (H) Itzcuauhtzin [i.e., he (H) is "It-is-a-Golden-Eagle" (*lit.*, obsidian eagle)]; both were

Key to the Exercises   195

high-born noblemen. And afterwards there came the commanding general (H) Tezcatzin [i.e., he (H) is "It-Is-a-Mirror"] and the general (H) Totozacatzin [i.e., he (H) is "It-Is-Bird-Grass"]. Both were elite-warrior noblemen, Mexihca noblemen.

1. The meaning of *Moquihuixtzin* (nonhonorific, *Moquihuix* or *Moquihuixtli*) is uncertain. Garibay translates it as "Cara sucia" ("Dirty Face"), but how he arrived at this is unknown; evidently he took *-ix-* to be the nounstem *(īx)-tli-*, "face." It might be, but what would *(moquiuh)-tli-* mean? Other possibilities for deciphering the name exist; for example, it might be formed on the perfective-patientive nounstem from the unattested verbstem *(moqu-i-hui-ya)*, for the derivation of which see § 54.2.3.*b.iii*. Neither this nor its source destockal verbstem *(moqu-i-hui)* is listed in any dictionary, however. The latter verbstem may even serve as the source for *(moqu-i-uh)-tli-* or *(moqu-i-hui)-tl-*.

EXERCISE 57

57A. 1. teuhyōhua = it is full of/covered with dust
   2. nōhuiyān = everywhere
   3. teōyōtica = it is by means of godliness/divinity; i.e., spiritually
   4. īmac ihcac = it stands in his/her hand
   5. ca = indeed (principal clause introducing particle); cah = he/she/it is (VNC)
   6. yohuan = at night; īhuān = with it/therewith
   7. tōlin = it is a rush/they are rushes
   8. yēceh = however
   9. tēhuān yōlqueh = they have lived with people; i.e., they are kinsfolk
   10. yōlilizzoh = it is a thing that has owned living/life in abundance; i.e., it is a thing filled with living/life; it is breath/a spiritual thing
   11. moyāōhuān = they are your (sg) enemies
   12. quicōloa = he/she bends it
   13. ihīyōtl = it is breath
   14. mātlālcuēyeh = she is the owner of a deep-green skirt
   15. in Ehcatitlan = adjr at/to/from the Place in the Vicinity of Breezes
   16. ihui oc = it is thus still; iihhuiyōc = in its plumage
   17. tlanelihtoāni = he/she is one who customarily says things truly; i.e., he/she is a creditable, truthful person
   18. ye = already (adverbial particle); yeh = he/she/it is that one (pronominal NNC)
   19. ahyēcyōtl = it is badness (*lit.*, it is nongoodness)
   20. tlaīhuani = it is an instrument for drinking; i.e., it is a cup/glass/goblet

57B. *The Owl*

   a. Tecolōtl ololtic, tapayoltic, cuitlaololtic. Īxtemahmalacachtic; īxpechtic. Cuācuahueh ihhuitica. Cuāteolōltic; cuātecontic. Ihhuitilāhuac; ihhuiyōtilāhuac. Īxmihmiquini in tlahcah. Texcalco, cuahuitl iihtic in tlācati. Yohualtica in tlacuācua, īpampa oc cencah huellachiya in yohuan. Tlatomāhua in īc tlahtoa. Quihtoa, "Tecolō, tecolō, ō, ō."

   b. An owl is round, ball-like; it is round backed [*lit.*, it is round at the back]. Its eyes are circular [*lit.*, it is like spindle whorls at the eyes]; it is flat faced [*lit.*, it is flat at the face]. It has horns of feathers [*lit.*, it is horned with feathers]. It is round headed; it is mug headed. Its feathers are dense [*lit*., it is dense at the feathers]; its plumage is dense. It is blind during the day. It is in crags or in a tree hollow that it is born. It is at night that it regularly eats, because it sees better at night [*lit*. it sees still very well]. It is deep voiced when it calls. It says, "Tecolo, tecolo, o, o."

57C. *A Skirmish*
  a. "Mēxihcahé, mā ye cuēl!"
   Niman ye īc tlahcahuaca īhuān tlapītzalo. Īhuān chīmallāza in yāōtlachixqui.
   Niman ye īc quintocah in Españoles, quimmāyauhtihuih, īhuān quimāntihuih. Caxtōltin in ānōqueh in Españoles; niman īc quinhuālhuīcaqueh. Auh in īmācal, niman īc quitzīnquīxtihqueh. Ānepantlah contēcatoh.
   Auh in ōquimahxītīcoh caxtōltin omēin in oncān miquizqueh, ītōcā [one would expect *ītōcāyōcān* since a place is what is being named] Tlacōchcalco; niman ye īc quinpehpetlāhuah. Moch quincuīlihqueh in īnyāōtlatqui īhuān in īmichcahuīpil, īhuān in ixquich in īntech catca. Moch quintepēhualtihqueh. Niman ye īc tlācohtih. Quinmictiah.
   Auh in īmicnīhuān quinhuālitztoqueh ānepantlah.
  b. "O Mexihcas, up and at 'em!"
   Immediately thereupon there was shouting along with blowing [of conch trumpets]. In addition, the sentinel brandished his shield.
   Immediately thereupon they chased the Spaniards, they went knocking them down, and (n.i.N.) moreover they went capturing them. The captured Spaniards were fifteen in number; immediately thereupon they brought them back. And as for their [i.e., the Spaniards'] boat, immediately thereupon they retired it. They stopped [*lit*., they went to place it] in the middle of the lake [*lit*., water].
   And when they had taken [*lit*., they came in order to make them arrive] the eighteen who would die there to the place called Tlacochcalco, immediately afterwards they stripped each of them naked. They took from them all their war equipment along with their cotton (protective) vests, as well as everything that was on them. They tore everything from them. Immediately thereupon they became slaves. They killed [i.e., sacrificed] them.
   And their friends remained watching them from the middle of the lake.

57D. *A Messenger from the Hereafter*
  a. Cē tlācatl cihuātl, īchān Tenōchtitlan, mic īca cocoliztli. Niman motōcac īithualco; īpan quitemanqueh. Ye iuh nāhuilhuitl motōcac in cihuātl micqui, mozcalih yōhualtica. Cencah tlamauhtih. In oncān motōcaca tlatatacco motlapoh, auh in tetl īc motemanca, huehca huehhuetzito.
   Auh in yehhuātl cihuātl, in ōiuh mozcalih, niman quinohnōtzato, quilhuīto in Motēuczōma in tleh in quittac. Quipōhuilih, quilhuih, "Ca in īc ōninozcalih: nimitzilhuīco, ca ye ixquich. Ca tehhuātl moca tzonquīza in tlahtohcāyōtl in Mēxihco. Ca tehhuātl mopan māntiyāz in āltepētl Mēxihco. Āc ihqueh in ye huītzeh, ca yehhuāntin tlālmahcēhuaquīhuih. Yehhuāntin onozqueh in Mēxihco."
   Auh in yehhuātl micca cihuātl, ye nō cempōhualxihuitl oncē īnen, īhuān oc cē quichīuh īconēuh oquichtli.
  b. A noble lady, whose home was at Tenochtitlan, died from a sickness. Then she was buried in her courtyard; they paved it with stones over her. When the dead woman

had been buried for four days, she revived during the night. She frightened people greatly. There where she had been buried, it opened up at the grave, and the stones with which she had been covered went severally to fall at a distance.

And this woman, after she had revived, then went in order to converse with Moteuczoma; she went in order to say to him what she had seen. She recounted it to him, she said to him, "Indeed for this purpose did I revive: I came in order to say to you, 'It is indeed already finished [*lit.*, it is a full/complete amount]. Indeed with <u>you</u> the kingdom in Mexihco is coming to an end. Indeed in <u>your</u> time the city of Mexihco will go being captured. The ones who already are coming, they are indeed the ones who are coming to merit the land. <u>They</u> will dwell in Mexihco.'"

And this woman who had died continued to live twenty-one years longer [*lit.*, her life was twenty-one years more], and (n.i.N.) moreover she gave birth to another child, which was a male.

EXERCISE 58

58A. First, it should be pointed out that what Siméon calls a "Root" (French, racine; Spanish, raíz) is never a root according to § 1.11.2, where "root" is defined as "a single major morpheme/morph." He gives what he considers the source for the entry.
   1. in oc īmonequiyān—The "root" is wrong; first, because the *c* on the *inoquic* has no possible justification (rewritten, *inoquic* would be *in oc īc*, which is totally inappropriate here); second, if Siméon had paid attention to his own entry for *monequian* (p. 288), he would have known that it has to be in the possessive state, here īmonequiyān (see § 46.4.1).
   2. icnēlīlmachītia: nitē *or* ninotē—There is no way for the embed *icnēlīl-* to come from *ninotē-(icn-ēl-i-liā)*, since both it and the embed in the entry come from *nitē-(icn-ēl-i-ā)*.
   3. yacahuīctic—There is no connection between this entry, which contains the passive patientive nounstem *(huīc)-tli-*, "digging stick" (see § 38.1.3.*b*), and *yacahuitzoa*, first, because this alleged source contains the nounstem *(huitz)-tli-*, "thorn," and, second, because it is a causative (!) verbstem, i.e., *tla-(yaca-huitz-o-ā)*, derived from the intransitive verbstem *(yaca-huitz-a-hui)*, "to become like a thorn (i.e., sharp pointed) at the nose/tip." There is NO way to jump from a verbstem built on the suffixal units *a-hui/o-ā* to a verbstem built on the inceptive/stative verbstem-forming suffix *ti*. The entry *(yaca-huīc-ti-Ø)-c-*, "one who has become like a digging-stick at the nose," is a preterit-agentive nounstem from the verbstem *(yaca-huīc-ti)*, "to become like a digging stick at the nose." [Incidentally, Siméon's translation is doubtful; "flat and broad" would be better, since evidently the digging end of the digging stick is the relevant part.]
   4. Huetzcatocātzin—This personal-name NNC has nothing to do with either of the alleged "roots." In his entry for *uetzcayotl*, "a beam, a piece of lumber for construction," Siméon says its root is *uetzca*, i.e., *(hue-tz-ca)*, "to laugh." (In fact it is from *(huetzi)*, "to fall"; for the type of formation exhibited by *(huetz-Ø-cā-yō)-tl-*, see § 39.3.6, *note*; *(hue-tz-ca-yō)-tl-* is not a legitimate form.) Why Siméon felt the need to involve *(-yō)-tl-* is a puzzle; he should have simply chosen *(hue-tz-ca)*. As for *(tōcāi)-tl-*, "name," it is a totally wrong choice. The nonhonorific form of

Huetzcatocātzin is *Huetzcatoc*, i.e., the personal-name NNC is formed on a stem that is a preterit-as-present tense connective-*t* compound-stemmed NNC (embed: the preterit predicate *(hue-tz-ca)Ø-*; matrix: *(o)*, i.e., the matrix form of *(on-o)*). It is translated as "he is (called) 'He Is Recumbent Laughing.'"

5. yamaztiya: ni—The source is not the derived *ya*-verbstem *(yam-ā-ni-ya)*. The entry is derived from the source of this, the destockal verbstem *(yam-ā-ni)*.

6. cococ—This cannot come from the derived causative verbstem *nino-(coco-ā)* (see § 24.3.2.c), since it comes from its *ya*-verbstem intransitive source *(coco-ya)*.

7. zoquittihuītz—The embed *zoquit-* cannot come from the derived *ya*-verbstem *(zoqui-ti-ya)* but comes from the source of this, the inceptive/stative *ti* verbstem *(zoqui-ti)*.

8. ēlleltia: nin—This first-type causative verbstem, which is formed on an intransitive "*ti*-of-possession" verbstem, cannot possibly come from the transitive verbstem *nitla-(ēl-le-l-o-ā)*, since there is no way to jump from an *o-ā* verbstem to a *ti* verbstem (compare 3 above). The source of both is the nounstem *(ēl-le-l)-li-*.

9. yēcahui—The adverbial particle *ye* is not involved here, nor is the transitive verbstem *tla-(cāhua)* (as Siméon indicated with his question mark, he himself doubted the correctness of his assertion). The entry is an intransitive *a-hui* verbstem formed on the nounstem *(yēc)-tli-*, "a finished thing; a good thing."

10. ihcīca: n—The compound intransitive verbstem *(ih-cī-ca)*, "to pant," is formed with the nounstem *(ih-)-* (see § 30.13) embedded in the matrix **(cī-ca)*, which comes from the unattested destockal verbstem **(cī-ni)*, formed according to § 24.5.9. It has nothing to do with *(ih-ci-hui)*, "to hurry," apropos of a source. (The fact that the act of hurrying might bring about an act of panting is not relevant. However, we are dealing with translations—distortions that hide the meaning of the constituent morphemes—and it is not impossible that the root morpheme *ci-* of the original destockal verbstem **(ci-ī-ni)* is somehow that of the verbstem *(ih-ci-hui)*. Even if this were true, however, Siméon's assertion would still be false.)

11. cacayachilia: nitētla—This is a derived double-object applicative frequentative verbstem that cannot possibly come from the intransitive (!) frequentative verbstem *(ca-cay-a-ca)*, "to become small pieces," first, because of the impossible jump from no verb object to two, and, second, because the shift of /k/ to [č] is not possible here. The correct source is the single-object causative frequentative verbstem *tla-(ca-cay-a-tz-a)*, "to cause s.th. to become small pieces," where the shift from /¢/ to [č] is unexceptional; see § 27.4.5.

12. cecepahtic—The intensified-adjective formation involving *(pah)-tli* (see § 41.1.4.*b*) has nothing to do with any derivation involving the intransitive verbstem-forming suffix *a-hui*. The fact that both items involve the nounstem *(ce)-tl-*, "ice," at some point in their structure in no way makes one the source of the other.

13. copāctli—This is the most absurd statement of "roots" in the entire exercise. By what logic did Siméon connect the notion of "palate, roof of the mouth" to a pot, *(cōmi)-tl-*, and becoming/being happy, *(pāqui)*? Also, what motivated him to dispense with the /m/ of *(cōmi)-tl-*? The source of *copāctli* is uncertain.

14. cuecuetzoca—The intransitive frequentative verbstem *(cue-cuetz-o-ca)* has nothing to do with the causative verbstem *tla-(cuech-o-ā)*, "to reduce s.th. to a powder."

Key to the Exercises 199

The *o* in the latter is a stock-formative occurring before the causative suffix *ā*; the *o* in *cuecuetzoca* is the stock-formative of the intransitive destockal verbstem *(cuetz-ō-ni)*. There is no relation between the two.

15. The entry should read *ihzolotza: nitla*. This is a compound verbstem whose embed is *(ih-)-* (see § 30.13). The source verbstem is the transitive destockal verbstem *tla-(zol-ō-ni-ā)*, from the intransitive destockal verbstem *(zol-ō-ni)*, "for flowing water to make a noisy sound."

58B. *Huitzilopochtli*

  a. Huitztzilōpōchtli zan mācēhualli, zan tlācatl catca. Nāhualli. Tētzāhuitl. Ahtlācacemēleh. Tēīxcuepani. Quiyōcoyani in yāōyōtl. Yāōtēcani; yāōtlahtoāni.

  Ca ītechpa mihtoāya, "Tēpan quitlāza in xiuhcōātl, in mamalhuāztli"—quihtōznequi "yāōyōtl," "teōātl tlachinōlli." Auh in ihcuāc ilhuiquīxtilōya, malmicohuaya, tlaāltīlmicohuaya. Tēāltiāyah in pōchtēcah.

  Auh in īc mochihchīhuaya: xiuhtōtōnacocheh catca; xiuhcōānāhualeh; xiuhtlalpīleh: mātacaxeh; tzitzileh, oyohualeh.

  b. Huitzilopochtli [i.e., he is (called) "It Is a Left Hand/Foot Like a Hummingbird"] was just a commoner, just a human being. He was a shaman. He was an apparition [~ a portent of evil]. He was a sadistic person. He was a deceiver. He customarily instigated [*lit.*, he customarily invents them] wars. He was a troop commander; he was a battle strategist [*lit.*, a war chief].

  Indeed, about him it was said, "He hurls upon people the turquoise snake [i.e., the fire snake] and (n.i.N.) the fire drill,"—which means "war" or "flood and (n.i.N.) scorched fields" [i.e., war]. And when people celebrated (his) festival, people sacrificed captives; people sacrificed "bathed ones" [*lit.*, people used to survive captives; people used to survive (ritually) "bathed ones"]. The merchants (ritually) "bathed" people [i.e., ones who were to be sacrificed].

  And thus was he adorned: he wore ear pendants of lovely-cotinga feathers [*lit.*, he was a turquoise-bird ear-pendant owner]; he had a fire-snake mask [*lit.*, he was a turquoise-snake mask owner]; he wore a turquoise sash [*lit.*, he was a turquoise-sash owner]; he had a maniple/maniples [*lit.*, he was a maniple owner]; he had jingles [*lit.*, he was a jingle owner]; he had bells [*lit.*, he was a bell owner].

58C. *The Eagle Falcon*

  a. Cuāuhtlohtli, īhuān tlohcuāuhtli: achi huēi in cihuātl, auh in oquichtli zan achi tepitōn. In cihuātl cencah yeh tlamāni. Ītōcā alcon.

  Tēncōztic. In iihhuiyo mochi tlīlnextic. In īcuitlapil mahtlāctli omōme. Īcxi cōztic.

  In īc tlama: zan īca in īzti. In ihcuāc īmpan mocahcanāuhtiuh tōtōmeh, mā zo ihui in īmpan mocahcanāhua, ahmō īc quinhuītequi in īāmatlapal, zan iztitica quimmotzolōznequi. Auh in yehhuāntin tōtōmeh ahoc mō huel patlānih. In patlānizneuquih, ahoc mō huel huih. Zā chahchapāntihuetzih. Auh in tlā centetl huel cahci, zan niman īēlpan quimotzoltzitzquia. Niman quiquechcoyōnia, cātli in īezzo. Huel quitlamia; ahmō tleh canah itlah quichipīnia in eztli. Auh in ihcuāc huel tlacua, achtopa quihuihhuitla in iihhuiyo in tōtōtl. In cemilhuitl ēxpa in tlacua. In īc ceppa ihcuāc in aye mō huālquīza tōnatiuh. In īc ōppa nepantlah tōnatiuh. In īc ēxpa ihcuāc in oncalac tōnatiuh.

Mopilhuahtia huel ohhuicān; texcalcamac in mochāntia. Zan ōntemeh in īpilhuān.

Īhuān in yehhuātl tlohtli quiyōllōtiāya in Huitztzilōpōchtli, īpampa ca quihtoāyah in yehhuāntin tlōtlohtin in īc ēxpa tlacuah in cemilhuitl iuhqui in mah cātlītiah in tōnatiuh, īhuān īpampa in ihcuāc cātlih eztli, moch quitlamiah.

Ahmō cualōni in īnacayo. Auh in īc mahcih tlōtlohtin, īīxpan quitlāliliah canauhtli, īhuān īēlpan, īēlchiquippan [for īēlchiquiuhpan] quitlālilia tzonhuāztli. Auh in cequīntin zan quiyahualochtiah in tzonhuāztli.

b. The eagle falcon, also [called] the falcon eagle: the female is larger than the male [*lit.*, the female is somewhat large, but the male is just somewhat small]. The female is an excellent hunter. Its [Spanish] name is halcón.

It has a yellow bill [*lit.*, it is yellow at the bill]. Its plumage is entirely dark gray. Its tail has twelve [feathers]. Its legs are yellow.

It hunts thus: it is just by means of its talons. When it goes into a dive [*lit.*, it goes making itself thin (by folding its wings in order to dive)] on birds, although it dives on them, it does not strike them with its wings but just tries to grapple them with its talons. And those birds are no longer able to fly. If they try to fly, they can no longer go. They just abruptly drop heavily/plop. And when it [the falcon] successfully catches one, it just immediately grips its breast with its talons. Immediately it pierces it at the neck and drinks its blood. It consumes it completely; it does not let a drop of blood fall anywhere [*lit.*, nothing anywhere that is something that is blood does it cause to sprinkle]. And when it is able to eat, first it plucks out the bird's feathers. During a day it eats three times [*lit.*, it is three times that it eats]. The first time is when the sun has not yet come forth. The second time is at midday. The third time is when the sun has set.

It raises its young in quite dangerous places; it builds its home in a cavity in a cliff. It has only two nestlings [*lit.*, its children are only two in number].

Moreover, Huitzilopochtli used to inspire this falcon, because, they used to say, when these falcons eat three times a day, it is as if they give it to the sun to drink, and (n.i.N.) in addition because when they drink blood they consume all of it.

Its flesh is not edible. But in order that falcons be caught, they set a duck before one of them, and (n.i.N.) therewith in its breast, in its chest they place a snare. But some only put the snare for it around it [i.e., the duck].

58D. *Distracted Messengers*

a. Quil mach Quetzalcōātl Tōllān tlahtoāni catca. Quil ōmentin cihuah mahāltiāyah in īneāltiāyān. In ōquinhuālittac, īc niman quinhuālihuah cequīntin quimittazqueh in āc ihqueh mahāltiah. Auh in yehhuāntin tītlantin, zan ye quimitzticateh in mahāltiah cihuah. Ahmō mah quinōnōtzatoh. In Quetzalcōātl oc ceppa zā tēpan conihuah in īxōlōuh (quihtōznequi "ītītlan") in quimittaz āc ihqueh in mahāltiah. Zan nō iuh quichīuh; ayoc mō quicuepato in īnetītlaniz.

Īc oncān tzīntic, nelhuayōhuac in mihtoa "moxōxōlōtītlani."

b. It is said that Quetzalcoatl was king in Tollan. It is said that two women were bathing in his bathing place. When he saw them, immediately he sent some people to see who were bathing. But these messengers just remained looking at the bathing women. They did not go to report to him [*lit.*, to advise him]. Quetzalcoatl later again sent off his "page" (which means "his messenger") to see who were the ones bathing. He also just did likewise; he never brought back [*lit.*, he never went in order to return it] his report [*lit.*, his message].

In this fashion there it began and took root that one says "an errand is being run in the manner of pages."

Introduction to the Vocabulary

For the most part the translations of the following vocabulary items are of those of Molina. One should remember, as pointed out in Lesson 1, that the life-worlds experienced and gauged by a Spanish speaker and by a Nahuatl speaker were quite different. Spaniards, like Europeans in general, not only were not sympathetic to native ways—they were obsessively hostile to them. Their aim was to convert the foreign into what they deemed the better and the right, not just in religion, where the conversion was deliberate and aggressive, but in every area of life, where it was often unconscious. Molina shared in this conversionary endeavor. It should be remembered, therefore, that while we are forced to accept his equivalences, we must be wary of them, knowing that they offer in varying degrees skewed denotations, unfaithful connotations, and deceptive pragmatics. Of course, even if Molina had been in accord with the Nahuatl speakers' culture, his translations would have suffered the inescapable distortion always present in translation; they would just not have been so indiscriminate. All intermeshing linguistic systems (phonology, morphology, syntax, semantics, etc.) are distinctive in their functioning within their particular language. Of them all, however, the semantic system is the most particularistic.

The entries in this vocabulary include only items used in the exercises. As a rule, verb + verb compound stems (see Lesson 28) are not listed unless they exhibit some peculiarity of meaning or form. Other regularly formed derived verbstems are not listed (such as frequentatives; see Lesson 27). Affective nounstems containing -TZIN, -TŌN, -PĪL, -PŌL (see Lesson 32) are included only in special instances.

In using this vocabulary one should be aware of the following considerations that affect search procedures:

1. The format of the listing was devised in the belief that speed in locating an item is of less importance than the furthering of an understanding of stem formation. That is to say, the vocabulary has been made an integral part of the learning project. The entries are therefore listed by "source" stems under which are included, as subentries, derived stems and compound stems in which a source stem serves as embed. The embed of a subentered compound stem is italicized. The notion of "source" stem is quite loose, being operationally defined as "the most basic stem in the corpus" (that is, it may be a derived stem or even a compound stem).

2. The main entries are alphabetized by *stems*; therefore, for example **etl**, i.e., (E)-TL-, is listed before **eh,** i.e., (EH)-∅-.

3. Since, as a rule, transitive verbstems are derived from intransitive ones, the intransitive is listed as the source stem; thus, to find TLA-(MAN-A) one must look under (MANI). (Incidentally, this description of the derivational facts contradicts earlier theories of grammarians who mistook the intransitive stem for a passive derivation [see Olmos, for example]. It is in fact an inchoative or stative.)

4. A nounstem beginning with TLA-, TĒ-, M-O-, M-☐-, NE-, or a combination of these, may be a derived form and, if so, will be listed under the source stem; for example, **tlaquēntli** is to be found under (QUĒMI):TLA-. Remember also that stems beginning with TLA- or M-O- (and more rarely NE-) followed by two consonants may indicate a source with a supportive [i]; for example, **tlahtōlli** is listed under (iHT-O-Ā):TLA-. An initial supportive [i] is indicated in an entry by a lowercase letter.

5. The spelling changes presented in Lesson 2 should be kept in mind. For example, a derived form with a **-co** may come from a source stem with -QUI; one with a **-z** may come from a source stem with -CI; etc.

6. The sound changes presented in Lesson 2 should be kept in mind. For example, a stem with **-x** may be derived from one with -ZA or -CI; etc.

7. Verbstems are listed by the imperfective stem followed by the perfective stem; e.g., (CATZ-Ā- HUA) > (CATZ-Ā-HUA) . When a transitive stem is listed, its verb object pronoun is given after the perfective stem; e.g., (CĀHUA) > (CĀUH):TLA-. A projective verb object pronoun is represented by the nonspecific form; i.e., TĒ- (for human), TLA- (for nonhuman). A reflexive verb object pronoun is represented by the nonfirst-person form M-O-; a reciprocative verb object pronoun is represented by the first-person plural form T-O-. When necessary, the nonspecific reflexive/reciprocative pronoun is represented by NE-.

8. Both restricted-use and general-use nounstems are listed only for **-tl-** class stems; however, both stems are also shown for other class nounstems in special instances. Derived general-use nounstems that obligatorily occur in possessive-state NNCs are indicated by the possessor pronoun, +TĒ(or +TLA(, where the leftward parenthesis indicates the beginning of the stem. As always, the class-identifying *num¹* morph is separated from the stem by a hyphen to indicate that only a stem and not an NNC is being presented. The hyphen after the *num¹* morph insists that one remember that in an NNC a *num²* morph must obligatorily follow. Therefore, in the listing -TLI-, -TL-, -IN-, -☐-, and -UH- are *always* followed in an NNC by the singular-number morph -Ø. For a nounstem that occurs in an NNC with a plural subject pronoun, -T- indicates the dyad -T-IN, -M- the dyad M-EH, and -HU- the dyad -HU-ĀN. A -Ø- in the *num¹* slot indicates the dyad -Ø-Ø, except when the *num²* slot is to be filled with the plural morph -H; in this case the full dyad, -Ø-H, is shown.

9. The arrangement of letters in the alphabetical sequence is as follows: A, C, CH, CU (~ UC), [D], E, (H), HU (~ UH), I, (L), M, N, O, P, QU, T, TL, TZ, [V], X, Y, Z. The parentheses around H, L, UC, and UH indicate that they do not occur in initial position (although L is so used in items borrowed from Spanish). The brackets around D and V indicate that they are foreign to the system and occur only in items borrowed from Spanish. Special attention must be paid to the digraphs CH, CU, HU, QU, TL, and TZ; each two-character unit symbolizes a single sound. They are alphabetized as such.

Note: For anyone interested, the names of the letters are a, ce, che, cue /kʷe/, e, ach, hue /we/, i, le, me, ne, o, pe, que /ke/, te, le, tze, xe /še/, ye, za /sa/. These names are, of course, pronounced with Nahuatl values; thus, for example, i is not pronounced /ai/ as in English but /i/ as in Nahuatl.

Vocabulary

A

*(Ā) > (Ā) = [*defec v, creates only pret-as-pres VNCs*], to be present; **nāc** = I am present; **āc** = he is present
  (Ā-Ø)-C- > (Ā-Ø-CĀ)-UH- = *pret agen*, one who is present; *interrog*, **āc?** = who is it/he/she? who are they? **āc in . . . ?** = who is it that . . . ? (*tradit sp*, **aquin**); **āc ihqueh?** = who are they? (*tradit sp*, **aquique**); *neg*, **ayāc** = it is no one
  (A-C-AH)-Ø- = someone
(Ā)-TL- > (Ā)-UH- = water/urine; the crown of the head [*Occasional emb*, (AH-)-. Sublistings involving this embed stem are placed at the end of this heading.]; **ātl tlacualli** = it is water and it is food; i.e., it is a repast/meal/banquet
  (Ā-HUAH-Ø)-☐- > (Ā-HUAH-Ø-CĀ)-UH- = *pret agen*, one who has owned water; i.e., a water owner; (Ā-HUAH-Ø-CĀ-N)-☐- = at/to/from a place of water owners
  (Ā-CA)-TL- > (Ā-CA)-UH- = water associate; i.e., reed; (Ā-CA-TŌNA-L-EH-Ø)-☐- > (Ā-CA-TŌNA-L-EH-Ø-CĀ)-UH- = *pret agen*, one who has owned a Reed day sign; i.e., a Reed day sign owner; (Ā-CA-TZĀLAN)-☐ = among the reeds
  (Ā-CAL)-LI = dugout canoe; boat; (Ā-CAL-CHĪMAL)-LI- = a shield in the form of a boat; i.e., a war dugout; a warship; (Ā-CAL-CHĪMAL-EH-Ø)-☐- > (Ā-CAL-CHĪMAL-EH-Ø-CĀ)-UH- = *pret agen*, one who has owned a war dugout; i.e., a war dugout owner; (Ā-CAL-HUAH-Ø)-☐- > (Ā-CAL-HUAH-Ø-CĀ)-UH- = *pret agen*, one who has owned a dugout canoe; i.e., a dugout canoe owner; T-☐-(Ā-CAL-HUĪ-TEQUI) > (Ā-CAL-HUĪ-TEC) = to bump into one another with boats; (Ā-CAL-OH)-TLI- = a road for dugout canoes; i.e., a canal; TLA-(Ā-CAL-TĒM-A) > (Ā-CAL-TĒN) = to fill s.th. into a dugout canoe/boat
  (Ā-CŌL)-LI- = a water bend; (Ā-CŌL-NĀHUA-C)-☐- = *place-name s*, Place within Hearing Distance of the Water Bend; (Ā-CŌL NĀHUA-☐-CA)-TL- = one associated with Acolnahuac/an inhabitant of Acolnahuac
  (Ā-HUĒ-HUĒ)-TL- > (Ā-HUĒ-HUĒ)-UH- = water-drum, i.e., cypress tree
  (Ā-L-TEPĒ)-TL- > (Ā-L-TEPĒ)-UH- = water-and-hill, i.e., town/city; (Ā-L-TEPĒ-TE-NĀMi)-TL- > (Ā-L-TEPĒ-TE-NĀN)-Ø- = town/city wall
  (Ā-L-TI-Ā) > (Ā-L-TI-H): M-☐- = to cause o.s. to have water; i.e., to bathe o.s./to take a bath; +TĒ(NE-Ā-L-TI-Ā-YĀ-N)-Ø- = *pos-st*, (s.o.'s) bathing place; TĒ-(Ā-L-TI-Ā) >

(Ā-L-TI-H) = to cause s.o. to have water, i.e., to bathe s.o.; (TLA-Ā-L-TĪ-L)-LI- = one who has been bathed, i.e., a bathed one/a ritually bathed one (i.e., a sacrificial victim); (TLA-Ā-L-TĪ-L-MIQUI) > (TLA-Ā-L-TĪ-L-MIC) = to die in relation to a (ritually) bathed one, i.e., to survive a (ritually) bathed one; i.e., to sacrifice a (ritually) bathed one

(Ā-MAL-Ī-N-A-L)-LI- = a twisted thing in the form of water, i.e., twisted water; (Ā-MAL-Ī-N-A-L-PAN)-☐- = *place-name s,* The Area of Twisted Water

(Ā-MĀXa)-TL- > (Ā-MĀX)-∅- = water bifurcation

(Ā-NĀHUA-C)-☐- = *place-name s,* Place within Hearing Distance of Water, i.e., Place Near Water [1. the area bordering the southern coasts (Gulf and Pacific) of Mexico; 2. the area around the lakes in the Valley of Mexico]; (Ā-NĀHUA-☐-CA)-TL- = a person associated with Anahuac; a person from Anahuac; an inhabitant of Anahuac

(Ā-NE-PAN-TLAH)-☐- = place in the middle of the water/lake

(Ā-PANŌ) > (Ā-PANŌ) = to cross over on/in water; to ford a stream

(Ā-POZ-Ō-N-A-L)-LI- = water foam; M-☐-(Ā-POZ-Ō-N-A-L-NEH-NEQUI) > (Ā-POZ-Ō-N-A-L-NEH-NEC) = to resemble amber/foam

(Ā-TATACA) > (Ā-TATACA) = to dig for water

(Ā-TE)-TL- > (Ā-TE)-UH- = rock/egg characterized by water/urine; i.e., testicle

(Ā-TĒN)-TLI- = water edge; shore/beach

(Ā-TEZ-CA)-TL- > (Ā-TEZ-CA)-UH- = a mirror made of water, i.e., a puddle/pool/pond/lake; (Ā-TEZ-CA-TĒN)-TLI- = pond edge/shore; lake edge/shore

(Ā-TI-YA) > (Ā-TI-YA) ~ (Ā-TI-X) = to become water/like water/liquid; (for metal or wax) to melt; to lose density; (Ā-TI-∅)-C- = a thing that has become water/like water/liquid, i.e., a melted thing; a transparent thing; TLA-(Ā-TI-LIĀ) > (Ā-TI-LIH) = to cause s.th. to become water/liquid; i.e., to melt s.th. (e.g., metal, wax)

(Ā-TOC-TIĀ) > (Ā-TOC-TIH): TLA- = to cause s.th. to be carried by a river

(Ā-TŌTOL)-IN- = turkey on water, i.e., pelican

(Ā-TŌY-A)-TL- > (Ā-TŌY-A)-UH- = a thing that pours forth in the form of water, i.e., river; (Ā-TŌY-A-PAN)-☐- = over a river; (Ā-TŌY-A-PAN-O-Ā) > (Ā-TŌY-A-PAN-O-H) = to ford a river; (Ā-TŌY-A-XĀL)-LI- = river sand

(Ā-TLA-COMŌL)-LI- = a pit/hole with water, a well

(Ā-TLA-CUI) > (Ā-TLA-CUI) = to fetch water

(A-TLAH)-☐- = place of abundant water; (Ā-TLAH-CA)-TL- = person associated with a place of much water, i.e., a lake dweller

(Ā-TLA-TLA) > (Ā-TLA-TLA) = to burn on water/in a liquid state [NOT "(for water) to burn"]; to become damaged as if by fire for lack of water; (Ā-TLA-TLA-YĀ-N)-☐- = at/to/from a place where there is burning on water/in a liquid state

(Ā-TL-Ī) > (Ā-TL-Ī) = to drink water; (Ā-TL-Ī-HUA-LŌ-NI)-∅- = a thing with which people drink water, i.e., a drinking vessel

(Ā-TL-IHTI-C)-☐- = at/to/from a place in the midst of water [*This might also be the double nucleus construction* **ātl iihtic,** "at/to/from a place in the water's midst."]

(Ā-YACa)-TL- > (Ā-YAC)-∅- = water nose/point, i.e., a point at the front of a rush of water; an inlet of water

(Ā-ZŌL)-IN- = water quail, i.e., Wilson snipe

(Ā-ZTA)-TL- > (Ā-ZTA)-UH- = white thing in water, i.e., an egret; egret feather; (Ā-ZTA-CAL)-LI- = egret feather house

(AH-HUETZI) > (AH-HUETZ) = to fall in the form of water; i.e., (for dew) to form; (AH-HUECH)-TLI- = a thing that has fallen in the form of water, i.e., dew [also (AH-HUACH)-TLI-]; (AH-HUACH-QUIY-A-HUI) = to drizzle lightly

(AH-PIL-O-Ā) > (AH-PIL-O-H) = to cause water to hang; i.e, to pour water; (AH-PIL-Ō-L)-LI- = a clay water jar/pitcher

(AH-QUETZA) > (AH-QUETZ) = to lift up the head (e.g., while lying down); to hold the head high (e.g., in arrogance)

ACH = possibly/maybe/perhaps; I don't know (+ *interrog*); **ach cān** = I don't know where [*as a response*]

(ĀCH-CĀUH)-TLI- = elder brother; master of youths [*abs af s*, (ĀCH-CĀ-CĀUH)-T-] [*The pos-st core* +TĒ(ĀCH-CĀUH)- *permits a secondary gen-use stem formation*, (TĒ-ACH-CĀUH)-∅- (*see § 15.1.5). Also,* +TĒ(ĀCH-CĀUH)- *has the variants* +TI(ĀCH-AUH)- *and* +T(ĀCH-CĀUH)-, *which permit secondary gen-use stem formations:* (TI-ĀCH-CĀUH)-∅- *and* (T-ĀCH-CĀUH)-∅-; *the latter is usually translated as* "a prime thing/a foremost thing/an excellent thing."]

(A-CHI)-∅- = a small amount or quantity; a few; (A-CHIH-TŌN-CA)-☐- = for/in a little time

(ACH-TO)-☐- = first; (ACH-TO-PA)-☐- = first; in the first place

(AH-)- = *glottalized emb. See* (Ā)-TL-.

AH- ~ AY- ~ A- = not; non-/in-; **ahca zo ah#** = not; **ahca no zo mō** = or perhaps not

(AH-CĀ-N)-☐- = no place

(AH-CO)-☐- = in no site, i.e., above/up there/up here/upstairs; TLA-(AH-CO-CUI) > (AH-CO-UC) ~ (AH-CO-C) = to lift s.th.; (AH-CO-HUETZI) > (AH-CO-HUETZ) = to go upward/rise

(AH-HUEL)-☐- = unsuccessfully badly; unable; impossible

(AH-MAN-A) > (AH-MAN): M-☐- = to become upset/alarmed/disturbed; TĒ-(AH-MAN-A) > (AH-MAN) = to upset/disturb s.o.

AH#∅-∅(MŌ)☐-∅# = in no way, by no means; no/not; **ahmō nō** = neither; **ahmō mah** = not as though/not such that; it is not the case that. . .

(AH-NE-ZCAL-I-H-∅-CĀ-YŌ)-TL- = what is characteristic of a person not well-bred, i.e., ill-breeding/lack of breeding. *See* (iZCAL-I-Ā): M-O-.

AHNŌ = neither/not either; **ahno zo** = perhaps otherwise; **ahno zo eh** = perhaps on the other hand

AHOC ~ AYOC ~ AOC = no longer/not any more

(AH-TLA)-TL- > (AH-TLA)-UH- = nonsling; i.e., spear thrower, atlatl. *See* (TLA)-TL-.

(AH-TLĀCA)-TL- > (AH-TLĀCA)-UH- = a nonperson, i.e., an inhuman person; an evil/vicious/malevolent person; (AH-TLĀCA-CEM-ĒL-EH-∅)-☐- > (AH-TLĀCA-CEM-ĒL-EH-∅-CĀ)-UH- = *pret agen*, one who has owned a whole/entire liver as an inhuman/vicious person; i.e., one who is happy/contented being an inhuman/vicious person; a cruel-hearted, sadistic person; (AH-TLĀCA-YŌ)-TL- = inhumanity

(AH-TLA-PA-L)-LI- = a nonside; i.e., a false side; i.e., a wing; a leaf

AHZA ZO = perhaps/perchance

AHZO = by chance/maybe

AYA = not yet; **aya mō** = not yet

AY#∅-∅(Ā-∅)C-∅# = it is no one. *See* (Ā-∅)-C-.

AY#∅-∅(ĀX-∅-CĀ-N)☐-∅#. *See* (ĀYA).

(AHCI) > (AHCI) = to arrive; +TĒ(AHCI-YĀ-N)-∅- = [*used in pos-st NNC*], (s.o.'s) place of arrival; **nahciyān** = it is my place of arrival; TĒ- ~ TLA-(AHCI) > (AHCI) = to overtake s.o./s.th.; to reach out and take s.th. [*applic obj unjustified by s's form*]
 (AHXĪ-TIĀ) > (AHXĪ-TIH): M-∅- = to cause o.s. to arrive; (H) to arrive; TĒ-(AHXĪ-TIĀ) > (AHXĪ-TIH) = to take s.o. (to a place);
(AHHUA) > (AHHUA): TĒ- = to scold/reprimand s.o.
(ĀHUI)-TL- > (ĀHUI)-∅- = aunt
(ĀHUI-YA) > (ĀHUI-YA) ~ (ĀHUI-X) = to become/be content; (ĀHUI-LŌ) = *nonac*; (ĀHUI-L)-LI- = pastime/recreation/toy/frivolity; M-O+TLA-(ĀHUI-L-TI-Ā) > (ĀHUI-L-TI-H) = to cause s.th. to be/serve as one's pastime/toy; i.e., to amuse o.s. with s.th.
(ĀMA)-TL- > (ĀMA)-UH- = paper/sheet of paper; *by extens,* book; (ĀMA-TLA-PA-L)-LI- = side like a sheet of paper, i.e., wing
(ĀMI) > (ĀN) = to go hunting
*(AM-I-Ā) > (AM-I-H) = [*defec v used only in pret VNC*], to exist (?); **quēn amih** = it is of such a nature; *interrog,* what is its nature? how is it? **quēn amihqueh** = they are of such a nature; *interrog,* what is their nature? how are they?
(ĀMOX)-TLI- = book
(ĀNA) > (ĀN): TLA- ~ TĒ- = to seize, take hold of s.th./s.o.; to catch s.th./s.o.; (TLA-ĀN)-TLI- = a thing that has been taken hold of; an unsheathed/disinterred/uprooted thing; M-∅-(ĀNA) > (ĀN) = to grow in height; (for a rope/cord) to give/stretch
ANCA = so that/so as to/in such a manner as to; if that is the case, then . . . ; judging from that, according to that
(AQUI) > (AC) = to enter; to fit in; TLA-(AQUI-Ā) > (AQUI-H) = to cause s.th. to enter, to insert s.th., to transplant s.th.; to drive s.th. (e.g., a stake) in the ground; to put s.th. in a hole; to add s.th. on; (TLA-AQUĪ-L)-LI- = a thing that has been added on; (TLA-AQUĪ-L-LŌ)-TL- > (TLA-AQUĪ-L-LO)-∅- = [*gen-use s used in org-pos NNCs*], an added-on thing; i.e., fruit
AT = perhaps
AUH = and
(ĀXCĀi)-TL- > (ĀXCĀ)-∅- = property/possessions
 (ĀXCĀ-HUAH-∅)-∅- > (ĀXCĀ-HUAH-∅-CĀ)-UH- = *pret agen*, one who has owned property, i.e., a propertied person
(ĀYA) > (ĀX) = to be fluent/easy/effortless (?); AY#∅-∅(ĀX-∅-CĀ-N)∅-∅# = hardly/barely/slowly/difficultly; **ayoc āxcān** = still barely
(ĀYI) > (ĀX): TLA- = to make/do s.th.; to till/work the land; TĒ+TLA-(ĀYĪ-TIĀ) > (ĀYĪ-TIH) = to make/urge s.o. to do/make s.th.
 (ĀX-∅-CĀ-N)-∅- = at present/now/today
 (ĀZ)-TLI- = tool/implement/device; (AH-ĀZ)-TLI- = a tool-like thing, i.e., wing; (ĀZ-CA)-TL- > (ĀZ-CA)-UH- = tool associate, i.e., mandible user; i.e., ant; (ĀZ-CA-PŌTZA-L)-LI- = ant mound; (ĀZ-TLĀ-N)-∅- = *place-name s*, At/To/From the Vicinity of Tools (?); (ĀZ-TĒ-∅-CA)-TL- = one associated with Aztlan; a dweller in Aztlan; an Aztec
(AYOH)-TLI- = squash

Vocabulary

C

(-C)-TLI-. *See* (-CO)-☐-.

*(C)-∅- > (C)-∅- = means/purpose/reason/cause; time [*Used only in a pos-st NNC and only with the 3rd sg pos pron* ī-∅- *and with a 3rd sg subj pron; therefore, it appears only in* ĪC, #∅-∅+Ī-∅(C)∅-∅#, "by means of it/with it/by way of it/through it/ . . ."]; **zan īc** = frequently/continually/ceaselessly; **īc cen** = for good/once and for all; **īc** = *interrog,* when? **īc in . . .** = *interrog,* when is it that? (*tradit sp,* **iquin**)

    (I-C-AH)-∅- = at some time/sometimes/occasionally; ever (*in questions*)

CA = indeed

*(CA)-∅- > (CA)-∅- = means [*used only in a pos-st NNC and as emb in conn-t comp*]; e.g., **moca** = with the help of you (sg)/by means of you/thanks to you; with you; against you; **huīctica** = by means of a digging stick

(CA)-TL- = [*predominantly used as matrix nounstem*] a being/entity; a being associated with (the embed) [*The association may be either actual or metaphorical.*]; e.g., **ācatl** = it is a thing associated with water, i.e., a reed; **ichcatl** = it is a thing associated with maguey fiber, i.e., cotton/wool; **Mēxihcatl** = a person associated with Mexihco; e.g., a dweller in/inhabitant of Mexihco [*Also source of the v* (CA-TI), "to become/be a being," i.e., "to be" (*see* (YE). *Also source of the n* (CA-L)-LI- (*see* (CAL)-LI-) *and the v* (CA-LI), *q.v.*]

(CĀ)-TL- = *interrog,* which entity?; *as matrix,* one who/that . . .

    (CĀ-TL-EH)-∅- = which one? (CĀ-TL-EH-HUĀ)-TL- = which one? (CĀ-TL-E-IN)-∅- = which one?

(CAC)-TLI- = sandal/shoe/footwear

    (CAC-COP-Ī-N-A) > (CAC-COP-Ī-N): M-O- = to pull o.s. off from the sandals/shoes, i.e., to pull off one's sandals/shoes

    (CAQU-EH-∅)-☐- > (CAQU-EH-∅-CĀ)-UH- = *pret agen,* one who has owned sandals/shoes; i.e., a sandal/shoe owner

    (CAC-NAMACA-∅)-C- > (CAC-NAMACA-∅-CĀ)-UH- = *pret agen,* one who has sold sandals/shoes, i.e., a sandal vendor/seller, a shoe vendor/seller

(CACA)-TL- = a type of frog

(CĀCĀ-L-Ō)-TL- > (CĀCĀ-L-Ō)-UH- = a crow

(CACAHUA)-TL > (CACAHUA)-UH- = cacao bean

(CA-H) ~ (CA-T). *See* (YE).

(CĀHUA) > (CĀHUA) = to last/abide/remain; (CĀHUi)-TL- > (CĀUH)-∅- = a thing that results from lasting/remaining; i.e., time

    (CĀHU-A) > (CĀUH): TLA- ~ TĒ- = to cause s.th./s.o. to remain; i.e., to leave/abandon s.th./s.o.; to let s.th./s.o. go; to carry s.th. elsewhere; to forsake s.o.; M-O-(CĀHU-A) > (CĀUH) = to cease/stop; to leave off speaking or doing s.th.; to hush/be quiet; to stop off (in a place); to stay; *reflex-as-pass,* to be left behind

    (TLA-CĀUH)-TLI- = an empty space; s.th. left behind/a leftover

    (TLA-CĀUH-∅)-QUI- > (TLA-CĀUH-∅-CĀ)-UH- = *pret agen,* one who has left s.th., i.e., a discarder/abandoner/leaver

    (CĀHU-A-L-TIĀ) > (CĀHU-A-L-TIH): M-O+TLA- = to cause o.s. to abandon s.th., i.e., to abstain from s.th./to refrain from s.th.

(CĀUH-∅-TI-QUĪZA) > (CĀUH-∅-TI-QUĪZ): M-O- = to abruptly stop off (at a place); (NE-CĀUH-∅-TI-QUĪZA-LIZ)-TLI- = action of abruptly stopping off (somewhere)

(CAL)-LI- = house [*Strictly analyzed, it is* (CA-L)-LI-, *with the* (CA)- *being the* (CA)-TL- *listed above but here used as an embed rather than as a matrix. This entry and all its subentries containing the stem as an emb should, technically speaking, be listed under* (CA)-TL-, *but it has seemed more convenient not to indicate the hyphen and to list it as a main entry.*]

(CAL-AQUI) > (CAL-AC) = to enter a house/to enter; +TĒ(CAL-AQUI-YĀ-N)-∅- = [*used in pos-st NNC*], (s.o.'s) entering place; (s.o.'s) entryway; (CAL-AC-O-HUA) > (CAL-AC-O-HUA) = *nonac*, [*used in impersonal NNCs*], (for people in general) to enter; TLA-(CAL-AQUI-Ā) > (CAL-AQUI-H) = to cause s.th. to enter

(CAL-COH-CŌL)-LI- = a manifoldly curved thing in the form of a house, i.e., a maze

(CAL-CUĀi)-TL- > (CAL-CUĀ)-∅- = head of a house, i.e., roof

(CAL-CUECH)-TLI- = soot of a house, i.e., soot

*(CAL-I) > (CAL) = to dwell/occupy a house; (CAL-∅)-QUI- = *pret agen*, a dweller/inhabitant

(CAL-IHTI-C)-▢- = in/to/from a place in the belly of a house; i.e., in/to/from the inside/interior of a house

(CAL-ĪX)-TLI- = face of a house; i.e., house front/entryway

(CAL-LAH)-▢- = place of abundant houses; i.e., a settlement, a group of houses, a small village; (CAH-CAL-LAH)-▢- = a village/settlement; villages/settlements

(CAL-LĀL)-LI- = land of a house, i.e., land on which a house sits

(CAL-ME-CA)-TL- = a rope of houses/rooms, i.e., a corridor; (CAL-ME-CA-C)-▢- = at a place of corridors, i.e., a monastery-like school where the sons of nobles and outstandingly qualified sons of commoners led austere, rigorously disciplined lives throughout most of their childhood and youth, being trained in religion, astrology, calendar reckoning, dream interpretation, history, literature, rhetoric, and correct social behavior

(CAL-MĪL)-LI- = field of a house, i.e., land around a house

(CAL-NACAZ)-TLI- = ear of a house, i.e., (outside) corner of a house

(CAL-NĀHUA-C)-▢- = at a place within hearing distance of a house, i.e., at a place in the vicinity of a/the house

(CAL-OH)-TLI- > (CAL-OH)-HUI- = path leading to a house, i.e., walk (leading to a house)

(CAL-PIYA) > (CAL-PIX) = to guard/be in charge of a house; (CAL-PIX-∅)-QUI- > (CAL-PIX-∅-CĀ)-UH- = *pret agen*, one who has guarded a house, a house guarder; i.e., a steward/majordomo

(CAL-PŌL)-LI- = big house, i.e., a quarter (of a town); city district/precinct/ward/quarter; suburb; *(CAL-PŌL-LŌ)-TL- > (CAL-PŌL-LŌ)-∅- = [*gen-use s used in org-pos NNCs*], (s.o.'s) integrally owned calpolli/(s.o.'s) own calpolli; (s.o.'s) home calpolli; **nocalpōllo** = it is my own calpolli

(CAL-TECH)-TLI = house side-surface, i.e., house facing/wall facing; (CAL-TECH)-▢- = [*2nd-degree adv*], in contact with a house/against a house wall

(CAMA)-TL- > (CAN)-∅- = mouth; cavity/opening

Vocabulary

(CAMOH)-TLI- = sweet potato
(CĀ-N)-◻- = at that place/there; *interrog*, at what place?/where? **cān in . . . ?** = where is it that . . . ? (*tradit sp*, **canin**)
  (CĀ-M-PA)-◻- = in/to/from/through what place? in/to/from/through where?
  (CA-N-AH)-◻- = at some place/somewhere
(CAN-Ā-HU-A) > (CAN-Ā-UH): TLA- = to make s.th. (e.g., a board) become thin
  (CAH-CAN-Ā-HU-A) > (CAH-CAN-Ā-UH): M-O- = (for a bird) to make itself thin (by folding its wings, as in a dive)
(CANAUH)-TLI- = duck
(CAQUI) > (CAC): TĒ- ~ TLA- = to hear s.o./s.th.; to listen to s.o./s.th.; TĒ+TLA-(CAQUI-LIĀ) > (CAQUI-LIH) = to hear s.th. from s.o.; TĒ+TĒ- ~ TĒ+TLA-(CAQUĪ-TIĀ) > (CAQUĪ-TIH) = to cause s.o. to hear s.o./s.th.; to inform s.o. of s.th.
(CA-T). *See* (YE).
(CATZ-Ā-HUA) ~ (CATZ-Ā-HUA) = to become/be dirty; (CATZ-Ā-HUA-∅)-C- = a dirty thing
  (CATZ-A-C)-TLI- = a thing that has been dirtied; a dirty/black thing
(CAXi)-TL- > (CAX)-∅- = bowl
  (CAX-PECH)-TLI- = platform serving as a bowl; i.e., a plate
(CAX-TŌL)-LI- = fifteen in number
  (CAX-TŌL-TE)-TL- = fifteen in number
(CAY-Ā-NI) > (CAY-Ā-N) = to become/be sparse/skimpy
  (CA-CAY-A-CA) = to become small pieces/crumbs
  (CA-CAY-A-TZ-A) > (CA-CAY-A-TZ): TLA- = to cause s.th. to become small pieces/crumbs; TĒ+TLA-(CA-CAY-A-CHI-LIĀ) > (CA-CAY-A-CHI-LIH): = to cause s.th. to become pieces/scraps/crumbs for s.o.; to crumble s.th. for s.o.; to take s.th. to pieces for s.o.
(CE)-TL- > (CE)-UH- = ice/icicle
  (CE-CE-YA) = to become/be like ice; i.e., to become/be cold; (CE-CE-∅)-C- = a thing that has become cold; a cold thing; (CE-CE-PAH-TI-∅)-C- = a thing that has become very cold; a very cold thing/a frozen thing; *metaph*., a very terrifying/dreadful thing; TLA-(CE-CE-LIĀ) > (CE-CE-LIH): = to chill s.th.
  (CE-CUI) > (CE-UC) ~ (CE-C) = *anim*, to be cold (CE-C)-TLI- = one who has become cold; a cold one; (CE-C-MIQUI) > (CE-C-MIC) = to die in the manner of a cold one; i.e., to suffer from/die of the cold
  (CĒ-HUA) > (CĒ-HUA) = (for the weather) to become/be cold [< *(CE-Ē-HUA)]; (CĒ-HUA-L)-LI- = shade/shadow (e.g., cast by a tree)
(CE-HUETZI) > (CE-HUETZ) = for there to be a freeze; (CE-HUETZI-LIZ)-TLI-, action of becoming frozen; (CE-HUETZI-LIZ-PAN)-◻- = in freezing weather time
(CE-HUI) > (CE-UH) = for an angry person) to become calmed down; (for a fire/a candle) to become extinguished; (for s.th. hot) to become cool
(CE-HUIĀ) > (CE-HUIH): M-O- = to use coolness in relation to o.s.; i.e., to rest/take a rest; M-O-(CEH-CE-HUIĀ) > (CEH-CE-HUIH) = to rest from time to time; (for each person) to take a rest; TĒ-(CE-HUIĀ) > (CE-HUIH) = to give a rest to s.o./to spell s.o.; to disencumber s.o.; to mollify s.o.; TLA-(CE-HUIĀ) > (CE-HUIH) = to extinguish s.th. (e.g., fire, candle)

(CE-PAY-A-HUI) > (CE-PAY-A-UH) = to snow; (CE-PAY-A-HUI)-TL- = snow
(CĒ-L)-∅-. *See* (CEM)-∅-.
(CEL-I-YA) > (CEL-I-YA) ~ (CEL-I-Z) = to sprout/burgeon; (CEL-I-∅)-C- = a fresh, green thing; +TLA(CEL-I-CA)-∅- = *pos-st only*, s.th.'s action of sprouting; (s.th.'s) new growth/fresh sprouting
(CE-LIĀ): TLA-. *See* (CE-YA).
(CEM)-∅- ~ CEN)-∅- ~ (CĒ)-∅- = one in number
   (CEM-ĒL-EH-∅)- > (CEM-ĒL-EH-∅-CĀ)-UH- = *pret agen*, one who has a liver that is one (i.e., entire/whole); i.e., a contented, tranquil person
   (CEM-IHCA) > (CEM-IHCA) = to stand as one (i.e., forever); (CEM-IHCA-∅)-C- = one that stands forever; s.th. eternal; *adv*, eternally/forever
   (CEM-ILHUI)-TL- = one day, a whole day; [*in 1st-decree advlzd NNC*], during one day/for a whole day; (CĒ-CEM-ILHUI)-TL- = every day
   (CEM-MĀ)-TL- = one fathom
   (CEM-PANA-HUIĀ) > (CEM-PANA-HUIH): TĒ- ~ TLA- = to surpass s.o./s.th.
   (CEM-PŌHUA-L)-LI- = one score/twenty in number; (CEM-PŌHUA-L-XIHUI)-TL = twenty years
   (CEM-POL-I-HUI) > (CEM-POL-I-UH) = to become destroyed forever/to perish forever; (CEM-POH-POL-I-HUI) > (CEM-POH-POL-I-UH) = to become completely and forever destroyed
(CEN)-∅- = *advlzd*, as one, i.e., completely/entirely; together; for once and all; **īc cen** = forever
(CEN-CA-H)- = [*prfv occuring in VNC with 3rd sg subj*], **cencah** = *advlzd VNC*, wholly/entirely/completely; much; very
(CEN-CĀHU-A) > (CEN-CĀUH): TLA- = to leave s.th. as one (i.e., complete); i.e., to get s.th. ready; to prepare s.th.; to adorn s.th./deck s.th. out; TĒ+TLA-(CEN-CĀHUI-LIĀ) > (CEN-CĀHUI-LIH) = to get s.th. ready for s.o.; to prepare s.th. for s.o.
(CEN-CHĪHUA) > (CEN-CHĪUH): TLA- = (for several persons) to make s.th. as one (i.e., together); to cooperate in making s.th.
(CEN-CUĀ) > (CEN-CUAH): TLA- = to eat s.th. entirely, to eat s.th. up completely
(CEN-HUETZI) > (CEN-HUETZ) = to fall as one (i.e., together); i.e., to sit down together as a group
(CEN-TE)-TL- = one in number; (CEN-TE-TI) > (CEN-TE-T) = to become a unity; to be in unison
(CEN-TECPĀN)-TLI- = one lined-up set, i.e., twenty in number
(CEN-TLA-HT-A-L-HUIĀ) > (CEN-TLA-HT-A-L-HUIH): TĒ- = to speak with one (idea/thought) about s.o., i.e., to make up one's mind about s.o.
(CEN-TLĀL-I-Ā) > (CEN-TLĀL-I-H): M-O- = to sit down together [*The subj pron must be pl.*]
(CEN-TLA-MAN)-TLI- = one thing/one part/one affair
(CEN-YOHUA-L)-LI- = one night; [*2nd-degree advlzd NNC*] **cenyohual** = during one night/for one whole night; (CĒ-CEN-YOHUA-L)-∅- = every night/night after night
(CEP-PA)-∅- = one time/once; **oc ceppa** = once more/once again
(CĒ)-∅- = one in number; **oc cē** = it is another one
*(CĒ-L)-LI- > (CĒ-L)-∅- = [*used only in pos-st NNC*], aloneness; alone; lone/solitary; **nocēl** = I am alone; **īcēl āzcatl** = it is the "lone ant" (~ the "solitary ant")

Vocabulary

(CE-QUI)-∅- > (CE-C-)-∅- = one/a certain amount or number; one/some/part (CE-C-CĀ-N)-☐- = in one place/in a certain place (CE-C-NI)-☐- = in one place/in a certain place
(CEN)-TLI- = dried ear of maize [*var. s*, (CIN)-TLI-]
(CE-YA) > (CE-Z) = to be willing/to consent/to agree; (CE-YA-LIZ)-TLI- = action of being willing; willingness; will; TLA-(CE-LIĀ) > (CE-LIH) = to be willing about s.th., i.e., to receive/accept s.th.; TĒ+TLA-(CE-LI-LIĀ) > (CE-LI-LIH) = to receive s.th. from s.o.; +TĒ(CE-YA-YA)-∅- = [*used in pos-st NNC*] (s.o.'s) will/volition; **noceyaya** = it is my means/faculty of willing; i.e., it is my will/volition
(CI-A-HUI). *See* (CIY-A-HUI).
(CIH)-TLI- = grandmother; jackrabbit/hare
(CIHUĀ)-TL- > (CIHUĀ)-UH- = woman/wife
  *(CIHUĀ-POH)-TLI- > (CIHUĀ-POH)-∅- = [*used only in pos-st NNCs*], a fellow woman; (female) companion (of a woman); kinswoman (of a woman); M-O+TĒ-(CIHUĀ-POH-TI-Ā) > (CIHUĀ-POH-TI-H) = (for a woman) to cause o.s. to become her fellow woman; i.e., (for a woman) to take s.o. (a woman) for a friend
  (CIHUĀ-TLĀ-N)-☐- = *place-name s*, In/To/From the Place in the Vicinity of Women; the Region of Women, i.e., the West; (CIHUĀ-TLĀ-M-PA)-☐- = Toward/From the Region of Women; i.e., Toward/From the West
(CIN)-TLI-. *See* (CEN)-TLI-.
(CĪTLAL)-IN- = star [*abs af s*, (CĪ-CĪTLAL)-T-]
(CIY-A-HUI) > (CIY-A-UH) = to become tired; TLA-(CIY-A-HUI) > (CIY-A-UH) = to become tired because of s.th. [*applic obj unjustified by form*]
(-CO)-☐- ~ (-C)-TLI- = [*defec loc n used only as a matrix s*], place/site
  (CŌĀ)-TL- > (CŌĀ)-UH- = snake; a sharer/twin/guest [*abs af s*, (CŌ-CŌA)-∅-H]
  (CŌĀ-CHĪHUA) > (CŌĀ-CHĪUH): TĒ- = to make s.o. a sharer, i.e., to be a host to s.o.
  (CŌĀ-CUA-LŌ) > (CŌĀ-CUA-LŌ) = to be eaten by means of snakes
  (CŌĀ-NŌTZA) > (CŌĀ-NŌTZ): TĒ- = to summon s.o. as a sharer, i.e., to invite s.o. to be a guest
  (CŌĀ-TEQUI)-TL- > (CŌĀ-TEQUI)-UH- = work with sharers, i.e., communal work
  (CŌĀ-TE)-TL- > (CŌĀ-TE)-UH- = rock from a snake, i.e. a snake egg
  (CŌĀ-TEPĒ)-TL- = Snake Mountain
  (CŌĀ-XĀ-YACa)-TL- > (CŌĀ-XĀ-YAC)-∅- = snake face/mask; (CŌĀ-XĀ-YACA-YO-H-∅)-☐- > (CŌĀ-XĀ-YACA-YO-H-∅-CĀ)-UH- = *pret agen*, a thing that has owned abundant snake masks; i.e., a thing covered/decorated with the snake-mask design(s)
(COCO-YA) > (COCO-X) = to become/be sick; (COCO-X-∅)-QUI- > (COCO-X-∅-CĀ)-UH- = *pret agen*, one who has become sick, i.e., a sick person; (COCO-X-∅-CĀ-NĀN)-TLI- = a sick mother; (COCO-∅)-C- > (COCO-∅-CĀ)-UH- = *pret agen*, one who has become sick, i.e., a sick one; (COCO-∅-CĀ-TLĀL)-LI- = miserable/sickly/unhealthy land; (COCO-∅-CĀ-YŌ)-TL- = destitution/indigence
(COCO-L)-LI- = ache/ailment; discomfort; anger
(COCO-LIZ)-TLI- = sickness; (COCO-LIZ-CUI) > (COCO-LIZ-CUI) = to take sick
(COCO-LIĀ) > (COCO-LIH): T-O- = to be sick in relation to one another, i.e., to hate one another; TĒ-(COCO-LIĀ) > (COCO-LIH) = to be sick in relation to s.o., i.e., to hate s.o.; (TĒ-COCO-LIĀ-NI)-∅- = *cuspres agen*, one who customarily is sick in relation to s.o., i.e., one who hates s.o.
(COCO-Ā) > (COCO-H): M-O- = to allow/let o.s. to become sick; i.e., to become/be sick

(COCHI) > (COCH) = to sleep

(CŌHUA) > (CŌUH): TLA- ~ TĒ- = to buy s.th./s.o.; (TLA-CŌHUA-LŌ-NI)-∅- = a thing with which people customarily buy things; i.e., a coin/money

   (CŌHU-IĀ) > (CŌHU-IH): M-O+TĒ- = to buy s.th. for o.s.

   (CŌHUI-LIĀ) > (CŌHUI-LIH): TĒ+TLA- = to buy s.th. for s.o.

(CŌL)-LI- = a bent-over one; i.e., a grandfather; (CŌL-HUAH-∅)-☐- > (CŌL-HUAH-∅-CĀ)-UH- = *pret agen*, one who has owned grandfathers; i.e., a dweller in Colhuahcan; (CŌL-HUAH-∅-CĀ-N)-☐- = *place-name s*, In/To/From a Place of Grandfather Owners; i.e., In/To/From a Place of Venerable Tradition

   (CŌL-O-Ā) > (CŌL-O-H): TLA- = to bend/fold s.th.; to curve s.th.; to detour around s.th.; (CŌL-Ō)-TL- > (CŌL-Ō)-UH- = a thing that is bent/curved (at the tail); i.e., a scorpion

(COLOH)-TLI- = a framework

(CŌMi)-TL- > (CŌN)-∅- = bowl/pot; barrel cactus; (CŌN-TŌN)-TLI- = a small bowl/pot; (CŌN-TŌN-CO)-☐- = in a small bowl/pot

   (CŌN-TLĪL)-LI- = black ink from the outside of a pot; i.e., pot soot

(COMŌL-O-Ā) > (COMŌL-O-H): TLA- = to make a hole/cavity in s.th.; to hollow/dig out s.th.; to excavate s.th.; (TLA-COMŌL)-LI- = a thing that results from excavating a pit, i.e., an excavation/pit/large hole

(COM-Ō-NI) > (COM-Ō-N) = to crackle, to catch fire; M-O-(COM-Ō-NI-Ā) > (COM-Ō-NI-H) = (for an individual) to become inflamed/agitated; (for a crowd) to riot; (for a fire) to flare up

(CONĒ)-TL- > (CONĒ)-UH- = child; offspring [*abs af s*, (CŌ-CONE)-∅-H] [*The stem has a female focus; e.g., a woman's child, a bear's cub.*]

(COPĀC)-TLI- = palate, roof of the mouth

(COP-Ī-N-A) > (COP-Ī-N): M-O- = to pull o.s. loose, to divest o.s.

   (COH-COP-Ī-N-A) > (COH-COP-Ī-N-A): TLA- = to pull thing after thing (e.g., button after button) loose (e.g., from buttonholes); (TLA-COH-COP-Ī-N)-TLI- = an unbuttoned thing

(COT-Ō-NI) > (COT-Ō-N) = (for thread/twine/cord/rope) to become broken

   (COT-Ō-N-A) > (COT-Ō-N): TLA- = to break/pinch s.th. off, to pick s.th. (i.e., fruit) from a tree; to cut s.th. asunder

(COY-Ō-NI) > (COY-Ō-N) = *nonan*, to become dug as a hole, to become a hole; *anim*, to make a yipping/howling sound; (COY-O-C)-TLI- = a thing that results from becoming dug as a hole; i.e., a hole; (TLA-COY-O-C)-TLI- = a thing that has been dug generally, i.e., a hole/burrow; cupboard; (COY-Ō)-TL- = one that yips/howls; i.e., a coyote

   (COY-Ō-NI-Ā) > (COY-Ō-NI-H): TLA- = to make a hole in s.th.; to pierce s.th.

(CŌZ)-TLI- = a yellow thing

   (CŌZ-A-HUI) > (CŌZ-A-UH) = to become/be yellow colored

   (CŌZ-CA)-TL- = a thing associated with yellow; i.e., a bead/round-shaped jewel; necklace; **cōzcatl quetzalli** = it is a necklace and it is a quetzal plume; i.e., it is a precious jewel

   (CŌZ-TI-YA) > (CŌZ-TI-YA) ~ (CŌZ-TI-X) = to become/turn yellow, to yellow; (CŌZ-TI-∅)-C- = a thing that has become yellow, a yellow thing

CH

(CHAL-Ā-NI) > (CHAL-Ā-N) = *nonan,* to become cracked; to clash/rattle/crunch; to make a grating/grinding sound; to be out of tune
    (CHAL-Ā-NI-Ā) > (CHAL-Ā-NI-H): T-O- = to clash with one another; to be out of harmony with one another; to be quarrelsome with one another
(CHĀL-CHIHUi)-TL- > (CHĀL-CHIUH)-∅- = greenstone/jade/jadite [*var s,* (CHĀL-CHIUH)-TLI-]
    (CHĀL-CHIUH-ĪXI-MATI) > (CHĀL-CHIUH-ĪXI-MAT) ~ (CHĀL-CHIUH-ĪXI-MAH) = to know/be an expert in greenstones/jade/jadite
(CHAL-O-Ā) > (CHAL-O-H): TLA- = to scold/chide about s.th.
(CHAM-Ā-HUA) > (CHAM-Ā-HUA) = (for a child) to grow/become chubby; (for maize, cacao, etc.) to begin to fill out and ripen
    (CHAM-A-C)-TLI- = a thick/filled-out thing; (CHAM-A-C-CAL-TI-∅)-C- = a thing that has become very thick; i.e., a very thick thing
*(CHĀN)-TLI > (CHĀN)-∅- = [*primarily used in pos-st NNC and as emb*] home; [*in advlzd NNC*] at/to/from (s.o.'s) home; **nochān** = at my home
    (CHĀN-EH-∅)-◻- > (CHĀN-EH-∅-CĀ)-UH- = *pret agen,* one who has owned a home, i.e., a home owner; (CHĀN-EH-∅-CĀ-CONĒ)-TL- > (CHĀN-EH-∅-CĀ-CONĒ)-UH- = a home owner's child, i.e., a legitimate child
    (CHĀN-TI-Ā) > (CHĀN-TI-H): M-O- = to cause o.s. to have a home; to make o.s. a home
(CHAP-Ā-NI) > (CHAP-Ā-N) = (for falling dough, wet clay, etc.) to make a thudding noise when striking a surface; (CHA-CHAP-Ā-NI) > (CHA-CHAP-Ā-N) = (for rain) to fall in large drops; (CHAH-CHAP-Ā-NI) > (CHAH-CHAP-Ā-N) = to drop with a dull thud/plop
(CHAPOL)-IN- = grasshopper
(CHIC-Ā-HUA) > (CHIC-Ā-HUA) = to become/be strong; (CHIC-Ā-HUA-∅)-C- = one who has become strong; a strong one
(CHIAN)-TLI-. *See* (CHIYAN)-TLI-.
(CHIC-)-. *See* (CHICO)-◻-.
(CHICO)-◻- = to one side; irregularly/badly; **chico tlanāhuac** = out of the way outside [*as emb in num s,* (CHIC-) ~ (CHICU-) ~ (CHICUA-) = five plus . . .]
    (CHICO-HUĪ-YA) > (CHICO-HUĪ-YA) = to become long irregularly; i.e., to become/be unequal in length [*var* (CHICO-HUĒ-I-YA)]
    (CHIC-ŌME)-∅- = seven in number [*anim,* (CHIC-ŌME-N)-T-]
        (CHIC-ŌM-ŌZTŌ-TL- = seven caves; (CHIC-ŌM-ŌZTŌ-C)-◻- = *place-name s,* At/To/From the Place of Seven Caves; (CHIC-ŌM-ŌZTŌ-◻-CA)-TL- = one associated with Chicomoztoc; a dweller in Chicomoztoc
    (CHICU-ĒI)-∅- = eight in number
    (CHICUA-CĒ)-∅- = six in number; (CHICUA-CEN-TE)-TL- = six rock, i.e., six in number; (CHICUA-CEN-TLA-MAN)-TLI- = six things
    (CHIUC-NĀHUI)-∅- = nine in number; (CHIUC-NĀUH-MIC-TLĀ-N)-◻- = *place-name s,* In/To/From the Ninth Region of the Dead (i.e., the lowest level of the afterworld); (CHIUC-NĀUH-ŌLŌ)-TL- = nine maize cobs
(CHICHI)-∅- = dog; (CHICHI-CONĒ)-TL- > (CHICHI-CONĒ)-UH- = dog child; i.e., puppy

(CHICHI-YA) > (CHICHI-YA) ~ (CHICHI-X) = to become/turn/be bitter;
   (CHICHI-∅)-C- = a thing that has become bitter; i.e., a bitter thing;
   (CHICHI-LIZ)-TLI- = action of becoming bitter
(CHĪCHĪ-MĀ-N)-∅- = *place-name s*, In/To/From the Place of the Area of Milk [*The emb is* (CHĪCHĪ)-TL-, "a thing that results from suckling," i.e., "milk", NOT (CHICHI)-∅-, "dog."]; (CHĪCHĪ-MĒ-∅-CA)-TL- = a person associated with Chichiman, a dweller in Chichiman, a Chichimec
(CHICUA-)-. See (CHICO)-∅-.
(CHIHCHA) > (CHIHCHA) = to spit; TĒ- ~ TLA-(CHIHCHA) > (CHIHCHA) = to spit on s.o./s.th. [*applic obj unjustified by form of stem*]
   (CHIHCHA-L)-LI- = a thing that results from spitting; i.e., spit/spittle; (CHIHCHA-L-EH-∅)-∅- > (CHIHCHA-L-EH-∅-CĀ)-UH- = *pret agen*, one that has owned spittle; i.e., a spittle owner, one that slobbers
(CHIH-CHIHCHA) > (CHIH-CHIHCHA) = to sputter
(CHĪHUA) > (CHĪUH): M-O- = to grow; to happen/occur; TLA- ~ TĒ-(CHĪHUA) > (CHĪUH) = to make/do s.th.; to engender s.o. (TLA-CHĪUH-∅)-QUI- > (TLA-CHĪUH-∅-CĀ)-UH- = *pret agen*, one who has made s.th.; i.e., a maker/craftsman
   (TLA-CHĪHUA-L)-LI- = a made thing/a work/an artifact [< TLA-(CHĪHUA)]; a creature/child [< TĒ-(CHĪHUA)]
   (TLA-CHĪUH)-TLI- = an artifact; worked/tilled land
(CHĪHUA-LŌ-NI)-∅- = a feasible/doable thing
(CHĪHUA-L-LANI) > (CHĪHUA-L-LAN): TĒ+TLA- = to tell s.o. to do s.th.
(CHĪHUA-L-TIĀ) > (CHĪHUA-L-TIH): TĒ+TLA- = to cause s.o. to make/do s.th.
(CHIH-CHĪHUA) > (CHIH-CHĪUH): M-O- = to dress/adorn/attire/bedeck o.s./to prepare/get ready; (CHIH-CHĪHUA) > (CHIH-CHĪHUA): TLA- ~ TĒ- = to prepare s.th./s.o.; to get s.th./s.o. ready; to embellish/adorn s.th.; to dress/adorn s.o.; (TLA-CHIH-CHĪHUA-L)-LI- = a thing that has been embellished/given a false appearance; a counterfeit/spurious thing
(CHĪHU-IĀ) > (CHĪHU-IH): TĒ+TLA- = to do s.th. to s.o.; TĒ-(TLA-CHĪHU-IĀ) > (TLA-CHĪHU-IH) = [tla-*fusion*] to put a spell on s.o.
(CHĪHUI-LIĀ) > (CHĪHUI-LIH): TĒ+TLA- = to do/make s.th. for s.o.
(CHĪL)-LI- = chili pepper
   (CHĪL-CUEMI)-TL- > (CHĪL-CUEN) = chili-pepper field/patch
   (CHĪL-LO-H-∅)-∅- > (CHĪL-LO-H-∅-CĀ)-UH- = *pret agen*, a thing that has owned abundant chili peppers; i.e., a thing highly seasoned with chili peppers
(CHĪMAL)-LI- = shield
   (CHĪMAL-HUAH-∅)-∅- > (CHĪMAL-HUAH-∅-CĀ)-UH- = *pret agen*, one who has owned a shield; i.e., a shield owner
   (CHĪMAL-LĀZA) > (CHĪMAL-LĀZ) = to throw a shield; to make a throwing motion with a shield, i.e., to brandish a shield
(CHIN-O-Ā) > (CHIN-O-H): TLA- = to scorch s.th.; (TLA-CHIN-Ō-L)-LI- = a scorched thing; e.g., scorched field/land
(CHIP-Ā-HUA) > (CHIP-Ā-HUA) = to become clean
   (CHIP-Ā-HU-A) > (CHIP-Ā-UH): M-O- = to purify/cleanse o.s., to become purified/cleaned
(CHIP-Ī-NI) > (CHIP-Ī-N) = to drip; (CHI-CHIP-Ī-NI) > (CHI-CHIP-Ī-N) = to fall in small drops; to drip frequently

Vocabulary

(CHIP-Ī-NI-Ā) > (CHIP-Ī-NI-H): TLA- = to sprinkle/besprinkle s.th.
(CHIQU-I-HUi)-TL- > (CHIQU-I-UH)-∅- = basket
*(CHIQU-I-UH-YŌ)-TL- > (CHIQU-I-UH-YŌ)-∅- = [gen-use s used in org-pos NNC] (s.o.'s) rib cage; **nochiquiuhyo** = it is my rib cage
(CHIT-Ō-NI) > (CHIT-Ō-N) = to pop off; to spring up/jump up; to splinter off; (for a fire) to emit sparks
(CHIT-Ō-NI-Ā) > (CHIT-Ō-NI-H): TLA- = to pop s.th. off; to eject s.th.
(CHIUC-). See (CHICO)-☐-.
(CHIYA) > (CHIX): TĒ- ~TLA- = to await/wait for s.o./s.th. [var sp, TĒ- ~ TLA-(CHIYE)]
    (CHIYA-LŌ-NI)-∅- = a thing worthy of being awaited
    +TĒ(CHIYE-LŌ-YĀ-N)-∅- = [used only in pos-st NNC] s.o.'s place of being waited for
    (TLA-CHIYA) > (TLA-CHIX) = [tla-*fusion*] to look; M-O-(TLA-CHIYE-L-TIĀ) > (TLA-CHIYE-L-TIH) = to cause o.s. to look, i.e., to be observant; TĒ-(TLAH-TLA-CHIYA-L-TIĀ) > (TLAH-TLA-CHIYA-L-TIH) = to cause s.o. to look and look, i.e., to teach s.o. to be observant
(CHIYAN)-TLI- = chia (The plant <u>Salvia chian</u> and its seeds; the seeds are used in a beverage and as a source for oil.)
(CHŌCA) > (CHŌCA) = to cry TĒ-(CHŌCA) > (CHŌCA) = to weep for s.o. [applic obj unjustified by the form of the s]
    (CHŌC-TIĀ) > (CHŌC-TIH): TĒ- = to cause s.o. to cry; (TĒ-CHŌC-TIH-∅)-☐- > (TĒ-CHŌC-TIH-∅-CĀ)-UH- = *pret agen*, a thing that makes people cry; i.e., a lamentable thing
    (CHŌQUI-LIĀ) > (CHŌQUI-LIH): TLA- = to cry about s.th., to lament s.th.
    (CHŌQUI-LĪ-LŌ-NI)-∅- = a thing worthy of being wept for; i.e., a lamentable thing
(CHOL)-LI- = hoof; (CHOL-O-Ā) > (CHOL-O-H) = to use hooves; i.e., to bound away/flee/jump; (CHOL-Ō-L)-LI- = one who results from fleeing, i.e., a refugee
    (CHOL-HUIĀ) > (CHOL-HUIH): TĒ- ~ TLA- = to use hooves in relation to s.o./s.th.; i.e., to spring/jump/step over s.o./s.th.

CU

(CUĀ) > (CUAH): TLA- ~ TĒ- = to eat s.th./s.o.
    (TĒ-CUĀ-NI)-☐- = one that customarily eats people; i.e., a wild beast; a cannibal [var s, (TĒ-CUĀ-NI)-TL-]; (TĒ-CUĀ-N-Ē-HU-A)-TL- > (TĒ-CUĀ-N-Ē-HU-A)-UH- = wild-animal skin; (TĒ-CUĀ-N-TŌNA-L)-LI- = a vicious/dire day sign; (TĒ-CUĀ-N-CUA-LŌ) = to be eaten by means of wild beasts; (TĒ-CUĀ-N-CUA-L)-LI- = food for wild animals, wild-animal food
(CUA-LŌ-NI)-∅- = an edible thing
+TLA(CUA-LŌ-CA)-∅- = [used only in pos-st NNC] (s.th.'s) action of being eaten; i.e., (s.th.'s) eclipse: **īcualōca in tōnatiuh** = it is the eclipse of the sun
+TĒ(TLA-CUĀ-YA)-∅- = [used only in pos-st NNCS] (s.o.'s) eating utensil
+TĒ(TLA-CUĀ-YĀ-N)-∅- = [used only in pos-st NNCs] (s.o.'s) eating place
(CUA-L)-LI- = a thing that can be eaten; i.e., s.th. good; (TLA-CUA-L)-LI= s.th. that can be eaten; i.e., food
(CUA-L-TIĀ) > (CUA-L-TIH): TĒ+TLA- = to cause s.o. to eat s.th.; i.e., to feed s.th. to s.o.; (TĒ-TLA-CUA-L-TIH-∅)-QUI- > (TĒ-TLA-CUA-L-TIH-∅-CĀ)-UH- = *pret agen*, food server/waiter
(CUA-CUĀ) > (CUA-CUAH): TLA- = to chew s.th./to gnaw s.th.

(CUĀ-CUĀ) > (CUĀ-CUAH): TLA- = to eat s.th. regularly/to eat time after time
(CUĀ-)-. See (CUĀi)-TL-.
(CUĀCH)-TLI- = large cotton blanket/cape
(CUAHUi)-TL- > (CUAUH)-∅- = tree; pole/stake/stick; wood; (CUAHUI-L-TE)-TL- > (CUAHUI-L-TE)-UH- = sticks and stones; i.e., punishment
  (CUAUH-Ā-CAL)-LI- = a wooden scoop; i.e., a half-fanega [fanega = Spanish grain measure (about 1.60 bu).]
  (CUAUH-AQUI-Ā) > (CUAUH-A-QUI-H) = to cause a tree to enter; i.e., to plant a tree
  (CUAUH-CAL)-LI- = housing made of wood; i.e., large wooden cage (serving as a prison)
  (CUAUH-HUĀ-C-∅)-QUI- = *pret agen*, a person who is dry like a piece of wood; i.e., an emaciated person
  (CUAUH-HUĀ-TZ-A-L)-LI- = dried-out wood; deadwood
  (CUAUH-MĀi)-TL > (CUAUH-MĀ)-∅- = a tree arm; i.e., a tree branch
  (CUAUH-MĀXa)-TL- > (CUAUH-MĀX)-∅- = crotch of a tree, a tree crotch
  (CUAUH-OCUIL)-IN- = tree worm
  (CUAUH-POZ-TEQUI) > (CUAUH-POZ-TEC): TLA- = to break s.th. like one would break a stick [*var s*, TLA-(CUAP-POZ-TEQUI)]
  (CUAUH-TE-CHAL-Ō)-TL- > (CUAUH-TE-CHAL-Ō)-UH- = tree squirrel
  (CUAUH-TE-NĀMi)-TL- > (CUAUH-TE-NĀN)-∅- = a wooden wall; i.e., a palisade; *(CUAUH-TE-NĀM-EH-∅-T-O) > (CUAUH-TE-NĀM-EH-∅-T-O) = [*a pret-as-pres v*] to lie owning a palisade; to be surrounded by a palisade
  *(CUAUH-TE-NĀN-YO-H-∅-T-O) > (CUAUH-TE-NĀN-YO-H-∅-T-O) = [*A pret-as-pres v.*] to lie owning a palisade in every part; i.e., to be surrounded by a palisade
  (CUAUH-TI-∅)-C- = *pret agen*, one that has become like a tree; i.e., a tall one
  (CUAUH-TLAH)-□- = place of abundant trees; i.e., a forest/grove
  (CUAUH-TLA-PECH)-TLI- = wooden platform/litter
  (CUAUH-XĪCAL)-LI- = a gourd like vessel made of wood; TLA-(CUAUH-XĪCAL-HUIĀ) > (CUAUH-XĪCAL-HUIH) = to use a wooden tray/vessel on s.th.; i.e., to pan for s.th. with a wooden tray
  (CUAUH-YOHUA-∅)-C- > (CUAUH-YOHUA-∅-CĀ)-UH- = *pret agen*, a thing that has become darkness because of trees; i.e., a dark forest
(CUĀi)-TL- > (CUĀ)-∅- = head
  (CUĀ-CHĪ-CHĪL-TI-∅)-C- = one that has become chili-red colored at the head; i.e., a bird with a bright red head
  (CUĀ-CUAHUi)-TL- > (CUĀ-CUAUH)-∅- = a tree on the head; i.e., antler/horn; (CUĀ-CUAHU-EH-∅)-□- > (CUĀ-CUAHU-EH-∅-CĀ)-UH- = *pret agen*, one that has owned antlers/horns; i.e., an owner of antlers/horns (e.g., a cow); (CUĀ-CUAUH-TIH-TĪC-E-C-TI-∅)-C- = one that has become chalk colored at the antlers; i.e., one with chalk-colored antlers; M-O-(CUĀ-CUAUH-TLĀZA) > (CUĀ-CUAUH-TLĀZ) = to throw o.s. from/rid o.s. of antlers; i.e., to cast off/discard antlers; (CUĀ-CUAUH-MĀ-TZŌL-TI-∅)-C- = one that has become tapered and branched at the antlers; i.e., one with tapered, branched antlers [*var s.* (CUĀ-CUAM-MĀ-TZŌL-TI-∅)-C-]
  (CUA-HCHIC)-TLI- = a head-shaved one; i.e., a high-ranking warrior
  (CUĀ-ILPI-Ā) > (CUĀ-ILPI-H): M-O- = to cause one's own head to become bound; i.e., to bind up one's head
  (CUĀ-IZTA-YA) > (CUĀ-IZTA-YA) ~ (CUĀ-IZTA-Z) = to become/be white at the head,

Vocabulary   219

  i.e., to become white-headed; (CUĀ-IZTĀ-∅)-C- = one white at the head; i.e., a
  white-headed one; (CUĀ-IZTA-L)-LI- = one who results from becoming white at the
  head; i.e., a white-headed one; (CUĀ-IZTA-L-EH-∅)-☐- = *pret agen*, one who has
  owned white at the head; i.e., a white-headed person
 (CUĀ-TE)-TL- > (CUĀ-TE)-UH- = rock at the head; i.e., a hard head
 (CUĀ-TE-CON-TI-∅)-C- = a thing pot shaped at the head; i.e., a pot-headed thing. *See*
  (TE-COMa)-TL-.
 (CUĀ-TE-OLOL-TI-∅)-C- = a thing that has become round at the head; i.e., a round-
  headed thing
 (CUĀ-NACa)-TL- > (CUĀ-NAC)-∅- = flesh on the head; i.e., chicken's comb [*in a
  flawed-subject NNC:* (CUĀ-NACA)-☐-, "chicken/rooster/hen"]
 (CUĀ-TZAY-Ā-N-A) > (CUĀ-TZAY-Ā-N): TĒ- = to tear/rip/cleave s.o. at the head; i.e.,
  to wound s.o. in the head
(CUAL-Ā-NI) > (CUAL-Ā-N) = to become/be angry; (CUAL-A-C)-TLI- = foam (at the
  mouth)/slaver/slobber
 (CUAL-Ā-NI-Ā) > (CUAL-Ā-NI-H): TĒ- = to cause s.o. to become angry; to anger s.o.
(CUAM-)-. See (CUAHUi)-TL-.
(CUAP-)-. See (CUAHUi)-TL-.
(CUĀUH)-TLI- > (CUĀUH)-∅- = eagle
  (CUĀUH-TL-ŌCĒLŌ)-TL- = an eagle-jaguar warrior; *by extens*, a real man [*also, as a
  conjoined NNC lexical item:* **cuāuhtli ōcēlōtl**, "he is an eagle and he is a jaguar"; i.e.,
  "he is an eagle-jaguar warrior"]
  (CUĀUH-PIL)-LI- = eagle-nobleman; i.e., elite-warrior nobleman
  (CUĀUH-TLA-HT-O-Ā) > (CUĀUH-TLA-HT-O-H) = to speak like an eagle; i.e., to rule
  by appointment in recognition of one's elite-warrior accomplishments; to rule as a mil-
  itary deputy ruler/a military governor; (CUĀUH-TLA-HT-O-H-∅)-☐- > (CUĀUH-TLA-
  HT-O-H-∅-CĀ)-UH- = one who has spoken like an eagle; i.e., a high-ranking warrior;
  a military deputy ruler; a military governor
  (CUĀUH-TLOH)-TLI- = an eagle falcon
(CUĒCH)-TLI- = pulverized substance/powder; soot/lampblack [*var s*, (CUĪCH)-TLI-]
  (CUĒCH-O-Ā) > (CUĒCH-O-H): TLA- = to cause s.th. to become pulverized; to reduce
  s.th. to powder; to grind s.th. to a fine powder
(CUECH-Ā-HUA) > (CUECH-Ā-HUA) = to become/be damp/moist; (TLA-CUECH-
  Ā-HUA-YĀ-N)-☐- = place where things in general are damp/moist
(CUĒi)-TL- > (CUĒ)-∅- = skirt; **cuēitl huīpilli** = she is a skirt and she is a blouse; i.e., she
  is a woman; **ticuēitl tihuīpilli** = you are a skirt and you are a blouse; i.e., you are a
  woman
(CUĒL)-☐- = briefly/quickly; already; **ye cuēl eh** = soon
(CUEMi)-TL- > (CUEN)-∅- = worked/tilled land; a ridge turned up by a spade (or by a plow,
  in colonial times)
  (CUEN-CHOL-HUIĀ) > (CUEN-CHOL-HUIH): TĒ- ~ TLA- = to jump over s.o./s.th. as
  if over a spade-turned ridge; i.e., to jump/step over s.o./s.th.
(CUEPI) > (CUEP) = to turn around
  (CUEP-A) > (CUEP): TLA- = to cause s.th. to return; i.e., to return s.th.; M-O- (CUEP-A)
  > (CUEP) = to cause o.s. to turn back; i.e., to return; to turn/change (into);
  (NE-CUEP-A-LIZ)-TLI- = action of returning; transformation; +TĒ(NE-CUEP-CĀ)-∅-

= [*used only in pos-st NNC*] (s.o.'s) action of returning; i.e., (s.o.'s) return
(CUEP-Ō-NI) > (CUEP-Ō-N) = to burst/burst open/explode; (for flowers) to burst into bloom; (for a flower) to open/bloom
  (CUE-CUEP-O-CA) > (CUE-CUEP-O-CA) = to burst/explode to pieces
(CUETL-Ā-CH)-TLI- = wolf
(CUETL-A-X)-TLI- = a thing that has become withered; cured hide, leather
  (<u>CUETL-A-X</u>-I-HUI) > (<u>CUETL-A-X</u>-I-UH) = to become discouraged; to become dispirited/fainthearted; to become indolent/listless
  (<u>CUETL-A-X</u>-O-Ā) > (<u>CUETL-A-X</u>-O-H): M-O- = to let/allow o.s. to become fainthearted; to faint/swoon
(CUETZ-Ō-NI) > (CUETZ-Ō-N) = to have an itchy sensation (?)
  (CUE-CUETZ-O-CA) > (CUE-CUETZ-O-CA) = to have an itch; to be agitated
(CUEX)-TLI- = mat/matting
  (<u>CUEX</u>-TLĀ-N)-∅- = *place-name s,* In/To/From the Place in the Vicinity of Mats;
  (<u>CUEX</u>-TĒ-∅-CA)-TL- = one associated with Cuextlan, a dweller in Cuextlan; a Cuextec (*later:* Huaxtec); M-O-(<u>CUEX</u>-TĒ-∅-CA-NEQUI) > (<u>CUEX</u>-TĒ-∅-CA-NEC) = to resemble the Cuextecs (i.e., the Huaxtecs)
(CUI) > (CUI): TLA- = to take s.th.; M-O-(CUI) > (CUI) = to consider o.s.; to esteem o.s.
  (CU-IĀ) > (CU-IH): M-O+TLA- = to take s.th. for o.s.; i.e., to borrow s.th.; to be in debt; (M-O-TLA-CU-IH-∅)-∅- > (NE-TLA-CU-IH-∅-CĀ)-UH- = *pret agen,* a person who has gotten himself into debt; i.e., a person in debt, a debtor
(CUĪ-LIĀ) > (<u>CUĪ</u>-LIH): TĒ+TLA- = to take s.th. from s.o.
(CUĪ-TLANI) > (<u>CUĪ</u>-TLAN): TĒ+TLA- = to tell s.o. to pick/take s.th. up
(CUIH-<u>CUI</u>) > (CUIH-<u>CUI</u>): TLA- = to pick up s.th. (i.e., litter); to carve s.th. (in wood or stone); (TLA-CUIH-CUI)-TL- > (TLA-CUIH-CUI)-UH- = a sculpted thing (in wood or stone)
(CUĪCA) > (CUĪCA) = to sing; (CUĪCa)-TL- > (CUĪC)-∅- = song; (<u>CUĪCA</u>-TLĀZA) > (<u>CUĪCA</u>-TLĀZ) = to throw a song; i.e., to begin singing
  (CUĪCA-T-IĀ) > (CUĪCA-T-IH): TĒ- = to have a song for s.o.; i.e., to sing for s.o.
  (CUIH-<u>CUĪCA</u>-T-IĀ) > (CUIH-<u>CUĪCA</u>-T-IH): TĒ- = to sing repeatedly for s.o.; to sing for a number of individuals separately
(CUIL-TŌN-O-Ā) > (CUIL-TŌN-O-H): M-O- = to be wealthy and happy/to enjoy life; (NE-CUIL-TŌN-Ō-L)-LI- = a thing that results from being rich; i.e., wealth/riches
(CUIL-TŌN-O-Ā) > (CUIL-TŌN-O-H): TĒ-= to enrich s.o.; (<u>TĒ-CUIL-TŌN-O-H-∅</u>)-∅- > (<u>TĒ-CUIL-TŌN-O-H-∅</u>-CĀ)-UH- = *pret agen,* a thing that has enriched people; i.e., a thing that enriches people
(CUITLa)-TL- > (CUITL)-∅- = excrement/dung; rump/lower back
  (<u>CUITLA</u>-CHĪHU-IĀ) > (<u>CUITLA</u>-CHĪHU-IH): TĒ- = to make excrement on s.o.; i.e., to accuse s.o. undeservedly
  (<u>CUITLA</u>-HUAH-∅)-∅- > (<u>CUITLA-HUAH-∅</u>-CĀ)-UH- = *pret agen,* one who has owned excrement; i.e., an excrement owner
  (<u>CUITLA</u>-HUIĀ) > (<u>CUITLA</u>-HUIH): M-O+TĒ- = to use one's excrement/fertilizer on s.o.; i.e., to take care of s.o.
  (<u>CUITLA</u>-MIZ)-TLI- = an excrement puma
  (<u>CUITLA</u>-OLOL-TI-∅)-C- = an entity round at the back; i.e., a round-backed entity

Vocabulary

(CUITLA-PIL)-LI- = an appendage to the rump; i.e., a tail
(CUITLA-XCOL)-LI- = intestines; (TĒ-CUITLA-XCOL-YĒC-TI-H-Ø)-▢- > (TĒ-CUITLA-XCOL-YĒC-TI-H-Ø-CĀ)-UH- = *pret agen,* a thing that has soothed s.o.'s intestines; i.e., a thing soothing to the intestines
CUIX = *interrog,* perchance? [*in an adjunct cl*], whether

E

(E)-TL- > (E)-UH- = bean
  (E-CUEMi)-TL- > (E-CUEN)-Ø- = bean field/patch
  (E-XŌ)-TL- > (E-XŌ)-UH- = a green thing in the form of a bean; i.e., a green bean; (E-XŌ-TI-Ø)-C- = a thing that has become like a green bean; i.e., a thing like a green bean
(EH)-Ø- = an entity; (EH-HUĀ)-TL- ~ -Ø- = that entity/that one: **nehhuātl** = I am that one/it is I [*The 3rd-person NNCs use a var s*: (YEH-HUĀ)-TL- ~ -Ø-; **yehhuātl** = he is that one/it is he; **yehhuāntin** = they are the ones/it is them.]
(EH-CA)-TL- > (EH-CA)-UH- = breeze; (EH-CA-TEPĒ)-TL- = Breeze Mountain/Hill; (EH-EH-CA)-TL- = strong breeze; i.e., wind
(EHCO) > (EHCO) = to arrive
  (EHCA-HUIĀ) > (EHCA-HUIH): TĒ- = to cause s.o. to arrive
(Ē-HUA) > (Ē-HUA) ~ (Ē-UH) = to depart [*frequently with the dir pref* ON-]; to start off/leave/go away; (for a bird) to take off flying [*The* (Ē-UH) *is an irreg prfv s.*]
(Ē-HU-A) > (Ē-UH): TĒ- = to raise/lift s.o. into a sitting position; to make s.o. get up (from a recumbent position)
(Ē-HU-A)-TL- > (Ē-HU-A)-UH- = skin/pelt/(raw) hide; rind/bark
(Ē-)-. See (ĒYI)-.
(ĒI)-Ø-. See (ĒYI)-.
*(EL)-Ø- > (EL)-Ø- = [*used only in pos-st NNC*] diligence, eagerness; diligent/eager; active: **īmel** = it is their diligence; i.e., they are diligent; [*in neg NNCs*] lazy; reluctant; **ahīmel** = they are lazy; **ahtel** = we are lazy
(ĒL)-LI- > (ĒL)-Ø- = liver; (*as the seat of emotions*) heart
  (ĒL-CI-H-CI-HUI) > (ĒL-CI-H-CI-UH) = to sigh
  (ĒL-CHIQU-I-HUi)-TL- > (ĒL-CHIQU-I-UH)-Ø- = liver basket; i.e., chest/rib cage
  (ĒL-Ē-HU-A) > (ĒL-Ē-UH) = to cause the liver to rise; i.e., to lift the liver; i.e., to involve/excite/stir up the heart; TLA-(ĒL-Ē-HU-IĀ) > (ĒL-Ē-HU-IH) = to lift the liver (i.e., heart) with regard to s.th.; i.e., to yearn for s.th.; (ĒL-Ē-HU-I-Z)-TLI- = s.th. worthy of being desired; s.th. desirable
  (ĒL-LACU-Ā-HU-A) > (ĒL-LACU-Ā-UH): M-▢- = to strengthen o.s. in the liver; i.e., to take courage
  (ĒL-LAHU-ĒL-Ī-LŌ-Ø)-C- = one who is a scoundrel in the liver; i.e., an evil-livered one; i.e., an evil-hearted one
  (ĒL-LE-L)-LI- = fiery sensation in the liver; i.e., affliction; depression/heartache/regret/sorrow [*For* the matrix stem (TLE-L)-LI-, "a fiery sensation," *see* § 57.7.]; TLA-(ĒL-LE-L-O-Ā) > (ĒL-LE-L-O-H) = to cause s.th. grief; TĒ-(ĒL-LE-L-QUĪX-TIĀ) > (ĒL-LE-L-QUĪX-TIH)- = to cause s.o. to go out from affliction/heartache; i.e., to dispel affliction/heartache for s.o.; M-▢-(ĒL-LE-L-TI-Ā) > (ĒL-LE-L-TI-H) = to cause o.s. to

have a fiery sensation in the liver; i.e., to be repentant/regretful; (ĒL-LE-L-TI) > (ĒL-LE-L-TI) = to have a fiery sensation in the liver; i.e., to be troubled/sorry
(ĒL-PAN)-TLI- = chest/breast
(ĒX-)-. See (ĒYI)-∅-.
 (ĒYI)-∅- ~ (ĒI)-∅- ~ (Ē-)- ~ (ĒX-)- = three in number. See also (YĒYI)-∅- ~ (YĒI)-∅-.
 (Ē-ILHUI)-TL, = three days; adv, for three days
 (Ē-TECPĀN)-TLI- = three rows, i.e., sixty in number
 (Ē-TLA-MAN-IX)-T- = all three entities; adv, in all three ways
 (ĒX-CĀ-N)-☐- = in/to/from/through three places
 (ĒX-PA)-☐- = three times
(EZ)-TLI- = blood
 *(EZ-ZŌ)-TL- > (EZ-ZO)-∅- = [gen-use s used in org-pos NNCs] (vital) blood
 (EZ-ZO-H-∅)-☐- > (EZ-ZO-H-∅-CĀ)-UH- = pret agen, a thing that has owned blood in abundance; i.e., a thing covered with blood

HU

HUĀL- = dir pref, hither; loc pref, here. [Contrast ON-.]
 (HUĀL-CA-H). See *(HUĀL-YE).
 (HUĀL-LĀ) ~ (HUĀL-LA-UH) ~ (HUĀL-HUI) > (HUĀL-LAH) ~ (HUĀL-HUI) = to come
 (HUĀL-YE) > (HUĀL-CA-H) ~ (HUĀL-CA-T) = to be here/to be in this direction; adv, **huālcah** = it is more; more [usually **oc huālcah**, "it is more/much more; more/much more"]
*(HUĀN)-∅- > (HUĀN)-∅- = [restr-use s not used] company; adv, in (s.o.'s/s.th.'s) company; with, along with, in addition to, furthermore, moreover; **nohuān** = in my company/with me; **īhuān** = in his/her/its company; with him/her/it; therewith, along with that, furthermore [**Īhuān** is NOT a conjunction. It does NOT mean "and."]
(HUAP-Ā-HUA) > (HUAP-Ā-HUA) = nonan, to become hard/knotty/stiff/rigid; anim, to get a cramp
 (HUAP-A-C)-TLI- = a thing that has become stiff; a stiff/hardened thing; (HUAP-A-C-PAH-TI-∅)-C- = a very stiff thing
(HUĀ-QUI) > (HUĀ-C) = to become dry; (HUĀ-C-∅)-QUI- = a thing that has become dry; i.e., a dry thing; (HUĀ-C)-TLI- = a thing that results from becoming dry; i.e., a dry thing
 (HUĀ-TZ-A) > (HUĀ-TZ): TLA- = to cause s.th. to become dry; to dry/dry out s.th.
(HUĀUH)-TLI- = amaranth
(HUEH-)-. See (HUĒ-I)-∅-.
(HUĒ-HUĒ)-TL- > (HUĒ-HUĒ)-UH- = upright cylindrical drum with a skin head
(HUĒ-I)-∅- [emb forms, (HUĒ-)- ~ (HUEH-)-] = a big/large/important one [abs pl s, (HUEH-HUĒ-I-N)-T- ~ -☐-]; **huēi ātl** = large water; i.e., lake/ocean; (HUĒ-I-TLA-TQUI)-TL- > (HUĒ-I-TLA-TQUI)-∅- = important property/equipment; (HUĒ-I-YA) > (HUĒ-I-YA) ~ (HUĒ-I-X) = to become/be big; to grow/grow up; to grow in honor and rank [var s, (HUĪ-YA)]; (HUĒ-I-YA-∅)-C- = a thing that has become long; i.e., a long thing [var s, (HUĪ-YA-∅)-C-]; (HUĒ-I-YA-∅-QU-I-YA) > (HUĒ-I-YA-∅-QU-I-X) = to become/be long
(HUĒ-HUĒ-TI) > (HUĒ-HUĒ-T) ~ (HUĒ-HUE-H) = to become/be an old man; (HUĒ-

Vocabulary

HUE-H-∅)-☐- > (HUĒ-HUĒ-T-∅-CĀ)-UH- = *pret agen*, one who has become an old man; i.e., an old man; (HUĒ-HUĒ-N)-TLI- = an old man; (HUĒ-HUĒ-N-TZIN)-☐- = a beloved/honored old man

(HUEH-CA)-TL- = distance; [*2nd-degree adv*], **huehca** = at/to/from a distance; distant/far away; from far away/from afar; (HUEH-CA-PAN)-☐- = in a high place; a high/tall thing

(HUEH-CĀHUA) > (HUEH-CĀHUA) = to be very old; to tarry/delay/wait a long time; (HUEH-CĀHUi)-TL- = (HUEH-CĀUH) = a long time [*2nd-decree adv*], **huehcāuh** = for a long time; **ye huehcāuh** = long ago/in the distant past/back in olden times; **oc huehcāuh** = a long time from now

(HUEH-XŌLŌ)-TL- > (HUEH-XŌLŌ)-UH- = turkey cock

(HUEL)-☐- = successfully; well; able; possible; very/fully; **huel achto** = first of all; **huel āxcān** = at this very moment; **huel cenyohual** = for an entire night; **huel miyecpa** = very many times/frequently; **huel zan icah** = quite seldom

(HUEL-ITT-A) > (HUEL-ITT-A): TLA- ~ TĒ- ~ M-O- = to look favorably/approvingly upon s.th./s.o./o.s.; to enjoy seeing s.th./s.o./o.s.; to like s.th./s.o. that is seen

(HUEL-NĒCI) > (HUEL-NĒZ) = to have a good appearance; to be obvious; +TĒ(HUEL-NĒZ-CA)-∅- = s.o.'s action of appearing pleasing; i.e., s.o.'s good/pleasant appearance

(HUELI)-☐- = successfully; able; possible; (HUELI-TI) > (HUELI-TI) = to be possible; to be able

(HUĒL-I-YA) > (HUĒL-I-YA) ~ (HUĒL-I-X) = to become/be tasty/delicious; (HUĒL-I-∅)-C- = a tasty/delicious thing

(HUĒL-TĪ-UH)-TLI- = elder sister

(HUEN)-TLI- = an offering/oblation/gift

(HUEN-CHĪHUA) > (HUEN-CHĪUH): TĒ- ~ TLA- = to make an offering/gift of s.o./s.th.

(HUE-TZ-CA) > (HUE-TZ-CA) = to laugh; TĒ-(HUE-TZ-QUĪ-TIĀ) > (HUE-TZ-QUĪ-TIH) = to make s.o. laugh; (TĒ-HUE-TZ-QUĪ-TIH-∅)-☐- > (TĒ-HUE-TZ-QUĪ-TIH-∅-CĀ)-UH- = *pret agen*, a laugh-provoking entity

(HUETZI) > (HUETZ) = to fall, to flop down; (for a gun) to fire

(HUEXŌ)-TL- > (HUEXŌ)-UH- = willow; (HUEXŌ-CANAUH)-TLI- = willow duck, i.e., black-crowned night heron

(HUEXŌ-TZIN-CO)-☐- = *place-name s,* At/To/From the Place of the Small Willows; (HUEXŌ-TZIN-☐-CA)-TL- = a person associated with Huexotzinco; a dweller in Huexotzinco

*(HUĪC)-☐- > (HUĪC)-∅- = [*gen-use s used only*] (in) a direction; **nohuīc** = in my direction; **mocuitlahuīc** = toward your rear

+TĒ- ~ TLA-(HUĪC-PA)-∅- = toward (s.o./s.th.)

(HUĪCA) > (HUĪCA): TLA- = to carry s.th.; (TLA-HUĪC)-TLI- = s.th. that has been carried; i.e., a carried thing; (HUĪC)-TLI- = s.th. that has been carried; i.e., a digging stick

(HUĪCA) > (HUĪCA): TĒ- = to carry s.o.; i.e., to go with s.o., to accompany s.o.

(HUĪCA) > (HUĪCA): M-O- = to carry o.s.; i.e., (H) to come

(HUI-HUIX-O-Ā) > (HUI-HUIX-O-H): TLA- ~ TĒ- = to shake/rock s.th./s.o.

(HUIL-ĀNA) > (HUIL-ĀN): TĒ- ~ TLA- = to drag s.o./s.th.

(HUĪ-PIL)-LI- [*for* (HUĪ-IPIL)-LI-] = (Indian woman's) blouse; sleeveless blouse; (warrior's) sleeveless jacket [C*f.,* (IPIL)-LI-.]

(HUĪP-TLA)-☐- = day after tomorrow

(HUĪ-TEQUI) > (HUĪ-TEC): TĒ- = to thrash/beat/strike/whip s.o.; (HUĪ-TEC-Ō) = *pass*, (for s.o./s.th.) to be struck by lightning; M-O-(HUĪ-TEQUI) > (HUĪ-TEC) = (for things) to bump/crash into one another; T-O-(HUĪ-TEQUI) > (HUĪ-TEC) = (for people) to bump/crash into one another

(HUĪ-TŌL-I-HUI) > (HUĪ-TŌL-I-UH) = to become bent/curved
  (HUĪ-TŌL-O-Ā) > (HUĪ-TŌL-O-H): TLA- = to curve/bend s.th.; (TLA-HUĪ-TŌL)-LI- = a bow

(HUITZ)-TLI- = a thorn; a thing like a thorn; a sharp-pointed thing
  (HUITZ-NĀHUA-C)-∅- = *place-name s,* In/To/From a Place in Hearing Distance of Thorns (one of the edifices in the Great Temple complex in Tenochtitlan); (HUITZ-NĀHUA-∅-CA)-TL- = one associated with Huitznahuac; (HUITZ-NĀHUA-∅-CA-TLĀL-PAN)-∅- = *place-name s,* In/To/From the Region of the Land of the Huitznahuacas (in Sahagún, identified as the area to the south)
  (HUITZ-TI-∅)-C- = a thing that has become like a thorn; i.e., a sharp, pointed thing
  (HUITZ-TZIL)-IN- = one that hums in the shape of a thorn; i.e., a hummingbird; (∅-∅-HUITZ-TZIL-ŌPŌCH-TLI-∅)-∅- = *pers name s,* "It is a Left-Hand/Foot Like A Hummingbird (in that it is swift, aggressive)" [NOT, as is usually said, "Southern Hummingbird," "Hummingbird to the South," etc.]; (HUITZ-TZĪ-TZIL)-IN- = one that hums constantly in the shape of a thorn

*(HUĪ-TZI) > (HUĪ-TZ) = [*defec v; a pret-as-pres v; the imprfv s is not used*], to come; **tihuītz** = you (sg) come; **tihuītza** = you (sg) came

(HUĪ-YA-∅)-C-. *See* (HUĒ-I)-∅-.

I

Note: When the stem-initial /i/ is merely a supportive vowel, it is represented in an entry by a lowercase letter.

(Ī) > (Ī): TLA- = to drink s.th.; (Ī-HUA) > (Ī-HUA) = *nonac s*; (Ī-HUA-NI)-∅- = s.th. that can be/is fit to be drunk; i.e., a drinkable/potable thing; (TLA-Ī-HUA-NI)-∅- = an instrument for drinking; i.e., a cup/glass/goblet
  (Ī-TIĀ) > (Ī-TIH): TĒ+TLA- = to cause s.o. to drink s.th.; to make/get s.o. to drink s.th.; to give s.o. a drink

*(∅-I-Ā) > (∅-I-H) = [*defec v, used only in pret-as-past tense VNCs*], to exist (?); **āc ihqueh?** = who are they? [*trad sp*, **aquique**]

ĪC, i.e., #∅-∅+Ī-∅(C)∅-∅#. *See* *(C)-∅-.

(IC-CĀUH)-TLI- > (IC-CĀUH)-∅- ~ (TĒ-IC-CĀUH)-∅- = younger brother; **niccāuh** ~ **notēiccāuh** = he is my younger brother

(ICI) > (IZ) = to be nearby; [*3rd-sg pres or pret VNC advlzd*], here; to/from/through here; **iz cah** ~ **iz catqui** = here it is; behold; **zan iz** = right here; **zan ici** = right here

(iCN-ĒL-I-Ā) > (iCN-ĒL-I-H): TĒ- = to do s.o. a favor; to do good to s.o.;
  (iCN-ĒL-Ī-L)-LI- = one to whom a favor has been done; i.e., a favored one; M-O-(iCN-ĒL-Ī-L-MATI) > (iCN-ĒL-Ī-L-MAT) ~ (iCN-ĒL-Ī-L-MAH) = to be grateful; to feel gratitude; TĒ-(iCN-ĒL-Ī-L-MATI) > (iCN-ĒL-Ī-L-MAT) ~ (iCN-ĒL-Ī-L-MAH) = to be grateful to s.o.; TĒ- ~ M-O+TĒ-(iCN-ĒL-Ī-L-MACH-Ī-TIĀ) > (iCN-EL-Ī-L-MACH-Ī-TIH) = to give thanks to s.o. for a benefit received
  (TĒ-iCN-ĒL-Ī-LIZ)-TLI- = a favor done to s.o.

(iCN-ĒL-I-Ā) > (iCN-ĒL-I-H): M-O- = to do o.s. a favor, to do good to/for o.s.
(iCNi)-TL- > (iCNi)-∅- = fellow/guy; rascal; **nocni** = he is my buddy; **nocné!** = hey buddy!/ hey fellow!
(iCN-ĪUH)-TLI- = friend; **nocnīuh** = he is my friend
   (iCN-ĪUH-TOCA) > (iCN-ĪUH-TOCA): TĒ- = to believe s.o. to be a friend; to consider s.o. a friend
(iCN-Ō)-TL- > (iCN-Ō)-UH- = orphan/pauper
   (iCN-Ō-ITT-A) > (iCN-Ō-ITT-A): TĒ- = to see s.o. as an orphan, i.e., to look kindly/compassionately upon s.o.; to pity/take pity on s.o.
   (iCN-Ō-MATI) > (iCN-Ō-MAT) ~ (ICN-Ō-MAH): TĒ- = to consider s.o. with compassion
   (iCN-Ō-TLĀCA)-TL- > (iCN-Ō-TLĀCA)-UH- = an indigent person
*(iCPA)-TL- > (iCPA)-∅- = [*gen-use s used only as emb s*] top/upper part/summit
   (iCPA-L)-LI- = high-backed seat
   (iCPA-C)-TLI- > (iCPA-C)-∅- = top location; i.e., top/head; **icpacxōchitl** = it is flowers for the head; i.e., it is a garland; *adv*, over/on top of/above; **nocpac** = on the top of my head; over/above my head; **tepēticpac** = on top of a/the mountain; over/above a/the mountain
(iCZA) > (iCZA): TLA- = to tread/step on s.th.; **nitlacza** = I step on s.th.; (iCX-Ō) ~ (iCZA-L-Ō) = *nonac s*
(iCXI)-TL- > (iCXI)-∅- = a thing that is tread on, a thing that treads on; foot; leg; **nocxi** = it is my foot; they are my feet; (iCX-EH-∅)-☐- > (iCX-EH-∅-CĀ)-UH- = *pret agen*, one that has owned feet; s.o./s.th. that has feet
(iCXI-PĀCA) > (iCXI-PĀCA) ~ (iCXI-PĀC): M-O- = to wash o.s. at the feet; i.e., to wash one's own feet
(iCXI-POL-AC-TIĀ) > (iCXI-POL-AC-TIH): TLA- = to cause s.th. to enter underwater with a foot; i.e., to push s.th. underwater with a foot
(iCH)-TLI- > (iCH)-HUI- ~ (iCH)-∅- = maguey hemp/fiber; **nochhui** ~ **noch** = it is my maguey fiber [*Var treats initial /i/ as a full vowel*: **nichhui** ~ **nich**.]
   (iCH-CA)-TL- > (iCH-CA)-UH- = maguey-fiber associate; i.e., cotton; [*in addition in postconquest times*], wool; *by extens*, sheep; (iCH-CA-HUĪ-PIL)-LI- = cotton (protective) vest (worn by warriors) [*For* (iCH-CA-HUĪ-IPIL)-LI-, *see* (IPIL)-LI.]; (iCH-CA-MĀX-TLa)-TL- > (iCH-CA-MĀX-TLI)-∅- = cotton breechcloth; (iCH-CA-YŌ)-TL- = s.th. pertaining to sheep
   (iCH-PĀNA) > (iCH-PĀN): TLA- = to sweep s.th.; [*usually with* tla-*fusion*], (TLA-CH-PĀNA) > (TLA-CH-PĀN) = to sweep/do the sweeping
   (iCH-PŌCH)-TLI- > (iCH-PŌCH)-∅- = maiden; daughter [*abs af s*, (iCH-PŌ-PŌCH)-T-]
   (iCH-TEQUI) > (iCH-TEC) = to cut maguey fiber; i.e., to steal; (*when transitive with a specific obj*) to steal (a specific thing); (iCH-TEC-Ō-NI)-∅- = a thing susceptible to theft; (iCH-TA-∅-CĀ)-☐- = furtively; stealthily; in secret/secretly/hiddenly [*an irreg pret agen with 2nd-degree adverbialization*]
   (iCH-TI) > (iCH-TI) = to become/be like maguey fiber; (iCH-TI-∅)-C- = a wiry thing; a sinewy and lean person
   (iCH-TIL-MAH)-TLI- = maguey-fiber blanket/cloak/cape
(iCHCUA) > (iCHCUA): TLA- = to dig up s.th. (a clod/chunk of earth); [*usually with*

tla-*fusion*], (TLA-CHCUA) > (TLA-CHCUA) = to dig up a clod/chunk of earth
(TLA-CHCUI)-TL- > (TLA-CHCUI)-UH- = sod/turf/clod; (TLA-CHCUI-TEQUI) >, (TLA-CHCUI-TEC) = to cut sod; (TLA-CHCUI-TEC)-TLI- = a sod-cut thing, a thing of cut sod
*(IHCA) > (IHCA) = [*shows pret-as-pres irregularity*], to be standing
(iH-CAHU-A-CA) > (iH-CAHU-A-CA) = to shrill/give a war whoop; **tlahcahuaca** = *impers*, there is shouting/an outcry/whooping (for battle) [*a freq s from* (CAHU-Ā-NI)]
(iH-CAHU-A-TZ-A) > (iH-CAHU-A-TZ): TĒ- ~ TLA- = *applic*, to yell at s.o./s.th.; *caus*, to cause s.o. to utter a shrill sound
(iHCALI) > (iHCAL): TĒ- = to skirmish/battle with s.o.
(IH-CĪ-CA) > (IH-CĪ-CA) = to pant [< *(CĪ-NI) < *(CI-Ī-NI)]; (IH-IH-CĪ-CA) > (IH-IH-CĪ-CA) = to pant continually
(iH-C-I-HUI) > (iH-C-I-UH) = to hurry; [*as matrix*], to suffer (an illness)
(iH-C-I-UH-∅-CĀ)-☐- = [*gen-use pret agen advlzd*], in the manner of one who hurries, i.e., quickly/hurriedly
(IH-COY-O-CA) > (IH-COY-O-CA) = (for wind/waves/rushing water/fire/etc.) to make a loud noise [*a freq s from* (COY-Ō-NI)]
(iHCHIQUI) > (iHCHIC): TLA- = to scrape s.th. clean
(IHCUĀC)-☐- = at that time; when
(IHCUAN-I-Ā) > (IHCUAN-I-H): TLA- ~ M-☐- = to move s.th.; to move away; **nitla-ihcuania** = I move s.th. [*Var s treats initial /i/ as a supportive vowel*: **nitlahcuania.**]; **mihcuanihqueh** = they moved; **ommihcuanihqueh** = they moved on
(iHCUIL-I-HUI) > (iHCUIL-I-UH) = to become written/painted
(iHCUIL-O-Ā) > (iHCUIL-O-H): TLA- = to write/paint s.th.
(IHHUI)-TL- > (IHHUI)-UH- = a feather; **nihhuiuh** = it is my feather; they are my feathers;
(IHHUI-TI-CA)-☐- = by means of/with feathers
(IHHUI-TIL-Ā-HUA-∅)-C- = a thing thick at the feathers; i.e., a thickly feathered thing
(IHHUI-YŌ)-TL- > (IHHUI-YŌ)-∅- = plumage; (IHHUI-YŌ-TIL-Ā-HUA-∅)-C- = a thing thick at the plumage; i.e., a thickly plumaged thing
(HUI-HHUI-TLA) > (HUI-HHUI-TLA): TLA- = to pluck the feathers off of s.th.
*(IH-Ī)-TL- = [*used only as emb*], breath [*redup of* *(Ī)-TL-*]
(IH-Ī-YŌ)-TL- > (IH-Ī-YŌ)-∅- = breath; essence; (IH-Ī-YŌ-CUI) > (IH-Ī-YŌ-CUI) = to catch one's breath, to refresh o.s., to take a refreshment
(IH-Ī-YO-H-∅)-☐- = *pret agen*, a thing that has owned abundant breath; i.e., a thing strong with alcoholic spirits
(IH-Ī-YŌ-HUIĀ) > (IH-Ī-YŌ-HUIH): TLA- = to use the breath on s.th.; i.e., to become winded because of s.th.; i.e., to suffer s.th. that is a hardship; to become exhausted because of s.th.
(iH-MATI) > (iH-MAT) ~ (iH-MAH): TĒ- = (for a god) to devise/design s.o.
(iH-MATI) > (iH-MAT) ~ (iH-MAH): TLA- = to be skilled/dexterous/clever with s.th.; (TLA-H-MATI) > (TLA-H-MAT) ~ (TLA-H-MAH) = [tla-*fusion*], (for a shaman, etc.) to carry out a deception/trick
(TLA-H-MACH)-TLI- = skill/dexterity; *by extens*, s.th. resulting from skill; e.g., needlework/embroidery; (TLA-H-MACH-TIL-MAH)-TLI- = a blanket with embroidery
(iH-NECUI) > (iH-NEUC): TLA- = to smell s.th./to inhale s.th.; **nitlahnecui** = I smell s.th.

Vocabulary

+TĒ(TLA-H-NECUI-YĀ)-∅- = [*used only in pos-st NNCs*], (s.o.'s) sense of smell
(IH-PĪTZA) > (IH-PĪTZ): TĒ- = to blow on s.o.; i.e., to cast a spell on s.o.; (TĒ-IH-PĪTZA-LIZ)-TLI- = action of blowing on s.o., i.e., action of casting a spell on s.o.
(IH-PŌ-CA) > (IH-PŌ-CA) = to emit fumes/vapors [< *(PŌ-NI) < *(PO-Ō-NI)]
(IHTACa)-TL- > (IHTAC)-∅- = victuals/provisions; larder/store of provisions; **nihtac** = they are my victuals/my provisions
(iHT-A-HUI) > (iHT-A-UH) = to become uttered; (for s.o.'s name) to become uttered; i.e., to become talked about/to acquire renown
  (iHT-O-Ā) > (iHT-O-H): TLA- = to cause s.th. to become uttered, i.e., to say s.th.; to promise s.th.; (iHT-Ō-Z-NEQUI) > (iHT-Ō-Z-NEC): TLA- = [*fut emb comp*] to want to say s.th.; i.e., to mean s.th.; **quihtoznequi** = it means…; (TLA-HT-O-Ā) > (TLA-HT-O-H) = [tla-*fusion*], to speak; (for birds) to sing; (for frogs) to croak; etc.
  (TLA-HT-O-Ā-NI)-∅- = one who customarily speaks; i.e., speaker; ruler/king/chief
  (TLA-HT-O-H-∅)-QUI- > (TLA-HT-O-H-∅-CĀ)-UH- = *pret agen*, a speaker/ruler/chief; (TLA-HT-O-H-∅-CĀ-TI) > (TLA-HT-O-H-∅-CĀ-T) = to become/be a ruler/king/chief; to rule/govern; (TLA-HT-O-H-∅-CĀ-TŌCĀi)-TL- > (TLA-HT-O-H-∅-CĀ-TŌCĀ)-∅- = name as a ruler/king; a kingly name; (TLA-HT-O-H-∅-CĀ-YŌ)-TL- = kingship/rulerhood; kingdom/sovereignty; eloquence
  (TLA-HT-Ō-L)-LI- = what is uttered/said; utterance/word/speech; language; (a bird's) song, (a frog's) croak, etc.; **tlahtōlli ihīyōtl** = it is an utterance and it is breath; i.e., it is a discourse; TĒ-(TLA-HT-Ō-L-CHIYA) > (TLA-HT-Ō-L-CHIX) = to await s.o. for words; i.e., to await s.o.'s words [*See* § 30.14.2.]; (TLA-HT-Ō-L-HUĒL-I-∅)-C- = pleasing of words/speech; M-O-(TLA-HT-Ō-L-HUEL-ITT-A) > (TLA-HT-Ō-L-HUEL-ITT-A) = to look well/favorably on o.s. with regard to words; i.e., to like one's own words; (TLA-HT-Ō-L-ITQUI) > (TLA-HT-Ō-L-ITQUI) = to carry words/speech; i.e., to serve as/be an ambassador; (TLA-HT-Ō-L-ITQUI-∅)-C- > (TLA-HT-Ō-L-ITQUI-∅-CĀ)-UH- = a word-carrier; i.e., an ambassador; (TLA-HT-Ō-L-LŌ)-TL- = wordiness; i.e., history/description
  (iHT-A-L-HUIĀ) > (iHT-A-L-HUIH): TĒ+TLA- = to say s.th. about/for s.o.; TĒ-(TLA-HT-A-L-HUIĀ) > (TLA-HT-A-L-HUIH) = [tla-*fusion*], to speak for s.o.
(IHTI)-TL- > (IHTI)-∅- = belly/stomach; inside part; **nihti** = it is my stomach [*var s*, (IHTE)-TL- > (IHTE)-∅-] +TLA(IHTI-C)-∅- = in s.th.'s interior/inside of s.th./within s.th.
(IHTŌ-TI-Ā) > (IHTŌ-TI-H): M-☐- = to dance; (M-☐-IHTŌ-TI-H-∅)-QUI- > (NE-IHTŌ-TI-H-∅-CĀ)-UH- = *pret agen*, one who has danced; i.e., a dancer
(iHTLAC-A-HUI) > (iHTLAC-A-UH) = to become/get spoiled/damaged/ruined; +TĒ(iH-TLAC-A-UH-CA)-∅- = (s.o.'s) action of becoming damaged/ruined; (s.o.'s) defect/faults/flaws; **nohtlacauhca** = it is my action of becoming ruined, it is my defect; **ihtlacauhca in petlatl** = it is the mat's defect, it is a defect in the mat [*The pos pron* **ī-∅** *has become* **i-∅** *because of the following glottal stop.*]
  (iHTLAC-O-Ā) > (iHTLAC-O-H): TLA- ~ TĒ- = to damage/harm/spoil/ruin s.th.; to harm s.o.; (TLA-HTLAC-Ō-L)-LI- = a flaw/fault/defect; [*in postconquest times*], sin
(iH-TLANI) > (iH-TLAN): TLA- = to request s.th.; to ask for s.th.; **nitlahtlani** = I request s.o.; M-O+TLA-(iH-TLAN-IĀ) > (iH-TLAN-IH) = to ask s.th. about o.s.; i.e., to examine one's conscience; TĒ+TLA-(iH-TLANI-LIĀ) > (iH-TLANI-LIH): = to request s.th. from s.o.

(iH-TZOMA) > (iH-TZON): TLA- = to sew s.th.; to thatch s.th. (a roof); **nitlahtzoma** = I sew/thatch s.th.

(iHXILI) > (iHXIL): TĒ- ~ TLA- = to spear/stab s.o.; to prick/goad s.th. (an animal); (TĒ-IHXIL-∅)-QUI- > (TĒ-IHXIL-∅-CĀ)-UH- = *pret agen*, one who has speared/stabbed s.o.; i.e., a spearer/stabber; (TLA-HXIL)-LI- = one that has been speared/stabbed

(XI-HXILI) > (XI-HXIL): TĒ- = to spear/stab s.o. repeatedly

(IHYĀNA) > (IHYĀN): M-∅- = to hide (o.s.); to take shelter from the rain

(IHYĀNI-LIĀ) > (IHYĀNI-LIH): TĒ+NE- = to hide (o.s.) from s.o.

(iHYĀ-YA) > (iHYĀ-YA) ~ (iHYĀ-X) = to stink; (iHYĀ-∅)-C- > (iHYĀ-∅-CĀ)-UH- = *pret agen*, a thing that has stunk; i.e., a stinking thing/a foul-smelling thing

(iHYE-L)-LI- = flatulence [< (iHYĀ-YA)]

(TLA-HYĀ-YA) > (TLA-HYĀ-YA) ~ (TLA-HYĀ-X) = [*Impers* tla-], (for a stench) to be in/permeate (some place)

(TLA-HYE-L)-LI- = s.th. foul; smelly filth; stench; dysentery [< (TLA-HYĀ-YA)]

(IHZA) > (IHZA) = to become awake; to wake up

(IH-ZŌ) > (IH-ZŌ): M-∅- = to puncture o.s., i.e., to bleed o.s.; to make a blood sacrifice

(iH-ZOM-O-CA) > (iH-ZOM-O-CA) = to hiss [*a freq s from* (ZOM-Ō-NI)]

+TLA(H-ZOM-O-CA-YĀ-N)-∅- = [*used only in pos-st NNCs*], (s.th.'s) hissing place]

(IHUĀ) > (IHUAH): TĒ- ~ TLA- = to send s.o. as a messenger; to send s.th. (i.e., a message)

(IHUI) > (IUH) = to become/be similar; to be thus; [*3rd-sg pres or pret VNC advlzd*], thus; in this way; **mā zo ihui** = although

+Ī-∅(HUI-YĀ-N)-∅- [*for* +Ī-∅(IHUI-YĀ-N)-∅-] = slowly/calmly/tranquilly; carefully

(IUH-∅)-QUI- > (IUH-∅-CĀ)-UH- = *pret agen*, one that has become thus; one like this; one in this manner; thus; in this way; **iuhqui in mah** = it is as if/though [*trad sp* **iuhquinma ~ iuhquimma**]

(IHUIN-TI) > (IHUIN-TI) = to become tipsy/drunk/intoxicated

(IHUIN-TI-Ā) > (IHUIN-TI-H): TĒ- = to make/get s.o. tipsy/drunk/intoxicated

(IL-)- = *emb s only*

(IL-ACA-CH-I-HUI) > (IL-ACA-CH-I-UH) = to swirl; (IL-ACA-CH)-TLI- = a swirl

(IL-AQUI) > (IL-AC) = to sink/to become submerged

(IL-AQUI-Ā) > (IL-AQUI-H): TLA- ~ TĒ- = to sink/submerge s.th./s.o.

(IL-AC-TIĀ) > (IL-AC-TIH): TLA- = to sink/submerge s.th.

(iL-)- = *emb s only*

(iL-CĀHU-A) > (iL-CĀUH): TLA- = to forget s.th.; (TLA-L-CĀUH)-TLI- = a forgotten thing

(iL-HUIĀ) > (iL-HUIH): TĒ+TLA- = to say s.th. to s.o.; to tell s.th. to s.o.

*(iLHUI-L)-LI- >(iLHUI-L)-∅- = [*used only in pos-st NNCs*], recompense/reward

(T-O-LHUI-L-TI) > (T-O-LHUI-L-TI) = to become/be our due reward/recompense [*The pos pron can, of course, be replaced by any other pos pron.*]

(iL-NĀMIQUI) > (iL-NĀMIC): TLA- = to remember s.th.

(iL-PĪTZA) > (iL-PĪTZ): TLA- = to blow on s.th.; (TLA-L-PĪTZ-∅)-QUI- > (TLA-L-PĪTZ-∅-CĀ)-UH- = *pret agen*, one who has blown on s.th.

(TLA-L-PĪTZ)-TLI- = a thing that is blown on

(iL-PĪTZA) > (iL-PĪTZ): TĒ= to prompt/inspire s.o.

Vocabulary

(ILAMa)-TL- > (ILAN)-∅- = old woman [*var s*, (ILAN)-TLI-]
(iLHUI)-TL- > (iLHUI)-UH- = day/festival
   (iLHUI-QUĪX-TIĀ) > (iLHUI-QUĪX-TIH) = to cause a festival to come out/pass; i.e., to celebrate a festival; (iLHUI-QUĪX-TI-LIĀ) > (iLHUI-QUĪX-TI-LIH): TĒ- = to cause a day/festival to come out/pass for s.o.; i.e., to celebrate a festival in honor of s.o.
   (iLHUI-CA)-TL- = a day associate; i.e., sky; (iLHUI-CA-Ā)-TL- = sky water; i.e., ocean/sea; (iLHUI-CA-Ā-TĒN)-TLI- = the edge of sky water; i.e., edge/shore of the ocean; seashore; (iLHUI-CA-YŌL-LO-H)-TLI- = the heart of the sky; i.e., the center of the sky
(ĪLŌ-TI) > (ĪLŌ-T) = to return
(iLPI) > (iLPI) = to become/be tied/knotted; (iLPI-Ā) > (iLPI-H): TLA- = to cause s.th. to become tied; i.e., to tie s.th.; (TLA-LPĪ-L)-LI- = a thing that people tie; i.e., a knot; a thing that can be knotted/tied; a sash; (iLPI-Ā) > (iLPI-H): M-O- = to gird o.s.; *reflex-as-pass*, (for s.th.) to undergo tying/be tied; (NE-LPĪ-LŌ-NI)-∅- = a thing by means of which people customarily gird themselves; i.e., a belt/sash
   (iLP-IĀ) > (iLP-IH): M-O- = (for things) to become tied to one another
   (iLPI-LIĀ) > (iLPI-LIH): M-O- = (for things) to become tied to one another
(ĪMACACI) > (ĪMACAZ): TĒ- = to respect s.o./to be respectful toward s.o.; to hold s.o. in awe; to fear s.o.; (ĪMACAX-Ō-NI)-∅- = one who is worthy of respect
(IM-MAN)-∅- = the proper/appropriate/opportune time; **ye imman īn** = this is the proper time; **ye imman in . . .** = now is the time that/to/for . . .
   (TLA-IM-MAN-TI) > (TLA-IM-MAN-TI) = [*impers tla-*] (for the proper/assigned time) to arrive (to put s.th. into effect)
(ĪN)-∅- = this one/these; **ihqueh īn** = these
(ĪNĀYA) > (ĪNĀX): TLA- = to hide s.th.
(IPIL)-LI- = pile/stack
(iT-HUI) > (iT-HUI) = to become discernible/seeable; (TLA-T-HUI) > (TLA-T-HUI) = [*impers tla-*] (for things in general) to become seeable; i.e., to dawn; (TLA-T-HUI)-TL- = dawn; (TLA-T-HUI-NĀHUA-C)-∅- = within hearing distance of dawn, i.e., near dawn; TĒ- (TLA-T-HUI-TI-Ā) > (TLA-T-HUI-TI-H): = to cause s.o. to be at dawn; i.e., to hold/detain s.o. at dawn
   (iT-HU-A) > (iT-HU-A): TLA- = to see s.th.; (iT-HU-A-L)-LI- = an inner courtyard; (iT-HU-A-L-NE-PAN-TLAH)-∅- = in/into/to/from the middle of a/the courtyard
(iTQUI) > (iTQUI): TLA- = to carry s.th.; (TLA-TQUI)-TL- > (TLA-TQUI)-∅- = a thing that is carried; i.e., equipment/property/belongings; (TLA-TQUI-HUAH-∅)-∅- > (TLA-TQUI-HUAH-∅-CĀ)-UH- = *pret agen*, one who has owned equipment; i.e., a person with equipment; an outfitted person; (TLA-TC-Ō-NI)-∅- = a means/instrument for carrying s.th; **tlatcōni tlamāmalōni** = it is a means for carrying s.th. and it is a means for bearing s.th. on the back; i.e., governance [here "s.th." = "people"]
   (TLA-TQUI-TI-Ā) > (TLA-TQUI-TI-H): M-O+TLA- = to cause s.th. to become one's own property
(iTT-A) > (iTT-A): TĒ- ~ TLA- = to see s.o./s.th.; T-O-(iTT-A) > (iTT-A) = to see one another; **mohottah** = *freq VNC*, they stare at one another
   (iTTI-LIĀ) > (iTTI-LIH): TĒ+TLA- ~ TĒ+TĒ- = to see s.th./s.o. for s.o.; M-O+TLA-
   (iTTI-LIĀ) > (iTTI-LIH): = to see s.th. for o.s.; i.e., to envision s.th.
   (iTT-Ī-TIĀ) > (iTT-Ī-TIH): TĒ+TLA- = to cause s.o. to see s.th. (by showing the object);

to show s.th. to s.o.; TĒ-(TLAH-TLA-TT-Ī-TIĀ) > (TLAH-TLA-TT-Ī-TIH) = [tla-*fusion plus redup*], to cause s.o. to see various things; i.e., to train s.o. to be observant

(ITL-AH)-∅- = something

(ĪTZ)-TLI- > (ĪTZ)-HUI- ~ -∅- = obsidian; piece of obsidian/obsidian fragment
    (ĪTZ-CUĀUH)-TLI- = obsidian eagle; i.e., golden eagle
    (ĪTZ-EH-EH-CA) > (ĪTZ-EH-EH-CA) = (for a wind) to blow with pieces of obsidian
    (ĪTZ-TI-YA) > (ĪTZ-TI-YA) = to become/be like obsidian; i.e., to become/be cold; (ĪTZ-TI-∅)-C- > (ĪTZ-TI-∅-CĀ)-UH- = *pret agen*, a thing that has become cold; i.e., a cold thing; (ĪTZ-TI-∅-CĀ-PAH-TI) > (ĪTZ-TI-∅-CĀ-PAH-TI) = to become/be very cold; (ĪTZ-TI-∅-CĀ-PAH-TI-∅)-C- = a very cold thing; a frigid thing

*(iTZ-A) > (iTZ) = to look/watch; * TĒ ~ TLA-(iTZ-A) > (iTZ): = to see s.o./s.th. [*Both of these stems (intrans and trans) are emb only.*]; **nēchitztoc** = he lies seeing/looking at me; he remains looking at me

(ITZ-CUIN)-TLI- = dog
    (ITZ-CUIN-CUĀ) > (ITZ-CUIN-CUAH) = to eat dogs; (ITZ-CUIN-CUĀ-NI)-∅- = one that customarily eats dogs; i.e., a ringtail
    (ITZ-CUIN-CUITLA-PIL)-LI- = a dog tail

(iTZ-MOL-Ī-NI) > (iTZ-MOL-Ī-N) = (for plants) to sprout

(ITZ-TAPAL-TE)-TL- > (ITZ-TAPAL-TE)-UH- = a rock with the shape of a flagstone; i.e., a flat stone

(iX-)-∅- = [*used only as emb or matrix*], total amount
    (iX-A-CHI)-∅- = a very large amount/number; much; many
    (iX-HUA) > (iX-HUA) = to germinate/sprout
    (iX-QUI-CH)-∅- = a total amount/quantity; all; finished thing; the end of the matter; (iX-QUI-CH-CA)-∅- = up to this/that time
    (iX-TLĀ-HUI) > (iX-TLĀ-UH) = to become restored; TLA-(iX-TLĀ-HU-A) > (iX-TLĀ-UH): = to repay s.th. (i.e., a debt); TĒ+TLA-(iX-TLĀ-HU-IĀ) > (iX-TLĀ-HU-IH): = to pay s.th. to s.o.
    (iX-HUI) > (iX-HUI) = to become sated

(ĪX)-TLI- = face; surface; eye
    (ĪX-CĀHU-IĀ) > (ĪX-CĀHU-IH): M-☐- = to pay attention to o.s.; i.e., to mind one's own business/affairs; to act by o.s.; (NE-ĪX-CĀHU-Ī-L)-LI- = a private thing/matter
    +TĒ-(ĪX-CO-H-YĀ-N)-∅- = [*used in pos-st NNCs only (advlzd)*], on (s.o.'s) personal initiative; by (s.o.'s) own free will; of (s.o.'s) own accord; (s.o.'s) personal/private thing
    (ĪX-CUĀCH-HUIĀ) > (ĪX-CUĀCH-HUIH): TLA- = to use a large cotton blanket on s.th. at the surface; M-☐-(ĪX-CUĀCH-HUIĀ) > (ĪX-CUĀCH-HUIH) = [*used in a reflex-as-pass VNC*] (for a large cotton blanket) to be used on a surface; i.e., to cover a surface
    (ĪX-CUEP-A) > (ĪX-CUEP): TĒ- = to deceive s.o.; (TĒ-ĪX-CUEP-A-NI)-∅- = one who customarily deceives people; i.e., a deceiver/deluder
    (ĪXI-MATI) > (ĪXI-MAT ~ ĪXI-MAH): TĒ- ~ TLA- = to know s.o./s.th. by the face; i.e., to recognize s.o./s.th.; to be acquainted with s.o./s.th.; (TLA-ĪXI-MATI-NI)-∅- = a knowledgeable/clever person; (TLA-ĪXI-MACH)-TLI- = a thing with which people have become acquainted; i.e., a discovery; +TĒ(ĪXI-MACH-∅-CA)-∅- = [*used only in pos-st NNCs*], (s.o.'s) action of being recognized; i.e., (s.o.'s) recognition (by others); the recognition of (s.o.)
    (ĪXI-MATI) > (ĪXI-MAT ~ ĪXI-MAH): M-☐- = to know o.s.; to be cautious/wary; T-☐-

(ĪXI-MATI) > (ĪXI-MAT) ~ (ĪXI-MAH) = to be acquainted with/know one another
(ĪX-MIH-MIQUI-NI)-Ø- = one that is customarily dead at the eyes; i.e., a blind one
(ĪX-NĀHUA-C)-□- = near the eyes
(ĪX-NĀMIQUI) > (ĪX-NĀMIC): TLA- = to meet s.th. at the face; i.e., to face toward s.th.
*(ĪX-PAN)-Ø- > (ĪX-PAN)-Ø- = [*used only in pos-st NNCs*], before the eyes of (s.o.); in front of (s.o.); in (s.o.'s) presence
(ĪX-PECH-TI-Ø)-C- = one that has become flat at the face; i.e., a flat-faced thing
(ĪX-TE)-TL- > (ĪX-TE)-UH- = egg of the face; i.e., eyeball; (ĪX-TE-MAH-MAL-ACA-CH-TI-Ø)-C- = a thing that has become like spindle whorls at the eyes; i.e., a circular-eyed thing
(ĪX-TEZ-CA)-TL- > (ĪX-TEZ-CA)-UH- = mirrors in front of the eyes; i.e., eyeglasses
(ĪX-TI-Ā) > (ĪX-TI-H): TĒ- = to cause s.o. to have eyes; i.e., to incite s.o.; to make s.o. confront an enemy
*(ĪX-TLAN)-Ø- > (ĪX-TLAN)-Ø- = [*used only in pos-st NNCs*], beneath (s.o.'s) eyes; i.e., in (s.o.'s) presence
(ĪX-TLA-PA-L)-□- = [*used only in advlzd NNC*], with the side as a face; i.e., crosswise
(ĪX-XĪP-TLA)-TL- > (ĪX-XĪP-TLA)-Ø- = representative/proxy/image/resemblance; TĒ-(ĪX-XĪP-TLA-YŌ-TI-Ā) > (ĪX-XĪP-TLA-YŌ-TI-H) = to cause s.o. to have a representational surrogate; i.e., to make an image of s.o.
(iXCA) > (iXCA): TLA- = to bake s.th.; (TLA-XCA-L)-LI- = a thing that people bake; i.e., tortilla/bread; (TLA-XCA-L-IXCA) > (TLA-XCA-L-IXCA) = to bake tortillas; (TLA-XCA-L-IXCA-Ø)-C- > (TLA-XCA-L-IXCA-Ø-CĀ)-UH- = *pret agen*, a tortilla baker; a baker
(TLA-XCA-L-CHĪHUA) > (TLA-XCA-L-CHĪUH) = to make tortillas
(TLA-XCA-L-LĀ-N)-□- = *place-name s*, In/To/From the Place in the Vicinity of Tortillas
(TLA-XCA-L-NAMACA) > (TLA-XCA-L-NAMACA) = to sell tortillas
(IXHU-ĪUH)-TLI- = grandchild
(IX-TLĀ-HUA)-TL- = treeless flatland; grassy plain; valley floor
(IY-Ā-HU-A) > (IY-Ā-UH): TLA- = to offer up s.th. (in sacrifice to a deity); to incense s.th.
(IY-E)-TL- > (IY-E)-UH- = tobacco smoke; tobacco tube; tobacco; tobacco plant
*(IY-O-Ā) > (IY-O-H) = [*defec v, only pret VNCs occur*], to be alone; *adv*, only; **zan niyoh** = I am alone; only I; **zan iyohqueh** = they are alone; only they
(ĪZ-A-HUI-Ā) > (ĪZ-A-HUI-H): TĒ- = to surprise/shock/ astonish s.o.
(iZCAL-I-Ā) > (iZCAL-I-H): M-O- = to come to/revive; to come to one's senses; to be discreet/prudent; (M-O-ZCAL-I-Ā-NI)-Ø- = one who customarily comes to his senses; i.e., an able/capable person; (M-O-ZCAL-I-H-Ø)-QUI- ~ (M-O-ZCAL-I-H-Ø)-□- > (NE-IZCAL-I-H-Ø-CĀ)-UH- = *pret agen*, one who has become prudent; i.e., a prudent/discreet person; a proficient/able person
(iZHUA)-TL- > (iZHUA)-UH- = leaf; TLA-(iZHUA-HUIĀ) > (iZHUA-HUIH) = to use leaves on s.th.; i.e., to scrub s.th. with leaves
(iZHUA-YŌ)-TL- > (iZHUA-YŌ)-Ø- = foliage; [*pos-st NNC used for org-pos*], leaf; foliage; M-O-(IZHUA-YŌ-TI-Ā) > (IZHUA-YŌ-TI-H) = (for a plant) to cause itself to have foliage; i.e., to sprout leaves
(iZ-)-Ø- = [*used only as emb*], equal amount
(iZ-QUI)-Ø- = an equal amount/number; as much; as many; so much; so many;

(iZ-QUI-TLA-MAN)-TLI- = an equal number of things
(IZTA)-TL- > (IZTA)-UH- = salt
  (IZTA-YA) > (IZTA-YA) ~ (IZTA-Z) = to become like salt; i.e., to become/be white; (IZTĀ-∅)-C- > (IZTĀ-∅-CĀ)-UH- = *pret agen*, a thing that has become white; i.e., a white thing; (IZTA-L)-LI- = a thing that results from becoming white; i.e., a white thing
(iZTE)-TL- > (iZTE)-∅- = fingernail/toenail; talon; claw [*var s*, (iZTI)-TL- > (iZTI)-∅-]
  (iZTE-HUEH-HUĒ-I-YA) > (iZTE-HUEH-HUĒ-I-YA) = to become long at the fingernails/toenails; i.e., to have long fingernails/toenails
(IZTLAC)-TLI- = saliva/drivel/slaver/spittle; *also*, venom; *by extens*, a lie
  (IZTLAC-MĪ-N-A)> (IZTLAC-MĪ-N): TĒ- ~ TLA- = to shoot s.o. with venom; (for a poisonous snake) to bite s.o.

M

MĀ = [*adv part introducing wishes and commands (with opt) or admonitions (with admon)*], if only; **mā ah#** = if only not (*with admon*); **mā ca#** ~ **mā camō** = if only not (*in wishes and commands*); **mā caye** = if only not yet; **mā cazo** = if only perhaps not; **mā nēn** = if only in vain (*in admonitions*); **mā ye cuēl!** ~ **mā ye cuēl eh!** = [*expression of encouragement*], come on! up and at 'em! let's get on with it!; **mā zo ihui** = although it be thus; provided that; as long as; assuming that; **mā zo iuhqui** = be it/that as it may; be it/that such and so; **mā zo tēl** = no matter if
(MĀ) > (MAH): TĒ- ~ TLA- = to capture s.o.; to hunt/catch s.th. (TLA-MĀ-NI)-∅- = one that customarily hunts/pursues s.th.; one that customarily catches/captures s.th.; i.e., a hunter/pursuer
  (MA-L)-LI- = captive [*abs af s*, (MĀ-MA-L)-T-]; (MA-L-MIQUI) > (MA-L-MIC) = to die in relation to a captive; i.e., to survive a captive; i.e., to incur the loss of a captive through sacrifice (TLAH-TLA-MĀ) > (TLAH-TLA-MAH) to seine, to fish [tla-*fusion plus redup*]
(MACA) > (MACA): TĒ+TLA- = to give s.th. to s.o.
  (TLA-MACA-Z)-QUI- > (TLA-MACA-Z-CĀ)-UH- = *fut agen*, priest/offering priest
  (TĒ-MAC)-TLI- = a thing that is given to s.o.; i.e., a gift
  (MAH-MACA) > (MAH-MACA): TĒ+TLA- = to give s.th. to each person
  (MACA) > (MACA): M-O+TĒ- = [*reflex-as-pas*], to be given to s.o.; M-O+TLA-(MACA) > (MACA) = to give s.th. to o.s.; i.e., to take s.th. as medicine
  (NE-MAC)-TLI- = a gift; TĒ+TLA-(NE-MAC-TI-Ā) > (NE-MAC-TI-H) = to cause s.th. to be s.o.'s gift; i.e., to endow s.o. with s.th.
(MACH)-☐-. *See* (MATI).
MAH = *adv part*, such that; **mah ca#** ~ **mah camō** = such that not
(MAHUI) > (MAUH) = to become/be afraid
  (MAUH-∅)-QUI- > (MAUH-∅-CĀ)-∅- = one who has become afraid; i.e., a timorous one; a coward; (MAUH-∅-CĀ)-☐- = *adv*, like a coward/in the manner of a coward; cowardly; fearfully; (MAUH-∅-CĀ-MIC-∅)-QUI- = *pret agen*, a dead one in the manner of a fearing person; i.e., one who has fainted with fear; (MAUH-∅-CĀ-QUĪZA) > (MAUH-∅-CĀ-QUĪZ) = to exit frightenedly; (MAUH-∅-CĀ-TLĀCA)-TL- = a cowardly person; a coward
  (MAHUI-Z)-TLI- = action of fearing/fear; a person worthy of fear; i.e., a person worthy

Vocabulary

of respect/honor; (MAHUI-Z-CUI) > (MAHUI-Z-CUI) = to take/get fear; i.e., to become frightened; (MAHUI-Z-TI) > (MAHUI-Z-TI) = to become/be a person/thing worthy of honor/esteem; (MAHUI-Z-TI-∅)-C- = *pret agen*, one that has become worthy of honor/esteem; i.e., a person/thing worthy of honor/esteem; a marvelous person/thing; (MAHUI-Z-ZŌ)-TL= a thing characteristic of a person worthy of honor; i.e., honor/dignity/honorableness

(MAH-MAHUI) > (MAH-MAUH) = to be afraid again and again; to be deeply afraid

(MAUH-TIĀ) > (MAUH-TIH): TĒ- ~ TLA- = to cause s.o./s.th. to be afraid; to frighten s.o./s.th.; M-O-(MAUH-TIĀ) > (MAUH-TIH) = to let/allow o.s. to be afraid; i.e., to become/be afraid; to give in to fear

(TĒ-MAH-MAUH-TIH-∅)-☐- = *pret agen*, a thing that has terrified people; i.e., a terrifying thing

(MĀi)-TL- > (MĀ)-∅- = hand; arm; *by extens.*, branch (of a tree) [*As an emb this stem occasionally has the glottalized shape* (MAH-)- *before a consonant and, before a vowel, the shape* (MĀY-)-.]; (MĀ-TI-CA)-☐- = with the hand(s)

+TĒ(MĀ-C)-∅- = in (s.o.'s) hand(s); **nomāc** = in my hand(s)

(TLA-MĀi)-TL- > (TLA-MĀ)-∅- = a quasi-arm; i.e., a sleeve

(MĀ-CĒ-HU-A) > (MĀ-CĒ-UH) = to cause the hands to become/be cool; i.e., to dance; (MĀ-CĒ-HU-A-L)-LI- = commoner/plebeian/peasant

(MĀ-CU-Ī-L)-LI- = s.th. taken as corresponding to a hand; s.th. having five members (like a hand); i.e., five in number; (MĀ-CU-Ī-L-MĒTZ)-TLI- = five months; (MĀ-CU-Ī-L-MĒTZ-TIĀ) > (MĀ-CU-Ī-L-MĒTZ-TIH) = to spend five months (in a place); (MĀ-CU-Ī-L-PŌHUA-L)-LI- = one hundred in number; (MĀ-CU-Ī-L-TE)-TL- = five stones; i.e., five things

(MĀ-NEH-NEMI) > (MĀ-NEH-NEN) = to walk on all fours; (MĀ-NEH-NEMI-NI)-∅- = *custpres agen*, one that customarily walks on all four; i.e., a four-footed animal

(MĀ-ŌPŌCH)-TLI- = left hand

(MĀ-PI-PĪTZ)-TLI- = a whistling sound made with the hand; (MĀ-PI-PĪTZ-O-Ā) > (MĀ-PI-PĪTZ-O-H) = to whistle by means of the hand; to whistle shrilly

(MĀ-PITZ-A-C)-TLI- = a thing (i.e., an arm) that is slender as arms go; i.e., a thing (i.e., a branch) that is slender as branches go; i.e., a slender branch

(MĀ-TACAX)-TLI- = a maniple; (MĀ-TACAX-EH-∅)-☐- = *pret agen*, one who has owned a maniple; i.e., a maniple owner

(MĀ-TOCA) > (MĀ-TOCA): TLA- = to follow s.th. by means of the hand; i.e., to touch/feel s.th.; to examine s.th. by touch; to grope s.th.; +TĒ(TLA-MĀ-TOCA-YĀ)-∅- = s.o.'s sense of touch; **notlamātocaya** = it is my sense of touch

(MĀ-TLa)-TL- > (MĀ-TL)-∅- = strips of cloth/leather serving as a hand; i.e., a net; (MĀ-TLA-TĒM-A) > (MĀ-TLA-TĒN): TLA- = to put s.th. into a net

(MAH-CĒ-HU-A) > (MAH-CĒ-UH): TLA- = to cause s.th. to become cool by means of the hands (?); i.e., to merit/deserve s.th.; to obtain s.th. merited; (MAH-CĒ-HU-A-L)-LI- = a thing that is deservedly obtained; i.e., a deserved/merited thing; reward/recompense/merit; **nomahcēhual** = it is my merit/recompense; (N-O-MAH-CĒ-HU-A-L-TI) > (N-O-MAH-CĒ-HU-A-L-TI) = to become/be my merit/recompense [*The pos pron inside the stem can be replaced by any of the others with a concomitant change in the s's meaning.*]

(MAH-CUEX)-TLI- = bracelet

(MAH-PIL)-LI- = an appendage of a hand; i.e., a finger

(MAH-TLĀC)-TLI- = ten in number; (MAH-TLĀC-TL-OM-ĒI-N)-T- = thirteen (animate) beings; (MAH-TLĀC-PĀN)-TLI- = ten rows; (MAH-TLĀC-PŌHUA-L)-LI- = two hundred in number; (MAH-TLĀC-XIHUI)-TL- = ten years

(MĀY-A-HUI) > (MĀY-A-UH) = to give a shove; to act aggressively/forcefully; TĒ-(MĀY-A-HUI) > (MĀY-A-UH) = to give a shove/push against s.o.; i.e., to shove/knock/push s.o. to the ground [*applic obj unjustified by s's form*]; (MĀY-A-UH)-TLI- = a thrown-down thing; (MĀY-A-UH-CĀ-N)-TLI- = right hand; (MĀY-A-UH-CĀ-M-PA)-◻- = toward the right hand

(MĀY-EH-∅)-◻- > (MĀY-EH-∅-CĀ)-UH- = *pret agen*, one who has owned hands; i.e., a farm laborer, a field hand

(MAL-ACA)-TL- > (MAL-ACA)-◻- = spindle; (MAL-ACA-TI) > (MAL-ACA-TI) = to become like a spindle; (MAL-ACA-CH)-TLI- = a thing that has become like a spindle; i.e., a spindle whorl; a circular thing; a circle; (MAL-ACA-CH-TI) > (MAL-ACA-CH-TI) = to become like a spindle whorl; i.e., to become a circle; (MAL-ACA-CH-TI-∅)-C- = *pret agen*, a thing that has become like a spindle whorl; i.e., a round/circular thing

(MAL-ACA-CH-I-HUI) > (MAL-ACA-CH-I-UH) = to revolve/rotate

(MĀMĀ) > (MĀMAH): TLA- ~ TĒ- = to carry s.th./s.o. on the back [*var s*, TLA-(MĒMĒ) > (MĒMEH)]; (TLA-MĀMAH-∅)-◻- > (TLA-MĀMAH-∅-CĀ)-UH- = *pret agen*, one who carries a load on his back; i.e., a carrier

(MAH-MĀMA-L-TIĀ) > (MAH-MĀMA-L-TIH): M-O+TLA- = (for various persons) to take s.th. as a load/burden upon themselves

(MAMALI) > (MAMAL): TLA- = to drill/bore a hole in s.th.

(MAMAL-HU-ĀZ)-TLI- = drilling instrument; i.e., fire drill; *also*, Castor and Pollux (the two brightest stars in the constellation Gemini); **xiuhcōātl mamalhuāztli** = it is the turquoise-snake and it is the fire drill; i.e., it is war [*Do not confuse this stem with* (MĀMA-L-HU-ĀZ)-TLI-, "carrying frame (for a back load)," *from* TLA-(MĀMĀ), "to carry s.th. on the back."]

(MĀ-NA-HUIĀ) > (MĀ-NA-HUIH), M-O- = to defend o.s.; to have a bowel movement/to defecate; +TĒ(NE-MĀ-NA-HUIĀ-YĀ)-∅- = (s.o.'s) means of defending o.s.; (s.o.'s) defense; **nonemānahuiāya** = it is my means of defending myself

(MANI) > (MAN) = to cover a flat surface; to extend over a flat surface; to extend over a surface; (for a flat-bottomed object) to sit/rest (somewhere); +TLA(MAN-CĀ-N)-∅- = [*used in pos-st NNC only*], (s.th.'s) location

(MAN-A) > (MAN): TLA- = to cause s.th. to extend over a surface; to set s.th. flat/flat-bottomed on the ground/floor; (TLA-MAN-A) > (TLA-MAN) = [tla-*fusion*] to make an oblation; (TLAH-TLA-MAN-A) > (TLAH-TLA-MAN) = [tla-*fusion plus redup*] to make repeated oblations; (for several people) to make oblations

(TLA-MAN)-TLI- = a set-down thing; i.e., a thing

(MANI-LIĀ) > (MANI-LIH): TĒ+TLA- = to set s.th. down for s.o.; i.e., to make an offering to s.o.

(MAN-A) > (MAN): M-O- = to place/situate o.s.; to be placed/situated

(MATI) > (MAT) ~ (MAH) = to become/be cognizant/knowledgeable; to become/be informed; *frequently used with the dir pref* ON-; e.g., **nonmati** = I know the way there/I know its whereabouts; (MAT-∅)-QUI- > (MAT-∅-CĀ)-UH- = *pret agen*, a composed/

calm person; +TĒ(<u>MATI</u>-YĀ-N)-Ø- = (s.o.'s) time of being cognizant; **nomatiyān** = in my time of cognizance; in my time; (<u>N-O-MATI-YĀ-N</u>-TI) > (<u>N-O-MATI-YĀ-N</u>-TI) = to become/be in my time of being cognizant; to happen in my time [*The pos pron inside the stem can be replaced by any of the others with a concomitant change in the s's meaning.*]; (MACH-Ō) = *nonac*; (MACH)-☐- = [*2nd-degree advlzd NNC*], as a known thing; i.e., positively/evidently/assuredly; especially/indeed; notably; namely; people say . . . ; ever; however: **mach eh** = particularly; especially, above all; **mach ahmō** = people say not

(MACH-TIĀ) > (MACH-TIH): TĒ- = to cause s.o. to be knowledgeable; i.e., to teach s.o.

(MACH-TIĀ) > (MACH-TIH): M-O- = to cause o.s. to be knowledgeable; i.e., to study/learn; (<u>M-O-MACH-TIH</u>-Ø)-QUI- > (<u>NE-MACH-TIH</u>-Ø-CĀ)-UH- = *pret agen*, a student; (<u>NE-MACH-TĪ</u>-LŌ-NI)-Ø- = a thing by means of which people study/learn; i.e., a textbook

(MATI) > (MAT) ~ (MAH): TLA- ~ TĒ- = to be cognizant of s.th./s.o.; i.e., to know s.th./s.o. [*applic obj unjustified by s's form*]; **īpan nitēmati** = I look upon s.o. as it (i.e., as whatever is identified by the supplement to the *pos pron* **ī-Ø-**); (<u>TLA-MATI</u>-NI)-Ø- = *cuspres agen*, one who customarily knows things; i.e., a wise/learned person

(<u>TLA-MAT</u>-Ø-TI-M-O-MAN-A) > (<u>TLA-MAT</u>-Ø-TI-M-O-MAN) = (for the wind/bad weather) to become calm

(TLA-MACH-TZIN)-☐- = [*2nd-degree advlzd NNC*], quietly

(MACH-TIĀ) > (MACH-TIH): TĒ+TLA- = to teach s.o. s.th.; M-O+TLA-(MACH-TIĀ) ~ (MACH-TIH) = to study/learn s.th.

(MACHI-L-TIĀ) > (MACHI-L-TIH): TĒ+TLA- = to cause s.o. to know s.th.; to inform s.o. of s.th.

(MACHI-TOCA) > (MACHI-TOCA): M-O+TLA- = to pretend to know s.th.

(<u>MACHI</u>-YŌ)-TL- = exemplariness; sign/example/model/sample; pattern [< *(MACHI)-TL- = a thing that results from being cognizant (?)]

(<u>MACHI</u>-Z)-TLI- = a thing that is worthy of being known; news; (<u>MACHI-Z</u>-TI) > (<u>MACHI-Z</u>-TI) = to become/be a known thing

(MATI) > (MAT) ~ (MAH): M-O- = to know o.s.; i.e., to dither/surmise/conjecture/be of an opinion; **ītech ninomati** = I know myself in contact with/regarding it; i.e., I am experienced/skilled with it; (NE-MACH)-TLI- = awareness/cognizance/mindfulness; +TĒ (<u>NE-MACH</u>-PAN)-Ø- = *advlzd*, in (s.o.'s) being aware; **ahmō nonemachpan** = without my being aware; (<u>NE-MACH</u>-TI-Ā) > (<u>NE-MACH</u>-TI-H): M-O- = to cause o.s. to have awareness/cognizance; i.e., to ready o.s./to get o.s. ready/to prepare o.s.

(MĀTLĀL)-IN- = deep/dark green color; blue-green; (<u>MĀTLĀL</u>-Ā)-TL- = dark green water; blue water; (<u>MĀTLĀL</u>-CUĒY-EH-Ø)-☐- = *pret agen*, one who has owned a a deep-green skirt; i.e., the owner of a deep-green skirt

(MĀXa)-TL- > (MĀX)-Ø- = bifurcation; crotch (of tree/human); fork (of road/stream); (MĀX-TLa)-TL- > (MĀX-TLI)-Ø- = a strip of cloth for the crotch; i.e., breechcloth

(MAZĀ)-TL- > (MAZĀ)-UH- = deer; (<u>MAZĀ</u>-TI) > (<u>MAZĀ</u>-TI) = to become a deer; i.e., to become a wild animal/lose one's humanity/become insane; M-O-(<u>MAZĀ-TI</u>-LIĀ) > (<u>MAZĀ-TI</u>-LIH): = to cause/allow o.s. to become a deer; i.e., to (intentionally) become a wild animal/lose one's humanity/give in to insanity/become insane

(<u>MAZĀ</u>-TLA-CUA-L)-LI- = fodder for animals; (<u>MAZĀ</u>-TLA-CUA-L-TI-Ā) >

(MAZĀ-TLA-CUA-L-TI-H) = to cause deer to have food; i.e., to feed horses, to give fodder to horses

(ME)-TL- > (ME)-UH- = maguey plant; maguey

(ME-CA)-TL- > (ME-CA)-UH- = maguey associate; i.e., rope, cord; TĒ-(ME-C-ĀN-IĀ) > (ME-C-ĀN-IH) [for ME-CA-ĀN-] = to take hold of rope with regard to s.o.; i.e., to use a rope on s.o.; i.e., to hang s.o.; TLA-(ME-CA-PĀ-TZ-CA) > (ME-CA-PĀ-TZ-CA) = to squeeze liquid from s.th. by means of ropes

MEC = *adv part*, then [*var s*, NEC]

(MEL-Ā-HUA) > (MEL-Ā-HUA) = to become/be straight/stretched out lengthwise; to lie stretched out full length; (MEL-Ā-HUA-Ø)-C- = a straight thing; a true/right thing; (MEL-A-C)-TLI = a thing that has become straight; a straight thing

(MEL-Ā-HU-A) > (MEL-Ā-UH): TLA- = to straighten s.th.; to pass straight by s.th. without stopping; to explicate s.th.; (TLA-MEL-Ā-UH-Ø)-QUI- > (TLA-MEL-Ā-UH-Ø-CĀ)-UH- = *pret agen*, one who has straightened things; i.e., a straightener (of things); one who has explicated things; i.e., an explicator; (TLA-MEL-Ā-UH-Ø-CĀ)-☐- = *advlzd*, in the manner of one who has straightened things; i.e., directly/unswervingly; (TLA-MEL-Ā-UH-Ø-CĀ-IHCA) > (TLA-MEL-Ā-UH-Ø-CĀ-IHCA) = *pret-as-pres*, to stand erect/stand up straight; (TLA-MEL-Ā-UH)-TLI- = an explicated thing

(MĒMĒ) > (MĒMEH): TLA-. *See* TLA-(MĀMĀ).

(METLa)-TL- > (METL)-Ø- = metate, grinding stone (stone on which women grind maize or cocoa)

(METZ)-TLI- = thigh; M-O-(METZ-POZ-TEQUI) > (METZ-POZ-TEC) = to break o.s. at the thigh; i.e., to break a thighbone

(MĒTZ)-TLI- = moon; month; (MĒ-XIH-CO)-☐- = *place-name s*, At/To/From the Place of the Moon's Navel [See § 48.4.1.a.]; (MĒ-XIH-☐-CA)-TL- = a person associated with Mexihco; a dweller in/an inhabitant of Mexihco; a Mexihca

(ME-XIH)-Ø- = a member of the Mexih tribe [*abs pl s*, (ME-XIH)-T-; **tiMexihtin** = we are Mexihs] [*Said to be a corruption of* (ME-CIH)-TLI-, "maguey jackrabbit/hare," *which served as the source for the personal-name nounstem* (Ø-Ø-ME-XIH-Ø-Ø)-Ø-, *supposedly an early leader of the Aztecs. The tribe allegedly bore his name.*]

(MIA-C)-. *See* (MIYE-)-.

(MĪ)-TL- > (MĪ)-UH- = arrow; **mītl chīmalli** = it is an arrow and it is a shield; i.e., it is war/a war/a battle; (MĪ-CŌMi)-TL- > (MĪ-CŌN)-Ø- = pot for arrows; i.e., quiver; (MĪ-HUAH-Ø)-☐- > (MĪ-HUAH-Ø-CĀ)-UH- = *pret agen*, one who has owned arrows; i.e., arrow owner

(MĪ-NI) > (MĪ-N) [*for* (MI-Ī-NI)] = to become pierced by an arrow; TLA- ~ TĒ-(MĪ-N-A) > (MĪ-N): = to cause s.th./s.o. to become pierced by an arrow; i.e., to shoot s.th./s.o. with an arrow; (for an insect) to sting s.o.; +TLA(TĒ-MĪ-N-A-YA)-Ø- = (s.th.'s; i.e., an insect's) instrument for stinging s.o.; (s.th.'s) stinger: (TLA-MĪ-N-Ø)-QUI- > (TLA-MĪ-N-Ø-CĀ)-UH- = *pret agen*, an archer/bowman

(MIC)-TLI-. *See* (MIQUI).

(MIC-Ø)-QUI-. *See* (MIQUI).

(MICH)-IN- > (MICH)-Ø- = fish; (MICH-HUAH-Ø)-☐- > (MICH-HUAH-Ø-CĀ)-UH- = *pret agen*, one who has owned fish; i.e., a fish owner; a fisherman

(MIE-C)-Ø-. *See* (MIYE-)-.

Vocabulary

(MĪL)-LI- = cultivated field; (MĪL-CHĪHUA) > (MĪL-CHĪUH) = to work a field; (MĪL-CHĪUH-Ø)-QUI- > (MĪL-CHĪUH-Ø-CĀ)-UH- = *pret agen*, one who has worked/tilled a field; i.e., a farm laborer; a farmer; TĒ-(MĪL-CHĪHUA) > (MĪL-CHĪUH): = to make s.o. at a field; i.e., to work as a field hand in s.o.'s field(s); to cultivate s.o.'s field(s) [*See § 30.14.2 for the creation of this "pos-st-NNC-to-incorp-adv" compound v.*]

(MĪL-EH-Ø)-☐- > (MĪL-EH-Ø-CĀ)-UH- = *pret agen*, one who has owned a field; i.e., a field owner; *(MĪL-EH-Ø-CĀ-POH)-TLI- > (MĪL-EH-Ø-CĀ-POH)-Ø- = [*used only in pos-st NNCs*], (s.o.'s) fellow field owner; a field owner like (s.o.)

(MĪL-LAH)-☐- = place of abundant cultivated fields; (MĪL-LAH-CA)-TL- = a person associated with abundant cultivated fields; i.e., a farmer; a peasant; a rustic

(MĪL-PAN)-☐- = in the field(s)/in the country

(MI-MIL)-LI- = a thing rounded lengthwise; a tubular/columnar/cylindrical thing; (MI-MIL-TI-Ø)-C- = a thing that has become tubular/columnar/cylindrical; i.e., a tubular/columnar/cylindrical thing

(MI-MIL-O-Ā) > (MI-MIL-O-H): TLA- = to cause s.th. to roll; to roll s.th.; to bowl s.th. over; to repeat s.th.

(MI-MIL-O-Ā) > (MI-MIL-O-H): M-O- = to roll/tumble over and over

(MĪ-MIL-O-Ā) > (MĪ-MIL-O-H): M-O- = to wallow

(MĪ-N-A): TLA-. *See* (MĪ)-TL-.

(MIQUI) > (MIC) = to die; (MIC-Ø)-QUI- > (MIC-Ø-CĀ)-UH- = *pret agen*, one who has died; i.e., a dead person [*abs af s*, (MĪ-MIC-Ø)-QU-]; (MIC-Ø-CĀ-ZĀ-YŌL)-IN- = deadman fly; (MIC-Ø-CĀ-TĒX)-TLI- = a widowed brother-in-law (of a man)

(MIC)-TLI- = a thing that results from dying; i.e., a dead body; a corpse; (MIC-TLĀ-N)-☐- = *place-name s,* Place in the Vicinity of Dead Bodies; the afterworld, the underworld; (MIC-TLĀ-M-PA)-☐- = *adv*, toward Dead-Body Land; i.e., toward the north

(MIC-TIĀ) > (MIC-TIH): TĒ- ~ TLA- ~ M-O- = to kill s.o./s.th./o.s.; to commit suicide; (TĒ-MIC-TĪ-LIZ)-TLI- = act of killing people; a massacre; +TĒ(MIC-TĪ-LŌ-CĀ)-Ø- = s.o.'s being murdered; i.e., the murder of s.o.; s.o.'s murder; **īmmictīlōca** = it is their murder; +TĒ(NE-MIC-TĪ-LŌ-CĀ)-Ø- = s.o.'s action of being self-killed; i.e., s.o.'s suicide; **īnemictīlōca** = it is his/her suicide

(MIC-O-HUA-NI)-Ø- = an instrument/means for dying; i.e., a deadly thing

(MIX)-TLI- = cloud; (MIX-CŌĀ)-TL- = cloud snake; tornado (Ø-Ø-MIX-CŌĀ-TL-Ø)-Ø-, *pers name s*, Cloud Snake [*name of a god; the abs af s,* (MĪ-MIX-CŌA)-Ø-H, *refers to his devotees, servants, etc.*]

(MIYE-)- ~ (MIYA-)- = [*emb only*], abundant

(MIYE-C)-Ø- ~ (MIYA-C)-Ø- ~ (MIYE-QUĪ)-Ø- ~ (MIYA-QUĪ)-Ø- = an abundant/large/numerous amount or quantity; much; many [*also* (MIE-C)-Ø- ~ (MIA-C)-Ø- ~ (MIE-QUĪ)-Ø- ~ (MIA-QUĪ)-Ø-; *abs pl s,* (MIYE-QUĪ-N)-☐- ~ -T-; etc.]

(MIY-Ā-HUA)-TL- > (MIY-Ā-HUA)-UH- = a thing that has become an abundant amount; i.e., maize tassel and flowers [< *(MIYA-Ā-HUA)]

(MIZ)-TLI- = puma, cougar [*abs af s,* (MĪ-MIZ)-T-]

(MIZQUI)-TL- > (MIZQUI)-UH- = mesquite

(MŌ)-☐- = probable/likely thing; *adv*, probably/in all likelihood; **ahmō** = it is not at all likely; i.e., not at all; no; **mā camō** = if only not at all [*used in wishes and commands*]

(MO-)-Ø- = [*used only as emb*], full; (MO-CA) = to seem to be full [*defec v, imprfv s only and used only in pres VNCs*]; **nimoca zoquitl** = I am full of mud; i.e, I am all muddy/I am covered with mud; **timocah zoquitl** = we are covered with mud

(MO-CHI)-∅- ~ (MO-CH)-∅- = a full/whole amount or number [*abs pl s*, (MO-CHĪ-N)-☐- ~ -T-]; (MO-CHI-PA)-☐- = at all times/always

(MOH-MŌCHI)-TL. *See* TLA-(MŌTLA).

(MŌL)-LI- = sauce; stew/ragout; mole; (MŌL-CAXi)-TL- > (MŌL-CAX)-∅- = a bowl for making sauce; i.e., a (stone) mortar (used with a pestle)

(MŌTLA) > (MŌTLA): TLA- ~ TĒ- = to throw a rock/rocks at s.th./s.o.; (MOH-MŌCHI)-TL- = a thing repeatedly or sporadically thrown; i.e., popcorn

(MŌTLA) > (MŌTLA): M-O- = to hurl o.s.

(MOTZOL)-LI- = grasping one (?) [*with abs pl subj*, (MOTZOL)-T- = avaricious ones]

(MOTZOL-O-Ā) > (MOTZOL-O-H): TLA- = to grapple/grab/grasp s.th.

(MOTZOL-TZĪTZQUI-Ā) > (MOTZOL-TZĪTZQUI-H): TLA- = to grip/grasp s.th. in the fist or a claw

(MOY-Ā-HUA) > (MOY-Ā-HUA) = (for paper) to blot; (for a stain/rumor) to spread; (for people) to disperse; (for water) to become turbid/muddy

(MŌY-Ō-NI) > (MŌY-Ō-N) = to swarm; (MŌY-Ō)-TL- > (MŌY-Ō)-UH- = a thing that swarms; i.e., gnat; mosquito [*abs af s*, (MŌ-MŌY-O)-∅-H]

(MŌZ-TLA)-☐- = tomorrow; **mōmōztla eh** = every tomorrow; i.e, every day/daily

(MŌZ-TLA-YŌ)-TL- > (MŌZ-TLA-YŌ)-∅- = s.th. pertaining to tomorrow; **īmōztlayōc** = on its morrow; i.e, on the next day; **oc īmōztlayōc** = on the day before, on the previous day

N

(-N)-TLI- = [*defec n used only as matrix*], place; **cān** = #∅-∅(CĀ-N)☐-∅# = at an entity place; i.e., at a place; where

(NACA)-TL- > (NAC)-∅- = meat; (NACA-MŌL)-LI- = sauce made from meat; i.e, meat stew

(NACA-YŌ)-TL- > (NACA-YŌ)-∅- = fleshiness; [*org-pos NNC*], flesh/body: **nonacayo** = it is my flesh/body

(NACA-YO-H-∅)-∅- > (NACA-YO-H-∅-CĀ)-UH- = *pret agen*, one that has owned flesh in abundance; i.e., an owner of abundant flesh; a bodily being; a fleshy/corpulent person; *(NACA-YO-H-∅-CĀ-POH)-TLI- > (NACA-YO-H-∅-CĀ-POH)-∅- = [*used only in pos-st NNC*], (s.o.'s) fellow flesh owner; i.e., a bodily being like (s.o.); **tinonacayohcāpoh** = you are a bodily being like me

(NA-NACA)-TL- > (NA-NAC)-∅- = quasi-meat; i.e., mushroom

(NACAZ)-TLI- = ear; (TLA-NACAZ)-TLI- = (outside) corner (of a building)

(NACAZ-TLA-CHIYA) > (NACAZ-TLA-CHIX) = to look toward an ear; i.e., to look toward one side

(NACAZ-TZATZA)-TL- = a deaf person; [*in a flawed-subj NNC*], a disparagingly-viewed deaf person. *See* §32.8.

(NACOCH)-TLI- = ear pendant

(NACHCA)-☐- = *adv*, at an unspecifiable distance; i.e., over there; off in the distance; in the beyond/in the hereafter

(NĀHUA)-TL- = a loud, clear sound; a clearly perceptible sound; the Nahuatl language; one

Vocabulary 239

who speaks a clear language, i.e., a Nahua

*(NĀHUA-C)-TLI- > (NĀHUA-C)-∅- = [*used in pos-st NNC or a matrix or emb only*], a place within hearing distance; i.e., vicinity/proximity; i.e., at a clearly audible distance; at a place near/close to; (NĀHUA-QU-EH-∅)-☐- = *pret agen*, one who has owned vicinity; i.e, a possessor of vicinity; **Tloqueh Nāhuaqueh** = he is "He-Has-Owned-Besideness-and-He-Has-Owned-Vicinity"; i.e., he is the One Who is Ever-Near (omnipresent god)

(NĀHUA-TI) > (NĀHUA-T) = (for a person) to have a clear sound; to speak out clearly/distinctly; (for a bell) to have a good sound; TĒ- ~ TLA-(NĀHUA-T-IĀ) > (NĀHUA-T-IH) = to be clearly audible with regard to s.o./s.th.; i.e., to give a command/order to s.o.; to give an order about s th.; (NĀHUA-T-Ī-L)-LI- = s.th. that is being commanded; i.e., a command; an obligation

(NĀHUA-T-I-LIĀ) > (NĀHUA-T-I-LIH): TĒ+TLA- = to cause s.th. to be clearly audible to s.o.; to have s.o. give an order about s.th.; TĒ-(TLA-NĀHUA-T-I-LIĀ) > (TLA-NĀHUA-T-I-LIH) = [tla-*fusion*] to have s.o. say that one is not at home; TĒ+TĒ-(NAH-NĀHUA-T-I-LIĀ) > (NAH-NĀHUA-T-I-LIH) = to give a command to several people regarding s.o.

(NĀHUA-L)-LI- = a sorcerer/shaman; disguise [*abs af s*, (NĀ-NĀHUA-L)-T- ~ (NĀHUA-L)-T-]; [*As an emb the s is usually translated as:* "with craftiness/cunning; on the sly; warily/cautiously/dissemblingly/deceitfully."]

(NĀHUA-L-ITT-A) > (NĀHUA-L-ITT-A): TĒ- = to look at s.o. in disguise; i.e., in secret/on the sly; to spy on s.o.

(NĀHUA-L-QUĪZA) > (NĀHUA-L-QUĪZ) = to exit in disguise (i.e., stealthily/by deceit/with cunning)

(NĀHUI)-∅- ~ (NĀUH-)- = four in number [*abs pl s*, (NĀHUI-N)-T-]
  (NĀUH-CĀ-M-PA)-☐- = to/from the four directions
  (NĀUH-CUAUH-Ā-CAL)-LI- = four half-fanegas [A fanega is about 1.60 bushels.]
  (NĀHU-ILHUI)-TL- = four days; for four days
  (NĀUH-MAH-PIL)-LI- = four fingers
  (NĀUH-PA)-☐- ~ (NĀP-PA)-☐- = four times
  (NĀUH-PŌHUA-L)-LI- = eighty in number; (NĀUH-PŌHUA-L-TE)-TL- = eighty rock in number; i.e., eighty things; (NĀP-PŌHUA-L-ILHUI)-TL- = eighty days
  (NĀUH-TE)-TL- = four rock in number; i.e, four things
  (NĀUH-XIHUI)-TL- = four years; (NĀUH-XIUH-TIĀ) > (NĀUH-XIUH-TIH) = to spend four years; to be four years old

*(NĀL)-LI- > (NĀL)-∅- = [*defec n, used in comp only (as embed or matrix)*], far side; on the far side; through/all the way through; beyond; (NĀL-QUĪZA) > (NĀL-QUĪZ) = to pass through and come out the other side: (NĀL-QUĪZ-∅)-QUI- > (NĀL-QUĪZ-∅-CĀ)-UH- = *pret agen,* a thing that has passed all the way through; i.e., a thoroughly penetrating thing; (NĀL-QUĪZ-∅-CĀ)-☐- = [*used in advlzd NNC*] in the manner of/like a thoroughly penetrating thing; entirely, thoroughly; TLA-(NĀL-QUĪZ-∅-CĀ-CAQUI) > (NĀL-QUĪZ-∅-CĀ-CAC) = to understand/comprehend s. th. perfectly/thoroughly

(NAMACA) > (NAMACA): TLA- = to sell s.th.
  (TLA-NAMACA-∅)-C- > (TLA-NAMACA-∅-CĀ)-UH- = *pret agen,* one who has sold things; i.e., a vender/seller/peddler
  (TLA-NAMAC)-TLI- = a thing that has been sold

(NAMAC-Ō-NI)-∅- = a thing that can be sold; i.e., a sellable thing
(NĀMIQUI) > (NĀMIC): TĒ- = to encounter s.o.; to intercept s.o.; to go out to meet s.o.; to compete with s.o.; +TĒ(NĀMIC-Ō-YĀ-N)-∅- = [*used only in pos-st NNCs*], (s.o.'s) meeting place; (NĀMIC)-TLI- = a match/equal/mate; a married person/a spouse; an opponent; (NĀMIC-TI) > (NĀMIC-TI) = to have a mate/spouse; M-O-(NĀMIC-TI-Ā) > (NĀMIC-TI-H) = to cause o.s. to have a mate/spouse; i.e., to get married
(NĀMIQUI) > (NĀMIC): TLA- = to incur s.th. (a fine, etc.); to run into s.th., to come across s.th.; to bring s.th. on o.s.; M-O+TLA- ~ M-O+TĒ-(NĀMIC-TIĀ) > (NĀMĪC-TIH) = to cause o.s. to meet s.th.; i.e., to bring s.th. on o.s.; to contend against s.o.
(NĀMOYA) > (NĀMOYA): TLA- ~ TĒ- = to rob/plunder/steal s.th.; to abduct/kidnap s.o.
(NĀN)-TLI- = mother; **nāntli tahtli** = he is a mother and he is a father; i.e., he is a parent; she is a mother and she is a father; i.e., she is a parent; he/she is a caregiver
(NĀN-EH-∅)-☐- > (NĀN-EH-∅-CĀ)-UH- = *pret agen,* one who has owned a mother; i.e., a person who has a mother
(NĀN-MIC-TIĀ) > (NĀN-MIC-TIH): M-O- = to kill o.s. by means of one's mother; i.e., to commit matricide; to kill one's mother
(NĀN-QUI-LIĀ) > (NĀN-QUI-LIH): TĒ- = to act like a mother in relation to s.o.; i.e., to respond to/answer s.o.
(NĀN-YŌ)-TL- = motherhood
(NĀPAL-O-Ā) > (NĀPAL-O-H): TLA- = to carry s.th. in the arms
NEC = *adv part*, then [*var*, MEC]
(NĒCI) > (NĒZ) = to become visible; to appear; to seem; **huālnēci** = it shows forth; (TLA-NĒCI) > (TLA-NĒZ) = *impers,* (for things in general) to become bright and clear; +TĒ(NĒZ-CĀ)-∅- = s.o.'s means of (continuing) to appear; i.e., s.o.'s trace/the trace(s) of s.o.
(NĒX-TIĀ) > (NĒX-TIH): M-O- = to reveal o.s.; to appear; (NE-NĒX-TĪ-LIZ)-TLI- = action of self-revelation
(NECOC)-☐- = *adv,* on/at/to/toward/from both sides; **necoc īxeh** = he is an owner of faces on both sides; i.e., he is a two-faced person; he is a scandalmonger/talebearer
(NECHIC-O-Ā) > (NECHIC-O-H): TLA- = to gather s.th. together; to collect s.th.; T-O-(NECHIC-O-Ā) > (NECHIC-O-H) = (for people) to come together; to meet/assemble; to reassemble
(NECUIL-I-HUI) > (NECUIL-I-UH) = to become twisted/flexed
(NECUIL-O-Ā) > (NECUIL-O-H): TLA- = to twist/bend/flex s.th.; to make s.th. crooked
(NEL)-LI- = a true thing; truth; (NEL)-☐- = [*used in advlzd NNCs*] in truth/truly/really
(NEL-TI) > (NEL-TI) = to become true; to prove true; to become verified; TLA-(NEL-TI-LIĀ) > (NEL-TI-LIH) = to prove s.th. to be true; to verify s.th.
(NEL-IHT-O-Ā) > (NEL-IHT-O-H): TLA- = to say s.th. truly; to be truthful/creditable
(NE-LHUA)-TL- = root; (NE-LHUA-YŌ)-TL- > (NE-LHUA-YŌ)-∅- = beginning/origin; [*gen-use s used in org-pos NNCs*], root; **īnelhuayo** = it is its root, they are its roots; (NE-LHUA-YŌ-HUA) > (NE-LHUA-YŌ-HUA) = to take root
(NEL-O-Ā) > (NEL-O-H): TLA- ~ TĒ- = to stir s.th.; to mingle with people; (TLA-NEL-O-Ā) > (TLA-NEL-O-H) = [tla-*fusion*] to paddle/row; (TLA-NEL-O-H-∅)-QUI- > (TLA-NEL-O-H-∅-CĀ)-UH- = *pret agen,* a paddler/rower
(NEMI) > (NEN) = to live/exist; (NEN)-TLI- = a thing that results from living; i.e., life

Vocabulary 241

(NEMI-LIĀ) > (NEMI-LIH): TLA- = to dwell on/think about s.th.
(NEMĪ-TIĀ) > (NEMĪ-TIH): TĒ- = to cause s.o. to live; i.e., to sustain s.o.
(NEH-NEMI) > (NEH-NEN) = to walk/get a move on/travel
(NĒN)-☐- = [*used in an advlzd NNC*], with failure; in vain; uselessly/worthlessly
(NENE)-TL- > (NENE)-UH- = doll; idol; clitoris
  (NENE-PIL)-LI- = doll-like appendage; i.e., tongue
(NE-PAN- . . .). *See* *(PAN)-Ø-.
(NEQUI) > (NEC): TLA- = to want s.th.; to use s.th.; +TĒ(TLA-NEQUI-YĀ)-Ø- = means of/faculty for wanting things; i.e., s.o.'s will/intention; M-O-(NEQUI) > (NEC) = [*reflex-as-pass; nonan*], to want itself; i.e., to be wanted/needed: **tētech monequi** = it is necessary to s.o.; +TLA(M-O-NEQUI-YĀ-N)-Ø- = s.th.'s time of being needed; i.e., s.th.'s appointed/proper time; **īmonequiyān** = at its needed time; i.e., while the moment is propitious/favorable for it
(NEQUI-Z)-TLI- = s.th. worthy of being desired; s.th. desirable
+TLA(NEC-Ō-CĀ)-Ø- = s.th.'s action of being needed; i.e., s.th.'s needfulness, the needfulness for s.th., the need for s.th.; s.th.'s usefulness
(NEC-Ō-NI)-Ø- = a desirable thing
(. . . -NEQUI) > (. . . -NEC): TĒ- = *as matrix,* to consider without foundation that s.o. is . . . ; to claim unjustly that s.o. is . . . ; M-O-(. . . -NEQUI) > (. . . -NEC) = *as matrix,* to pretend (to be . . .), to feign (to be . . .)
(NEH-NEQUI) > (NEH-NEC): M-O- = to resemble/mimic; to impersonate; M-O-(. . . -NEH-NEQUI) > (. . . -NEH-NEC) = *as matrix,* to pretend o.s. (to be . . .); to feign (to be . . .)
(NEUC)-TLI- = honey; (NEUC-YO-H-Ø)-☐- > (NEUC-YO-H-Ø-CĀ)-UH- = *pret agen,* a thing that has owned honey in every part; i.e., a honey-covered thing; a honeyed thing
(NEX)-TLI- = ash/ashes; *(NEX-XŌ)-TL- > (NEX-XO)-Ø- [*gen-use s used in org-pos NNCs*], ash/ashes; **ocotl īnexxo** they are the pinewood's ashes
  (NEX-XO-H-Ø)-☐- > (NEX-XO-H-Ø-CĀ)-UH- = a thing that possesses abundant ashes; i.e., a thing covered with ashes
(NI-CĀ-N)-☐- = *adv,* at this place; here
(NI-MAN)-☐- = *adv,* at this moment; then; immediately afterward; [*as intensifier*], absolutely; **niman ahcān** = absolutely nowhere, nowhere at all; **niman ahmō** = absolutely not, in no way, not at all; **niman ye** = immediately afterward; **niman īc** = immediately thereupon
NŌ = *adv part,* also; **no zo ~ no zo eh** (*with syncope,* **no ceh**) = also maybe
  (NŌ-HUI-YĀ-N)-☐- = everywhere
(NŌCH)-TLI- = prickly-pear fruit
(NO-HMAH) = [*prfv s used in advlzd 3rd-sg pret VNC*], still; spontaneously; **oc nohmah** = still
(NOHPAL)-LI- = prickly-pear cactus plant
(NŌNCUAH)-☐- = [*advlzd NNC*], apart/to one side/separately; individually/by oneself
(NŌTZA) > (NŌTZ): TĒ- = to call/summon s.o.; to invite s.o.; to address s.o./to speak to s.o.; (TLA-NŌTZ)-TLI- = one who has been summoned
  (NŌCHI-LIĀ) > (NŌCHI-LIH): TĒ+TĒ- = to call/summon s.o. for s.o.
  (NŌTZA) > (NŌTZ): T-O- = to summon one another; to address one another;

(T-O-NŌTZ-∅)-QU- = ones who have summoned one another; mutual summoners; (NE-NŌTZ)-TLI- = a thing that results from mutual summoning; i.e., an accord/compact/mutual agreement/mutual decision

(NŌ-NŌTZA) >(NŌ-NŌTZ): T-O- ~ TĒ- = to take counsel with one another/to confer with one another; to advise/inform s.o.; TĒ+TĒ-(NŌ-NŌCHI-LIĀ) > (NŌ-NŌCHI-LIH) = to advise/counsel s.o. for s.o.

(NOH-NŌTZA) > (NOH-NŌTZ): TĒ- ~ T-O- = to converse with s.o./one another

O

OC = *adv part*, still, yet; for now; for a moment; while; in the meantime; first; in addition/besides; **oc achi** = a little more; **oc achto** = first; **oc cencah** = especially, much more; **oc ceppa** = again, once again; **oc nohmah** = still; **oc īhuān** = in further addition to it/this; **oc nō** = also, likewise, furthermore; **oc nō īhuān** = also in further addition to it/this

(OC)-TLI- = pulque (i.e., fermented juice of the maguey)

(ŌCĒLŌ)-TL- > (ŌCĒLŌ)-UH- = jaguar [*abs af s*, (Ō-ŌCĒLŌ)-O-H ~ (ŌCĒLŌ)-M-]

(OCO)-TL- > (OCO)-UH- = pine torchwood/pine wood/pine splinter; (OCO-CIN)-TLI- = pine cone

(OCUIL)-IN- = worm

(OH)-TLI- > (OH)-HUI- = path/road; **ohtlica** (i.e., **ohtli īca**) = by means of a road; on a road

    (OH-HUI-H-∅)-☐- > (OH-HUI-H-∅-CĀ)-UH- = *pret agen,* a difficult thing; a dangerous/hazardous thing; (OH-HUI-H-∅-CĀ)-☐- = [*used in an advlzd NNC*], with difficulty/dangerously; (OH-HUI-H-∅-CĀ-N)-☐- = in a dangerous place

    (OH-QUETZA) > (OH-QUETZ) = to erect a path/road; i.e., to open up a path/road; (OH-QUECHI-LIĀ) > (OH-QUECHI-LIH): TĒ- = to erect a path/road for s.o.; i.e., to open up a path/road for s.o.

    (OH-TĒN)-TLI- = edge of a path/road; i.e., pathside/roadside

    (OH-TLA-TOCA) > (OH-TLA-TOCA) = to follow a path/road

    (OH-TLĀZA) > (OH-TLĀZ) = to hurl a path/road; i.e., to block a path/road; to close a path/road; (OH-TLĀXI-LIĀ) > (OH-TLĀXI-LIH) = to hurl a path/road from s.o.; i.e., to block a path/road to s.o.

    (OH-ZOL)-LI- = a road/path in disrepair

(OHUA)-TL- > (OHUA)-UH- = stalk of green maize; (OHUA-MĪL)-LI- = field of green maize stalks

(ŌL)-LI- = rubber/latex/liquid rubber; (ŌL-LO-H-∅)-☐- > (ŌL-LO-H-∅-CĀ)-UH- = a thing that has owned abundant rubber/liquid rubber; i.e., a thing that is covered with rubber/liquid rubber

    (ŌL-CHIP-Ī-NI-Ā) > (ŌL-CHIP-Ī-NI-H): TLA- = to besprinkle s.th. with liquid rubber; (TLA-ŌL-CHIP-Ī-NĪ-L)-LI- = a thing splattered with liquid rubber

    (ŌL-Ī-NI) > (ŌL-Ī-N) = to move/budge/be in motion/quake; (ŌL-Ī-N-∅)-☐- = *pret agen*, a thing that has moved/budged; i.e., an earthquake; the sun [*This pret agen s does* NOT *mean "movement," as Siméon says. It is not an action s.*]; +TLA(ŌL-Ī-N-CĀ)-∅- = s.th.'s action of moving; i.e., s.th.'s movement

(ŌLŌ)-TL- > (ŌLŌ)-UH- = maize cob (with kernels removed)

Vocabulary 243

(OLOL)-LI- = ball/sphere; TĒ ~ TLA-(OLOL-HUIĀ) > (OLOL-HUIH) = to be in/form a circle around s.o./s.th.; to encircle s.o./s.th.; to round up people/animals;
    (OLOL-O-Ā) > (OLOL-O-H): TĒ ~ TLA- = to wrap s.o./s.th. up; to roll s.th. into a ball; (OLOL-HUIĀ) > (OLOL-HUIH): TĒ+TLA- = to wrap s.th. up for s.o.; to roll s.th. into a ball for s.o.
    (OLOL-TI-Ø)-C- = a round/ball-shaped/spherical thing
(ŌME)-Ø- ~ (ŌM-)- ~ (ŌN-)- ~ (ŌP-)- = two in number; [*gross pl s*], (ŌME-X)-T- = all two; both; (Ø-Ø-ŌME-CIHUĀ-TL-Ø)-Ø- = *pers name s*, "She-is-the-Lady-of-Duality"; (Ø-Ø-ŌME-TĒUC-TLI-Ø)-Ø- = *pers name s*, "He-Is-the-Lord-of-Duality"; **nŌmetēuctli nŌmecihuātl** = [*conjunctive-comp stemmed personal name*] I am "He/She-Is-the-Lord-of-Duality-and-He/She-Is-the-Lady-of-Duality" (the androgynous goddess-god of the duality principle at work in generation and creation); (ŌME-YŌ)-TL- = duality; (ŌME-YŌ-CĀ-N)-☐- = *place-name s*, In/To/From the Place of Duality (the dwelling place of Ometeuctli-Omecihuatl)
(ŌM-ILHUI)-TL- = two days; [*in 1st-degree advlzd NNC*], for two days
(ŌM-PŌHUA-L)-LI- = forty in number; (ŌM-PŌHUA-L-XIHUI)-TL- = forty days
(ŌN-TE)-TL- = two rock in number; i.e., two in number; (ŌN-TLA-MAN)-TLI- = two things; (ŌN-TLA-PAL)-☐- = *advlzd*, on two sides
(ŌP-PA)-☐- = *adv*, two times/twice
(OMI)-TL- > (OMI)-UH- = bone
ON- = *dir pref*, thither; *loc pref*, there [*Contrast* HUĀL-.]; (ON-CĀ-N)-☐- = at/in/to/from/through that place; there; to/from/through there
    *(ON-O) > (ON-O) = *pret-as-pres v*, to be lying down/to be recumbent; *(TLA-ON-O) > (TLA-ON-O) = [*impers tla-*], (for everyone) to be recumbent; (for everything) to be in place (for a social gathering); **tlaonoc** = all is there; i.e., everything necessary for the feast is ready
(ŌN)-Ø- = that one/those: **ihqueh ōn** = they are those; (ŌM-PA)-☐- = at/to/from/through that place; there; to/from/through there
(ŌP-PA)-☐-. *See* (ŌME)-Ø-.
(ŌPŌCH)-TLI- = left side/hand/foot
(OQUICH)-TLI- > (OQUICH)-HUI- ~ -Ø- = man; male; (OQUICH-YŌ)-TL= manhood/manliness; heroic deed
    (OQUICH-TLĀL-I-Ā) > (OQUICH-TLĀL-I-H): M-☐- = to sit like a man
(OTOMI)-TL- > (OTON)-Ø- = a member of the Otomi tribe; an Otomi; [*in Tetzcohco and Tenochtitlan*], a warrior in one of the prestigious military orders
(ŌTZ)-TLI- = a pregnant woman; [*abs af s*, (Ō-ŌTZ)-T-]
(Ō-YA) > (Ō-X): TLA- = to shell s.th. (maize, peas, etc.)
    (TLA-Ō-L)-LI- = a thing that has been shelled; i.e., shelled maize kernels; (TLA-Ō-L-PĀ-HUA-X)-TLI- = dried-maize-kernel stew
(OYO-HUA) > (OYO-UH) = to howl; (OYO-HUA-L)-LI- = bell; (OYO-HUA-L-EH-Ø)-☐- > (OYO-HUA-L-EH-Ø-CĀ)-UH- = *pret agen*, one who has owned bells; i.e., a bell owner
(OYO-HU-IĀ) > (OYO-HU-IH): TĒ- = to howl at/for s.o.
(OZOMAH)-TLI- = monkey
(ŌZTŌ)-TL- > (ŌZTŌ)-UH- = cave; (ŌZTŌ-MĀ-N)-☐- = *place-name s*, In/To/From the Area of Caves; (ŌZTŌ-MĒ-☐-CA)-TL- = a person associated with Oztoman; a dweller in Oztoman; *by extens*, a vanguard merchant

P

(-PA)-◌- = [*defec loc/dir n that occurs only as a matrix s*], at/in/to/from the place of; to/in/from the direction of; **nīxpampa xēhua** = depart from in front of me; i.e., get out of my sight

(-PA)-◌- = [*defec frequency n that occurs only as a matrix s that embeds only numeral or quantity ns*], occasion(s), time(s); *mācuīlpa* = five times

(PĀ) > (PAH): TLA- = to dye s.th.; (TLA-PAH-∅)-QUI- > (TLA-PAH-∅-CĀ)-UH- = *pret agen,* one who has dyed things; i.e., a dyer

  (PA-L)-LI- = a thing that can be used for dyeing; i.e., black clay

  (TLA-PA-L)-LI- = a dyed thing; a dye; a color for painting; a red color; *by extens,* a side (because of the assignment of colors to the cardinal directions); (CEN-TLA-PA-L)-◌- = on/from one side

(PĀCA) > (PĀCA) ~ (PĀC): TLA- = to wash s.th.; M-O+TLA-(PĀQUI-LIĀ) > (PĀQUI-LIH) = to wash s.th. for o.s.

(PACH-I-HUI) > (PACH-I-UH) = (for a building) to settle/sag/slump; (for a tomb/house/granary) to cave in/collapse

  (PACH-O-Ā) > (PACH-O-H): TLA- = to press down on s.th.; to govern s.th.; (for a fowl) to sit on s.th. (i.e., its eggs)/to brood; (TLA-PACH-Ō-L)-LI- = a governed one/a subject

  (PACH-O-Ā) > (PACH-O-H): M-O- = to press o.s. (against s.th.)

(PACH-I-HUI) > (PACH-I-UH) = (for a person) to become/be sated; to eat one's fill/become satisfied

  (PACH-I-HUĪ-TIĀ) > (PACH-I-HUĪ-TIH): TĒ- = to cause s.o. to become sated; to cause s.o. to become satisfied

(PAH)-TLI- = medicine; (PAH-TI) > (PAH-TI) = to have (good) medicine; i.e., to get well; to recuperate

  (PAH-TI-Ā) > (PAH-TI-H): TĒ- ~ TLA- = to cause s.o./s.th. to have (good) medicine; i.e., to cure s.o./s.th.; to remedy s.o./s.th.; to repair/restore s.th.; (TLA-PAH-TĬ-L)-LI- = a person restored to health; a cured/healed/well person

  (PAH-TI-Ā) > (PAH-TI-H): M-O- = to cause o.s. to have (good) medicine; i.e., to cure o.s.; (NE-PAH-TI-LŌ-NI)-∅- = a thing with which one cures o.s.; i.e., a curative

(PĀ-HUA-CI) > (PĀ-HUA-Z): TLA- = to cook s.th. in water; i.e., to cook s.th. in a pot/to stew s.th.; M-O+TLA-(PĀ-HUA-XI-LIĀ) > (PĀ-HUA-XI-LIH) = to stew s.th. for o.s.

*(PAL)-LI- > (PAL)-∅- = [*used only in advlzd pos-st NNC or as emb*], grace; favor/sake/help; *advlzd,* by (s.o.'s) grace; **mopal** = by your grace

  (PAL-Ē-HU-IĀ) > (PAL-Ē-HU-IH): TĒ- ~ TLA- = to cause a favor to rise for s.o.; i.e., to do a favor for s.o., to help s.o.; to do a favor in relation to s.th.; i.e., to help s.th.; (TLA-PAL-Ē-HU-IĀ) > (TLA-PAL-Ē-HU-IH) = [Tla-*fusion.*] to help/be helpful; +TLA(PAL-Ē-HU-Ī-LŌ-CĀ)-∅- = s.th.'s (action of) being helped; i.e., s.th.'s alleviation, the alleviation of s.th.

(PAL-Ā-NI) > (PAL-Ā-N) = to fester/decay/rot

(PAL-O-Ā) > (PAL-O-H): TLA- = to taste/sample/sip s.th.; to sop s.th. (e.g., bread) in soup or gravy

  (PĀ-PAL-Ō)-TL- > (PĀ-PAL-Ō)-UH- = one that constantly sips; i.e., a butterfly

(PĀMi)-TL- > (PĀN)-∅- = flag/banner

-(PAM-PA)-∅-. *See* *(PAN)-∅-.

Vocabulary 245

*(PAN)-Ø-> (PAN)-Ø- = [*used only in advlzd pos-st NNCs or as emb*], upper surface; surface appearance; superior location; place/area; time; **īpan** = on it; in his time; **zā tēpan** = then; later/afterwards; **nepan** = upon one another; mutually; (NE-PAN-TLAH)-☐- = place of abundant crossing over one another; i.e., the point of intersecting lines; i.e., the middle point/the middle; (NE-PAN-I-HUI) > (NE-PAN-I-UH) = to be/lie upon one another; +TLA(NE-PAN-I-UH-YĀ-N)-Ø- = s.th.'s converging/intersecting place; (NE-PAN-Ō)-TL- = mutuality, reciprocity; *advlzd,* mutually [*Not used as an emb*; (NE-PAN)-☐- *is used instead.*]; +NE(PĀ-PAN)-Ø- = one another's layered surfaces; i.e., on top of one another; i.e., diverse/various things; (TLA-PAN)-TLI- = an above-things thing; i.e., roof/flat roof; +TLA(PAM-PA)-Ø- = s.th.'s reason/cause/support; **īpampa** = by reason of it; because of it; about it; +TĒ(PAM-PA)-Ø- = s.o.'s behalf; s.o.'s regard/respect/virtue; **mopampa** = with regard to you, by virtue of you; on your behalf
  (PAN-Ē-HU-A)-TL- = skin at the surface; skin surface/epidermis; (PAN-Ē-HU-A-YŌ)-TL- > (PAN-Ē-HUA-YŌ)-Ø- = a characteristic/feature of the epidermis; [*gen-use s used in org-pos NNCs*], skin surface; epidermis: **nopanēhuayo** = it is my epidermis

(PANŌ) > (PANŌ) = to cross/pass over; to cross a river/stream/etc.; (PANŌ-NI)-Ø- = one who customarily crosses a river; i.e., a boat passenger; (PANŌ-HUA) > (PANŌ-HUA) = [*nonac s (used only in impers VNCs)*], (for people in general) to cross/pass over; (PANŌ-HUA-NI)-Ø- = a passage on a boat; a bridge

(PANA-HUIĀ) > (PANA-HUIH): TĒ- ~ TLA- = to carry s.o./s.th. across a river/stream; to overtake and pass s.o.; to surpass/excel s.o.; to go/pass beyond s.th. (e.g., a stream/river)

(PĀQUI) > (PĀC) = to become/be happy/glad; (PĀC-Ø)-QUI- > (PĀC-Ø-CĀ)-UH- *pret agen,* one who has become happy; i.e., a happy/merry one; (PĀC-Ø-CĀ)-☐- = *advlzd,* in the manner of a happy one; i.e., happily
  (PAH-PĀQUI) > (PAH-PĀC) = to be happy (on various occasions); TLA-(PAH-PĀQUI) > (PAH-PĀC) = to take joy/pleasure in s.th. on various occasions; to enjoy s.th. a number of times [*applic obj unjustified by s's form*]
  (PAH-PĀQUI-L-TIĀ) > (PAH-PĀQUI-L-TIH): TĒ- = to cause s.o. to be happy on various occasions; (TĒ-PAH-PĀQUI-L-TIH-Ø)-☐- > (TĒ-PAH-PĀQUI-L-TIH-Ø-CĀ)-UH- = *pret agen,* s.o./s.th. that has made people happy; i.e., s.o./s.th. that delights people; (TĒ-PAH-PĀQUI-L-TIH-Ø-CĀ-N)-☐- = a place where s.o./s.th. delights people; i.e., a delightful/pleasing place; in/to/from a delightful/pleasing place

(PA-TLA) > (PA-TLA): TLA- = to exchange/change s.th.
  (PA-TI-UH)-TLI- = an exchange item/value; price; payment; salary/wages

(PATL-Ā-NI) > (PATL-Ā-N) = to fly
  +TLA(PATL-Ā-NI-YĀ-N)-☐- = s.th.'s flying place

(PĀ-TZ-CA) > (PĀ-TZ-CA): TLA- = to squeeze liquid from s.th.; to wring water from s.th. (e.g., wet clothes)
  (TLA-PĀ-TZ-CA-LŌ-NI)-Ø- = a thing by means of which people press out liquid; i.e., a juice press/a milk pail
  (TLA-PĀ-TZ-C-Ō-NI)-Ø- = a thing by means of which people press out liquid; i.e., a juice press/a milk pail

(PECH)-TLI- = a horizontal flat surface; a platform. See (CAX-PECH)-TLI-.
  (PECH-A-HUI) > (PECH-A-UH) = to become/be a horizontal flat surface

(PECH-O-Ā) > (PECH-O-H): TLA- = to give s.th. a flat foundation; (TLA-PECH)-TLI- = a thing that serves as a flat foundation; i.e., a platform/litter/bier/bedstead
(PEH-PENA) > (PEH-PEN): TĒ- ~ TLA- = to pick/choose/select s.o./s.th.; to gather up s.th. scattered on the ground
(PĒHUA) > (PĒUH) = to begin/to start off
  (PĒHUA-L-TIĀ) > (PĒHUA-L-TIH): TLA- = to cause s.th. to begin; to begin/start s.th.
(PĒHUA) > (PĒUH): TĒ- = to conquer/vanquish s.o.
(PETLa)-TL- > (PETL)-∅- = mat; **petlatl icpalli** = it is a mat and it is a seat; i.e., it is authority
  (PETLA-CAL)-LI- = a structure made of mats; i.e., a wickerwork chest/coffer
(PETL-Ā-HU-A) > (PETL-Ā-UH): TĒ- = to cause s.o. to become naked; i.e., to undress s.o.; to strip s.o. naked
(PETZ-C-A-HUI) > (PETZ-C-A-UH) = to become slippery
  (PETZ-C-O-Ā) > (PETZ-C-O-H): M-O- = to slip/slide; M-O-(PEH-PETZ-C-O-Ā) > (PEH-PETZ-C-O-H) = to slip and slide
(PETZ-I-HUI)- > (PETZ-I-UH) = to become/be polished/shiny
  (PETZ)-TLI- = pyrite (mineral used for making mirrors)
(PEY-Ō)-TL- > (PEY-Ō)-UH- = peyote (a spineless, globe-shaped cactus having buttonlike tubercles that are dried and chewed as a drug) [< (PEY-Ō-NI), "to glisten"]
(PIL)-LI- = a pendent/dependent thing; an appendage; a child (of a family): **nopilhuān** = they are my children; (PIL-TŌN)-TLI- = a child; a boy; a girl; (PIL-TZIN)-TLI- = a child; a boy; a girl
  (PIL-HUAH-∅)-◌- > (PIL-HUAH-∅-CĀ)-UH- = *pret agen,* one who has owned a child; i.e., a parent; (PIL-HUAH-∅-CĀ-TEUH)-◌- = *adv,* in the likeness of a child owner; i.e., like a parent; (PIL-HUAH-∅-CĀ-TEUH-TLA-MATI) > (PIL-HUAH-∅-CĀ-TEUH-TLA-MAT) ~ (PIL-HUAH-∅-CĀ-TEUH-TLA-MAH) = to know things like a parent; to consider o.s. a parent
  (PIL-HUAH-TI-Ā) > (PIL-HUAH-TI-H): M-O- = to cause o.s. to have an acquired child; i.e., to beget a child; to raise one's young
  (PIL-NEQUI) > (PIL-NEC) = to want a child; (PIL-NEC-∅)-QUI > (PIL-NEC-∅-CĀ)-UH- = *pret agen,* one who has wanted a child; (PIL-NEC-∅-CĀ-YŌ)-TL- > (PIL-NEC-∅-CĀ-YŌ)-∅- = what is characteristic of one who has wanted a child, i.e., the natural impulse to have an offspring
  (PIL-QUĪX-TIĀ) > (PIL-QUĪX-TIH): TĒ- = to cause s.o. to come out as a child; i.e., to rejuvenate s.o.; TLA-(PIL-QUĪX-TIĀ) > (PIL-QUĪX-TIH) = to cause s.th. to come out young; to grow s.th. anew
  (PIL)-LI- > (PIL-LŌ)-∅- = child (of a clan, tribe, etc.), i.e., a special-privilege child; i.e., a nobleman, noble lady; **pilli** = he/she is a noble; **nopillo** = he/she is my noble [*abs af s,* (PĪ-PIL)-T-]
  (PIL-CA) > (PIL-CA) = to be pendant; to be hanging
  (PIL-O-Ā) > (PIL-O-H): TLA- = to cause s.th. to become pendant; i.e, to hang s.th. up
(PĪN-Ā-HUA) > (PĪN-Ā-HUA) ~ (PĪN-Ā-UH) = to become/be ashamed [*The prfv s* (PĪN-Ā-UH) *is an irregular formation.*]
(PI-PI-TZ-CA) > (PI-PI-TZ-CA) = to squeak/screech; +TLA(PI-PI-TZ-CA-YĀ-N)-∅- = s.th.'s screeching place

Vocabulary

(PĪTZA) > (PĪTZ): TLA- = to blow on s.th. (e.g., a fire); to play s.th. (i.e., a wind instrument); to smelt s.th.
(PITZ-Ā-HUA) > (PITZ-Ā-HUA) = to become/be thin/slender; (PITZ-Ā-HUA-∅)-C = a thing that has become thin/slender; i.e., a thin/slender thing
  (PITZ-A-C)-TLI- = a thing that results from becoming slender; i.e., a slender thing
(PIX-A-HUI) > (PIX-A-UH) = *impers,* to drizzle
(PIX-O-Ā) > (PIX-O-H): TLA- = to broadcast/scatter s.th. (e.g., seeds); to sow s.th. by scattering seeds; (TLA-PIX-O-H-∅)-◻- > (TLA-PIX-O-H-∅-CĀ)-UH- = a sower/broadcaster
(PIYA) > (PIX): TLA- = to guard/keep s.th. [*var sp,* TLA-(PIYE)]; (PIYA-L)-LI- = s.th. that is kept/guarded; i.e., a cache/store of goods; a deposit TĒ+TLA-(PIYA-LIĀ) > (PIYA-LIH) = to guard s.th. for s.o.
  (PIYA) > (PIX): M-O- = to guard o.s.; i.e., to to aloof/be on one's guard
  (PIYA-L-TIĀ) > (PIYA-L-TIH): M-O+TĒ- = to cause s.o. to guard o.s.; to put o.s. in s.o.'s safekeeping; to entrust o.s. to s.o. *See* § 25.11.3.b.
*(POH)-TLI- > (POH)-∅- = [*restr-use s not used*], companion/match/equal/peer; **nimopoh** = I am your equal; **mocihuāpoh** = she is a woman like you
(PŌHUI) > (PŌUH) = to be of account/be taken account of/be noticed; to be counted in/belong: **tētech nipōhui** = I am dedicated to/belong to s.o.
  (PŌHU-A) > (PŌUH): TLA- = to cause s.th. to be taken account of; to count s.th.; to recount/relate s.th.; to give an account of s.th.; to read s.th.; (PŌHU-A-LŌ-NI)-∅- = a thing that can be counted; a countable thing; TĒ-+TLA-(PŌHUI-LIĀ) > (PŌHUI-LIH) = to recount/relate s.th. to s.o.; to read s.th. to s.o.
  (PŌHU-A) > (PŌUH): TĒ- = to respect/esteem s.o.; to pay respect to s.o.
(POL-AQUI) > (POL-AC) = to enter under water; to become submerged
  (POL-AC-TIĀ) > (POL-AC-TIH): TLA- = to cause s.th. to enter under water; to push s.th. under water; to submerge s.th.
(POL-I-HUI) > (POL-I-UH) = to become lost/destroyed; to perish/disappear
  (POL-O-Ā) > (POL-O-H): TLA- = to lose s.th.; to destroy s.th.; to waste s.th. (e.g., wealth)
  (POL-Ō-L-TIĀ) > (POL-Ō-L-TIH): TĒ+TLA- = to cause s.o. to lose s.th. (e.g., his reason); to rid s.o. of s.th.
  (POH-POL-Ō-L-TIĀ) > (POH-POL-Ō-L-TIH): TĒ+TLA- = to cause s.o. to lose s.th. (e.g., troubles); to banish s.o.'s s.th. (e.g., s.o.'s sorrows)
(POL-Ō-NI) > (POL-Ō-N) = to stutter
  (PO-POL-O-CA) > (PO-POL-O-CA) = to stutter badly; to speak one's language badly; to speak a foreign or unintelligible language
*(PŌ-NI) > *(PŌ-N) = to give off smoke [*an obsolete destockal v, from* *(PO-Ō-NI), *whose meaning is now expressed by its freq s* (PO-PŌ-CA) *but whose derived nounstems remain in use*]; (PŌ-C)-TLI- = smoke; (PŌ-C-CŌZ-TI-YA) > (PŌ-C-CŌZ-TI-YA) = to become yellow like smoke; i.e., to become/be smoke yellow: (PŌ-C-CŌZ-TI-∅)-C- = a smoke-yellow thing; i.e., a dull yellow thing; (PŌ-C-YŌ)-TL- > (PŌ-C-YŌ)-∅ = smokiness; [*gen-use s used in org-pos NNC*], smoke: **īpōcyo tletl** it is the fire's smoke; (PŌ-CH)-TLI- = incense smoke; fumes; haze; (PŌ-CH-TLĀ-N)-◻- = *place-name s,* At/To/From the Place in the Vicinity of Fumes; (PŌ-CH-TĒ-◻-CA)-TL- = a person associated with Pochtlan; an inhabitant of Pochtlan; *by extens,* a merchant

(PO-PŌ-CA) > (PO-PŌ-CA) = to emit smoke; (for a heated surface) to shimmer
(PO-PŌ-TZ-A) > (PO-PŌ-TZ): TLA- = to make s.th. emit smoke
(POZ-Ō-N-A-L)-LI- = a thing that results from being boiled; i.e., foam
(POZ-TEQUI) > (POZ-TEC) = to become broken/to break; (POZ-TEC-∅)-QUI- = a thing (e.g., leg, stick) that gets broken; (POZ-TEC)-TLI- = a broken thing (e.g., leg, stick)
(POZ-TEQUI) > (POZ-TEC): TLA- = to break s.th. (e.g., stick, bone); (TLA-POZ-TEC-∅)-QUI- = one who breaks things (such as sticks, tree branches, etc.); (TLA-POZ-TEC)-TLI- = a broken thing (e.g., stick/leg/arm)

QU

(QUECH)-TLI-. *See* TLA-(QUETZA).
(QUĒMI) > (QUĒN): TLA- = to put s.th. on; to wear s.th.; (TLA-QUĒMI)-TL- > (TLA-QUĒN)-∅- = s.th. put on/worn, i.e., clothing; (TLA-QUĒN)-TLI- = a thing people wear; i.e., clothing
(QUĒN-TIĀ) > (QUĒN-TIH): TĒ+TLA- = to cause s.o. to put s.th. on; to dress s.o. in s.th.
(QUĒ-N)-☐- ~ (QUĒ-)- = *interrog*, how? in what manner? **quēn amih** = how? what sort? **quēn mach amih** = what ever sort? **quēn in** . . . ? = in what manner is it that . . . ? **quēn mach** = how is it possible . . . ? how ever . . . ?
(QUĒ-M-MAN)-☐- = *interrog*, at what time (today)? [< (IM-MAN)-☐-]; *noninterrog*, from time to time, at times; **zan quēmman** = seldom, rarely
(QUĒ-X-QUI-CH)-∅- = how large a total amount/quantity? how much? how many (in general)?
(QUĒ-Z-QUI)-∅- = how large or full a number? how many (specifically)? how large a sum? +Ī-∅(QUĒ-Z-QUI-LHUI-YŌ-C)-∅- = some days after it/that; some days later; (QUĒ-Z-QUI-TE)-TL- = how many rock? I.e., how many (nonhuman)?
(QUETZA) > (QUETZ): TLA- = to stand s.th. up/erect; (TLA-QUETZA) > (TLA-QUETZ) = [tla-*fusion*], to tell a story/stories; (TLA-QUETZ-∅)-QUI- > (TLA-QUETZ-∅-CĀ)-UH- = *pret agen*, a storyteller; (TLA-QUETZ)-TLI- = a neatly stacked pile of firewood; (QUETZA-L)-LI- = s.th. that can be stood upright; i.e., a quetzal plume; *by extens*, s.th. rich/precious/dear/valuable; (∅-∅-QUETZA-L-CŌĀ-TL-∅)-∅- = *pers name s*, "It-Is-a-Quetzal-Plume-Snake/a-Precious-Snake"; (QUETZA-L-PATZ-A-C)-TLI- = a quetzal-plume crest device; (QUETZA-L-QUĒMI)-TL- > (QUETZA-L-QUĒN)-∅- = clothing as valuable/beautiful as quetzal plumes; i.e., a rich/precious costume; (TLA-QUETZA-L)-LI- = a thing that has been stood upright; i.e., a column/pillar; a fable/story
(QUETZA) > (QUETZ): M-O- = to stand up; +TLA(NE-QUETZA-YĀ-N)-∅- = s.th.'s standing-up place
(QUECH)-TLI- = a thing held erect; i.e., a neck; (QUECH-ŌL)-LI- = rubber at the neck, i.e., flexible neck; *by synecdoche*, roseate spoonbill [*Other translations have been suggested, but "swan" is* NOT *a possibility; there were no swans in the Nahuatl-speaking area, which explains why "cisne" (swan) never occurs in Molina's dictionary.*]
(QUECH-COT-Ō-N-A) > (QUECH-COT-Ō-N): TLA- = to break s.th. off at the neck; i.e., to cut s.th. off at/from the neck; to cut off s.th.'s neck/head
(QUECH-COY-Ō-NI-Ā) > (QUECH-COY-Ō-NI-H): TLA- = to pierce s.th. in the throat/neck
(QUECHI-LIĀ) > (QUECHI-LIH): TĒ+TLA- = to tell s.th. (i.e., a story, stories) to s.o.

Vocabulary

*(-QUI) > *(-QUI): TLA- = to will/want s.th. [*Defec v; used only as a matrix in a "future embed" compound v and only in the imperfect tense. See § 28.11.2.*]

QUIL = people say/it is said

(QUIMICH)-IN- = mouse

(QUIMIL)-LI- = bundle; (QUIMIL-PA-TLA) > (QUIMIL-PA-TLA): TĒ- = to exchange s.o. at a bundle; i.e., to take over s.o.'s bundle

   (QUIMIL-O-Ā) > (QUIMIL-O-H): TLA- = to wrap s.th. up

QUIN = [*with past tense*] just now; [*with future tense*] next, then, later, afterward; presently; **quin āxcān** = recently/a little while ago; **quin ihcuāc** = a little while after that time/then; **quin tēpan** = at last; afterward; later; finally

(QUIN-Ā-NI) > (QUIN-Ā-N) = to produce a thin, high-pitched sound

   (QUI-QUIN-A-CA) > (QUI-QUIN-A-CA) = to whine/buzz

(QUIQUICI) > (QUIQUIZ) = to make a blaring/honking/whistling sound; (QUIQUIZ)-TLI- = conch-shell trumpet

(QUIY-Ā-HUA)-TL- = doorway/entryway; (QUIY-Ā-HUA-TĒN)-TLI- = entry threshold; +TLA(QUIY-Ā-HUA-TĒN-YŌ)-Ø- = [*used in inh-pos NNCs*], s.th.'s entry threshold

(QUIY-A-HUI) > (QUIY-A-UH) = to rain; (QUIY-A-HUI)-TL- = rain

(QUĪZA) > (QUĪZ) = to exit/leave; **tētech quīza** = it comes out in contact with s.o.; i.e., it affects s.o.

   (QUĪX-TIĀ) > (QUĪX-TIH): TLA- = to cause s.th. to exit; i.e., to let s.th. out/to put s.th. out(side)

   (QUĪX-TIĀ) > (QUĪX-TIH): TĒ- = to resemble one's father (in looks or in action); to make s.o. leave

T

TĀCHCĀUH. *See* (ĀCH-CĀUH)-TLI-.

(TAH)-TLI- = father

(TAMAL)-LI- = tamale; (TAMAL-TEPI-TŌN)-Ø- = small tamale

   (TAMAL-HUIĀ) > (TAMAL-HUIH): TĒ- ~ M-O- ~ T-O- = to make tamales for s.o./o.s./one another

(TAMAZOL)-IN- = toad

(TAPAYOL)-LI- = a ball; (TAPAYOL-TI) > (TAPAYOL-TI) = to become round like a ball; (TAPAYOL-TI-Ø)-C- > (TAPAYOL-TI-Ø-CĀ)-UH- = *pret agen*, a thing that has become round like a ball; i.e., a thing that is round like ball; (TAPAYOL-TI-Ø-CĀ-TŌN)-TLI- = a thing that is slightly round like a ball

(TATACA) > (TATACA): TLA- = to dig/scratch s.th. in the earth; (TLA-TATAC)-TLI- = a thing that results from s.o. digging; i.e., a pit/hole; a grave; an excavation

(TE)-TL- > (TE)-UH- = rock/egg

   (TE-CAL)-LI- = house made of rock; i.e., vaulted chamber

   (TE-COMa)-TL- > (TE-CON)-Ø- = a clay pot; cup/mug; (TE-CON-TI-Ø)-C- = a pot-shaped thing

   (TE-CPA)-TL- > (TE-CPA)-UH- = flint; (TE-CPA-YO-H-Ø)-☐- = *pret agen*, one that has owned abundant flint; i.e., owner of abundant flint

   (TE-CHAL-O-Ā) > (TE-CHAL-O-H): TLA- = to scold s.th. from a rock; (TE-CHAL-Ō)-TL- > (TE-CHAL-Ō)-UH- = one that scolds/grumbles from a rock; i.e., a ground squirrel

(TE-CUĀCH)-TLI- = small cotton blanket
(TE-ILPI-Ā) > (TE-ILPI-H): TLA- = to tie s.th. like a rock; i.e., to tie s.th. firmly/tightly
(TE-MAN-A) > (TE-MAN): TLA- = to pave s.th. with stones/flagstones/slabs
(TE-MĀ-TLa)-TL- = a net for a rock; i.e., a sling; (TE-MĀ-TL-EH-∅)-☐- > (TE-MĀ-TL-EH-∅-CĀ)-UH- = one who has owned a sling; i.e., a sling owner
(TE-NĀMi) -TL- > (TE-NĀN)-∅- = stone barrier; i.e., wall; (TE-NĀM-EH-∅)-☐- = *pret agen*, one that has owned a wall; i.e., a walled one
(TE-NŌCH)-TLI- = rock-prickly-pear fruit; (TE-NŌCH-TI-TLAN)-☐- = *place-name s*, At/To/From the Place Beside Rock-Prickly-Pear Fruit; (TE-NŌCH-☐-CA)-TL- = person associated with Tenochco or Tenochtitlan; an inhabitant of Tenochco or of Tenochtitlan [*The derivation from* Tenōchtitlan *is irregular.*]
(TE-PACH-O-Ā) > (TE-PACH-O-H): TĒ- = to press s.o. down with rocks; i.e., to stone s.o.
(TE-PAN)-☐- = *place-name s*, At/To/From the Place Above Rocks; (TE-PAN-Ē-CA)-TL- = a person associated with Tepan, an inhabitant of Tepan, a Tepanec
(TE-PĀN)-TLI- = rock row; i.e., wall; (TE-PĀN-TLEHCŌ) > (TE-PĀN-TLEHCŌ) = to climb up on a wall; i.e., to climb a wall
(TE-PETLa)-TL- > (TE-PETL)-∅- = stone mat; i.e., tufa
(TE-POZ)-TLI- = hard metal (copper/iron); (TE-POZ-MĪ)-TL- > (TE-POZ-MĪ)-UH- = arrow made of hard metal; i.e., bolt (as used in a crossbow); (TE-POZ-TŌPĪL)-LI- = iron staff/rod/shaft; (TE-POZ-TLA-TEC-Ō-NI)-∅- = a thing with which people cut things that is made of hard metal; i.e., a metal ax
(TE-TAMAZOL)-LI- = stone toad
(TE-TEUH)-☐- = like a rock/rocklike; firmly/tightly; TLA-(TE-TEUH-ILPI-Ā) > (TE-TEUH-ILPI-H) = to tie s.th. like a rock; i.e., to tie s.th. firmly/tightly
(TE-TLA-QUETZA-L)-LI- = a stone column
(TE-TZO-TZONA) > (TE-TZO-TZON): TĒ- = to strike s.o. repeatedly with rocks; i.e., to pelt s.o. with rocks
(TE-XCA-L)-LI- = baked thing of stone; i.e., boulder/crag/cliff; oven; (TE-XCA-L-CAMA-C)-☐- = in/to/from a place of the/a mouth of/in a cliff; in a cavity in a cliff
(TĒC)-TLI-. *See* (TĒUC)-TLI-.
(TĒCA) > (TĒCA): TLA- = to stretch/lay out s.th. long/lengthwise on the ground/floor; to pour s.th. liquid (into a container); to dispose of s.th.; to cause s.th. (i.e., a boat) to ride/be/rest at anchor
(TĒCA) > (TĒCA): M-O- = to lie down; to stretch o.s. at full length
(TĒQUI-LIĀ) > (TĒQUI-LIH): TĒ+TLA- = to stretch out s.th. long on the ground for s.o.
(TECI)- > (TEZ) = to make meal/flour by grinding; (TEXĪ-HUA) > (TEXĪ-HUA) = *nonac s*; TLA-(TECI) > (TEZ) = to grind s.th. into meal/flour; (TEX-Ō) > (TEX-Ō) = *nonac s*.
(TEZ)-TLI- = an abraded thing; (TEZ-CA)-TL- = an abraded-thing associate; i.e., a mirror; **niTezcatl-Ihpōca**, i.e., #NI-∅(∅-∅-TEZ-CA-TL-∅+∅-∅-IH-PŌ-CA-∅-∅-∅)∅-∅# = [*personal-name NNC*], I am "It-Is-a-Mirror-That-Fumes"
(TEX-Ō-NI)-∅- = a thing with which people customarily grind; i.e., a pestle/a pounder
(TEX)-TLI- = a thing that results from grinding; i.e., meal/flour
(TE-C-I-HUI) > (TE-C-I-UH) = to hail; (TĒ-C-I-HUI)-TL- = hail/hailstone

Vocabulary

(TE-C-I-HU-IĀ) > (TE-C-I-HU-IH): TLA- = to hail on s.th.
(TECOL)-LI- = charcoal; +TLA(TECOL-LŌ)-∅- = [*used in org-pos NNC*], charcoal; **ītecollo cuahuitl** = it is the wood's charcoal
(TECOL-Ō)-TL- = owl [*abs af s*, (TĒ-TECOL-Ō)-∅-H ~ (TECOL-Ō)-M-]
*(TECH)-TLI- > (TECH)-∅- = [*used only in advlzd pos-st NNCs and in compound s*], side surface; contact: **notech** = in my contact, in contact with me; concerning/about me
   (TECH-TI-Ā) > (TECH-TI-H): M-O+TLA- = to cause o.s. to be in contact with s.th.; i.e., to appropriate s.th. for o.s.
(TECU-Ī-NI) > (TECU-Ī-N) = (for fire) to flare up/blaze up; (for the heart) to pound; (TE-TECU-I-CA) > (TE-TECU-I-CA) = (for a fire) to be noisy; (for a wound) to throb
   (TECU-Ī-NI-Ā) > (TECU-Ī-NI-H): M-O- = to stumble
(TE-Ī-NI-Ā) > (TE-Ī-NI-H): TLA- = to smash/shatter s.th; to break s.th. fragile into pieces
   (TE-TE-I-TZ-A) > (TE-TE-I-TZ): TLA- = to shatter s.th. fragile into many pieces; to gnaw s.th. (e.g., a bone)
TĒL = *part*, nevertheless; however; on the other hand
(TĒL-PŌCH)-TLI- = young man [*abs af s*, (TĒL-PŌ-PŌCH)-T-]
   (TĒL-PŌCH-CAL)-LI- = a young men's house; [*in a 1st-degree advlzd NNC*], into a young men's house
   (TĒL-PŌCH-NĒCI) > (TĒL-PŌCH-NĒZ) = to appear/seem to be a young man; to look like a young man
   (TĒL-PŌCH-YAH-∅)-☐- > (TĒL-PŌCH-YAH-∅-CĀ)-UH- = *pret agen*, a youthful goer; i.e., a young warrior; (TĒL-PŌCH-YAH-∅-CĀ-TI) > (TĒL-PŌCH-YAH-∅-CĀ-TI) = to become/be a young warrior
(TEMA > (TEN): M-O- = to take a steam bath
   (TEM-ĀZ)-TLI- = steam-bath implement; i.e., heated stone(s)/heated wall used for creating steam in a steam bath; (TEM-ĀZ-CAL)-LI- = a small structure containing a steam-producing device; i.e., a steam-bath shed/hut
(TĒMI) > (TĒN) = to become/be brimming full
   (TĒM-A) > (TĒN): TLA- = to fill s.th.; to put s.th. (e.g., maize) [somewhere]
(TĒMIQUI) > (TĒMIC) = to dream; TĒ- ~ TLA-(TĒMIQUI) > (TĒMIC) = to dream about s.o./s.th. [*applic obj unjustified by s's form*]
(TEMŌ) > (TEMŌ) = to descend; (for food) to become digested; **ahtemo** = it does not descend; i.e., it is indigestible; (TEMŌ-∅)-C- > (TEMŌ-∅-CĀ)-UH- = *pret agen*, one who has descended; i.e., a descender
   (TEMO-HUIĀ) > (TEMO-HUIH): TLA- = to cause s.th. to descend; to lower s.th.; to digest s.th
(TĒM-O-Ā) > (TĒM-O-H): TLA- = to seek s.th.
   (TĒM-O-LIĀ) > (TĒM-O-LIH): TĒ+TLA- = to seek s.th. for s.o.; to seek s.th. (i.e., information) about s.o.
(TĒN)-TLI- = lip/edge/brim; (TĒN-EH-∅)-☐- = *pret agen*, a thing that has owned an edge; i.e., a sharp-edged thing
   (TĒN-Ē-HU-A) > (TĒN-Ē-UH): TLA- = to cause s.th. to depart from the lips; i.e., to mention s.th.; to pronounce s.th.; (TĒN-Ē-HU-I-LIĀ) > (TĒN-Ē-HU-I-LIH): TĒ+TLA- = to mention s.th. to s.o.

(TĒN-HUĪ-TEQUI) > (TĒN-HUĪ-TEC): M-O- = to strike o.s. on the lips; i.e., to whoop/ululate

(TĒN-CŌZ-TI-∅)-C- = one yellow at the bill; i.e., a yellow-billed one

(TĒN-HUĪ-YA-∅)-C- = one long at the bill; i.e., a long-billed one

(TĒN-QUĪX-TIĀ)> (TĒN-QUĪX-TIH): TLA- = to cause s.th. to leave from the lips; i.e., to utter/divulge s.th.

(TĒN-TE)-TL- > (TĒN-TE)-UH- = stone for beneath the lower lip; i.e., a lip plug/labret

(TĒN-TLAHU-ĒL-Ī-LŌ-∅)-C- >(TĒN-TLAHU-ĒL-Ī-LŌ-∅-CĀ)-UH- = *pret pat s*, one who is evil at the lips; i.e., evil-tongued person

(TĒN-TLA-PA-L-LO-H-∅)-☐- > (TĒN-TLA-PA-L-LO-H-∅-CĀ)-UH- = *pret agen*, a thing that has owned abundant red color on the edges; i.e., a thing that has a red border

(TĒN-TZON)-TLI- = hair around the lips; i.e., a beard

(TĒN-YO-H-∅)-☐- > (TĒN-YO-H-∅-CĀ)-UH- = *pret agen*, one who has owned lips in abundance (because of being on everyone's lips as a topic of conversation); i.e., a famous person

(TĒN-YŌ)-TL- = a thing characterized by lips; i.e., the result of being on everyone's lips; i.e., fame/renown

*(TĒM-PAN)-∅- > (TĒM-PAN)-∅- = [*Only gen-use s is used.*], lip surface; **notēmpan** = on the surface of my lips

(TĒM-PAH-PAN-HUIĀ) > (TĒM-PAH-PAN-HUIH): M-O- = to shrill (while slapping the lips) [*trad sp*, M-O-(TEM-PA-PA-HUIA)]

(TE-NĀMi)-TL-. *See* (TE)-TL-.

(TĒNI)-TL- = foreigner/barbarian

(TEŌ)-TL- > (TEŌ)-UH- = god [*var emb s*, (TEOH-)-]

(TEŌ-Ā)-TL- = god water; i.e., exceptional/dangerous water (e.g., flood): **teōātl tlachinōlli** = it is a flood and it is scorched things (i.e., fields); i.e., it is war

(TEŌ-CATZ-A-C)-TLI- = a black one in the form of a god; i.e., a sacred black one

(TEŌ-CHĪCHĪ-MĒ-☐-CA)-TL- = a God Chichimec; i.e., a Supreme Chichimec, an Original/Source Chichimec, a Dangerous Chichimec

(TEŌ-CUITLa)-TL- > (TEŌ-CUITL)-∅- = god excrement; i.e., noble metal; gold/silver; (TEŌ-CUITLA-TĒN-TE)-TL- > (TEŌ-CUITLA-TĒN-TE)-UH- = a labret/lip plug made of gold

(TEŌ-IT-HUA-L)-LI- = a divine/sacred courtyard; i.e., a temple courtyard; (TEŌ-IT-HUA-L-TĒM-A) > (TEŌ-IT-HUA-L-TĒN): M-O- = to put o.s. into a temple courtyard; i.e., to participate in crowding into a temple courtyard

(TEŌ-MĀMĀ) > (TEŌ-MĀMAH) = to carry a god (an idol) on the back; (TEŌ-MĀMAH-∅)-☐- > (TEŌ-MĀMAH-∅-CĀ)-UH- = *pret agen*, one who has carried a god on the back; i.e., a god-bearer

(TEŌ-MATI) > (TEŌ-MAT) ~ (TEŌ-MAH): TĒ- ~ TLA- = to know s.o./s.th. to be a god; i.e., to worship s.o./s.th.; to consider s.o./s.th. divine

(TEŌ-NĀHUA-T-Ī-L)-LI- = a divine command

(TEŌ-PAN)-TLI- = sacred precinct/temple/church

(TEŌ-PIYA) > (TEŌ-PIX) = to guard a god; (TEŌ-PIX-∅)-QUI- > (TEŌ-PIX-∅-CĀ)-UH- = *pret agen*, a god guarder; i.e., a priest

(TEŌ-TE)-TL- > (TEŌ-TE)-UH- = rock of god; i.e., an outstanding/out of the ordinary rock; i.e., jet

Vocabulary

(TEŌ-TLĀC)-TLI- = god's (i.e., the sun's) torso/upper body; (TEŌ-TLĀC)-◻ [*used in 2nd-degree advlzd NNC*], at the time the god's (i.e., the Sun's) torso is at the zenith (because the god's face is already beyond the zenith), i.e., in the afternoon

(TEŌ-XĀHUA-L)-LI- = divine facial paint

(TEŌ-YŌ)-TL- = a thing characteristic of god; i.e., divinity; spirituality; (TEŌ-YŌ-TI-CA)-◻- = *adv*, by means of godliness/divinity; i.e., spiritually

(TEOH-CAL)-LI- = structure for a god; i.e., a temple;

(TEOH-CAL-HUĪ-YA-∅)-C- = *pret agen*, a long thing in the form of a temple; i.e., a long temple

(TEOH-TLĀL)-LI- = dangerous land, i.e., desert land/desert plain; (TEOH-TLĀL-PAN)-◻- = in the desert-plain region

TĒPAN. *See* (PAN)-◻-.

(TE-PĀN)-TLI-. *See* (TE)-TL-.

(TEPĒ)-TL- > (TEPĒ)-UH- = hill/mountain; (TEPĒ-TI-TLAN)-◻- = among the hills/mountains; (TEPĒ-TLAH)-◻- = place of abundant hills/mountains; a hilly area, a mountainous area; a mountain chain

(TEP-Ē-HUI) > (TEP-Ē-UH) = (for seed, etc.) to spill out and scatter on the ground; (for leaves) to fall from trees

(TEP-Ē-HU-A) > (TEP-Ē-UH): TLA- = to cause s.th. to spill/fall to the ground; to scatter s.th. on the ground: TĒ+TLA-(TEP-Ē-HU-A-L-TI-Ā) > (TEP-Ē-HU-A-L-TIH) = to cause s.o. to scatter s.th., to rip/tear s.th. from s.o.

(TEPI)-∅- = a small thing; (TEPI-TŌN)-∅- = a tiny thing, a very small thing

(TE-POZ)-TLI-. *See* (TE)-TL-.

(TEQUI) > (TEC): TLA- = to cut s.th.; (TLA-TEC-Ō-NI)-∅- = a thing with which people cut things; i.e., an ax/a knife

(TEQUI)-TL- > (TEQUI)-UH- = job/work/task; effort; tribute; *advlzd*, **zan tequitl** = just; nothing else but

(TEQUI-CĀHU-A) > (TEQUI-CĀUH) = to leave a job; i.e., to retire

(TEQUI-CUĀ) > (TEQUI-CUAH): TLA- = to eat s.th. busily/energetically

(TEQUI-HUAH-∅)-◻- > (TEQUI-HUAH-∅-CĀ)-UH- = *pret agen*, one who has owned tribute; i.e., a tribute owner; a veteran warrior; (TEQUI-HUAH-∅-CĀ-TI) > (TEQUI-HUAH-∅-CĀ-TI) = to become/be a tribute owner

(TEQUI-MĀ-CĒ-HU-A-L-LŌ)-TL- > (TEQUI-MĀ-CĒ-HU-A-L-LŌ)-∅- = commonerhood by means of effort; deliberate commonerhood (as when a noble disgraces himself by acting like a commoner)

(TEQUI-PACH-O-Ā) > (TEQUI-PACH-O-H): M-O- = to press o.s. down with effort; i.e., to worry; to be unhappy, to be troubled

(TEQUI-TI-Ā) > (TEQUI-TI-H): M-O+TLA- = to cause s.th. to be one's work; i.e., to busy o.s. with s.th.; to undertake s.th.

(TEQUI-TLA-NEL-O-Ā) > (TEQUI-TLA-NEL-O-H) = to paddle/row with effort; i.e., to paddle/row vigorously/diligently

(TĒTZ-Ā-HUI)-TL- > (TĒTZ-Ā-UH)-∅- = (bad) omen/portent; s.th. terrifying

(TĒTZ-Ā-HUIĀ) > (TĒTZ-Ā-HUIH): M-O+TLA- = to consider s.th. as an evil omen for o.s. [*for* (TĒTZ-Ā-UH-HUIĀ)]

(TĒTZ-Ā-M-MATI) > (TĒTZ-Ā-M-MAT) ~ (TĒTZ-Ā-M-MAH): TLA- = to know s.th. to be a bad omen; i.e., to consider s.th. a bad omen; to believe s.th. to be a bad omen [*var sp of* TLA-(TĒTZ-Ā-UH-MATI)]

(TĒUC)-TLI- > (TĒUC-YŌ)-∅- = lord; high-ranking noble [*Since Nahuatl allows the delabialization of /kw/ to [k], this stem has the var shape of* (TĒC)-TLI-, *absolute proof that the sp preferred among modern writers,* **tecuhtli** (*inviting one to replace a single consonant sound with an entire syllable*), *is ill advised and suggests ignorance of the language.*]
  (TĒUC-PAN)-∅- ~ (TĒC-PAN)-∅- = an area of a lord; a site for a lord; i.e., a palace
(TEUH)-TLI- = dust; (TEUH-YO-H-∅)-☐- = *pret agen*, a thing that has owned abundant dust; i.e., a dust-covered thing; a dusty thing
  (TEUH-YŌ)-TL- > (TEUH-YŌ)-∅- = dustiness; (TEUH-YŌ-HUA) > (TEUH-YŌ-HUA) = to be full of/covered with dust
(-TEUH)-☐- = [*defec n used only as matrix*], similarity/resemblance; *adv,* in the manner of; like: **chālchiuhteuh** = like greenstone/jadeite
(TĒX)-TLI- = a brother-in-law (of a man)
+TI(ĀCH-CĀUH)-∅-. *See* (ĀCH-CĀUH)-TLI-.
(TIĀNQUI-Z)-TLI- = market
(TĪCI)-TL- > (TĪCI)-UH- = healer, midwife, doctor
(TIL-Ā-HUA) > (TIL-Ā-HUA) = *nonan*, to become/be thickly/closely woven; *impers*, to rain hard/heavily
  (TIL-Ā-HUA-∅)-C- = *pret agen*, a thing that has become thickly woven; i.e., a thickly woven thing (e.g., a blanket; a thatched roof); a thick flat thing (e.g., a board, paper, tortilla, mat); a dense thing (e.g., a hedge)
  (TIL-MAH)-TLI- = blanket/cape/robe/cloak/mantle; clothes
(TĪTLANI).> (TĪTLAN): TĒ- ~ TLA- = to send s.o. (as a messenger); to send s.th. (e.g., a message); to use s.th.
  (TĪTLAN)-TLI- = one sent with a message; i.e., a messenger
  (NE-TĪTLANI-Z)-TLI- = message/errand
+TI(YAH-∅-CĀ)-UH-. *See* (YĀ).
(TĪZA)-TL- > (TĪZA)-UH- = white clay/chalk; white varnish
  (TĪZA-Ā-PAN)-☐- = In/To/From the Area of Chalk Water (~ Chalk River)
  (TĪC-E-C-TI-∅)-C- = a chalk-colored thing
  (TĪZA-HUIĀ) > (TĪZA-HUIH): TLA- = to apply white varnish to s.th.; to use white varnish on s.th.
(TOCA) > (TOCA): TĒ- ~ TLA- = to follow/pursue s.o./s.th. [*as a matrix*, to believe s.o./s.th. to be . . . ; to consider s.o./s.th. to be . . .]
  (TŌ-TOCA) > (TŌ-TOCA): TLA- = to pursue/chase s.th.
(TŌCA) > (TŌCA) = to do the planting/sowing
  (TŌCA) > (TŌCA): TLA- ~ TĒ- = to plant/sow s.th. (maize, beans, melons, etc.); to bury s.o.
  (TŌC)-TLI- = a thing that results from planting; i.e., a young maize plant
  (TŌCA) > (TŌCA): M-O- = *reflex-as-pass*, to be buried; +TĒ(NE-TŌCA-YĀ-N)-∅- = s.o.'s burial place
(TŌCĀi)-TL- > (TŌCĀ)-∅- = name; fame/honor; (TŌCĀ-YŌ)-TL- > (TŌCĀ-YŌ)-∅- = namehood; [*gen-use s used in org-pos NNCs*], name; fame/honor
  (TŌCĀ-TLĀL-I-Ā) > (TŌCĀ-TLĀL-I-H): TĒ- = to set s.o. down by name; i.e., to enroll s.o.
  (TŌCĀ-YŌ-TI-Ā) > (TŌCĀ-YŌ-TI-H): TLA- ~ TĒ- = to cause s.th./s.o. to have a name; i.e., to name s.th./s.o.; to give a name to s.th./s.o.

Vocabulary 255

(TŌCĀ-YŌ-TI-Ā) > (TŌCĀ-YŌ-TI-H): M-O- = to cause o.s. to have a name; i.e., to be named/called

(TŌ-CH)-IN- ~ -TLI-. See *(TŌ-NI).

(TOHMI)-TL- = body hair/fur/fuzz/down; (TOHMI-YŌ)-TL- > (TOHMI-YŌ)-∅- = furriness; [*gen-use s used only in pos-st NNC*], fur/fuzz/down: **tōchin ītohmiyo** = it is the rabbit's fur

(TŌL)-IN- = rush (a marsh plant)

    (TŌL-LĀ-N)-☐- = *place-name s,* At/To/From the Vicinity of Rushes

    (TŌL-LO-H-∅)-☐- > (TŌL-LO-H-∅-CĀ)-UH- = *pret agen,* one that has owned abundant rushes; i.e., a thing covered with/characterized by rushes

    (TŌL-O-Ā) > (TŌL-O-H) = to act like a rush; i.e., to nod/bow the head

    (TŌL-PETLa)-TL-> (TŌL-PETL)-∅- = a mat made of rushes; a rush mat

    (TŌL-TZĀLAN)-☐- = *adv,* among rushes

(TOL-Ī-NI-Ā) > (TOL-Ī-NI-H): M-O- = to be poor; to suffer

    (M-O-TOL-Ī-NI-H-∅)-QUI- > (NE-TOL-Ī-NI-H-∅-CĀ)-UH- = *pret agen,* one who has become poor; i.e., a poor person/a pauper

(TOL-O-Ā) > (TOL-O-H): TLA- = to swallow s.th.; TLA-(TOH-TOL-O-Ā) > (TOH-TOL-O-H) = to swallow s.th. hard; (for various persons) to swallow things

    (TOL-Ō-L-TIĀ) > (TOL-Ō-L-TIH): TĒ+TLA- = to cause s.o. to swallow s.th.

(TOM-Ā-HUA) > (TOM-Ā-HUA) = to become/be plump; (TOM-Ā-HUA-∅)-C- = a thing that has became plump; i.e., a plump/thick thing

(TOM-Ā-HU-A) > (TOM-Ā-UH): TLA- = to fatten s.th.; to speak with a deep/low-pitched voice

(TOMI) > (TON) = to become/be untied/loose

    (TOM-A) > (TON): TLA- = to untie/loose/undo s.th.

    (TOM-A)> (TON): M-O- = to ungird o.s.; (for a bird) to open its wings; +TLA(NE-TOM-A-YĀ-N)-∅- = s.th.'s (i.e., a bird's) wing-opening place

    (TOH-TOM-A) > (TOH-TON): TLA- = to undo/untie/loosen a number of things

(TŌ-NA) > (TŌ-NA) = (for the sun) to shine; (for the weather) to be sunny/warm; (TLA-TŌ-NA) > (TLA-TŌ-NA) = [*impers* tla-], (for heavenly bodies in general) to shine

    (TŌ-NA-∅)-C- > (TŌ-NA-∅-CĀ)-UH- = *pret agen,* s.th. (i.e., plants/agricultural crops/etc.) that has become fruitful/productive/luxuriant; (TŌ-NA-∅-CĀ-YŌ)-TL- = agricultural produce; agricultural foodstuffs; s.th. characterized by the warm/dry season

    (TŌ-NA-L)-LI- = heat of the sun; dry season (fall and winter); day sign; birth sign; birthright

    (TŌ-NA-∅-TI-UH) > (TŌ-NA-∅-TI-YAH) = (for the sun) to go warming/shining; (TŌ-NA-∅-TI-UH-∅)-∅- = *pret agen,* that which goes warming/shining; i.e., the sun: **tōnatiuh īcalaquiyān** = it is the sun's entering place; i.e., it is the west; **tōnatiuh īquīzayān** = it is the sun's exiting place; i.e., it is the east

    (TO-TŌ-N-I-Ā) > (TO-TŌ-N-I-H): TLA- = to warm/heat s.th.; (TLA-TO-TŌ-N-I-H) > (TLA-TO-TŌ-N-I-H) = [tla-*fusion*], to burn/offer up incense

(TŌ-NI) > *(TŌ-N) = to run [*an obsolete destockal v, from* *(TO-Ō-NI), *whose meaning is now expressed by its freq s,* (TO-TŌ-CA), *but whose derived nounstems remain in use*]

    (TŌ-CH)-IN- ~ -TLI- > (TŌ-CH)-∅- = a thing that runs fast; i.e., a rabbit; (TŌ-CH-TI) > (TŌ-CH-TI) = to become a rabbit; i.e., to turn into/become a wild animal, to lose one's humanity, to become insane; M-O-(TŌ-CH-TI-LIĀ) > (TŌ-CH-TI-LIH= to cause o.s. to become a rabbit; i.e., to turn into a wild animal; to drive o.s. insane

(TO-TŌ-CA) > (TO-TŌ-CA) = to run; (TLA-TO-TŌ-CA) > (TLA-TO-TŌ-CA) = [*impers* tla-], (for people/things in general) to run

(TO-TŌ-TZ-A) > (TO-TŌ-TZ-A): TĒ- = to cause s.o. to run; to hasten s.o.

(TŌPĪL)-LI- = rod, staff of office or authority; (TŌPĪL-EH-∅)-☐-> (TŌPĪL-EH-∅-CĀ)-UH- = *pret agen*, one who has owned a staff of office; i.e., a constable

(TŌTŌ)-TL- > (TŌTŌ)-UH- = bird
  (TŌTŌ-TE)-TL- > (TŌTŌ-TE)-UH- = bird egg
  (TŌTŌ-ZACA)-TL = bird grass

(TO-TŌ-CA). *See* *(TŌ-NI).

(TŌ-TOCA). *See* (TOCA): TLA-.

(TŌTOL)-IN- = turkey hen
  (TŌTOL-CAL)-LI- = house for turkey hens; i.e., turkey coop; (*after the conquest*) hen house; chicken coop
  (TŌTOL-EH-∅)-☐- > (TŌTOL-EH-∅-CĀ)-UH- = one who has owned turkeys; i.e., a turkey owner
  (TŌTOL-NAMACA) > (TŌTOL-NAMACA) = to sell turkeys; (TŌTOL-NAMACA-∅)-C- > (TŌTOL-NAMACA-∅-CĀ)-UH- = *pret agen*, one who has sold turkeys; a turkey seller/vender
  (TŌTOL-TE)-TL- = turkey egg; (TŌTOL-TE-TAMAL)-LI- = turkey-egg tamale

(TŌZ)-TLI- = adult yellow-headed parrot; (TŌZ-PA-L)-LI- = color like feathers of a yellow-headed parrot; (TŌZ-PA-L-Ā)-TL- = yellow-colored water

TL

TLĀ = [*adv part introducing wish and command sentences*], if (it may be that), may (it be that), would that; **in tlā** = [*used in adjoined clauses*], if (it is the case that); **in tlā nel** = if in truth; even though/although; assuming that/provided that; **in tlā no zo** = if even also; if otherwise; if maybe; **in tlā ca#** ~ **in tlā camō** = if not; **in tlā canel** ~ **in tlā canel mō** = even though in truth not; although not; in as much as not; provided that not

(TLA)-TL- > (TLA)-∅- = strip of cloth/leather

(TLĀ)-TL- > (TLĀ)-UH- covering, cover
  (TLĀ-PACH-O-Ā) > (TLĀ-PACH-O-H): M-O- ~ TĒ- ~ TLA- = to press down on o.s./s.o./s.th. with a covering; i.e., to put o.s./s.o./s.th. under covers, to cover o.s./s.o./s.th. (with a sheet, blanket, etc.) [*See § 30.7; the* TLĀ- *inside the s is not the obj pron* TLA (*as it is apparently usually taken to be, since in tradit sp the /a:/ never has the length indicated*), *but the v is strictly a single-obj v and the embedded* TLĀ- *is a nounstem incorporated as an adv.*]
  (TLĀ-TI-Ā) > (TLĀ-TI-H): M-Ō- ~ TĒ- ~ TLA- = to cause o.s./s.o./s.th. to have a cover/covering; i.e., to hide o.s./s.o./s.th.; *metaph.*, to kill s.o.; TĒ+NE-(TLĀ-TI-LIĀ) > (TLĀ-TI-LIH) = to hide/conceal (o.s.) from s.o.

(TLĀC)-TLI- > (TLĀC)-∅- = upper body, torso

(TLĀCA)-TL- = [*used only as abs-st NNC and as emb*], man; lord; human [*The gen-use s,* (TLĀCA)-TL-, *when used in pos-st NNCs, is translated "slave"; see* (TLĀCOH)-TLI-.]

Vocabulary

(TLĀCA-Ē-HU-A)-TL- = a human skin; [*in 1st degree advlzd NNC*], in a human skin: **ahnonnaquīz tlācaēhuatl** = I shall not cause myself to enter in a (flayed) human skin; i.e., I shall not wear a flayed skin

(TLĀCA-HUAH-∅)-☐- > (TLĀCA-HUAH-∅-CĀ)-UH- = *pret agen,* one who has owned a person; i.e., a slave owner

(TLĀCA-HUĒ-I-YA-∅)-C- ~ (TLĀCA-HUĪ-YA-∅)-C- = a long one in the form of a man; i.e., a tall man

(TLĀCA-MATI) > (TLĀCA-MAT) ~ (TLĀCA-MAH): TĒ- = to know s.o. to be a master; i.e., to obey s.o.

(TLĀCA-MIC-TIĀ)> (TLĀCA-MIC-TIH) = to kill a human being; i.e., to perform a human sacrifice

(TLĀCA-TECOL-Ō)-TL- = an owl in the form of a person, a human owl; i.e., a necromancer/sorcerer [*In postconquest times, churchmen imposed the concept of "devil" onto this s.*]

(TLĀCA-TĒUC)-TLI- ~ (TLĀCA-TĒC)-TLI- = lord of persons; i.e., high lord/sovereign; (TLĀCA-TĒC-CO)-☐- = *place-name s,* In/At/From the Place of the Lord/Sovereign (a temple in Tenochtitlan); (TLĀCA-TĒC-☐-CA)-TL = person associated with the Tlacatecco; i.e., a general

(TLĀCA-TI) > (TLĀCA-T) = to become a person; i.e., to be born (*not limited to VNCs with a human subject*); (TLĀCA-TI-LIĀ) > (TLĀCA-TI-LIH): TĒ- to cause/help s.o. be born

(TLACŌ)-TL- > (TLACŌ)-UH- = stick/twig/switch; (TLACŌ-TI) > (TLACŌ-T) = to become/be a stick; (TLACŌ-CH)-TLI- = arrow; (TLACŌ-CH-CAL)-LI- = house for storing arrows; armory; (TLACŌ-CH-CAL-CO)-☐- = *place-name s,* At/To/From the Place of the Armory (a building in Tenochtitlan); (TLACŌ-CH-CAL-CO-PA)-☐- = toward the Place of the Armory; i.e., toward the north; (TLACŌ-CH-CAL-☐-CA)-TL- = person associated with the Tlacochcalco; i.e., a commanding general

(TLĀCOH)-TLI- > (TLĀCA)-UH- = slave

(TLĀCOH-CUEPA) > (TLĀCOH-CUEP): M-O- = to turn o.s. into a slave; to become a slave

(TLĀCOH-TI) > (TLĀCOH-TI) = to become/be a slave; i.e., to work like a slave; to labor industriously

(TLACH)-TLI- = a ceremonial ball game in which the ball is struck only with elbows, hips, or legs to score a goal by passing it through a vertically set ring; (TLACH-CO)-☐- = place of the ball game; i.e., ball court

(TLA-CHCUI)-TL-. *See* TLA-(iCHCUA).

(TLACU-Ā-HU-A) > (TLACU-Ā-UH): M-O- = to strengthen o.s.

(TLACU-Ā-UH)-TLI- = a strengthened/hardened/toughened one; (TLACU-Ā-UH)-☐- = [*used in 2nd-degree advlzd NNC*], strongly; especially

(-TLAH)-TLI- = place where there is an abundance of . . . place characterized by . . . [*Defec n used only as matrix; the comp it forms is frequently advlzd.*], (-TLAH)-☐- = *adv*, in/to/from a place where there is an abundance of . . .

(TLAH)-TLI- = uncle (brother of father or mother)

(TLAHCAH)-TLI- = daylight; daytime; (TLAHCAH)-☐- = [*used in 2nd-degree advlzd NNC*], during the day/in the daytime

(TLA-HC-I-UH-∅)-QUI- = *pret agen*, an astrologer

(TLAHPAL)-LI- = effort/exertion/energy/vigor/force
  (TLAHPAL-TI) > (TLAHPAL-TI) = to become/be robust/vigorous/strong; (TLAH-PAL-TI-∅)-C- > (TLAHPAL-TI-∅-CĀ)-UH- = *pret agen*, one that has become robust/vigorous/strong; i.e., a robust/vigorous/strong one; (TLAHPAL-TI-∅-CĀ-PŌL)-∅- = a quite firm/strong/robust/vigorous entity
  (TLAHPAL-I-HUI) > (TLAHPAL-I-UH) = to become/be energetic
  (TLAHPAL-O-Ā) > (TLAHPAL-O-H): TĒ- = to cause/prompt/urge/encourage s.o. to be energetic/healthy; i.e., to greet s.o.; +TĒ(TĒ-TLAHPAL-O-Ā-YĀ)-∅- = s.o.'s means by which to greet people; i.e., s.o.'s salutation/words of greeting/greeting gift; (TĒ-TLAHPAL-Ō-LIZ)-TLI- = action of greeting people
(TLAHU-ĒL)-LI- = indignation/anger/ire
  (TLAHU-ĒL-CUI) > (TLAHU-ĒL-CUI) = to take anger; i.e., to get angry
  (TLAHU-ĒL-I-Ā) > (TLAHU-ĒL-I-H): TĒ- = to be enraged at s.o.; to hate and despise s.o.; (TLAHU-ĒL-Ī-LŌ-∅)-C- > (TLAHU-EL-Ī-LŌ-∅-CĀ)-UH- = *pret pat*, one who has been hated and despised; i.e., a scoundrel/villain/knave; a malicious/vicious person; (TLAHU-ĒL-Ī-LŌ-∅-CĀ)-☐- = [*used in advlzd NNC*], like/in the manner of a scoundrel/villain; TĒ-(TLAHU-ĒL-Ī-LŌ-∅-CĀ-MATI) > (TLAHU-ĒL-Ī-LŌ-∅-CĀ-MAT) ~ (TLAHU-ĒL-Ī-LŌ-∅-CĀ-MAH) = to consider s.o. a scoundrel; (TLAHU-ĒL-Ī-LŌ-∅-CĀ-TLA-HT-Ō-L)-LI = a word/speech of an evil one; i.e., an evil/wicked word/speech
(TLĀHUi)-TL- = red ochre
  (TLĀHUI-Ā) > (TLĀHUI-H) = to be like red ochre; i.e., (for a candle, etc.) to glow/shed light; to cast a light/radiate light; (for a person with a torch, etc.) to light the way; (TLĀHUI-Z)-TLI- = action of shedding light/lighting the way; emblem/insignia
  (TLĀHU-ĀNA) > (TLĀHU-ĀN) = to take red ochre; i.e., to get a glow on; to become tipsy/inebriated; (TLĀHU-ĀNA-NI)-∅- = *cuspres agen*, one who customarily becomes tipsy; i.e., a drunkard; (TLĀHU-ĀN-∅)-QUI > (TLĀHU-ĀN-∅-CĀ)-UH- = *pret agen*, one who has become tipsy; i.e., a drunkard
  (TLĀHU-ĀN-TIĀ) ~ (TLĀHU-ĀN-TIH): M-O- ~ TĒ- = to make o.s./s.o. become tipsy/drunk; to deliberately become tipsy/drunk
  (TLA-TLĀHUi)-TL-, "a thing resembling red ochre." *See* § 53.1.1.
  (TLA-TLĀ-HUI) > (TLA-TLĀ-UH) = to become like red ochre; i.e., to become red [*for* (TLA-TLĀUH-HUI)]; (TLA-TLA-C)-TLI- = a reddish colored thing; a red thing; (TLA-TLA-C-TI) > (TLA-TLA-C-TI) = to become/be reddish colored; to become/be bright reddish; (TLA-TLA-C-TI-∅)-C- = a thing that has become bright reddish; i.e., a bright reddish thing
(TLĀL)-LI- = earth/ground/soil/dirt
  (TLĀL-CĀHUA) > (TLĀL-CĀUH) = to abandon land; (TLĀL-CĀHUA-L)-LI- = an abandoned thing in the form of land; i.e., abandoned land; TLA- ~ TĒ-(TLĀL-CĀHU-IĀ) > (TLĀL-CĀHU-IH) = to abandon land to s.th./s.o.; i.e., to make way for s.th./s.o., to get out of the way of s.th./s.o.
  (TLĀL-CHĪHUA) > (TLĀL-CHĪUH) = to work/till land; to farm; (TLĀL-CHĪUH-∅)-QUI- > (TLĀL-CHĪUH-∅-CĀ)-UH- = *pret agen*, one who has tilled land; i.e., a farmer
  (TLĀL-CUĀ) > (TLĀL-CUAH) = to eat earth (a gesture of reverence and fidelity made by touching one finger to the ground and then to the mouth)

(TLĀL-HUĀ-QUI) > (TLĀL-HUĀ-C) = to become dry in the form of land; (TLĀL-HUĀ-C)-TLI- = a thing that results from drying in the form of land; i.e., dry land; an island; (TLĀL-HUĀ-C-∅)-QUI- > (TLĀL-HUĀ-C-∅-CĀ)-UH- = *pret agen*, a thing that has become dry in the form of land; i.e., dry land; (TLĀL-HUĀ-C-∅-CĀ-QUĪZA) > (TLĀL-HUĀ-C-∅-CĀ-QUĪZ) = to come out onto dry land

(TLĀL-I-Ā) > (TLĀL-I-H): TLA- ~ TĒ- = to ground s.th./s.o.; i.e., to set s.th./s.o. down; to put s.th./s.o. (somewhere); to erect s.th.; to settle s.o.; *by extens*, to compose s.th.; to devise s.th.; to construct s.th.; M-Ō-(TLĀL-I-Ā) > (TLĀL-I-H) = to seat o.s.; to sit/settle down; (NE-TLĀL-I-LŌ-NI)-∅- = a thing by means of which one sits down; i.e., a seat

(TLĀL-I-LIĀ) > (TLĀL-I-LIH): TĒ+TLA- = to set down/establish s.th. for s.o.

(TLĀL-LAN)-▢- = under the ground; underground

(TLĀL-LĀ-N)-▢- = *place-name s*, At/To/From/Through the Place in the Vicinity of Land; (TLĀL-TĒ-▢-CĀ)-TL- = one associated with Tlallan; an inhabitant of Tlallan

(TLĀL-LO-H-∅)-▢- = a thing that has owned dirt/earth/soil in abundance; a thing filled/covered with dirt

(TLĀL-LŌ)-TL- > (TLĀL-LŌ)-∅- = a thing characteristic of land/soil/dirt; (TLĀL-LŌ-HUA) > (TLĀL-LŌ-HUA) = to become characterized by dirt; i.e., to become/be covered with dirt

(TLĀL-MAH-CĒ-HU-A) > (TLĀL-MAH-CĒ-UH) = to merit/deserve land; to subjugate land; to acquire land by meritorious action

(TLĀL-MIQUI) > (TLĀL-MIC) = to die on the land; i.e., to die at home (not in battle); to die outside of battle; to die in time of peace

(TLĀL-MOMOZ)-TLI- = an earthen altar

(TLĀL-ŌL-Ī-NI) > (TLĀL-ŌL-Ī-N) = to move in the form of the land; i.e., (for the earth) to quake; (for an earthquake) to occur

(TLĀL-OMI)-TL- > (TLĀL-OMI)-UH- = earth bone (a certain kind of worm)

(TLĀL-PŌHU-A) > (TLĀL-PŌUH) = to measure land, to survey land; (TLĀL-PŌHU-A-LŌ-NI)-∅- = a thing with which one customarily measures land; i.e., an instrument for surveying

(TLĀL-POL-I-HUI) > (TLĀL-POL-I-UH) = to perish on the land/earth; to perish during a time of peace (by pestilence, etc.)

(TLĀL-TĒM-O-Ā) > (TLĀL-TĒM-O-H) = to seek land

(TLĀL-T-ICPA-C)-TLI- = earth; (TLĀL-T-ICPA-C)-▢- = [*used in 2nd degree advlzd NNC*], on the top of the land; i.e., on earth

(TLAL-I-HUI) > (TLAL-I-UH) = to become/be hasty/speedy

(TLAL-O-Ā) > (TLAL-O-H): M-O- ~ TĒ- = to cause o.s./s.o. to be hasty; i.e., to run/sprint; to make haste; to make s.o. run

(TLAMI) > (TLAN) = *nonan*, to come to an end; to become/be finished; to come to a conclusion; to become/be used up; (TLAN-∅)-QUI- = *pret agen*, a finished/concluded thing; (TLAMI-∅)-C- = a thing that has reached the end of a twenty-count; i.e., twenty things

(TLAMI-Ā) > (TLAMI-H): TLA- = to cause s.th. to end; to bring s.th. to an end; to finish/conclude s.th.; to consume s.th.

(TLAN)-TLI- = tooth

(TLAN-COT-Ō-NI) > (TLAN-COT-Ō-N) = to become broken at a tooth; to lose a tooth; (TLAN-COT-O-C-TI-Ø)-C- = one who has lost a tooth, one who is missing a tooth; a toothless person

*(TLAN)-Ø- > (TLAN)-Ø- = [*defec n, used only in advlzd pos-st NNCs and in a comp s*], bottom surface/undersurface; low-down location; adjacent location; a location overshadowed by s.th.; a location in the shelter of s.th.; under/beneath; near: **notlan ximotlāli** = sit next to me; **ātlan** = in the water/under the water; **nocaltitlan** = near my house; **ihhuititlan** = among feathers

(TLAN-A-HUI) > (TLAN-A-UH) = (for a sick person) to become downward; i.e., to worsen/take a turn for the worse, to get worse

(TLAN-CUĀi)-TL- > (TLAN-CUĀ)-Ø- = a head that is down below; i.e., a knee

(TLAN-XĪMA) > (TLAN-XĪN): TĒ- = to commit adultery; to be adulterous to s.o. [*tradit sp*, TE-(TLA-XIMA)]

(-TLĀ-N)-☐- = [*A matrix-only n, used only in place-names; see* (-N)-TLI-.], At/To/From the Place in the Vicinity of/Place Near . . . ; **Tlaxcallān** = At/To/From the Place in the Vicinity of Tortillas

(-TLANI) > (-TLAN): M-O- ~ TĒ- ~ TLA- = [*A matrix-only v, see* § 39.7.1.c *and* § 39.7.2.b.] to desire/want o.s./s.o./s.th. to become/be regarded as . . . ; to request/permit/command s.o./s.th. to . . .

(TLAŌCO-YA) > (TLAŌCO-X) = to be sad; (TLAŌCO-X-Ø)-QUI- > (TLAŌCO-X-Ø-CĀ)-UH- = *pret agen*, one who has become sad; a sad one; (TLAŌCO-X-Ø-CĀ)-☐- = [*used in 2nd-degree advlzd NNCs*], in the manner of a sad one; i.e., sadly

(TLAŌCO-L)-LI- = a thing that results from being sad; i.e., sorrow; pity, compassion, mercifulness; TĒ-(TLAŌCO-L-NŌ-NŌTZA) > (TLAŌCO-L-NŌ-NŌTZ) = to call out to s.o. in contrition/for compassion

(TLAP)-TLI- = box/coffer; (TLAP-CO)-☐- = in a coffer; (TLAP-CO-PA)-☐- = toward/from within a box; i.e., toward/from the East

(TLA-PAN)-TLI-. See (PAN)-☐-.

(TLAP-Ā-NI) > (TLAP-Ā-N) = *nonan,* to become broken; *anim,* to hatch; (TLAP-Ā-N-Ø)-QUI- = *pret agen,* a thing that has become broken; i.e, a broken thing

(TLAP-O-HUI) > (TLAP-O-UH) = (for a door, letter, etc.) to become/be open

(TLAP-O-Ā) > (TLAP-O-H): TLA- = to open s.th.; to uncover s.th.; +TĒ(TLAP-Ō-LŌ-CĀ)-Ø- = s.o.'s action of being opened; i.e., s.o.'s openness/accessibility; **notlapōlōca** = it is my openness; (TLA-TLAP-Ō-LŌ-NI)-Ø- = a thing by which one opens things; i.e., a key

(TLAP-O-L-HUIĀ) > (TLAP-O-L-HUIH): TĒ+TLA- = to open s.th. for s.o.

(TLA-TE-L)-LI- ~ (TLA-TI-L)-LI- = a large mound; (TLA-TI-L-Ō-L)-LI- = a mounded-up thing; (TLA-TI-L-Ō-L-CO)-☐- = *place-name s,* At/To/From the Place of Mounded-Up Land

(TLA-T-HUI). *See* (iT-HUI).

(TLA-TI-Ā): TLA-. *See* (TLE)-TL-.

(TLĀ-TI-Ā): TLA-. *See* (TLĀ)-TL-.

(TLA-TO-TŌ-CA). *See* *(TŌ-NI).

(TLA-TLA). *See* (TLE)-TL-.

(TLA-TQUI)-TL-. *See* (iTQUI): TLA-.

Vocabulary 261

(TLA-TLA-C-TI). *See* (TLĀHUi)-TL-.

(TLĀTL-A-UH-TIĀ) > (TLĀTL-A-UH-TIH): TLA- = to beg/pray for s.th. [*presupposes* *(TLĀTL-A-HUI)]

(TLATZ-I-HUI) > (TLATZ-I-UH) = to become/be lazy; (TLATZ-I-UH-∅)-QUI- = *pret agen*, one who has become lazy; i.e., a lazy person

(TLA-XĪMA): TĒ-. *See* (TLAN-XĪMA): TĒ-.

(TLĀZA) > (TLĀZ): TLA- = to throw/hurl s.th.; to make a throwing motion/gesture with s.th.; to brandish s.th.

  (TLA-TLĀX-Ō-NI)-∅- = a thing with which people hurl things; i.e., a catapult

  (TLĀXI-LIĀ) > (TLĀXI-LIH): TĒ+TLA- = to throw s.th. from s.o.; i.e., to cause s.o. to have an abortion

(TLA-ZO-H)-TLI-. *See* (ZO-Ā): TLA-.

(TLE)-TL- > (TLE)-UH- = fire

  (TLE-CAL)-LI- = housing over fire; i.e., chimney

  (TLE-CĀHU-IĀ) > (TLE-CĀHU-IH): TLA- = to leave fire to s.th.; i.e., to set fire to s.th.

  (TLE-CAXi)-TL- > (TLE-CAX)-∅- = bowl to contain fire; i.e., clay censer

  (TLE-CO)-☐- = *adv*, in a place of fire; i.e., in/on/to/from a fire; in/from a hearth

  (TLE-CŌĀ)-TL- > (TLE-CŌĀ)-UH- = a snake as painful as fire; i.e., a snake with a deadly bite

  (TLE-CŌMi)-TL- > (TLE-CŌN)-∅- = pot for over fire; i.e, crucible

  (TLE-CUAHUi)-TL- > (TLE-CUAUH)-∅- = a stick for producing fire; i.e., a fire drill

  (TLE-CUI-L)-LI- = fire receptacle; i.e., fire pit, hearth

  (TLE-HUĀ-TZ-A) > (TLE-HUĀ-TZ): TLA- = to cause s.th. to become dry by fire; i.e., to roast s.th. on a fire; TĒ+TLA- ~ M-O+TLA-(TLE-HUĀ-CH-I-LIĀ) > (TLE-HUĀ-CH-I-LIH) = to roast s.th. for s.o./o.s. on a fire

  (TLE-HUĪC-Ō-L)-LI- = a clay censer

  (TLE-MĀi)-TL- > (TLE-MĀ)-∅- = hand for fire; i.e., fire shovel; (TLE-MĀ)-TL- > (TLE-MĀ)-UH- = hand for fire; i.e., incense ladle

  (TLE-MĪ-N-A) > (TLE-MĪ-N): TLA- = to shoot s.th. with fire arrows

  (TLE-MIY-Ā-HUA)-TL- > (TLE-MIY-Ā-HUA)-UH- = a tassel made of fire; i.e., a flame

  (TLE-MŌY-Ō)-TL- > (TLE-MŌY-Ō)-UH- = a mosquito/gnat made of fire; i.e., a spark

  (TLE-NENE-PIL)-LI- = tongue of fire; i.e., flame

  (TLE-PAN-TLĀZA) > (TLE-PAN-TLĀZ): M-O- ~ TĒ- = to throw o.s./s.o. onto a fire

  (TLE-QUIQUIZ)-TLI- = a trumpet that produces fire; i.e., a cannon; a lombard gun; a firearm

  (TLE-TLĀL-I-Ā) > (TLE-TLĀL-I-H) = to set down a fire; i.e., to make a fire, to light a fire

  (TLE-XŌ-CH)-TLI- = a bloom/flower made by fire; i.e., a live coal, red-hot coal; ember

  (TLA-TI-Ā) > (TLA-TI-H): TLA- = to cause s.th. to be fire; i.e., to burn s.th. [*The TLA- inside the s is a var of* (TLE)-TL-.]; M-O+TLA-(TLAH-TLA-TI-LIĀ) > (TLAH-TLA-TI-LIH) = to burn various things belonging to o.s.; to burn one's various belongings

  (TLA-TLA) > (TLA-TLA) = to burn/be on fire [*The first TLA- is a variant of* (TLE)-TL-.]

(TL-EH)-∅- = *interrog*, what entity? what? **tleh in . . .** = what is it that . . . ? *neg*, **ahtleh** = it is nothing [*var s*, (TL-E-IN)-∅- ~ (TL-E-I)-∅-]

(TLEHCŌ) > (TLEHCŌ) = to ascend

(TLEHCA-HUIĀ) > (TLEHCA-HUIH): TĒ- ~ TLA- = to make s.o./s.th. go up/ascend; to take/carry/accompany s.o./s.th. upward
(TLĪL)-LI- = black ink; a black thing; black color
 (TLĪL-Ā)-TL- > water like black ink; i.e., murky depths of deep water
 (TLĪL-I-HUI) > (TLĪL-I-UH) to become/turn/be black
 (TLĪL-NEX-TI-Ø)-C- = one that has become blackish gray; i.e., a dark gray one
 (TLĪL-TI-Ø)-C- = a thing that has become black; i.e., a black thing
 (TLĪL-TI-YA) > (TLĪL-TI-YA) ~ (TLĪL-TI-X) = to become/be like black ink; i.e., to become/be black
*(TLOC)-Ø- > (TLOC)-Ø- = [*gen-use s used in advlzd pos-st NNC and as emb*], side; proximity; **notloc** = at my side; along with me; (TLOQU-EH-Ø)-▢- = *pret agen*, one who has owned alongsideness; i.e., an owner of nearness: **Tloqueh Nāhuaqueh** = he is "He is the Possessor of Nearness and of Vicinity"; i.e., he is the Omnipresent (God)
(TLOH)-TLI- = hawk/falcon
 (TLOH-CUĀUH)-TLI- = a falcon-eagle

TZ

(TZACU-A) > (TZAUC): TLA- = to cause s.th. to become closed/shut; i.e., to close/shut s.th.; (TZACU-A) > (TZAUC): TĒ- = to lock s.o. up; to imprison s.o.
 (TZACU-A-L)-LI- = a thing that has been closed; i.e., a pyramid; TĒ-(TZACU-A-L-TI-Ā) > (TZACU-A-L-TI-H) = to cause s.o. to have a pyramid; i.e., to build a pyramid to/for s.o.
 (TZAH-TZACU-A) > (TZAH-TZAUC): TLA- = to close/block a number of things (e.g., doors, exits); to close s.th. repeatedly
(TZAHTZI) > (TZAHTZI) = to shout/call out; (TZAHTZI-LIZ)-TLI- = action of shouting
 (TZAHTZI-LIĀ) > (TZAHTZI-LIH): TĒ- = to call to s.o.
(TZĀLAN)-TLI- > (TZĀLAN)-Ø- = [*used only in advlzd pos-st NNCs and as matrix*], area between/midst: **totzālan** = in our midst; **cuauhtzālan** among the trees/in the midst of the trees
(TZAPA)-TL- > (TZAPA)-UH- = dwarf
(TZAP-Ī-NI) > (TZAP-Ī-N) = to become pricked; (TZAP)-TLI- = a thing that pricks, i.e., a thorn
(TZAY-Ā-N-A) > (TZAY-Ā-N): TLA- = to cause s.th. to become torn/ripped; to tear/rip/rend s.th.
(TZEL-I-HUI) > (TZEL-I-UH) = to sift down; to fall as through a sieve
 (TZE-TZEL-I-HUI) > (TZE-TZEL-I-UH) = to sift down in quantity; to drizzle
(TZIHUAC)-TLI- = a cactus with elongated, spiny, maguey like leaves (stalks?), which apparently in primitive times could be used as a weapon; (Ø-Ø-TZIHUAC-PO-PŌ-CA-Ø-Ø-Ø)-Ø- = *pers name s*, "One-that-Emits-an-Aura-from/by-means-of-a-Tzihuactli" [*possibly translated freely as* "Earns-Fame/Honor-Wielding-a-Tzihuactli"]
(TZIL-Ī-NI) > (TZIL-Ī-N) = (for s.th. metallic) to make a sound; to clink/jingle/jangle/tinkle; (for a bell) to ring
 (TZI-TZIL)-IN- = a thing that makes a jingling/humming sound; a jingle bell; (TZI-TZIL-EH-Ø)-▢- = *pret agen*, one who has owned jingle bells; i.e., a jingle-bell owner
(TZĪN)-TLI- = buttocks/anus; base/foundation

Vocabulary

 (TZĪN-Ē-HU-A) > (TZĪN-Ē-UH): TLA- = to cause s.th. to depart from the base; i.e., to raze/devastate s.th.; *metaph.*, to uproot s.th.
 (TZĪN-HUITZ-TI-∅)-C- = a thing pointed at the base
 (TZĪN-QUĪZA) > (TZĪN-QUĪZ) = to exit/leave by means of the buttocks; i.e., to back up/away; to retreat; (TZĪN-QUĪX-TIĀ) > (TZĪN-QUĪX-TIH): TĒ- = to cause s.o. to back away/retreat
 (TZĪN-TEPOZ)-TLI- = hard metal at the butt/base; i.e., ferrule (i.e., metal cap attached at the end of a pole/lance/staff/etc., to prevent splitting)
 (TZĪN-TI) > (TZĪN-TI) = to have a foundation/base; i.e., to have a beginning, to begin
 (TZĪN-TLA-CZA) > (TZĪN-TLA-CZA) = to trample backwards
 (TZĪN-TLAN)-TLI- = down-below part that serves as a foundation; i.e., buttock; base
(TZIUH-CŌĀ)-TL- = turquoise (?) snake
(TZOHUAL)-LI- = dough made with amaranth seeds; amaranth dough
(TZO)-TL- = filth/dirt/sweat
 (TZO-PIL-Ō)-TL- = s.th. hung over filth; i.e., a turkey buzzard
(TZŌL-I-HUI) > (TZŌL-I-UH) = to become/be narrow/tapered/compressed; (TZŌL)-LI- = a thing that results from becoming narrowed/tapered/contracted, i.e., a narrowed/tapered/contracted thing
(TZOM-Ō-NI-Ā) > (TZOM-Ō-NI-H): TLA- = to cause s.th. to become torn/ripped/split; to tear/rip/split s.th.
(TZON)-TLI- = hair; feather barb [*as matrix in numeral s*], four hundred
 (TZON-CAL)-LI- = a structure made of hair; i.e., a wig
 (TZON-HU-ĀZ)-TLI- = an instrument made from hair; i.e., a snare; a noose for trapping birds and small animals
 (TZON-IC-QUETZA) > (TZON-IC-QUETZ): TLA- ~ TĒ- = to turn s.th. (e.g., bowl/bucket/basket) upside down; to empty s.th. containing water (e.g., a pitcher) into another container; to throw s.o. headfirst into water or over a cliff, etc.; M-O-(TZON-IC-QUETZA) > (TZON-IC-QUETZ) = to plunge/fall headfirst
 (TZON-IZTA-YA) > (TZON-IZTA-Z) = to become white at the hair; i.e., to become white-haired
 (TZON-QUĪZA) > (TZON-QUĪZ) = to come to an end
 (TZON-TE-COMa)-TL- > (TZON-TE-CON)-∅- = a hair pot; i.e., a head skull
 (TZO-TZONA) > (TZO-TZON): TĒ- ~ TLA- = to strike/beat s.o./s.th. repeatedly; to beat s.th. (e.g., gold/a drum)
 (TZO-TZONI-LIĀ) > (TZO-TZONI-LIH): TLA- = to beat s.th. rhythmically (e.g., a drum) for s.o.

V

(VINOH)-∅- = [*from Span*], wine

X

(XAH)-TLI- = thatch (?)
 (XAH-CAL)-LI- = house made of thatch (?); i.e., a pole-and-thatch hut
(XĀ-HU-A) > (XĀ-UH): M-O- = (for an Indian woman) to apply traditional face paint; (for fruit) to begin to ripen

(XĀ-HU-A-L)-LI- = traditional face paint/decoration (of an Indian woman)
(XĀL)-LI- = sand; (XĀL-LO-H-∅)-☐- = *pret agen*, a thing that has owned sand in abundance; i.e., a thing full of/covered with sand
(XĀL-TE)-TL- > (XĀL-TE)-UH- = rock made of sand; i.e., sandstone
(XĀMi)-TL- > (XĀN)-∅- = adobe, adobe brick
  (XĀM-Ā-CAL)-LI- = a dugout-like thing for forming adobe bricks; i.e., an adobe-brick mold
(XĀ-YACA)-TL- > (XĀ-YAC)-∅- = face/mask
(XEL-I-HUI) > (XEL-I-UH) = to become split/divided in half
(XIC)-TLI- = an encasing thing (like a tube, sock, sleeve, pullover vest, etc.)
  (XIQU-IPIL)-LI- = an encased, enclosed stack/pile; i.e., sack/bag; [*as matrix in numeral n*], eight thousand
(XĪCAL)-LI- = a gourd vessel/bowl
(XĪC-O-Ā) > (XĪC-O-H): TĒ- = to deceive s.o.
(XĪCOH)-TLI- = large honeybee; bumblebee
  (XĪCOH-CUITLa)-TL- > (XĪCOH-CUITL)-∅- = large honeybee excrement; i.e., beeswax
(XIHUi)-TL- > (XIUH)-∅- = herb/grass; turquoise; year
  (XIUH-CŌĀ)-TL- = turquoise snake; fire snake (a weapon of the god Huitztzilopochtli); **xiuhcōātl mamalhuāztli** = it is the turquoise snake and it is the fire drill; i.e., it is war; (XIUH-CŌĀ-NĀHUA-L-EH-∅)-☐- = one who has owned a fire-snake disguise, i.e., an owner of a fire-snake disguise/mask
  (∅-∅-XIUH-NEL-TZIN-☐-∅)-∅- = *pers name s*, "It-Is-Truth-in-the-Form-of-Turquoise (H)"
  (XIUH-TŌTŌ)-TL- = turquoise bird; i.e., lovely cotinga; (XIUH-TŌTŌ-NACOCH-EH-∅)-☐- = *pret agen*, one who has owned ear pendants of lovely-cotinga feathers; i.e., an owner of ear pendants of lovely-cotinga feathers
  (XIUH-TLA-LPĪ-L)-LI- = a turquoise sash; (XIUH-TLA-LPĪ-L-EH-∅)-☐- = *pret agen*, one who has owned a turquoise sash; i.e., a turquoise-sash owner
  (∅-∅-XIUH-TLA-MĪ-N-∅-☐-∅)-∅- = *pers name s*, "He-Has-Pierced-Things-with-Turquoise"
(XĪHUi)-TL- = a comet
(XIH-XICUIN)-☐- = glutton
(XI-HXILI): TĒ-. *See* TĒ-(iHXILI).
(XĪLŌ)-TL- > (XĪLŌ)-UH- = tender ear of maize before the kernels are fully formed; ear of unripe maize; (XĪLŌ-TEPĒ)-TL- = Tender-Maize-Ear Mountain
  (XĪLŌ-TI) > (XĪLŌ-TI) = (for a maize plant) to begin to put forth maize ears
(XĪMA) > (XĪN): TLA- = to cut away s.th.; to hew s.th. (wood/stone)
(XINĀCH)-TLI- = seed; (XINĀCH-YŌ)-TL- > (XINĀCH-YŌ)-∅- = s.th. characteristic of seed; [*gen-use s used in org-pos NNC*], semen; **toxināchyo** = it is our semen; it is semen (in general)
(XĪP-Ē-HU-A) > (XĪP-Ē-UH): TLA- = to flay s.th.; to bark/peel s.th.; to hull/shell s.th. (e.g., peas)
(XIQU-IPIL)-LI-. *See* (XIC)-TLI-.
(XO)-TL- > (XO)-∅- = foot/leg
  (XO-HUEH-HUĒ-I-YA-∅-)-C- = a thing that has become long at the legs; i.e., a long-legged thing [*var s*, (XO-HUIH-HUĪ-YA-∅)-C-]; (XO-HUEH-HUĒ-I-YA-∅-QU-I-YA) > (XO-HUEH-HUĒ-I-YA-∅-QU-I-X) = to become/be long at the legs; i.e., to be long-legged

Vocabulary

   (XO-TIH-TĪC-E-C-TI-∅)-C- = a thing that has become chalk-colored at the feet; i.e., a thing with chalk-colored feet
*(XŌ)-TL- > (XŌ)-UH- = [*defec n that occurs only in comp ss*], a green thing
   (XŌ-PAN-TLAH)-□- = season of the green time; i.e., rainy season
   (XO-XŌ-HUI)> (XO-XŌ-UH) = to become/be green; (XO-XŌ-UH-∅)-QUI- > (XO-XŌ-UH-∅-CĀ)-UH- = *pret agen*, a thing that has become green; i.e., a green/raw thing; (XO-XŌ-UH-Ō-CĀ-CUA-LŌ-NI)-∅- = s.th. edible green/raw; (XO-XO-C)-TLI- = a green-colored thing
   (XŌ-TLA) > (XŌ-TLA) = (for charcoal) to catch fire; (for land) to burn/swelter; (for flowers) to burst into bloom; to blossom; (for a person) to have a fever; (XŌ-CHI)-TL-> (XŌ-CHI)-UH- = a thing that results from blooming/blossoming; i.e., a bloom/flower/blossom; (XŌ-CHI-CHI-NĀN-CAL)-LI- = an area enclosed by a fence for flowers; i.e., a flower garden; (XŌ-CHIH-CUA-L)-LI- = flowerlike food; i.e., fruit; (XŌ-CHIH-CUA-L-LŌ)-TL- > (XŌ-CHIH-CUA-L-LŌ)-∅- = s.th. characteristic of fruit; [*gen-use s used in org-pos NNC*], fruit; (XŌ-CHI-TĒN-YO-H-∅)-□- > (XŌ-CHI-TĒN-YO-H-∅-CĀ)-UH- = a thing that has owned abundant edges with flowers; i.e., a thing with flowered/flowery borders
(XOC)-TLI- = a pot/stew pot
   (XOQU-IHYĀ-∅)-C- = a thing foul-smelling like a stew pot
(XOCO)-TL- > (XOCO)-UH- = plum, fruit with a tart taste
   (XOCO-YA) > (XOCO-YA) = to become/be like tart fruit; i.e., to become tart/sour/acidic; (XOCO-∅)-C- = a thing that has become tart/sour; i.e., a tart/sour thing
   (XOCO-HUAH-∅)-□- = *pret agen*, one who has owned plums/tart fruit; i.e., a plum/tart-fruit owner
   (XOCO-YŌ)-TL- > (XOCO-YŌ)-UH- = s.th. characteristic of tart fruit; [*gen-use s used in org-pos NNCs*], fruit; *metaph.*, offspring, youngest child
(XŌ-CHI)-TL-. *See* (XŌ)-TL-.
(XŌLŌ)-∅- > (XŌLŌ)-UH- = page, boy servant
   (XOH-XŌLŌ-TĪTLANI) > (XOH-XŌLŌ-TĪTLAN): M-Ō- = (for an errand) to be run in the manner of pages (i.e., defectively/badly)
(XOLO-PIH)-TLI- = a fool/dolt/booby
   (XOLO-PIH-CUĒP-A) > (XOLO-PIH-CUEP): M-O- = to turn o.s. into a fool; i.e., to become/be a fool
(XOMAH)-TLI- = spoon
(XŌ-TLA). *See* (XŌ)-TL-.
(XŌXA) > (XŌX): TĒ- = to bewitch s.o.; to put s.o. under a spell, to cast a spell on s.o.; (TĒ-XŌXA-LIZ)-TLI- = action of bewitching s.o.
(XO-XŌ-HUI). *See* (XŌ)-TL-.

Y

(YĀ) ~ (YA-UH) ~ (HUI) > (YAH) ~ (HUI) = to go
   (YAH-∅)-QUI- > (YAH-∅-CĀ)-UH- = *pret agen*, one who has gone; i.e., a goer; +TI(YAH-∅-CĀ)-UH- = a goer of the people; i.e., a warrior [*for* +TĒ(YAH-∅-CĀ)-UH-]
(YACa)-TL- > (YAC)-∅- = nose/point/tip
   +TLA(YACA-CEL-I-CĀ)-∅- = s.th.'s action of becoming green at the tip; i.e., s.th.'s (i.e., a plant's) new growth/fresh sprouts

(YACA-HUITZ-TI) > (YACA-HUITZ-TI) = to become/be like a thorn at the point/tip; (YACA-HUITZ-TI-∅)-C- = a thing with a pointed end; i.e., a sharp-pointed thing

(YACA-HUITZ-O-Ā) > (YACA-HUITZ-O-H): TLA- = to cause s.th. to become like a thorn at the nose; i.e., to put a sharp point on s.th.; to sharpen the point of s.th.

(YACA-HUĪC-TI-∅)-C- = one that has become like a digging stick at the nose; i.e., one with a long, wide nose

(YAC-ĀNA) > (YAC-ĀN): TĒ- = to take s.o. by the nose; i.e., to lead/guide s.o.; (TĒ-YAC-ĀN-∅)-QUI- > (TĒ-YAC-ĀN-∅-CĀ)-UH- = *pret agen*, one who has led people; i.e., a leader/guide

(YACA-TI) > (YACA-T) = to become/be a nose/point; i.e., to come in the lead/out in front; TĒ-(YACA-T-IĀ) > (YACA-T-IH) = to become/be the nose/point for people; i.e., to come along out in front of people

(YACA-TZACUI-LIĀ) > (YACA-TZACUI-LIH): TĒ- = to close the nose for s.o.; i.e., to intercept s.o., to head off s.o.

(YAQU-EH-∅)-☐- > (YAQU-EH-∅-CĀ)-UH- = *pret agen*, a thing that has owned a point; i.e., a pointed thing

(YAHUAL-O-Ā) > (YAHUAL-O-H): TĒ- ~ TLA- = to surround/encircle s.o./s.th.

(YAHUAL-Ō-CH-TI-Ā) > (YAHUAL-Ō-CH-TI-H): TĒ+TLA- ~ TLA+TLA- = to cause s.o./s.th. to surround s.th.; i.e., to put s.th. around s.o./s.th.

(YAM-Ā-NI) > (YAM-Ā-N) = to become/be soft/pliant

(YAM-A-Z)-TLI- = a thing that results from becoming soft/pliant; i.e., a soft/pliant thing; (YAM-A-Z-TI-YA) > (YAM-A-Z-TI-Z) = to become/be soft/pliant

(YANCUI-YA) > (YANCUI-YA) ~ (YANCUI-X) = to become/be new/recent; (YAN-CUI-∅)-C- = a thing that has become new/recent; i.e., a new/recent thing

(YĀŌ)-TL- > (YĀŌ)-UH- = enemy [*As an emb, this n frequently represents* (YAŌ-YŌ)-TL-, "s.th. characteristic of enemies," *i.e.,* "emity, warfare, war."]

(YĀŌ-CHIH-CHĪHUA) > (YĀŌ-CHIH-CHĪUH): M-Ō- = to dress/adorn/attire/bedeck o.s. for war; i.e., to ready/prepare o.s. for war

(YĀŌ-CHĪHUA) > (YĀŌ-CHĪUH): TĒ- = to make s.o. be an enemy; i.e., to make war on s.o.; (TĒ-YĀŌ-CHĪHUA-NI)-∅- = *cuspres agen*, one who customarily makes s.o. an enemy; i.e., a warrior

(YĀŌ-HUIĀ) > (YĀŌ-HUIH) = to act as if in battle

(YĀŌ-MIQUI) > (YĀŌ-MIC) = to die in battle

(YĀŌ-QUĪZA) > (YĀŌ-QUĪZ) = to go out to war, to go to war; (YĀŌ-QUĪZ-∅)-QUI- > (YĀŌ-QUĪZ-∅-CĀ)-UH- = *pret agen*, one who has left for war; i.e., a warrior/soldier; (YĀŌ-QUĪZ-∅-CĀ-YAC-ĀNA) > (YĀŌ-QUĪZ-∅-CĀ-YAC-ĀN) = to serve as a leader/captain of warriors/soldiers; (YĀŌ-QUĪZ-∅-CĀ-YAC-ĀN-∅)-QUI- = *pret agen*, one who has led warriors/soldiers; i.e., a leader/captain of warriors/soldiers

(YĀŌ-TĒCA) > (YĀŌ-TĒCA) = to lay out a battle; i.e., to command in battle; (YĀŌ-TĒCA-NI)-∅- = *cuspres agen*, one who customarily commands in battle; i.e., a battle commander; a troop commander

(YĀŌ-TLA-CHIX-∅)-QUI- = *pret agen*, one who has guarded things against enemies; i.e., a sentinel/guardsman

(YĀŌ-TLAHU-ĒL-Ī-LŌ-∅)-C- = *pret pat*, one who is evil/vicious in war; i.e., a war hellion/fiend/hothead

Vocabulary

(YAŌ-TLA-TQUI)-TL- > (YAŌ-TLA-TQUI)-∅- = war/battle equipment
(YA-UH). *See* (YĀ).
YE = already; formerly; **yeh** [*for* ye eh] = on the other hand
(YE) > (YE) ~ (CA-T) ~ (CA-H) [*The last two are from the archaic imprfv s* (CA-TI), *"to become a being," i.e., "to be."*] = to be/exist; to be found in a place; **oncah** = it is there/they are there; i.e., there is/are; (YE-LIZ)-TLI- = action of living; i.e., life
+TĒ(CA-TI-YĀ-N)-∅- = [*used in pos-st NNC only*], s.o.'s place of being; *advlzd*, in/to/from s.o.'s place of being
(YĒC-A-HUI)- > (YĒC-A-UH) = to become/be finished/completed
 (YĒC)-TLI- = a thing that results from becoming finished/completed; i.e., a finished thing; i.e., a good thing; (YĒC-YŌ)-TL- = what is characteristic of a good thing; i.e., goodness
(YĒCEH)-◻- = nevertheless
YEH. *See* YE.
(YEH)-∅-. *See* (EH)-∅-.
(YEH-HUĀ)-TL-. *See* (EH-HUĀ)-TL-.
(YĒ-HUA) > (YĒ-UH) = [*defec v, used in 3rd sg pres-tense VNC as an adv*], a little while ago; *(YĒ-UH)-TLI- = [*used in 2nd degree advlzd NNC*], **yēuh** = a little while ago; [*used as emb*], (YĒ-P-PA)-◻-, *adv*, formerly
(YĒI)-∅- ~ (YĒYI)-∅- ~ (YĒ-)- = three in number. *See also* (ĒI)-∅-.
 (YĒ-PŌHU-A-L-TE)-TL- = sixty rock in number; i.e., sixty in number; (YĒ-TE-YE) > (YĒ-TE-YE) ~ (YE-TE-CA-T) ~ (YE-TE-CA-H) = to be in three parts
*(-YŌ)-TL- = [*defec n used as matrix only*], a thing pertaining to; what is characteristic of
(YŌCO-YA) > (YŌCO-X): TĒ- ~ TLA- = to create s.o./s.th.; to contrive/devise/invent s.th.
(YOHUA) > (YOHUA) = to become night; (for night) to fall
 (YOHUA-L)-LI- = s.th. that has become night; i.e., night; (YOHUA-L-TI-CA)-◻- = [*used only in advlzd NNC*], by means of night; i.e., at night
 (YOHUA)-TL- = s.th. that results from nightfall; i.e., night; (YOHUA-N)-◻- = [*used only in advlzd NNC*], at the time of night; at nighttime; in/into the night; during the night
 (TLA-YOHUA) > (TLA-YOHUA) = [*impers* tla-], (for things in general) to become darkness/night
(YŌLI) > (YŌL) = to become alive; to live; (for a bird/fowl) to hatch; (YŌL-∅)-QUI- > (YŌL-∅-CĀ)-UH- = *pret agen*, one that has lived; a living being; an animal; **tēhuān niyōlqui** = I am one who has lived with s.o.; i.e., I am s.o.'s kinsperson; +TĒ(YŌL-CĀ)-∅- = [*used only in pos-st NNCs*], s.o.'s means of living; i.e., s.o.'s sustenance; (YŌLI-LIZ)-TLI- = action of living; life; (YŌLI-LIZ-ZO-H-∅)-◻- = *pret agen*, a thing that has owned living/life in abundance; i.e., a thing filled with living/life; i.e., breath/a spiritual thing; +TĒ(YŌLI-YĀ)-∅- = [*used only in pos-st NNCs*], s.o.'s instrument for living; i.e., s.o.'s soul
 (YŌL)-LI- = a thing that results from living; i.e., life/vitality [*As an emb, this n frequently represents* (YŌL-LŌ)-TL-, "heart."]; (YŌL-CA)-TL- > (YŌL-CA)-UH- = vitality-associate; i.e., bug/insect; small animal; (YŌL-IHTLAC-O-Ā,) > (YŌL-IHTLAC-O-H): TĒ- = to damage s.o. in the heart; i.e., to cause s.o. distress; (YŌL-LŌ)-TL- > (YŌL-LŌ)-∅- = what is characteristic of life/vitality; i.e., a heart; (YŌL-LŌ-TI-Ā) > (YŌL-LŌ-TI-H): TĒ- = to cause s.o. to have a heart; i.e., to inspire s.o.; to confide in

a friend; (YŌL-LO-H)-TLI- = a thing characterized by vitality; i.e., a heart; (YŌL-LO-H-CHIC-Ā-HUA-Ø)-C- = one who is strong at heart; i.e., a strong-hearted one; (YŌL-LO-H-TLAHPAL-I-HUI) > (YŌL-LO-H-TLAHPAL-I-UH) = to be energetic in the heart; i.e., to be brave-hearted; TĒ-(YŌL-LO-H-TLAHU-ĒL-Ī-LŌ-Ø-CĀ-TI-LIĀ) > (YŌL-LO-H-TLAHU-ĒL-Ī-LŌ-Ø-CĀ-TI-LIH) = to cause s.o. to become evil/a scoundrel in the heart; i.e., to make s.o. become crazy

(YO-YŌLI)-◻- = small creature; small nasty insect

(YŌLI-C)-◻- = adv, calmly; slowly; cautiously: īyōlic in its/his/her calmness/deliberate pace; i.e., calmly, slowly, cautiously

Z

ZĀ = adv part, only (as a diminution from a prior situation), now only; **zā tēpan** = only in s.o.'s time, i.e., afterward/finally; **zā zo** = no matter, any-; **zā zo canah** = no matter where; anywhere; **zā zan** = now only and just; i.e., any which way; foolishly/nonsensically

(ZĀ-ZAN-Ī-L)-LI- = a now-only and nothing-else-but thing; i.e., a fable/tale/short fiction; a funny anecdote/yarn; a riddle/puzzle

(ZACA) > (ZACA): TLA- = to transport/carry s.th.

(ZACA)-TL- > (ZACA)-UH- = straw/hay/bunchgrass/blades of grass; (ZACA-YO-H-Ø)-◻- = a thing that has owned straw/hay/grass in abundance; i.e., a thing filled/covered with straw/hay/grass

(ZĀCUĀN)-Ø- = a troupial

(ZAHU-A) > (ZAUH): M-Ō- = to deprive o.s. of food; to refrain from eating; to fast; (NE-ZAHU-A-LIZ)-TLI- = the action of fasting; (NE-ZAHU-A-L)-LI- = one that results from having undergone a fast; TĒ+NE- ~ TLA+NE-(ZAHU-I-LIĀ) > (ZAHU-I-LIH) = to fast for s.o./s.th.

(ZĀL-I-HUI) > (ZĀL-I-UH) = to become stuck together; to become glued

(ZĀL-O-Ā) > (ZĀL-O-H): TLA- = to glue/solder s.th.

ZAN = only (unqualified by previous situation); just; nothing else but; **zan cuēl** = soon, in a short time; **zan niman** = immediately

(ZĀ-YŌL)-IN- = a fly

(ZŌ) > (ZŌ): TLA- ~ TĒ- = to pierce/puncture s.th./s.o.; to take/draw blood from s.o.; (TLA-ZŌ)-TL- > (TLA-ZŌ)-UH- = a thing (e.g., a bead) strung on a cord/thread; a bled thing

(ZŌ) > (ZŌ): M-O- = to prick o.s.; to bleed o.s.

*(ZO-Ā) > *(ZO-H): TLA- = [*obsolete v*], to cherish/prize/treasure s.th.

(TLA-ZO-H)-TLI- = a thing that is cherished/prized; i.e., a precious/expensive thing; (TLA-ZO-H-CUĒi)-TL- > (TLA-ZO-H-CUĒ)-Ø- = a precious/expensive skirt; (TLA-ZO-H-PIL)-LI- = a precious dependent; i.e., a high-born noble; a legitimate child; (TLA-ZO-H-TE)-TL- > (TLA-ZO-H-TE)-UH- = a precious stone; (TLA-ZO-H-TIL-MAH)-TLI- = a precious/expensive blanket/cloak/cape; (TLA-ZO-H-TLAN-Ø)-QUI- = a richly finished thing

(TLA-ZO-H-TLA) > (TLA-ZO-H-TLA): TĒ- ~ M-O- ~ T-O- = to consider s.o./o.s./one another dear; i.e., to love s.o./o.s./one another; (NE-TLA-ZO-H-TLA-LIZ)-TLI- = the action of loving o.s./one another; i.e., self-esteem/mutual affection

Vocabulary

(ZŌHUA) > (ZŌUH): M-O- = (for a bird) to spread its wings/tail; (for a person) to open wide his/her arms
(ZŌL)-IN- = quail
  (ZŌL-NEH-NEQUI) > (ZŌL-NEH-NEC): M-O- = to pretend o.s. is a quail; i.e., to resemble a quail
(ZOL-Ō-NI) > (ZOL-Ō-N) = (for flowing water) to make a noisy sound
  (ZOL-Ō-NI-Ā) > (ZOL-Ō-NI-H): TLA- = to cause s.th. to make a sloshing/splashing/swashing sound
  (iH-ZOL-O-TZ-A) > (iH-ZOL-O-TZ): TLA- = to cause s.th. to become a gurgling/sloshing sound; i.e., to slurp/suck s.th. up; to noisily gulp s.th. down
(ZŌMĀ) > (ZŌMAH): M-O- = to frown in anger
  (ZŌMA-L-TIĀ) > (ZŌMA-L-TIH): TĒ+NE- = to make s.o. frown in anger
(ZOQUI)-TL- > (ZOQUI)-UH- = mud/clay
  (ZOQUI-TI) > (ZOQUI-T) = to become/be wet; (ZOQUI-TI-YA) > (ZOQUI-TI-YA) = to become/be soaking wet
  (ZOQUI-TLAH)-☐- = a place of abundant mud; i.e., a mud hole/quagmire/bog
  (ZOQUI-YŌ-HUA) > (ZOQUI-YŌ-HUA) = to become/be characterized by mud; i.e., to become/be covered with mud